ROck

THE ESSENTIAL GUIDE

David Sinclair was born in Giffnock, Renfrewshire. He grew up in Birmingham and London, where he went to school at Eltham College. After graduating from Warwick University with a degree in politics, he played drums with groups including London Zoo, TV Smith's Explorers and Laughing Sam's Dice. He worked as a BBC TV researcher on programmes including *The Rock and Roll Years* and *Wogan*. Rock critic of *The Times* since 1985, and a contributor to *Q* magazine since 1986, he edits the Global Music Pulse column in *Billboard* magazine, and makes regular appearances on Sky TV's *Sunrise* and Barry Johnston's *Sunday Edition* on BBC Radio 5.

ROcK on CD

THE ESSENTIAL GUIDE

DAVID SINCLAIR

First published in Great Britain in 1992 by
Kyle Cathie Limited
3 Vincent Square London SW1P 2LX

ISBN 1 85626 058 5

A CIP catalogue record for this book is available from the British Library.

Designed by Lorraine Estelle
Typeset by DP Photosetting
Printed and bound in Great Britain by
Biddles Ltd, Guildford, Surrey

FOR MY
MOTHER and FATHER

ACKNOWLEDGEMENTS

There are many people who have helped to make the writing of this book possible. Thanks are due to my editor at *The Times*, Richard Morrison, both for phoning when he did and for not phoning when he didn't; to Paul Du Noyer and John Aizlewood at *Q* for a similarly understanding approach; and to Andrew Harvey, editor of *The Times Saturday Review*, for commissioning the A–Z of Rock series, from which the idea for this book was initially developed. Some of the reviews incorporated here were previously published, in different forms, in *The Times* and *Q*.

Special mention must go to my unflappable agent, John Pawsey, to my consistently cheerful editor, Caroline Taggart, and to Kyle Cathie.

I would like to express my gratitude to the following people either for practical help or for inspiration, and in some cases both: Sian Davies, Paul Henderson, Claire Horton, Andrew Kenny, Dimple Lota, Jo Pratt, Philip Savil, Jill Sinclair, Pru Sinclair, John Street, Debbie Walker, Adam White and Richard Wootton.

My family has endured the writing of this book with grace and fortitude and my love and special thanks go, as ever, to Pru, Faith and Jack.

INTRODUCTION

L IKE MOST baby boomers I started listening to pop music as a child. I have no idea what make our family gramophone was in those days, but I remember that it was a weighty, oblong device with a single knob, which controlled the volume. The platen was covered in the sort of short brown fur that you might nowadays expect to find insulating an anorak. It had started to rise in places, like the wealds on an old dartboard. The needle, which was about the size of a small tack without the head, was supposed to be changed after *every single record played!* In practice, you could get away with playing both sides of two or maybe three 45-rpm discs without changing the needle, but that really was the limit. You bought the needles in quantities of 50 or 100. They came packaged in little metal tins.

I won't pretend that this was state-of-the-art equipment for the late Fifties, but it certainly wasn't as antediluvian then as it seems now. For a while my favourite record was a cheerful ditty by Tommy Steele called 'Handful of Songs'. I played it so often that eventually the record wore out, literally. The needle simply obliterated the grooves of the disc, wiping it as clean as a blank tape.

Thankfully, it wasn't too long before my parents invested in one of the brand new Dansette machines that were by this time all the rage. The Dansette was designed primarily for playing the 7-inch 45-rpm single. It came with a modern, rubberised turntable attachment and, on the more advanced models, a spindle sticking up from the centre on to which you could load up to half a dozen singles. When the first single had finished playing, the playing arm lifted itself out of the way and the next piece of vinyl came crashing down on top of the first one. The needle swung back into position and, *violà*, the next record began playing. Quite often, you found that the record on top could not get an adequate purchase on the one underneath and there would be the most terrible scraping and grinding noise. When that happened, the whole operation would have to be suspended, the offending disc removed, and the process started again.

You could play albums on the Dansette (you could even stack them up like the singles if you had sufficient nerve), but the 12-inch discs would overhang the platen by a good inch and a half all round. The slightest warp was thus enough to send the needle skating across the first track and halfway into the second before it finally settled down.

Yet even that imperfect system was an advance on the 78-rpm records in my Dad's collection. As kids, we used to find stacks of the old things lying forgotten in the attic, dusty relics of a bygone age. It was impossible to imagine a time when they could actually have been of contemporary value.

Now vinyl itself stands on the brink of a similar obsolescence and I can all too easily imagine the incredulity with which my own kids will greet my explanation of what those funny-looking black records stacked in the corner were once used for. 'You mean you physically had to scrape a piece of plastic with a needle? Come off it, Dad.' It will be like trying to explain what a typewriter was, or what it used to be like when there were only four TV channels.

The end of vinyl is clearly in sight. At the start of 1992, over the whole range of recorded music, the compact-disc format accounted for 46% of album sales while vinyl had slipped to just 8%. On January 6, the high-street retailer W.H. Smith announced its intention 'to phase out vinyl LPs over the next three months'. By that time, vinyl LPs were accounting for less than 3% of Smith's turnover in recorded music. During the run-up to Christmas in the preceding year, the store's branches were reporting sales of less than one copy per week of some new albums on vinyl.

This is hardly surprising, given the manifest superiority of CD over vinyl. At their launch in 1983, CDs were ritually smeared with honey and even ground underfoot, then slipped into a machine and played perfectly to demonstrate their durability. This was misleading. CDs are not indestructible and should be cared for in much the same way that vinyl LPs are. The point is that in an imperfect world CDs will not *automatically* deteriorate if they are subjected to *some* degree of rough handling.

Furthermore, the way in which CDs work, by digitally encoding information that is then translated into sound by a laser, means that there will be no intrinsic deterioration in the quality of the sound through normal use. In other words, a CD version of my old Tommy Steele record would still be reproducing its sound with exactly the same pristine accuracy as the day I first played it.

Even when vinyl is played on state-of-the-art equipment, it deteriorates every time the needle slices its way through the groove. Thus, certain high frequencies, such as the sound of cymbals, will never again sound as good as they did the very first time that the record was played.

CD offers a broader dynamic range, crystal clear sound, instant access to any track on the album, a timing display, remote control facilities and a vastly more dependable way of listening to music the way it was intended to be heard. There is no hiss, crackle or pop; no intrusive static or odd clicks. They have a gorgeous iridescent look, a longer playing-time than vinyl, and they are easier to carry, to store and to file.

Yet, incredibly, there are people who still say that they prefer vinyl to CD, and indeed among an ageing group of citizens this has become a fashionable view to take. Their arguments tend to be emotional rather than empirical, witness DJ John Peel writing in 1991: 'What about surface noise, I hear you whine. Listen, mate, life has surface noise and I like it. So there.'

Neil YOUNG, another hippy recidivist, goes further, describing digital music as 'the dark ages of recorded sound'. In an interview with Robert Sandall of *The Sunday Times*, YOUNG said:

'Rock used to be this wonderfully resonant, vibrating thing. And then we were all fooled by the clarity and control that digital brought. It seemed like a step forward – no hiss, but along with the hiss went depth of sound and the myriad possibilities of the high end where everything is like the cosmos, exploding stars, echo. . . . Your mind was challenged and your heart was moved.'

There are certainly no shortage of resonant, vibrating, extraneous noise on YOUNG's recent CDs and indeed his *Arc-Weld* live album has one of the grungiest sound mixes in the history of recorded rock. His complaint is more to do with rock tidying itself up in general. While digital recording techniques and the enhanced clarity of CD has undoubtedly helped to facilitate the clean-cut production values of say Phil COLLINS and DIRE STRAITS, what YOUNG is railing against is undue technical sophistication *of any sort*, something which he believes to be inimicable to the spirit of good old rock'n'roll.

He may have a point, but no art form can exist in its original state of primitive beauty for ever. A compact disc will sound exactly as clean or 'dirty' as the sound of the music that it is encoded to reproduce, and the fact that most musicians, producers and engineers choose to make their music sound cleaner and clearer than in the days of tape is hardly the fault of digital recording techniques.

Other more prosaic complaints about the new format range from the reduced scope for cover graphics to the higher price of CDs, and there are some specialist objections from club DJs and hip-hop acts, who point out that techniques such as mixing and scratching can only be achieved with vinyl records.

Then there are the tweakies: the kind of obsessive buffs who listen to the equipment, not the music. Armed with a top-of-the-range Linn record deck (power supply, turntable, pick-up arm and cartridge, costing well over £3,000, before you even think about the amplifier and speakers), the tweakies will tell you that their vinyl version of *Tubular Bells* has got much more 'warmth' than its CD equivalent. Some of them, such as Julian Vereker, MD of a hi-fi manufacturing company called Naim Audio, get quite hysterical, describing the sound of CD as 'diabolical' and 'impossible to live with'. They will complain about the over-bright, 'aggressive' sound of CD, the 'unreal' way in which it eliminates certain unintended, but nevertheless essential, ambient frequencies in its pursuit of a sterile digitalised perfection.

They might be right. Who knows? But this is the point at which the debate itself reaches a sterile impasse. Neither I, nor the vast majority of people, will spend anything like that amount of money on a turntable, let alone feel inclined to ponder such minutely perceived differences of sound quality. The fact is that in every practical sense CD is demonstrably superior to vinyl; and even that Linn deck has a needle which is eating its way into those grooves. The ineluctable truth is that if the tweakie listens to his vinyl version of *Tubular Bells* often enough *it will deteriorate*, no matter how good it sounded to begin with.

There have undoubtedly been teething troubles with CD,

particularly in the transfer of old analogue (tape) recordings to the new digital format. In their haste to get product on to the market on CD, record companies have not always got hold of the original master tapes of the albums concerned. Early CD versions of PINK FLOYD's *Dark Side of the Moon* were not transferred to CD from the master tape. Similarly, various LED ZEPPELIN albums were initially transferred from second- and even third-generation tape copies.

The process whereby old, analogue recordings are transferred into digital format is complex and subject to mishap. The multi-track master tapes *are* the original source of the material, but they are not the final sound that goes on to the disc. Engineers and producers will have adjusted the sound in a variety of ways in preparing the two-track (stereo) master mix that will have been used for manufacturing LPs and cassettes, in order to compensate for shortcomings and to correct any problems that may have developed in the recording session.

Strictly speaking, therefore, in order to transfer an album from analogue to digital, it is necessary to remaster the sound of the original recordings, but often, in the early days of CD, the old stereo mix-masters (which were intended for LP and/or cassette) were used, and the results were substandard.

A notable cock-up of this sort occurred with the Steely Dan back catalogue. Steely Dan's original recordings, from 1972–1980, were widely considered to have featured some of the finest studio engineering of all time. But even by 1981, due to improper storage and poor fidelity, the original analogue master tapes of the albums had deteriorated. An engineer was detailed to transfer the material on to digital masters, which he did with meticulous care, and the first batch of Steely Dan albums manufactured from the new digital masters was released on CD in 1985 to much acclaim. But subsequent batches were mistakenly made using the old analogue masters, which had continued to deteriorate, and those CDs were clearly not as good as the first batch. There were comparable errors involving early CD releases by Elton JOHN, the WHO, Diana ROSS, George HARRISON and doubtless many others.

It sounds serious, but interestingly the record company reported that it had received *no consumer complaints* about the second batch of Steely Dan CDs. So how bad could the reduction of sound quality have been? In the real world – not the world of the professional sound engineer or the hypercritical tweakie – the answer is: bad enough to notice a difference if you listen carefully to one straight after the other but, obviously, nothing like bad enough to warrant returning the CD to the shop.

In any case, such problems are now very rare, and all new albums are, of course, digitally recorded and mastered in the first place.

The argument that CDs cost too much has long been regarded as self-evident. For sure, we'd all like to see the price come down, but some of the claims about profit margins have been exaggerated. The often-quoted figure is that CDs cost £1 to produce. This is true as far as simply pressing the disc is concerned, but doesn't take into account artists' fees, mastering and post-production charges, typesetting, printing, packaging, distribution costs, copyright payments and other expenses. When all these are taken into consideration the real cost of producing a CD is nearer to £3. The manufacturer sells to the distributor for about £5, who sells to the retailer for £7.25, who sells to the public for about £12. If those mark-ups look severe, they are the same in percentage terms as the mark-ups on vinyl and tapes.

Obviously, the costs of production in manufacturing CDs of old material are greatly reduced and there has undoubtedly been a killing made on certain individual items, albums which had already recouped their costs many times over before they were even transferred to CD. Yet the very fact that people have bought CDs in preference to cheaper (and, let's face it, inferior) formats in sufficient quantities to render vinyl obsolete so quickly, suggests that the price of CDs is at least consistent with what the market will bear. And when you consider that the price of a ticket to see a show at Wembley Arena is now about £20–£25, can £10–£12 really be such a lot to pay for something that will probably last a lifetime?

The vinyl-vs-CD argument has in any case become academic. For we are now poised on the brink of the *next* technological revolution, and all the signs are that the launch of the digital compact cassette (DCC) format in September 1992 will do for cassettes what compact discs have done for vinyl. This is one innovation which the tweakies are unlikely to resist, since they have never got used to cassettes in the first place, still regarding them with a mixture of suspicion and contempt.

There are, at the time of writing, 120 million compact-disc

players in use worldwide, and one of the effects of the CD revolution has been to reawaken interest among rock-music fans whose enthusiasm had waned during the latter part of the Seventies and early Eighties. It was no coincidence that as sales of CDs picked up momentum, so this older generation of consumers re-emerged from the shadows, people who had given up reading *NME* and *Melody Maker* many years before, but welcomed the broad-minded and informed approach of *Q* magazine with open arms.

In more recent years a new breed of younger fan has also begun to appear, who, far from being alienated by the music of their elder siblings and parents, are hungry to discover more about the back catalogue available from acts like PINK FLOYD, QUEEN and Lou REED.

When *Q* was launched in 1986, the first issue came with a free booklet called *Key CDS – The Best Music on Compact Disc*. It was a slight volume. At that time there was only one AC/DC album listed (*Fly on the Wall*); only one by Crosby Stills Nash and Young (*Déjà Vu*); one by the BEACH BOYS and none of The BEATLES' proper recordings, which were still the subject of contractual wrangling between EMI and the members of the group.

Now, of course, almost everything is available on CD, and a book like this cannot hope to be comprehensive. Instead I have focused on the acts which have played a key rôle in the development of rock and tried to give a general indication of which are the best recordings available in their catalogue. The aim is to provide newer fans with an introduction to this wealth of material and to remind older listeners of what made these performances so great in the first place.

The emphasis is necessarily, though by no means entirely, on the more established acts, and since I didn't want to produce another heavy-metal manual, I have kept my definition of 'rock' fairly loose, assuming the scope to cover the more obvious of the country, soul, rap and blues artists whose work has had a significant impact on the rock mainstream.

The omissions are legion and regretted, but I hope there is enough here to spark enthusiasm and encourage wider investigation of the music that has become the most vibrant and all-pervasive popular art form of the 20th century.

Notes on the format of the book

For a while I toyed with the idea of organising the book into sections: the Fifties; the Sixties; heavy rock, singer-songwriters, soul, etc – but there were simply too many overlapping acts and too many grey areas to make it feasible. The book is thus organised as a straightforward alphabetical directory. The following points will, I hope, help to clarify the information given:

• Listed at the top of each act's entry is a group line-up (where applicable) and their highest charted album(s) in either the UK or the US, or both if they have reached the same peak in both markets. All No.1 albums by an act are automatically listed at the top. If an act has reached No.2 on two occasions, then both No.2 albums are listed, and so forth.

A No.1 album does not necessarily denote the highest sales, especially in America, where, until recently, chart positions were allocated according to a combination of sales and radio play. Often it is the follow-up to a huge (but possibly slow) selling album which rockets to the top as people rush out to buy it as soon as it is released. Even so, there is still no clearer indication of when an act's stock is buoyant than when it is sitting at, or near, the top of the chart.

• If a band is still functioning, the current personnel are listed. (f) next to a name indicates that the musician was a founding member of the group. 'Founding members' are defined as those who were in the ranks at the time of the group's first commercially available recorded release.

e.g.: Gary Husband – drums/vocals; Mark King (f) – vocals/bass; Mike Lindup (f) – keyboards/vocals.

• If a band has split up, the 'classic' line-up is given; i.e. the line-up at the time of the band's greatest success or the line-up for which the band is best remembered (usually the same thing).

• The entries are not comprehensive, but it is hoped that all the most important albums by an act, available on CD, will have been mentioned and their catalogue number quoted. The intention is for top-charted albums to be listed at the beginning; best albums (especially compilations) to be reviewed at the end; and any others worthy of note to be mentioned somewhere in the text. However, I don't claim infallibility.

• Albums which have not been released on CD in Britain may often be available as imports, usually from America or Japan. This is an area fraught with misunderstanding. Often these imports cost way over the odds, and their availability fluctuates week by week. You can usually get what you want at a Virgin or HMV Megastore, but smaller regional outlets may not be much good. I have therefore tended to steer clear of this whole area and where an album is not available on UK release (i.e. a retailer could not order it from his usual wholesaler), then I have marked it 'unavailable'.

• Italics in the text indicate an album title:
e.g.: PINK FLOYD's *Dark Side of the Moon*.

• 'Inverted commas' indicate a song title:
e.g.: 'Love in an Elevator' from the album *Pump* was a No.13 hit for AEROSMITH.

• SMALL CAPS indicate that an act has its own entry in the book.
e.g.: . . . providing the basis for songs by Sinead O'Connor, George MICHAEL, Fine Young Cannibals and no doubt many others besides . . .

• Information in (ordinary brackets) refers to *current* record label and most recent *CD catalogue number*. Dates in [square brackets] refer to *original* year of album release (in UK unless otherwise stated):
e.g.: *Music From Big Pink* (Capitol CDP 746 069-2) [1968]
NOTE: This may not be the same as the year that the album reached its highest chart position:
e.g. entry under Elton John:
Uk No.1 album: 1989: *Sleeping With the Past* (Rocket 838 839-2) (The album was released in Sept 1989, but first reached No.1 in June 1990.)

• If the album is mentioned in the text, but not considered separately, then the same information will appear in one (ordinary bracket). Again it refers to the *current* CD catalogue number and *original* album release date.
e.g.: After the initial burst of astounding creativity which produced *Stage Fright* (Capitol CDP 793 593-2; 1970), The Band went through a lull in the Seventies.

AC/DC

Convened: 1973, Sydney, Australia
Brian Johnson – vocals; Chris Slade – drums; Cliff Williams –
bass; Angus Young (f) – guitar; Malcolm Young (f) – guitar
UK No.1 album: 1980: *Back in Black* (Atco K250735)
US No.1 album: 1981: *For Those About to Rock (We Salute
You)* (Atco K250851)

From the land that brought you Crocodile Dundee, John Pilger
and dodgy lager commercials, AC/DC is one group that really
couldn't give a XXXX about the dictates of fashion, musical or
otherwise. 'We put out the same album every year with a
different cover,' guitarist Angus Young once quipped, and
whatever else you might say about the group's repertoire you
can't argue with its consistency.

Having established a rogue, highly risqué, heavy rock formula
with their début *High Voltage* (Atco K250257), released in Australia in December 1974, they have done little more than tweak the
fine-tuning right through to their most recent offering *The Razors
Edge* (Atco 7567-91413-2) in 1990. Rhythm guitarist Malcolm
Young once explained their philosophy thus:

'If you look at The BEATLES, they started out as a rock'n'roll band,
playing in Hamburg. They became really successful. And then
they started doing things like *Sergeant Pepper* and *The Magical
Mystery Tour*, but eventually they came back to playing straightforward rock'n'roll like "Get Back". The STONES did much the
same. We've learnt from bands like that that it's best just to stay
where you're at, because you're going to come back there anyway.
So why leave in the first place? Why not simply work better and
harder at what you've got?'

The band derives the hard core of its clientèle from the specialist heavy metal market where they are regarded as one of the genre's deities. Angus in full head-banging mode, wearing his perennial schoolboy stage uniform, was the cover star of the first issue of *Kerrang!* magazine, now something of a collectors' item. They headlined the Castle Donington Monsters of Rock festival in 1981, 1984 and 1991, the only act ever to do so three times.

But they have also touched a much broader populist nerve. Sales of their 1979 album *Highway to Hell* (Atco K250628) have topped six million, while those of *Back in Black* (see below) are approaching the 13 million mark and still going strong, an achievement which, but for the lack of big hit singles, puts them within spitting distance of the BON JOVI/DEF LEPPARD superleague.

With their take-no-prisoners approach, AC/DC have not so much transcended international boundaries of taste as jumped on them until they collapsed under the weight. In 1990, an item in *Newsweek* revealed that since the Berlin Wall had come down, business in West Berlin record shops had gone up by 300%. The magazine reported that the top sellers were AC/DC and the *Dirty Dancing* soundtrack. A strong blast of AC/DC's industrial-strength boogie was a vital plank in the surreal tactics adopted in 1989 by American troops bent on flushing out General Noriega by playing non-stop heavy metal music in the vicinity of his Panamanian hideout.

Angus and Malcolm Young were born in Glasgow, the two youngest of seven brothers and one sister. In the early Sixties the family emigrated to Sydney, Australia, where an older brother, George, founded a group called the Easybeats – famous for their 1966 hit 'Friday on my Mind' – in an immigrant hostel. He encouraged Angus and Malcolm to found AC/DC, and was instrumental in securing the band its first recording deal.

They recruited singer Bon Scott, brought up in Perth, but also an expatriate Scotsman. According to Malcolm, 'Bon was the biggest single influence on the band. When Bon came in it pulled us all together. He had that real stick-it-to-'em attitude. We all had it in us, but it took Bon to really bring it out.'

The group arrived in London for its first UK visit in April 1976 and within a year they were headlining Hammersmith Odeon, with success in America soon following. But early in 1980, a heavily boozed-up Scott choked to death on his vomit in the back of a friend's car in London. His replacement was Brian Johnson, who had previously enjoyed a spell as frontman in Geordie, an English band in the Sweet/Slade glam-pop tradition, which scored four hit singles in 1973.

Since Johnson has been on board there have been periodic attempts by producers or (American) record companies to 'smooth out' the AC/DC sound – Malcolm is particularly scathing about *For Those About To Rock*, complaining of 'too much time spent fucking around with the sound' – but the band has clung to its raw musical essence through thick and thin.

Lewd, loud and a generally taste-free antidote to all forms of subtlety or pretentiousness, AC/DC is a group that remains firmly in touch with the eternal verities of its trade, its music a perennial expression of rock as an exclusively delinquent pastime.

● *Back in Black* (Atco K250735) [1980]

The definitive AC/DC album. Recorded immediately after the death of Bon Scott, it was the first release to feature Brian Johnson, a man whose impossibly gruff, high-pitched shriek has been known to strip paint. 'Hells Bells', 'Rock and Roll Ain't Noise Pollution' and the immensely engaging 'You Shook Me All Night Long' remain some of the best riffs in the band's entire portfolio.

● *Who Made Who* (Atco K7816502) [1986]

After something of a lean patch AC/DC bounced back with this semi-compilation which provided the soundtrack to the Stephen King movie *Maximum Overdrive*. A mixture of old and new material it includes 'You Shook Me All Night Long', 'Hells Bells' and the epic 'For Those About to Rock (We Salute You)', the song which, to this day, they use as the grand finale of their live shows, complete with a deafening fusillade of cannon fire.

Bryan Adams

Born: November 5 1959, Kingston, Ontario
UK No.1 album: 1991: *Waking Up the Neighbours* (A&M 397
164-2)
US No.1 album: 1984: *Reckless* (A&M CDA 5013)

In the year that GUNS N' ROSES arranged for a consignment of *Use Your Illusion* to be delivered to a central London record store by Sherman tank, when PRINCE promoted the 'Gett Off' single with one of his most salacious videos yet and MADONNA invited us all into bed with her, it was a modestly promoted song by the mild-mannered Bryan Adams which swept the board in charts the world over. In the UK '(Everything I Do) I Do It For You' stayed at No.1 for a record-breaking 16 weeks, almost a third of the year.

As far as attention-grabbing is concerned, Adams has perfected one of the more original techniques. 'I believe that if you can maintain a really high standard of songwriting then you will rise above,' he explained in 1987. 'You don't have to be a rock'n'roll myth, you don't have to be a drug-taking alcoholic, you don't have to be a fashionable pop idol. All you have to be is a good songwriter. That's all I've ever believed. A lot of people think I've tried to develop a kind of working class, regular guy thing, but all I do is I go up on stage and I do my show, and all I'm saying is: These are just songs, and this is just me and my band. I never believed the myth that pop music is any bigger than just pop music, I don't care who it is.'

Adams formed his first band in Vancouver when he was 16. In January 1978 he met Jim Vallance, a withdrawn, low-key man who had studied classical composition and cello at university. They began writing together and while Vallance never actually joined Adams' band, he remained, for 12 years, a Bernie Taupin figure to Adams' Elton JOHN. The partnership eventually dissolved during the preparations for *Waking up the Neighbours* (see below) and, ironically, 'Everything I Do' is one of the very few Bryan Adams songs which Vallance did not have a hand in writing.

Unlike just about any other Canadian rock star – and Adams is the biggest there's ever been – he still lives in his home country, in north-west Vancouver on a rock bluff which he's named Cliff-hanger. Together with Vallance he wrote the Canadian Band Aid record, 'Tears are not Enough' and in 1986 he accompanied STING, Peter GABRIEL and U2 on the 1986 Amnesty International concerts.

But it is the sheer spread of his appeal in the niche marketing era of the Nineties that is truly remarkable. In 1991 he was simultaneously featured on the covers of the teeny girls' magazine *Smash Hits*, the head-bangers' Bible *Kerrang!* and the sober adult-rock forum of *Q* magazine. What is the man's secret?

His throaty voice is both macho and vulnerable, his looks manly enough for the boys and sexy enough for the girls. His songs, and the minimalism of his stage show, hark back to a mythical golden era in rock, when groups simply stood on stage and played great music. Clearly, this direct approach has touched a chord with a vast audience whose collective palate has become jaded by the excesses of modern gizmology and larger-than-life showmanship.

A young head on old shoulders, Adams was six when 'My Generation' came out, and nine during the summer of '69; although steeped in the music of the Sixties, he brings fresh professionalism and a relatively youthful enthusiasm to bear on a catalogue of fourth generation rock'n'roll songs which are minted with unerring efficiency. An arresting, finely honed amalgam of SPRINGSTEEN without the mystique, The STONES without the sleaze and The Faces without the booze, it has been Adams' unique achievement to crack open a hype-obsessed worldwide industry with so little fuss it verges on the eerie.

- *Bryan Adams* (A&M CDMID 100) [Canada 1980]
- *You Want It, You Got It* (A&M CDMID 101) [1981]
- *Cuts Like a Knife* (A&M CDMID 102) [1983]

Adams' eponymous début went gold in Canada (50,000) but that was about it. 'If you listen to this album now, it's pretty convoluted,' Adams says. 'There's a bit of rock, some funky stuff, some real pop. We just didn't know what we were doing. I look back on it now as being quite a good demo. It's an amusing record.'

The follow-up, *You Want It, You Got It*, was given a worldwide release, and reflected Adams' increasing maturity as a singer, but it was his third album, *Cuts Like a Knife*, that achieved the breakthrough, yielding three US hits – 'Straight From the Heart', the title track and 'This Time' – and becoming a certified million-seller by July of 1983.

All three albums are now available on mid-price CD.

- *Reckless* (A&M CDA 5013) [1984]

This elevated Adams to the first division and remains his finest achievement on disc. By his own admission, recording it was an obsessive experience. 'I was struggling with the idea of doing a

5

record that would outdo *Cuts Like a Knife*. I was very demanding with those working around me, the band, the engineer, Bob Clearmountain. You just get so into it that nothing else exists. I lost a lot of innocence on this album. People saw a different side of me, more brutal.'

In America *Reckless* yielded six Top 20 hits, among them the US No.1, 'Heaven', an earthy duet with Tina TURNER 'It's Only Love', his first UK hit 'Run to You' and the perennial live favourite 'Summer of '69'. It sold well in excess of seven million copies, and deservedly so.

● *Into the Fire* (A&M CDA 3907) [1987]

A disappointing follow-up to *Reckless* that finds Adams getting a bit serious and trying to make Big Statements, not his forte at all. 'Heat of the Night' and 'Hearts on Fire' are the best tracks by far, but the rest of it is forgettable.

● *Waking Up the Neighbours* (A&M 397 164-2) [1991]

Although on previous albums Adams has injected real emotion and a pleasing boy-next-door personality into his rabble-rousing anthems and sway-along ballads, there has always been a slightly calculating quality to his clean-cut, gung-ho rock'n'roll. Here he has sculpted a collection of such finely tuned blockbuster rock that it begins to sound like a cynical exercise in pushing the right buttons.

Producer Mutt Lange must shoulder a share of the responsibility for this. Renowned for his commercial ear and stringent quality control, Lange (who produced two similarly failsafe multi-million sellers for DEF LEPPARD) takes a co-writer credit on every track.

The result is a succession of muscle-bound rockers and bathetic ballads, most of them rather too neatly stylised for comfort. Highlights include 'Can't Stop This Thing We Started', 'House Arrest' and 'There Will Never Be Another Tonight'. Oh yes, and some ballad thingy called 'I Do It For You'.

Aerosmith

Convened: 1970, Sunapee, New Hampshire
Tom Hamilton (f) – bass; Joey Kramer (f) – drums; Joe Perry
(f) – guitar; Steven Tyler (f) – vocals; Brad Whitford (f) –
guitar
US No.3 album: 1976: *Rocks* (Columbia CD 32360)
UK No.3 album: 1989: *Pump* (Geffen GEFD 24254)

Like ZZ Top, Aerosmith spent most of the Seventies locked into
a Herculean American touring schedule that earned the band
massive domestic popularity while etching only the faintest of
marks on the UK psyche. Not one of their million-selling albums
from that period even registered in the British chart. For the
record they were: *Aerosmith* (unavailable; 1973), *Toys in the Attic* (see
below), *Rocks* (see above), *Draw the Line* (1978, available as two-in-
one CD together with *Toys in the Attic* Columbia 467385-2) and
Live! Bootleg (unavailable; 1978).

With his canyon-sized mouth and dainty physique, vocalist
Steven Tyler has often been likened to Mick Jagger, while his
guitar-slinging partner Joe Perry has something of the saturnine
elegance of the young Jimmy Page. Such comparisons go more
than skin-deep, since at its best Aerosmith's music combines the
sleazy raunch of The ROLLING STONES with the muscular power-
chord rock of LED ZEPPELIN.

In keeping with the spirit of those who had influenced them,
the band opted for the bare knuckle approach to the rock'n'roll
lifestyle, riding out the Seventies in a haze of drugged-out excess.
The explanation for their reluctance to tour outside America? 'We
were afraid to go through customs,' they told Q magazine in 1989.

Eventually such working practices produced diminishing
returns. The quality of their recorded output became erratic,
touring became a grind, they fell out with each other. When Perry
quit in 1979 it was the end of a golden era that had already begun
to tarnish.

The band struggled on in various permutations until 1984
when the original line-up reunited for another bite of the cherry.
In 1986 RUN DMC's hit version of 'Walk This Way', which featured
Tyler and Perry, gave the band a new lease of life and provided the
springboard to belated recognition in Britain. In 1987 they
enjoyed their first UK chart album with *Permanent Vacation* (Geffen

GEFD 24162), an agile collection of tuneful heavy rock including the minor hits 'Dude (Looks Like a Lady)' and 'Angel'.

Rehabilitated both musically and physically, Aerosmith now sound as hungry to play their bluesy hard rock as a new generation of fans is to hear it. A bunch of old warhorses perhaps, but still well able to take on the young bucks at their own game.

● *Toys in the Attic* (Columbia CD 80773) [1975]

A *tour de force* of two-guitar blues-rock, combining a typically high-energy attack with a sharp ear for melody, this recording was the high-water mark of a band that had an enduring impact on succeeding generations of American heavy rockers from VAN HALEN to BON JOVI to GUNS N' ROSES. But, as later became apparent, *Toys in the Attic* also addressed a broader constituency. The title track was covered by art-rock savants R.E.M. on their 1987 album *Dead Letter Office*, while 'Walk This Way' (a US No.10 hit in 1977) was converted into an international rap'n'roll smash in 1986 by RUN DMC.

● *Pump* (Geffen GEFD 24254) [1989]

An album of riotous charm, crammed with cock-of-the-walk riffs and blessed with a ridiculously hot mix, *Pump* underlines why advancing age can no longer in itself be considered a stumbling block in the making of prime rock music. Indeed, some groups, like wines, have acquired a vintage flavour that simply can't be matched by the fizzy bouquets of the latest overnight sensations. Certainly, when five musicians of this calibre, who started playing together more than 20 years ago, hit their stride, they boast a musical cohesion that is simply not available off the peg.

'Love in an Elevator' (their first UK Top 20 hit) clunks along with its catchy, chanted chorus; 'Janie's Got a Gun' is a confident incursion into BON JOVI's melodic territory, 'My Girl' and 'The Other Side' are great belts of post-STONES rock'n'roll; and 'What it Takes' is a big ballad finale with a touch of the BEATLES about it.

Joan Armatrading

Born: December 9 1950, St Kitts, West Indies
UK No.5 album: 1980: _Me Myself I_ (A&M CDMID 106)

Her fans have followed her from their Seventies bedsits to the suburbia of the Nineties, but that wasn't quite how Joan Armatrading planned it.

'I made my first album with the notion that I was doing a super-demo, and that other artists would then start doing my songs and I would be this anonymous, very successful songwriter. But it didn't quite work out like that. People seemed to want me to sing the songs . . . Now I can't imagine doing anything else. I would have trouble fitting into a band and not being the person in charge.'

That first 'super-demo', _Whatever's For Us_ (Castle Communications CLACD 143; 1974), was a flop, and Armatrading fared no better with her second release, _Back to the Night_ (unavailable; 1975). But far from sliding into anonymity, she has since blossomed into a star who remains, curiously enough, one of the least-covered major songwriters in rock.

Armatrading arrived in Birmingham, England when she was seven. Her mother bought a piano 'because it looked nice', and Armatrading Jr, always a rather quiet and introverted child, taught herself to play and write songs on it.

Nowadays she rubs shoulders with the biggest names in rock at shows like the 1987 Prince's Trust concert, where she knocked out a fraught but firm guitar solo with both Mark Knopfler and Eric CLAPTON breathing down her neck. While she is hardly a grandstanding performer, her calm composure has seen her through appearances at such vast outdoor events as the 1988 Mandela concert at Wembley Stadium and the Amnesty concert at Giants Stadium in New York.

A senior member of rock's landed gentry, she now lives in Guildford, where she owns a stud farm and has built and equipped her own home-recording studio.

Too fond of rock to be a folk singer and too much her own woman either to follow or to lead any movement or trend, Armatrading has remained unique in all respects but one: the curious case of her doppleganger Tracy Chapman. While anyone with ears has noted the uncanny resemblance between the musical styles of the two performers, Armatrading has remained resolutely coy on the subject. The two actually appeared, at separate times, on the same stage at the Mandela concert. Indeed it was that globally televised appearance which bounced Chapman's début, *Tracy Chapman* (Elektra 960 774-2; 1988), into multi-platinum overdrive. But the two didn't meet, and Armatrading claims never to have heard Chapman's first album, a feat which must have called for a stringently evasive pattern of listening behaviour during the first half of 1988.

Evidently her thoughts on Chapman, as on so many subjects, are destined to remain her own. For although Armatrading will happily strip down to the emotional raw in the lyrics of her songs, she strenuously guards against invasions of her privacy. A vegetarian who neither drinks nor smokes, her social life remains strictly divorced from the glare of the celebrity circuit. 'I wouldn't even be able to tell you where Stringfellows is,' she says, 'and that's the way I'd like to keep it.'

● *Joan Armatrading* (A&M CDMID 104) [1976]

It was this, her third album, that provided the break-through. A compelling, sparsely arranged fusion of folk, funk and gently smouldering introspection, it yielded the hit single 'Love and Affection', and effectively put Armatrading in a class of her own. The album was produced by the great Glyn Johns, who later averred that it was the best album he had ever made. Coming from a supervisor of recordings by The WHO and The ROLLING STONES among many others, this was serious praise indeed. Johns subsequently produced *Show Some Emotion* (A&M CDMID 105; 1977) and *To The Limit* (A&M CDA 4732; 1978), both strong collections of vintage Armatrading material.

● *The Shouting Stage* (A&M CDA 5211) [1988]
● *Hearts and Flowers* (A&M 395 298-2) [1990]

In more recent times Armatrading has tended to hire the best musicians that money can buy – Mark Knopfler, Pino Palladino, Manu Katche, Mark Brzezicki *et al* – and the (self-)production on these albums has become richer and smoother, an adult rock sound tailor-made for the CD medium.

Unfortunately, the instrumental structures of her later songs suffer from the rather arid, calculated quality that tends to beset the work of singer-songwriters who labour for long periods in their own recording studios (see Kate BUSH). But her lyrics are still turbulent despatches from the emotional front line and beneath that calm, retiring exterior Armatrading is either experiencing a maelstrom of interpersonal ferment or has the benefit of a very vivid imagination.

● *The Very Best of Joan Armatrading* (A&M 397 122-2) [1991]

This comprehensive collection revisits high points including 'Me Myself I', 'Drop the Pilot', 'Willow' and 'Down to Zero', while the perennial 'Love and Affection' (still her only Top 10 single) succumbs to the subtle charms of a Hugh Padgham remix, and comes out sounding pretty much the way it always did.

Aswad

Convened: 1975, London
Brinsley Forde (f) – guitar/vocals; Tony Gad – bass; Angus Drummie Zeb (f) – drums/vocals
UK No.10 album: 1988: *Distant Thunder* (Mango RRCD 27)

Initially a five-piece band, Aswad came together in the Metro Youth Club at the hub of Ladbroke Grove in London. They became the first UK reggae act to win a contract with a major label when they joined the roster at Island in 1976. They also signed up for the Rock Against Racism movement and thus became unlikely collaborators in the punk revolution.

But although they shared a militant attitude, Aswad's music abounded with fluid harmonies, deep, undulating rhythms and a languid grace that was the antithesis of punk's harsh clamour. 'There was a tension,' Drummie Zeb admitted later. 'We did the Chelmsford punk festival and as soon as we came on stage they started to throw toilet rolls and tomato ketchup bottles, which we didn't like at all. The organiser said, "They love you. That's how they show their appreciation." But frankly that wasn't the kind of appreciation we were looking for.'

Born in Britain of parents from Grenada (Zeb), Jamaica (Gad) and Guyana (Forde), Aswad were well placed to draw up the ground plans for British roots reggae. One of the earliest live bands to experiment with dub, they exerted considerable influence on contemporaries such as Birmingham's Steel Pulse. But despite an energetic recording schedule (over the years they have also been signed to Columbia, Stylus, Grove and run their own Simba label), they enjoyed limited commercial success and sustained themselves for the best part of a decade by bundling into transit vans and embarking on endless rounds of the UK club and college circuit.

Their break eventually came in 1988 with the No.1 success of 'Don't Turn Around', making theirs one of the longest group apprenticeships for 'overnight' stardom on record. Like the songs that provided the biggest hits for Boris Gardiner ('I Want to Wake Up With You'; 1986), Maxi Priest ('Close to You'; 1990) and Freddie McGregor ('Just Don't Want to be Lonely'; 1987), 'Don't Turn Around' is a light, tuneful slice of lovers' rock that represents the sprightlier side of the heavily rhythmic reggae coin. It was composed by Dianne Warren and Albert Hammond, the bespoke songwriting partnership responsible for many AOR hits including Starship's 1987 No.1 'Nothing's Gonna Stop Us Now'.

One of Aswad's great strengths, apart from patience, has been their ability to retain musical and political credibility, without shying away from the popular end of the market. It is Zeb's boast that Aswad is the only British group to have worked with three of the original Wailers – with Bunny Wailer on Jamaican TV, with Bob MARLEY on 'Punky Reggae Party' and with Peter Tosh on 'Johnny B Goode'. But he also says it is no less a source of pride that they were asked to produce a track for Cliff RICHARD, and invited to perform at his Wembley Stadium concerts in 1989.

● *Renaissance* (Stylus SMD 866) [1988]

This 20-track summary of Aswad's recording career, from the measured gait and jazzy inflections of their first single, 'Back To Africa', through to the breezy lovers' rock of 'Don't Turn Around' and 'Give a Little Love', is a perfect introduction to Britain's longest serving indigenous reggae group. Early (minor) hits such as 'Chasing for the Breeze' and an eloquent reworking of Toots and the Maytals' '54-46 Was My Number ('88 Remix)' underline the band's longstanding commitment to melody, while the depth-charged bass and drum-beats of the instrumentals 'Warrior Charge' and 'Dub Fire' provide solid evidence of their heavy dance-floor credentials. Not a group to belabour their political points, Aswad's generally upbeat songs are underpinned by other material of a tougher mien. 'Three Babylon', with its ominous burst of police sirens weaving through the back of the mix during the intro, is a pungent evocation of campaigns waged in the front line.

Bad Company See FREE

The Band

Convened: 1967, Woodstock, New York. Split up: 1976
Rick Danko (f) – bass/vocals; Levon Helm (f) – drums/vocals; Garth Hudson (f) – keyboards; Richard Manuel (f) (died 4.3.86) – keyboards/vocals; Robbie Robertson (f) – guitar/vocals
US No.5 album: 1970: *Stage Fright* (Capitol CDP 793 593-2)

If ever a collection of individuals deserved a name that was both anonymous and élite it was The Band. In America, where they never even put a single in the Top 20, these five musicians, four of them Canadian (Helm came from Arkansas), made a pivotal contribution to the development of rock while remaining essentially a cult phenomenon.

For one thing, as Bob DYLAN's backing group, they facilitated his transition from folk laureate to rock messiah, and on his early 'electric' dates of 1965/6 got booed nightly for their troubles. Then, in 1968, at the height of psychedelia, they appeared on the inside cover of their début, *Music From Big Pink* (see below), in a grainy, sepia-tinted photograph dressed, of all things, like ancient hillbilly farmers.

'We were rebelling against the rebellion,' was how Robertson explained the philosophy of this multi-talented ensemble. 'Whatever was happening. If everybody was going east, then we were going west and we never once discussed it. There was this kind of ingrained thing from us all along. We were these kind of rebels with an absolute cause. It was an instinct to separate ourselves from the pack.'

Such natural and idiosyncratic musical cohesion was a function of the many years the five of them had spent playing together, first in Canada as Ronnie Hawkins' backing band The Hawks, and then with DYLAN, before even contemplating a recording session of their own. What seems a lazy, sleepy-sounding musical feel is actually the product of razor-sharp, road-hardened reflexes and the musicians' complete confidence in each other's playing.

After the initial burst of astounding creativity which produced *Music From Big Pink* (see below), *The Band* (see below) and *Stage Fright* (Capitol CDP 793 593-2; 1970), The Band went through a lull in the Seventies. They toured again with DYLAN and backed him on his album *Planet Waves* (Columbia CD 32154; 1974), but once the decision to split had been taken, they elected to go out in style with one final show, recorded and filmed for posterity as *The Last Waltz* (see below).

The group reconvened in 1983 for live work, but without Robertson, who was replaced by James Wieder. The personal pressures which had forced them off the road in the Seventies finally took a grisly toll when Manuel, apparently suffering from a fit of depression, hanged himself from the shower-curtain rail in a Florida hotel room.

● *Music From Big Pink* (Capitol CDP 746 069-2) [1968]

In stark contrast to the then-prevailing vogue for hard rock and militant psychedelia, songs like 'Chest Fever' and 'The Weight' from this counter-revolutionary first album follow a pulse that is like the stately if occasionally erratic ticking of a grandfather clock. They also give voice to a lyrical lexicon that encompasses a wealth of traditional Americana of a sort that most hippies in 1968 had considered dead and buried. As the critic Greil Marcus remarked, 'Their music gave us a sense that the country was richer than we guessed.'

- **The Band** (Capitol CDP 746 493-2) [1969]

Incorporating 'Up On Cripple Creek' (their biggest US hit), 'The Night They Drove Old Dixie Down' (a hit for Joan Baez), 'Rag Mama Rag' (their biggest UK hit) and 'King Harvest (Has Surely Come)', this remains the definitive Band album.

The old-fashioned production values that hold sway on these early recordings could not be further removed from modern studio techniques. Instead of the bright, resonant instrumental tones that we have become conditioned to expect, there is the dull thud of Helm's dead-damped toms, Robertson's rubber-band guitar tone, Hudson's tinny, swirling organ sound and a rousing chorus of hick harmony vocals. It is a tonal assemblage that sounded dated at the time and which is now irredeemably locked into a bygone age.

Yet the warm-blooded, wholly expressive quality of the playing, born of The Band's unique musical camaraderie, is a commodity that all the click tracks and cannon-shot snare sounds in the world couldn't reproduce. What is on these discs is what was played at the sessions; there has been no hi-tech fairy-dust sprinkled here.

- **Rock of Ages** (Capitol CDP 746 617-2) [1972]

The Band's rough-hewn musical charm was always well suited to the live environment, and here they proved themselves especially adroit at capturing a sense of occasion. The album was recorded at a New Year's Eve show in New York at the end of 1971 for which a six-part horn section had been specially recruited. As well as the obvious stage favourites – 'Rag Mama Rag', 'The Weight' *et al* – there are several rarer inclusions such as 'Get Up Jake' (a little-known B-side) and a dynamic interpretation of Marvin GAYE's 'Don't Do It'.

- **The Last Waltz** (Warner Bros K266076) [1978]

Following their 1976 tour, The Band played one final show on Thanksgiving Day at the Winterland hall in San Francisco. They were joined by a stellar cast of guests including DYLAN, Neil YOUNG, Eric CLAPTON, Van MORRISON, Dr John, Neil Diamond, Joni

MITCHELL and Muddy WATERS and the resulting, highly emotional event was subsequently made into a remarkable film and live album, *The Last Waltz*. Thus was the legend of The Band cast in stone.

● *To Kingdom Come* (Capitol CDS 792 169-2) [1989]

This is an impressive, 31-track, remastered compilation which renders most of the other 'Best of . . .' collections redundant. As well as rounding up all the usual suspects it incorporates a smattering of rare material and copious sleeve notes. It is recommended with the caveat that it includes nothing from *The Last Waltz*.

Robbie Robertson

Born: Jaime Robertson, July 5 1944, Toronto, Canada
UK No.23 album: 1987: *Robbie Robertson* (Geffen GEFD
24160)

Although he was the most prolific writer and guiding spirit of The Band, Robertson rarely sang the songs himself, and he practically never wrote the lyrics. Called to explain the 11-year hiatus between the demise of The Band and the release of his solo début, Robinson said, 'I wasn't so sure I had something to say.'

● *Robbie Robertson* (Geffen GEFD 24160) [1987]

Recorded in New Orleans, London, Woodstock and Dublin, Robertson's first solo album was a good three years and $750,000 in the making – not a lot for Madonna, perhaps, but more than you might expect from someone in Robertson's reduced circumstances. In constructing it he worked from historical foundations – both Danko and Hudson were enlisted as sidemen – and then imported modern influences and modern expertise in roughly equal part. All four members of U2 feature on 'Sweet Fire of Love' and the hard rocking 'Testimony', while Peter GABRIEL lends vocals to 'Fallen Angel' and keyboards to 'Broken Arrow'. Although Robertson hauls out a marvellously gruff narrative on the album's surprise UK hit 'Somewhere Down the Crazy River', elsewhere he tends to sound disconcertingly like STING, especially on the biblical rant 'Showdown at Big Sky'. It is still a tough, tuneful album by an old dog committed to learning a few new tricks.

The Beach Boys

Convened: 1961, Los Angeles, California
Al Jardine (f) – vocals/guitar; Bruce Johnston – vocals/ keyboards; Mike Love (f) – vocals/saxophone/percussion; Carl Wilson (f) vocals/guitar
UK No.1 albums: 1976: *20 Golden Greats* (Capitol CDP 746 738-2)
              1983: *The Very Best of The Beach Boys* (unavailable)
US No.1 albums: 1964: *Beach Boys Concert* (coupled with *Live in London* [1969] (Capitol CDP 793 697-2)
              1974: *Endless Summer* (Capitol CDP 746 467-2)

At one point in the Sixties, The Beach Boys were plausibly described as 'the most popular American band of all time'. Certainly they were the only American group seriously to challenge the pre-eminence of The BEATLES, and as such they enjoyed a similarly blanket appeal among all age groups.

In a grand succession of hit singles, they defined an ideal adolescent Californian lifestyle revolving around sun, surf, sexy girls and speedy hot-rods. But rarely has such a carefree image been so at odds with the reality.

The band was started as a family affair by the teenaged brothers Brian (vocals/bass/keyboards), Dennis (vocals/drums) and Carl Wilson, together with their cousin Mike Love and a close friend Al Jardine. The Wilson boys were kept on a tight leash by their father Murry, a bullying martinet who reserved his harshest treatment for Brian, the eldest and most gifted of his sons and the creative mastermind of the group.

As well as verbal and physical abuse, one of Murry's strangest 'punishments' was to take out his glass eye and force Brian to look at the empty socket. The boy became a nervous and introverted young man, deaf in one ear, who never ventured on to a surfboard in his life, while Murry became the group's manager until he was sacked in 1964.

The Beach Boys' output in the early days was phenomenal, but although they had released 11 albums by the end of 1965, these are of patchy quality. It was the era when albums were an adjunct to singles – not, as today, the other way round – and these early collections tend to consist of two or three hits, the odd hidden gem and varying amounts of padding.

They are not very long either, and Capitol records has adopted a benign policy of 'doubling up' the early albums and releasing them on single CDs. Of the many two-in-one packages on offer, the best are:

– *Surfer Girl* (US 1963) with *Shut Down Volume 2* (US 1964) (Capitol CDP 793 622-2): a coupling which shows the clear development from the surfing theme to the related activity of beach buggies, hot-rods and drag racing on *Shut Down Volume 2*.

– *Little Deuce Coupe* (US 1963) with *All Summer Long* (US 1964) (Capitol CDP 793 694-2): much the same mixture, incorporating US hits 'Be True to Your School' and 'I Get Around' (No.1).

– *The Beach Boys Today!* (US 1965) with *Summer Days (and Summer Nights!!)* (US 1965) (Capitol CDP 793 694-2): on which clear evidence of Brian Wilson's capacity for a more complex and reflective style of songwriting emerges; despite their paperweight titles (and excessive use of exclamation marks), these albums prefigure the more ambitious work that was to come to fruition on *Pet Sounds* (see below).

It would be difficult to imagine a man less cut out for coping with the rigours of touring in a group than Brian Wilson. His first breakdown occurred in December 1964 when he suffered a catatonic fit aboard a plane bound for Houston from LA. He retired from the road, and from the world, but continued to work in his role as the group's writer and producer. His mood was obsessive. 'Holed up in his Bel Air mansion for months on end, he fed his depression with a diet of milkshakes, hashish brownies and random psychedelic drugs', according to *Billboard*'s editor-in-chief Timothy White.

Brian Wilson was replaced in the touring line-up by the amiable, clean-living and uncomplicated Bruce Johnston and the band carried on, with Brian operating from the wings to a greater or lesser degree depending on his mental and physical well-being.

The Beach Boys were a spent force in the studio long before the hell-raising Dennis Wilson (the only surfer in the group) drowned while swimming from his boat in the harbour at Marina Del Ray on December 28 1983. They released their last 'new' album in 1985, a half-hearted mélange of second-string material called *The Beach Boys* (Caribou CD 26378; deleted 1987) and apart from a fluke US No.1 hit with 'Kokomo' from the soundtrack of the movie *Cocktail* (Elektra 960 806-2; 1988) and the 1987 novelty hit 'Wipe-Out', a collaboration with roly-poly rappers The Fat Boys, the band has continued as an essentially nostalgic, touring attraction until the present.

'The Beach Boys need to make a studio album that we're proud of, an album that is as wonderful as [Paul SIMON's] *Graceland*,' said Bruce Johnston in 1991. Putting his finger on the problem, he continued: 'For that to happen Brian Wilson must be involved. His timbre must be on future recordings.'

The omens are not good even though in 1988 Brian finally released his critically acclaimed but commercially disastrous solo début *Brian Wilson* (Warner Bros 925 669-2; deleted July 1990), and last performed with The Beach Boys as recently as May 1990 (at the Cow Palace, San Francisco).

For although fit and apparently *compos mentis*, Brian has fallen under the spell of his controversial therapist-cum-manager, Eugene Landy, a sinister, Svengali-like character who has stamped his mark on virtually every aspect of his client's life, and who has firmly resisted any attempts to foster closer contacts between Brian and the group.

● *Pet Sounds* (Capitol CDP 748 421-2) [1966]

Brian Wilson's and The Beach Boys' masterwork, *Pet Sounds* is thought to have inspired The BEATLES in the writing and recording of *Sergeant Pepper's Lonely Hearts Club Band*. Like The BEATLES' *magnum opus*, it incorporates a wealth of non-rock instrumentation on tracks like 'God Only Knows' and 'Let's Go Away for a While', and is essentially a product of the studio environment.

But there is a mood of deep melancholia which emotionally

earths the album in a way that the flip witticisms and hazy hippy rhetoric of *Sergeant Pepper* were not able to do. Brian Wilson poured enough of his troubled soul into songs like 'I Know There's an Answer' and 'I Just Wasn't Made for These Times' to make this a searing, if sometimes faintly depressing, listening experience.

The CD comes with additional material from the sessions which didn't get used on the album at the time, three items of limited curiosity value only.

● *Smiley Smile* [1967]/*Wild Honey* [1968] (Capitol CDP 793 696-2)

Despite winning enduring critical acclaim, *Pet Sounds* was not a great commercial success and although The Beach Boys were a singles band *par excellence*, they never fully made the transition to albums. The follow-up, originally to have been called *Smile*, was intended to change that, but Brian lost heart and all but abandoned the project midway through its production. After interminable delays and alterations, *Smiley Smile* was salvaged from the wreckage, and although it is a a disappointingly patched-up version of the original grand plan, it nevertheless incorporates two of the group's all-time classics, 'Heroes and Villains' and 'Good Vibrations'. The latter, a long and complex 'pocket symphony', topped the charts in both the UK and the US and was, arguably, the pinnacle of the group's achievements. Although it remains a *bona fide* classic, it now seems a rather overwrought affair; was this where Freddie Mercury first got the idea for 'Bohemian Rhapsody'?

Smiley Smile is coupled with its follow-up, *Wild Honey*, an unremarkable 'back-to-basics' job, recorded in Brian's living room.

● *20 Golden Greats* (Capitol CDP 746 738-2) [1976]

Here in one breathless rush is what all the fuss was about in the first place. The Beach Boys' sound was built on a three-cornered foundation of gliding instrumental surf music, tightly knit doo-wop harmonies and sanitised Chuck BERRY guitar riffs. Indeed, their 1963 hit 'Surfin' USA', which kicks off this compilation, is so similar to BERRY's 'Sweet Little Sixteen' that, after legal representations were made, BERRY was retrospectively awarded a co-writing credit.

From such shaky beginnings a string of classics ensued : 'I Get Around', 'Help Me Rhonda', 'California Girls', 'Barbara-Ann' and 'Sloop John B' for starters.

As the collection wends its way past the 1965 watershed, so the songwriting matures, and the melodies, structures and emotions of 'God Only Knows', 'Wouldn't It Be Nice', 'Heroes and Villains' and the inevitable 'Good Vibrations' take on a far more involved quality.

Here in one handy collection is the core of the repertoire which has sustained affection and interest in The Beach Boys for more than twenty years after the passing of their singularly beleaguered glory days.

The Beatles

Convened: 1960, Liverpool. Split up: 1970

George HARRISON (f) – guitar/vocals/sitar; John LENNON (f) (died 8.12.80) – vocals/guitar/keyboards; Paul McCARTNEY (f) – vocals/bass/keyboards; Ringo Starr (f) – drums/vocals

US/UK No.1 albums: 1964: *A Hard Day's Night*(Parlophone CDP 746 437-2)

1965: *Help* (Parlophone CDP 746 439-2)

1966: *Rubber Soul* (Parlophone CDP 746 440-2)

1966: *Revolver* (Parlophone CDP 746 441-2)

1967: *Sergeant Pepper's Lonely Hearts Club Band* (Parlophone CDP 746 442-2)

1968: *The Beatles* (Parlophone CDP 746 443-2)

1969: *Abbey Road* (Parlophone CDP 774 6446-2)

1970: *Let It Be* (Parlophone CDP 746 447-2)

UK No.1 albums: 1963: *Please Please Me* (Parlophone CDP 746 435-2)

1963: **With The Beatles** (Parlophone CDP 746 436-2)

1964: **Beatles For Sale** (Parlophone CDP 746 438-2)

1977: **The Beatles at the Hollywood Bowl** (unavailable)

US No.1 albums: 1964: **Meet The Beatles** (unavailable)

1964: **The Beatles' Second Album** (unavailable)

1964: **Beatles '65** (unavailable)

1965: **Beatles VI** (unavailable)

1966: **'Yesterday' . . . and Today** (unavailable)

1967: **Magical Mystery Tour** (Parlophone CDP 748 062-2)

1973: **The Beatles 1967–1970** (unavailable)

The most important group in the history of rock, The Beatles provided the catalyst for a revolution in popular music and fashion. They were the first pop group to write their own music and to break with the custom of having a leader or lead vocalist to act as the main focus of attention. Instead their image, as McCARTNEY once described it, was that of 'four parts of the same person'.

The Beatles reigned supreme throughout the Sixties and many of their feats have never been equalled. Between 1963 and 1969 they enjoyed an incredible total of 17 UK No.1 hit singles. In America on April 4 1964 they held all top five places on the singles chart with 'Can't Buy Me Love', 'Twist and Shout', 'She Loves You', 'I Want to Hold Your Hand' and 'Please Please Me'.

They inspired a new form of worshipful mass hysteria among teenagers, dubbed by the *Daily Mirror* as Beatlemania. But they also redefined perceptions of rock music's aesthetic worth, prompting the critic of *The Times*, William Mann, to comment famously on the use of 'Aeolian cadences' and 'pandiatonic clusters' in their music. Like it or not, *Sergeant Pepper's Lonely Hearts Club Band* is still one of the most revered recordings ever released by a rock act.

Official recognition of their achievements was conferred on

June 12 1965 when all four Beatles were awarded the MBE in the Queen's Birthday Honours list, an unprecedented and unrepeated distinction in the milieu of rock.

More than two decades later, the re-release of the first four Beatles albums in March 1987 was a watershed in the marketing of rock on CD. So confident was EMI (Parlophone's parent company) of the demand for this repackaged product that it aimed its advertising campaign, in part, at people who didn't even own a CD player. The assumption was that newly available versions of the original Beatles albums would be enough to prompt the ditherers into making a capital investment in compact disc hardware. Such confidence, both in the merits of laser technology and in the enduring appeal of the most hallowed group in the history of rock'n'roll, proved well founded. Yet it remains a telling irony that it should be a monumental exercise in Fab Four nostalgia which heralded the final flowering of the brave new world of digital hi-tech.

Having initially been wrong-footed by the contractual wrangling that had kept Beatles product off the CD racks for so long, EMI set about marketing this newly restored treasure trove with a vengeance. Back in 1987, CDs were still not in wide circulation. Record companies did not send them to journalists as a matter of course, least of all EMI (which to this day operates the stingiest mail-out policy of all the major record labels).

In the case of the Beatles CDs, to forestall the expected high demand, the company took a policy decision that there were to be no review copies sent out *whatsoever*. Instead, any reviewer who wished to sample this 'new' aural experience in advance had to attend one of several pre-arranged playback sessions at EMI's Abbey Road studios. It was a bizarre experience sitting in a little room, full of journalists, all listening with earnest concentration to a body of material that had been recorded when two-track magnetic tape was still state of the art. What was for many people the first test of this most sophisticated of audio reproduction systems was being made in relation to an album which, in the case of *Please Please Me*, had been recorded in mono in one day (February 11 1963, to be precise); 14 tracks knocked out in less time than many bands now spend fixing the drum sound.

Producer and 'fifth Beatle' George Martin had been called in personally to supervise the remastering of the recordings, and much play was made of the fact that the early Beatles albums were transferred to CD in glorious mono. For although there were stereo* mixes done at the original sessions, these amounted to nothing more than a quick piece of post-production doctoring by the engineer, and were hardly a true representation of The Beatles' intentions when they recorded the songs in the first place.

All the albums were rendered in their original UK versions and the various American configurations have rightly been consigned to the dustbin of history (unlike The ROLLING STONES' catalogue where there has been an unsatisfactory mixture of UK and US versions of early albums floating around).

There was a distinct sense of revelation at hearing those Beatles albums for the first time on CD. The lack of scratches, crackle, hiss or any other interference was uncanny and it was explained that there is even a specially encoded 'digital silence' between tracks. Many instrumental features of the recordings became plainly audible for the first time: Starr's brushes on 'A Taste of Honey' for example, or certain harmonic shades to HARRISON's guitar on 'Do You Want To Know a Secret'. It was like suddenly seeing a familiar view from a window that had had a layer of grime removed from it, or returning to an old haunt to find that all the buildings had been sandblasted clean, their brickwork restored from sooty black to spotless beige.

But the pristine quality of CD reproduction is a two-sided coin. Without going in to all the 'warm' vinyl versus 'cold' silver disc controversy discussed in the introduction, it undoubtedly leaves the musicians' efforts painfully vulnerable to critical study. Did HARRISON intend the guitar intro to 'Roll Over Beethoven' to sound like a rubber band being twanged? Did McCARTNEY forget to plug in the bass during 'Hold Me Tight'? And were The Beatles really a barber shop vocal unit masquerading as a beat group, something you could be forgiven for thinking given the unfa-

---

* Stereo was a novelty in 1963, and the vast majority of records and record players were still mono. Thus, most acts did their recording and mixing in mono, leaving the engineer to concoct what would now be regarded as a 'fake' stereo image after the producer and musicians had gone home. Such stereo mixes sometimes presented a very odd aural picture. For instance, the voice might be stuck completely over on one side and the drums on the other. Other stereo enhancement tricks included adding a lot of needless echo on the voice or reverb on the instruments.

shionably prominent mixing of their extraordinarily versatile harmonies?

The launch of The Beatles catalogue on CD generated sufficient interest to earn each of the initial batch of reissues a place in the Top 50, no mean feat given the small proportion of CD to vinyl sales at that time. *Please Please Me, With The Beatles, A Hard Day's Night* and *Beatles for Sale* all re-entered the album chart on March 7 1987. They were followed by *Help, Rubber Soul* and *Revolver* on May 9 1987. However, the hype surrounding that little lot was but a whisper compared to the orchestrated clamour which surrounded the 20th anniversary of the release of The Beatles' magnum opus, *Sergeant Pepper's Lonely Hearts Club Band*, in June 1987.

'It Was Twenty Years Ago Today' trumpeted the headlines of a legion of dozy newspaper and colour supplement sub-editors, while on the day in question, June 1, a party held at Abbey Road studios to celebrate the 'event' was reported on *The Six O'Clock News*. Later the same evening, a two-hour Granada TV documentary, entitled *It Was Twenty Years Ago Today*, was broadcast. Naturally, EMI was waiting to pounce with the newly digitalised version of that historic album. Released bang on cue, it duly re-entered the chart the following week, winging its way with no great difficulty up to No.3.

The Beatles, unofficially known as *The White Album*, also did surprisingly brisk business, peaking at No.18 in September 1987, but already the excitement had passed. The rest of the albums – *Yellow Submarine* (Parlophone CDP 746 445-2; 1969), *Magical Mystery Tour, Abbey Road* and *Let It Be* – were pushed out on CD with little more fuss, in nice time for Christmas.

One side effect of this tidal wave of Beatles nostalgia was a spate of Beatles 'homages' by latterday acts who should have known better. Tears For Fears and XTC both put out albums that were little more than pastiches of the Fab Four's style, while it was suddenly cool for everyone from PRINCE to recidivist newcomers like Lenny KRAVITZ and Jellyfish to flaunt a broad streak of Beatles-ish psychedelia in their range of retro-influences.

Perhaps more to the point, the new digital hi-fi system had received the ultimate endorsement. A decade of musical invention and revolution had been recalled and compressed into 12 months, while a new technological revolution had simultaneously been completed. The compact disc was here to stay, at least for a while.

- **With The Beatles** (Parlophone CDP 746 436-2) [1963]

All the early Beatles albums are worth renewed attention, but it is the second which best evokes the bold, effervescent belt of pure harmony pop that sparked the rock revolution in the first place. Among many of their finest early performances, it houses original compositions such as 'All My Loving' along with covers like 'You Really Got a Hold On Me' and Chuck BERRY's immortal 'Roll Over Beethoven'.

- **Revolver** (Parlophone CDP 746 441-2) [1966]

Although it was *Sergeant Pepper* which won the bouquets, this is a considerably stronger selection of songs, and arguably The Beatles' finest hour. In terms of liberating pop from the guitar/ bass/drums convention, there had never been anything in rock like 'Eleanor Rigby', a song which George Martin scored for four violins, two violas and two cellos and on which none of The Beatles actually played a note. 'Tomorrow Never Knows' is similarly adventurous, while 'Love to You' marks HARRISON's first fully developed excursion into the world of Indian music. And despite its deceptively childish simplicity there is still an unsettling air about 'Yellow Submarine' and its stoned nursery rhyme sound effects. The strikingly insurgent quality of other numbers, especially 'Taxman' and 'Got To Get You Into My Life', remains intact to this day.

- **Sergeant Pepper's Lonely Hearts Club Band** (Parlophone CDP 746 442-2) [1967]

A collection of cute, catchy tunes infused with a musty, vaudevillian flavour by its lysergically inspired lyrics, *Sergeant Pepper's Lonely Hearts Club Band* is probably the most overrated album in the history of rock. Indeed, it was hailed as a masterpiece *on the day of its release* and its Toytown visions were soon being implausibly compared to the works of Schubert, Tennyson and Pinter.

It certainly stamped its mark on the collective psyche of the rock world, but in hindsight, the album's grand experimental visions led nowhere. Compare its influence with that of Jimi HENDRIX's *Are You Experienced*, which in 1967 languished at No.2 in the chart for much of *Sergeant Pepper's* run at the top. While HENDRIX's album opened up a world of infinite possibilities, the Beatles' *magnum opus* beckoned only in the direction of a stylistic cul de sac.

Most of the fuss was undoubtedly due to the timing of its release at the woozy apogee of the 1967 'Summer of Love', and to George Martin's innovative production which somehow shaped songs as diverse as HARRISON's unlistenable raga 'Within You, Without You' and McCARTNEY's ineffably twee 'When I'm 64' into an overall 'concept', thereby stretching – in people's minds at least – the boundaries of what was then called pop. Pop became rock and rock became art. 'Album rock' was born and suddenly everybody was in a mood to 'progress'. The otiose horrors of the rock opera lay just around the corner.

- *The Beatles* (Parlophone CDP 746 443-2) [1968]

While the rest of the rock world struggled to match the innovations of *Sergeant Pepper* with varying degrees of success, The Beatles went 'back to basics' (of a sort) with a double-album follow-up that could not have been more simply titled and designed. Notwithstanding the four songs by HARRISON, (including 'While My Guitar Gently Weeps') and even a singular credit to Starr for 'Don't Pass Me By', *The White Album* stands as a towering monument to the fecund songwriting talent of LENNON and McCARTNEY. From the rollicking 'Back in the USSR' to the gritty 'Revolution' and the fatuous 'Ob-La-Di, Ob-La-Da', even at this late stage in the game, there were few who could hold a candle to their incredible creative zest.

- *CD Singles Collection* (Parlophone 203 566-0) [1989]

An expensive and unwieldy boxed set, this comprises 22 three-inch CD singles from 'Love Me Do' to 'Let It Be' complete with B-sides. Singles were not generally included on UK albums in the Sixties. So apart from two patchy compilations – *Past Masters Volume 1* (Parlophone CDP 790 043-2; 1988) and *Past Masters Volume 2* (Parlophone CDP 790 044-2; 1988) – which include some but by no means all of The Beatles' singles, this is, unfortunately, the only way of getting them on CD.

Ringo Starr

Born Richard Starkey, July 7 1940, Liverpool
US No.2 album: 1973: *Ringo* (Parlophone CDEMS 1386)

Although his friendly, humorous disposition and adequate playing skills secured his place aboard the Beatles charabanc, Starr was never the man at the wheel.

The group's epoch-making achievements lent considerable initial momentum to his solo career, which he squandered by opening his account with an indulgent collection of showbiz standards, intended as a gift for his mother (*Sentimental Journey* 1970; unavailable), followed by a collection of poorly sung country songs (*Beaucoups of Blues* 1971; unavailable).

Even so, he enjoyed international hit singles with 'It Don't Come Easy' (1971) and 'Back Off Boogaloo' (1972) and found his métier as a singer of light, innocuous pop fare with *Ringo* (see above), by far his best album, providing him with two US No.1 hits – 'Photograph' and 'You're Sixteen'. His winning streak continued up to *Goodnight Vienna* (1974; unavailable), after which the hits tailed off.

Starr nevertheless remained a part of the rock aristocracy, appearing in 1976 with a host of stars at The BAND's farewell concert *The Last Waltz*. But throughout the rest of the Seventies his recording and acting work brought him little in the way of either critical approval or commercial success.

After dabbling unsuccessfully in projects ranging from film-making to furniture design and founding his own short-lived record label, Ring O'Records, his forays into the public eye became less frequent throughout the Eighties. In fact, his biggest success of the decade was in his rôle as narrator of the children's TV series *Thomas the Tank Engine and Friends*.

'I get by with a little help from my friends,' Starr sang in 1967 in his typically casual, down-beat fashion, and although he was one of the prime movers in the moulding of rock, there is a telling resonance in the gentle modesty of those words.

Jeff Beck

Born: June 24 1944, Surrey
US No.4 album: 1975: *Blow by Blow* (Epic CD 32367)

Jeff Beck is the greatest living rock guitarist, and that's official. In 1990, in a regular feature called 'The Experts' Expert', *The Observer* canvassed a cross-section of celebrity guitarists (Hank Marvin, Gary Moore, Brian May and others) on who they rated as the top man in their trade. Beck came out in front by a mile.

His pioneering work in the Sixties with The Yardbirds and the first Jeff Beck Group earned him a place in the original holy trinity of English guitarists. Eric CLAPTON sold out, Jimmy Page burned out and Beck . . . ? He dropped out. His profile these days is all but invisible and much of his back catalogue is available on CD only on import from America.

Even so, the handful of shows which he played in 1990, his first in Britain since 1981, were devastating displays of virtuoso delicacy and heavy metal brutality. Having given so sparingly of himself – just three albums released in the 13 years to 1991 – he has, paradoxically, been able to preserve the take-no-prisoners approach that has long since deserted his contemporaries.

A moody, self-contained maverick, Beck has blazed an erratic trail littered with the detritus of broken guitars and broken bands. When director Michelangelo Antonioni was looking for a group to symbolise the nihilistic side of Swinging London in his notorious counter-culture movie *Blow Up*, it was the Yardbirds who got the job. Beck was required to smash his guitar and amp to pieces, a duty which he performed with sinister relish during a number called 'Stroll On'.

After Beck left The Yardbirds in 1966, he formed The Jeff Beck Group with the then unknown vocalist Rod STEWART and Ron Wood who, although he would later play guitar in The ROLLING STONES, was relegated to playing bass while in the presence of the maestro (as was Jimmy Page, initially, when he and Beck both played in The Yardbirds).

In the Seventies Beck turned his hand to jazz fusion, producing a succession of superlative, predominantly instrumental albums with ever-longer stretches of inactivity in between.

There is no great mystery as to why Beck's catalogue is so poorly represented on CD. Despite unstinting critical acclaim, his albums no longer sell in sufficient quantities in this country to set product managers' pulses racing. In 1986, after he had just collected a Grammy award for Best Rock Instrumental for 'Escape' from the album *Flash* (Epic CD 26112; 1985), Beck said, 'For what little amount of work I do, I don't deserve anything.' It was a theme he returned to when commenting on his lack of public presence on the eve of his 1990 dates. 'One of Eric CLAPTON's tours is more than the sum total of my live work since 1980. I just can't withstand endless nights playing. The pitch that I play at is so intense that I just can't do it every night.'

While the lack of a strategy has kept Beck out of the limelight, it is, ironically, his obstinate unwillingness to play the big numbers game that has enabled him to be, in the words of David Gilmour of PINK FLOYD, 'the most consistently brilliant guitarist over the past 25 years'.

● *Truth* [1968]/*Beck-Ola* [1969] (EMI CDP 7954692)

These two albums, re-issued together on one mid-price CD in 1991, offer an excellent value-for-money summary of the recorded exploits of the first Jeff Beck Group, with Rod STEWART and Ron Wood. *Truth* is a brutish, innovative affair that Beck believes laid the ground-plan for the first LED ZEPPELIN album. Indeed, on hearing *Led Zeppelin I*, Beck pronounced himself 'stunned, shocked, annoyed, flattered and just a bit miffed by the whole thing.' Tracks include heavy-duty reworkings of Tim Rose's 'Morning Dew' (with STEWART in particularly fine voice), Willie Dixon's 'You Shook Me' and 'I Ain't Superstitious', and The Yardbirds' 'Shapes of Things'.

Beck-Ola is cast in a similar mould, with STEWART's raucous singing providing a fine counterpoint to the savage beauty of Beck's playing on a high quota of riff and blues numbers, including 'Plynth (Water Down the Drain)' and two Elvis PRESLEY favourites, 'Jailhouse Rock' and 'All Shook Up'.

The production (by Mickie Most) on both these albums is dreadful, but the belt of raw energy is nevertheless unmistakable and they remain flawed but dynamically intense statements of their time.

- **Blow by Blow** (Epic CD 32367) [1975]

Produced by George Martin, this album marked the start of Beck's purple patch as a solo jazz fusionist, aided by keyboard player Jan Hammer. His mercurial style is showcased on numbers like 'Freeway Jam' and a heart-stopping 'Cause We've Ended as Lovers', music which forged the missing link between the hard rock of LED ZEPPELIN and the esoteric jazz-rock of virtuosos like The Mahavishnu Orchestra and Weather Report.

- **Wired** (Epic CD 86012 deleted January 1989) [1976]
- **There and Back** (Epic CD 83288 deleted January 1989) [1980]

The twin peaks of his achievements, artistically speaking, these two albums have been deleted in the UK but are readily available as imports. *Wired* continued the George Martin liaison, and boasts epic performances of 'Led Boots', 'Come Dancing' and Charlie Mingus' 'Goodbye Pork Pie Hat'. *There and Back*, featuring Jan Hammer and drummer Simon Phillips, is a boggling *tour de force*, welding melody, technique and bloody-minded aggression into a blitzkrieg of pure, dazzling genius. The opening track, 'Star Cycle', was adopted as the the theme tune of the Channel 4 TV series *The Tube*.

- **Late 60s with Rod Stewart** (EMI CDP 746710 2) [1988]

Between February 1967 and July 1969, under the guidance of manager Mickie Most, Beck cut a succession of pop hit singles: 'Tallyman', 'Love is Blue' and by far the best known song he has ever recorded 'Hi Ho Silver Lining', which peaked at a surprisingly modest No.14 in the hit parade of 1967. Beck hates the disproportionate amount of attention given to the song, still describing it in 1990 as a 'ball and chain round my ankle'. This compilation scoops up these singles together with the best material from *Truth* and *Beck-Ola*.

- **Beckology** (Epic/Legacy EPC 469262 2) [US 1991/UK 1992]

Given the paucity of Beck's back catalogue available on CD, I suppose we should be grateful for this three-disc boxed set spanning his entire career, but in truth it is an irritating compilation that seems to have been spoilt for a ha'p'orth of tar.

The box itself is designed to look like an oblong guitar case, a neat idea, but made out of poorly finished, cheap cardboard. Likewise the accompanying booklet which features a solidly researched essay by Gene Santoro and a Pete Frame family tree (microscopically reproduced in white against a beige background) has a tacky look and feel.

Musically, like so many of these boxed sets, it's a mixture of the indispensable and the otherwise unreleasable. The three tracks by Beck's first group, The Tridents, which start the package off – 'Trouble in Mind', 'Nursery Rhyme' and 'Wandering Man Blues' – are performances of primitive incompetence.

Most of The Yardbirds' hits are present and correct: 'Heart Full of Soul', 'Over Under Sideways Down', 'Shapes of Things', 'Happenings Ten Years Time Ago', together with some pretty flaky album tracks and B-sides. The liaisons with Rod STEWART are also well represented, from raucous rockers like 'Plynth (Water Down the Drain)' and 'I've Been Drinking' through to the gorgeous 1984 recording of Curtis Mayfield's 'People Get Ready', and it is a jolt to recall what a strong blues shouter STEWART once was.

And of course there are many superlative instrumental performances from Beck's solo years (1975–present), notably the Grammy-award-winning 'Escape', the full-tilt version of 'Freeway Jam' (with The Jan Hammer Group) and his heart-wrenching interpretation of the Charlie Mingus standard 'Goodbye Pork Pie Hat'.

But there are several alarming omissions, too. The perennial live favourite 'Blue Wind' and the awesome thunder of 'Space Boogie' are two which spring to mind, but most glaring of all is the absence of 'Star Cycle' – thanks to *The Tube* TV series probably Beck's best known recording in this country. Surely someone could have alerted the American compilers to this fact? However, his one claim to pop star immortality, the *faux-naif* hit single 'Hi Ho Silver Lining', is included.

There is only one track ('The Pump') taken from 1980's landmark *There and Back* collection, and two each from *Wired* and *Blow By Blow*, which wouldn't seem so bad if there weren't four lumbering numbers from his regrettable dalliance with the Beck

Bogert and Appice 'supergroup' to wade through, where one ('Superstition') would have been plenty.

Beck is a genius, but this oddly lopsided collection is more of a curiosity trove than a tribute, and fails to do justice to his astounding and long-neglected legacy.

Chuck Berry

Born: Charles Berry, October 18 1926, San José, California
UK No.6 album: 1963: *Chuck Berry on Stage* (unavailable)

Chuck Berry's exuberantly poetic facility for chronicling the joys and frustrations of teenage life in the Fifties while neatly drawing together the strands of R'n'B and pop, made him one of the handful of performers who were instrumental in the invention of rock'n'roll.

Although he has released more than 20 albums, Berry's place in the history books was guaranteed by a glorious run of singles, beginning in 1955 with the million-selling 'Maybellene', interrupted by a spell of imprisonment between 1961-63 and then petering out after a final burst of glory with 'No Particular Place to Go' and 'Promised Land' in 1964. Ironically his biggest hit came years later with the tediously risqué 'My Ding-a-Ling', which reached No.1 on both sides of the Atlantic in 1972. Berry has insisted that he had been playing the song live since 'before "Maybellene"', but it is out of keeping with the rest of his repertoire, to put it mildly.

Berry learnt to play guitar while at school in St Louis, Missouri, but for several years he earned a living either by hairdressing or by assembly-line labouring. He was nearly 30, and married with two children, when Muddy WATERS introduced him to Leonard Chess, owner of Chess records in 1955. By the end of that year 'Maybellene' had scaled the US Top 5 and popular music would never be the same again.

His stretch in the Indiana federal prison in 1962 for 'transporting a minor across a state line for immoral purposes' – a contravention of the Mann Act – undoubtedly took some of the shine off Berry's golden period and as the Sixties progressed he began to tread water, increasingly trading on past glories.

His celebrity did not preclude further brushes with the law. In July 1979, only one month after performing by special request of Jimmy Carter at the White House, he was jailed for income tax evasion on his accounts of 1973.

In 1986 Keith Richards helped to organise a special concert at the Fox Theatre in St Louis to celebrate Berry's 60th birthday. The event was filmed by Taylor Hackford and the resulting movie *Hail! Hail! Rock'n'Roll* [1987] boasted some remarkable fly-on-the-wall sequences, including one scene in rehearsals where Berry was shouting the odds at Richards for not playing his (Berry's) riffs correctly.

'Chuck thought that all those rehearsals were for the band,' Richards later recalled. 'He didn't realise that they were for him. He wouldn't have thought in a million years that it was him who needed to rehearse, and it's not the sort of thing you can tell him.'

Plainly, Berry is not the sort of man to be told anything that he does not want to hear, yet for all his contrariness he *has* contributed one of the central repertoires of rock'n'roll. His songs romp along with an irresistible swing, their narrative lyrics – usually about cars, girls or school – delivered with a spry, mischievous twinkle. As a wordsmith he has few peers, while his distinctive style of guitar playing, with its racy sound and double-string bends, provided the blueprint for key figures from Keith Richards to Steve Jones of The SEX PISTOLS.

But the real beauty of Berry's music is that his songs, with their chord progressions loosely adapted from the familiar framework of the blues, have proved inspiring and accessible to musicians of all standards right down the years. Virtually anyone who has ever managed to string three chords together on a guitar – from the kid next door to Jimi HENDRIX – has at some time had a crack at 'Johnny B Goode' or 'Sweet Little Sixteen'.

In latter years Berry has depended on this widespread familiarity with his work to the point where he no longer bothers to take a group with him on tour, requiring the promoters to supply a local backing band at each gig. The musicians hired in this way may count themselves fortunate if they even meet Berry before the show, let alone find out beforehand what songs he is going to play and in which keys. His by-the-book approach to performing is legendary. He is paid in cash in advance; he plays strictly in accordance with the times specified in his contract; whether it be press interviews, TV appearances or even his own recording sessions, nothing is given beyond the bare minimum.

Perhaps he figures he has already given enough. Such is the universality of Berry's appeal that his work was among the key recordings from all walks of life to be encapsulated on the gold-plated copper record sent out on the *Voyager* space probe in 1977. The audio equipment which went with it was designed to last a billion years. As far as leaving something to posterity is concerned, you can't do much better than that.

- **The Chess Box** (Chess CHD 38) [1989]

'Johnny B Goode', 'Bye Bye Johnny', 'Sweet Little Rock'n'Roller', 'Promised Land', 'Memphis', 'Rock and Roll Music' and so many other titles on this chronologically organised, three-disc, 71-track sweep through Berry's career provided the very warp and woof from which the fabric of modern rock music was created. These original recordings, digitally remastered but many of them primitive in the extreme, teem with invention and a generosity of spirit that few performers have subsequently been able to match.

In Britain many of the songs are perhaps more clearly remembered for other artists' versions than for the originals. Berry's most assiduous disciples were undoubtedly The ROLLING STONES, who recorded significant cover versions of 'Come On', 'Around and Around', 'Carol' and about a dozen others. 'Roll Over Beethoven' was co-opted by The BEATLES; The Yardbirds (with Eric CLAPTON) opened their ground-breaking album *Five Live Yardbirds* (Charly CDCHARLY 182; 1964) with an absolutely scorching version of 'Too Much Monkey Business'; Buddy Holly scored a posthumous No.3 hit with 'Brown-Eyed Handsome Man' in 1963, and so on.

Some of the later material, including 'My Ding-a-Ling', is disposable, and at a price of around £40 the coat may not be cut according to everyone's cloth, but this would nevertheless be a marvellous addition to virtually any CD collection.

- **The Great Twenty-Eight** (Chess CHD 92500) [1990]

For those who want only the best, here are the edited highlights of Berry's most creative period on one disc, with not a ding-a-ling in sight.

Big Country

Convened: 1981, Dunfermline
Stuart Adamson (f) – vocals/guitar; Tony Butler (f) – bass/
vocals; Bruce Watson (f) – guitar
UK No.1 album: 1984: *Steeltown* (Mercury 822831-2)

In the early Eighties rock had been temporarily hijacked by a wave
of synthesiser bands – Depeche Mode, Yazoo, Soft Cell, EURYTH-
MICS, The HUMAN LEAGUE, Orchestral Manoeuvres In The Dark,
Ultravox and Blancmange to name a few – and the idea of
launching a new group that featured prominent guitars and no
keyboards ran counter to every fashionable precept of the day.
The fact that in 1983, 'Fields of Fire', only the second single
released by Big Country, managed to thrive in such a hostile
commercial environment, spoke volumes for the stirring quality
and steadfast integrity of the group's music.

Stuart Adamson had been a leading light in Dunfermline-based
desperados The Skids, one of the first Scottish groups to convert
the do-it-yourself ethos of punk from local enthusiasm into
national chart success with a portfolio of hits including 'Into the
Valley' and the incomparable 'Working for the Yankee Dollar'
(collected with others on *Dunfermline*, Virgin COMCD; 1987).
Their vocalist, Richard Jobson, went on to be a radio and TV
personality of modest repute.

Although Big Country enjoyed rapid success in Britain and
America, they were gradually overtaken by their contemporaries
U2 and SIMPLE MINDS, and much of the initial shine wore off. They
invested heavily in a promotional visit to the Soviet Union to
launch their unremarkable 1988 album *Peace in our Time* (Mercury
836325-2), flying 258 members of the world's TV, radio and press
to Moscow for the second of five concerts at the Palace of Sports.
This unprecedented junket behind the fraying iron curtain
guaranteed an impressive crescendo of media coverage and a vast
bill for promotional expenses, which their record company was
prepared to foot only in part.

They returned home, exhausted, dispirited and out of pocket.
Officially the group split up – and drummer Mark Brzezicki did
indeed quit – but within a couple of weeks the others were back
together again, already planning the next campaign.

- **The Crossing** (Mercury 812870-2) [1983]

A stunning debut which defined the unique Big Country sound: skirling guitars, windswept choruses and much romantic, north-of-the-border imagery. Notable for the hits 'In a Big Country', 'Fields of Fire' and the perennial stage favourite 'Harvest Home' – the group's first (and only non-chart) single.

- **Through a Big Country** (Mercury 846022-2) [1990]

This is the greatest hits album which, coming after the Moscow débâcle and the departure of Mark Brzezicki, drew a line under the first phase of the group's career. They had enjoyed no fewer than 16 chart singles since 1983 – several more than U2 during the same period – providing abundant material for such a compilation. All the best ones are here – 'Fields of Fire', 'Chance', 'Wonderland', 'Look Away' – and many more besides.

- **No Place Like Home** (Vertigo 510230-2) [1991]

The new Big Country emerged gleaming and chrysalis-like from the gloom of their peacenik period at the end of the Eighties. Having been lumbered for so long with the bagpipe guitars/checked-shirt rockers tag, they now cut loose with an upfront roots-rock approach that reaped dividends.

With Brzezicki's rôle confined to that of guest contributor, the intricate mosaic of syncopations and galloping tom-tom tattoos that was such a recognisable (some would say hackneyed) feature of the old Big Country sound had gone. A new tone was set right from the opening bars of the first single, 'Republican Party Reptile', which boasts a howling slide-guitar motif that is more dust-bowl blues than Highland fling. While Big Country had used mandolins and acoustic guitars before, the banjo and honky-tonk piano which contributes to the mellow Celtic-country swing of 'Beautiful People' was a first.

With its crisp, open-ended production – courtesy of Pat Moran and the band – this inspired collection quarries deep into the rock face, tapping the traditions of country, folk and Southern blues, while never losing the emotional integrity that has always been the cornerstone of Big Country's music.

The Black Crowes

Convened: 1989, Atlanta, Georgia
Johnny Colt – bass/vocals; Marc Ford – guitar; Steve Gorman
– drums; Chris Robinson (f) – vocals; Rich Robinson (f) –
guitar/vocals
US No.4 album: 1990: *Shake Your Money Maker* (Def American 842 515-2)

Although in their early twenties, The Black Crowes play old-
fashioned, rebel-yell rock. Their hair is long, their rôle models are
groups like The Faces, The ROLLING STONES, The Allman Brothers
Band and FREE, and their attitude is not so much about letting the
good times roll as it is a crusade to reassert the anti-establishment
values and abandoned working practices of rock in its heyday.
They don't use synthesisers or click tracks to keep time in the
studio, and their distaste for hi-tech trickery even extended on
one occasion to asking Reeves Gabrels (of David BOWIE's Tin
Machine) not to use his headless Steinberger guitar when they
invited him to jam with them on stage (Gabrels used it anyway).

The Robinson brothers played their first gig in 1984 as Mr
Crowe's Garden at a bar in Chattanooga, Tennessee. As the sons
of folk musician Stan Robinson, a career in music seemed
ordained. 'Chris and I didn't decide be in a band,' guitarist Rich
Robinson told *Rolling Stone*, 'we just assumed it.'

Spotted playing in a New York bar in 1988 by A & R man
George Drakoulias, the brothers recruited new personnel,
changed their name to The Black Crowes and, with Drakoulias
producing, recorded their début album *Shake Your Money Maker*
(see below) in the summer of 1989.

They embarked on 18 months of solid touring, slotting their
own shows in between treks supporting AEROSMITH, Heart, Robert
Plant, ZZ TOP and AC/DC. After a slow start, the album took off,
eventually selling in excess of three million copies in America
alone.

Chris Robinson has a reputation for shooting his mouth off
first and thinking about the consequences later, and the band
acquired a helpful frisson of controversy when they were booted
off ZZ TOP's *Recycler* tour in the wake of one too many snide
remarks about the beer company which was sponsoring the
event.

It's only rock'n'roll, but liking it is not enough for these guys. They're determined to love it to death.

● *Shake Your Money Maker* (Def American 842 515-2) [1990]

As soon as they lurch in to the mid-paced chug of the opener, 'Twice as Hard', followed by the even grittier 'Jealous Again', you know this album is something special.

For one thing, The Crowes have mastered the lost art of the measured rock'n'roll tempo: not slow, never speedy, but a loose, tugging style of playing that is as precise as it sounds relaxed.

For another, the beaky Chris Robinson is a charismatic singer with the kind of rich, throaty timbre that was the hallmark of Seventies heroes like Paul Rodgers (FREE, Bad Company) and Rod STEWART. And in Rich Robinson they have a gutsy rhythm and slide guitarist who makes highly distinctive use of open tunings.

They stamp a mark of complete authority on just about every song here. Typical of the set is 'Stare It Cold', an infectious slice of raunch propelled by a Rich Robinson riff which lurches to either side of the beat like a drunk weaving along the top of a garden wall. From the burning Southern soul of 'Seeing Things' and the *Sticky Fingers*-era grind of 'Sister Luck' to the aching ballad 'She Talks to Angels' and the funky, soul-man strut of Otis Redding's 'Hard to Handle', these boys play like they care.

Bon Jovi

Convened: 1983, Sayreville, New Jersey
David Bryan (f) – keyboards/vocals; Jon Bon Jovi (f) – vocals/
guitar/harmonica; Richie Sambora (f) – guitar/vocals; Alec
John Such (f) – bass/vocals; Tico Torres (f) – drums
UK/US No.1 album: 1988: *New Jersey* (Vertigo 836 345-2)
US No.1 album: 1986: *Slippery When Wet* (Vertigo 830
            264-2)

In 1986 heavy rock found its answer to The BEATLES. Although acts like Iron Maiden, DEF LEPPARD and VAN HALEN had previously sold albums in prodigious quantities, especially in America, Bon Jovi was the first *bona fide* metal group to enjoy blanket crossover success. Their needle shot off the graph with the release of *Slippery When Wet* (see below). A series of singles taken from it sailed to the top of the charts worldwide, greasing the way for a staggering sales tally of 17 million albums, a figure well into the rarified atmosphere of the HOUSTON/JACKSON super-league.

Bon Jovi was the brainchild of singer Jon Bongiovi (the original spelling of his name), who recruited musicians from among his friends and contacts playing the bars and juke-joints of New Jersey, the same circuit that in earlier days had nurtured Bruce SPRINGSTEEN and his E Street Band.

Bon Jovi's subsequent success undoubtedly hinges on the group's ability to appeal as much to the (predominantly male) gig-goers at a heavy-metal rough-house like Castle Donington as to the (predominantly female) teenage viewers of *Top of the Pops*. With their sleek figures and long blow-dried hair cascading over a uniform of sleeveless tops and tattooed shoulders, the boys look simultaneously tough and pretty, like their music.

Their shows are energetic, barnstorming displays performed with a nimble touch and a rousing generosity of spirit capable of dispelling all but the most cynical reservations about their music's lack of depth. For theirs is the sound and look by which an era of heavy rock has come to be defined. A slew of successful, but inevitably lesser bands, all flying the metal-with-melody flag, followed in their wake – among them Skid Row, Poison and Cinderella – while old stagers from Alice Cooper to WHITESNAKE started to pay just that little bit more attention to melodic detail and soon reaped the benefits of the new, metal-friendly environment which Bon Jovi had created.

● *Slippery When Wet* (Vertigo 830 264-2) [1986]

This was the album which took metal to the heart of the mainstream: a cheerful compendium of chunky, power-chord riffs, squealing, rapid-fire guitar solos and high pitched singing that on the surface sounds little different from any number of groups who favour those uncomfortable-looking, tight, striped trousers.

What sets it apart from the competition is the group's uncommon facility with a melody. One of their neatest tricks is to hit you with a catchy sequence that sounds like a great chorus immediately before going into the real chorus. This tried and tested Tin Pan Alley strategy – the musical equivalent to the old one-two combination in boxing – is employed to particularly devastating effect on 'You Give Love a Bad Name' and 'Livin' on a Prayer', two hugely successful singles which both topped the US chart.

- *New Jersey* (Vertigo 836 345-2) [1988]

The appeal of Bon Jovi's welterweight sound is further enhanced on the follow-up to *Slippery When Wet* by a clearly discernible SPRINGSTEEN influence, particularly on songs like 'Born to be my Baby' and 'Wild is the Wind'. SPRINGSTEEN himself had recently appeared on stage with Bon Jovi at the Stone Pony in Asbury Park, and the album's title serves further to underline the group's geographical and spiritual connections with NJ's most adored son.

The essence of the collection is a number like 'Blood on Blood', the sort of rousing, anthemic celebration of male adolescence which Bryan ADAMS pulled off with definitive panache on his 'Summer of '69'. Glib dismissals of a band which sums up in such explicit clichés the romantic notion of boys running free ('One for all and all for one', etc) are, of course, two a penny. But this is still diligently assembled stuff, and its continuing power to affect and inspire remains undeniable.

- *Bon Jovi CD Box Set* (Vertigo 838 605-2) [1989]

This complete collection of Bon Jovi albums released to date, at the stiff price of approximately £50, was deleted in March 1991, but some stores may still have it in stock. The set incorporates: *Bon Jovi (Vertigo 814 982-2; 1984), 7800 Degrees Fahrenheit* (Vertigo 824 509-2), *Slippery When Wet* (see above) and *New Jersey* (see above).

David Bowie

Born: David Robert Jones, January 8, 1947, London
UK No.1 albums: 1973: *Aladdin Sane* (EMI CDP 794 768-2)
                 1973: *Pin-Ups* (EMI CDEMC 3580)

1974: ***Diamond Dogs*** (EMI CDEMC 3584)
1980: ***Scary Monsters and Super Creeps*** (EMI
CDEMD 1029)
1983: ***Let's Dance*** (EMI America CDP 746
002-2)
1984: ***Tonight*** (EMI America CDP 746
047-2)

The constant, unsubtle rewriting of history that prompted journalist/broadcaster David Hepworth to the conclusion that 'Stalin would have loved the music press' has resulted in a persistent downgrading of David Bowie's colossal contribution to the scheme of things. Anyone coming to rock later than 1985 could be forgiven for thinking that here is an addled, Seventies relic of meagre talent, whose chameleon-like changes of image and style, although lauded at the time, amounted to little more than a knack for ripping off the prevailing musical trends of an era.

Yet Bowie's presence during the preceding decade coloured the entire fabric of popular music, leaving an indelible impression on everything from the silky textures of English art-rock (Bryan Ferry, David Sylvian) to the ragged fringes of American punk (Lou REED, Iggy POP) and beyond.

The majority of his back catalogue was released on compact disc in the usual way throughout the Eighties, but when his contract with RCA expired, there was a hiatus of about 18 months between that label's deletion of his albums and their subsequent re-release on his new label EMI.

Instead of putting out these vintage albums in their original form (a scrupulously observed policy when they reissued The BEATLES' back catalogue) EMI has in all cases tacked on rare and previously unreleased material to the end of the original track listings. Most of the extra songs bear little more than curiosity value ('rare' and 'previously unreleased' recordings have usually acquired such status for a good reason) and it wasn't long before some critics were complaining that the presence of this substandard material was a violation of the original albums' integrity.

Personally, I could live without the great majority of these bonus tracks, but given the persistent criticism of wasted capacity on CD versions of old 30–40 minute albums, it seems a churlish point to make. Record companies, it seems, are damned if they do and damned if they don't.

- **The Man Who Sold the World** (EMI CDEMC 3573) [US 1970/UK 1971]

Bowie was already posing in discreet make-up and a provocative dress on this notorious gender-bender cover, reproduced on CD now, but swiftly replaced with different artwork in the USA, UK and most European territories the first time round. More importantly, he had also recruited guitarist Mick Ronson and drummer Woody Woodmansey, who would become the nucleus of his Spiders From Mars band.

Tony Visconti, who produced and played bass, failed to distinguish himself in either department, but despite the paper-weight drum sound and fat, burping bass noises, there is an expectant tang to these performances, a metallic taste of excitement in the air.

The album is full of shadowy, edgy narratives like 'All the Madmen' that sit uneasily on some overly convoluted, progressive rock arrangements. 'The Width of a Circle' is a flawed epic, boasting some of the grittiest soloing Ronson ever committed to tape.

Lulu, of all people, took the title track to No.3 in 1974, but the really interesting thing about this album is that more than any other in Bowie's back catalogue it prefigures the eventual direction his work would take almost twenty years later with Tin Machine.

- **The Rise and Fall of Ziggy Stardust and the Spiders From Mars** (EMI CDEMC 3577) [1972]

A collection of flamboyant, titillating riches, Ziggy Stardust was the album which flagged Bowie's status as a Seventies godhead. In presenting himself as a theatrical, pseudo-alien, rock'n'roll fantasy figure, Bowie single-handedly swept away any lingering notions of tie-die hippy idealism and replaced them with a new manifesto of glittering sci-fi artifice and mysteriously ambiguous sexuality. Musically, he was still dealing in the conventional, three-minute rock song idiom, but the startling personae which inhabited the

43

lyrics of 'Starman', 'Ziggy Stardust', 'Suffragette City', *et al* gave it a challenging and exotic twist.

An extra track that *is* well worth h aving is 'John, I'm Only Dancing', the 1972 hit which should have been on the album in the first place. This remains an awesomely realised piece of work, and still his finest hour.

● *Young Americans* (CDEMD 1021) [1975]

Although Bowie had shed various personae since the Ziggy Stardust days, here was the first truly dramatic switch in musical direction, as he swung from the straight rock'n'roll of *Diamond Dogs* (see above) to the blue-eyed soul of *Young Americans*. Recorded at Sigma Sound studios in Philadelphia and in New York with a stellar cast of American musicians including Willie Weeks (bass), Andy Newmark (drums) and Carlos Alomar (guitar), it yielded the massive-selling US No.1 single 'Fame', co-written with John LENNON.

● *Low* (CDEMD 1025) [1977]
● *Heroes* (CDEMD 1027) [1977]

Austere, experimental and largely instrumental, these were two of three albums recorded in Berlin and produced in collaboration with Brian Eno. Bowie seemed to be making a conscious effort to distance himself from the mainstream, despite the obvious hits of 'Sound and Vision' (from *Low*) and the title track of *Heroes*.

Not that easy to listen to, these albums are nevertheless remarkable for their effect on the development of English pop. Within four years a new wave of musicians from The HUMAN LEAGUE to Depeche Mode were kitted out with synthesiser technology and a memory of what Bowie had accomplished here. A revolution had begun.

● *Let's Dance* (EMI America CDP 746 002-2) [1983]

After a string of changes in image and musical presentation, Bowie finally 'came out' as a relatively normal human being and recorded his best set of songs since *Ziggy Stardust*. Produced by Nile Rogers, *Let's Dance* features the Texas blues guitar of the late Stevie

Ray Vaughan, the Asbury Jukes's horn section, and no synthesisers whatsoever. In temperament it recalls the rock'n'roll big-band sound of American R'n'B originators like Johnny Otis, Louis Jordan and even James BROWN, but brought bang up to date and given that slightly odd Bowie tilt.

'Modern Love', 'China Girl', 'Cat People (Putting Out Fire)' and, of course, the title track are among the album's bountiful charms.

● *ChangesBowie* (EMI CDDBTV 1) [1990]

This superlative retrospective combines on one disc both of Bowie's two previous greatest hits compilations, *ChangesoneBowie* (unavailable; 1976) and *ChangestwoBowie* (unavailable; 1981). Between the poles of 'Space Oddity' (1969) and 'Blue Jean' (1984) lies a continent of outstanding material.

The one thread that has remained consistent throughout a career larded with so many improbable changes of costume is Bowie's excellence as a songwriter. Clearly, that has been the bedrock of his success while all else has been as shifting sand, a point underlined by this embarrassment of riches: 'Ziggy Stardust', 'Jean Genie', 'Diamond Dogs', 'Rebel Rebel', 'Fame' (a rather tinny ' '90 Remix'), 'Ashes to Ashes', 'Fashion' and 'Let's Dance' to list a few.

In a perverse and irritating reversal of the usual procedure, the CD version is missing three tracks which are included on the vinyl and cassette formats – 'Starman', 'Life on Mars' and 'Sound and Vision' – none of them exactly piffling items, either.

Tin Machine

Convened: 1989, Montreux, Switzerland
David Bowie (f) – vocals/guitar/saxophone; Reeves Gabrels (f) – guitar; Hunt Sales (f) – drums/vocals; Tony Sales (f) – bass/vocals
UK No.3 album: 1989 *Tin Machine* (EMI USA CDP 791 990-2)

From a peak of creative and commercial success with *Let's Dance* (see above), Bowie started on a downwards spiral, eventually hitting rock bottom with the critical savaging which he suffered for *Never Let Me Down* (EMI America CDP 746 677-2; 1987) and its unwieldy accompanying *Glass Spider* tour. One of England's all-time vocal stylists, he was now sounding like the legion of acts which had copied him; sometimes not even that good.

In forming Tin Machine, a sort of middle-aged metal band with class, he slapped a tourniquet on the haemorrhaged muse with such suddenness and brute force that it made you wince.

Bowie first met the Sales brothers when he and they played as part of Iggy POP's backing band in 1977. His involvement with Gabrels stemmed from a brief collaboration with the Montreal-based dance troupe La La La Human Steps in 1988. The four of them met together for the first time and within 36 hours they had put down the first track of what was to become the Tin Machine début.

● *Tin Machine* (EMI USA CDP 791 990-2) [1989]

Many fans greeted the scathing, bruising noise of this album with shocked disbelief. Underpinned by Hunt Sales's huge, ambient snare and kick-drum sound and dominated by the wailing sonic extremes of Gabrels's guitarr, the songs surge and teeter, many of them simply falling apart at the end, where they are left twitching on the floor, unrepaired by any invisible engineer's hand.

In a musical sense, Tin Machine is Bowie's wilder and rougher version of The Power Station, but whereas Robert PALMER maintained an academic air and a discreet distance from his accomplices, Bowie has flung himself into this project heart and soul.

A truly inspired album, *Tin Machine* was released at a time when heavy metal's stock had never been higher, its musical vocabulary accepted as the *lingua franca* of groups ranging from BON JOVI to Sonic Youth. The album sold a million worldwide, which was better than any of Bowie's solo releases since *Let's Dance* (see above).

But it also produced a reservoire of ill-feeling among a generation of Bowie snobs, the more blinkered of his fans who had once idolised him as a paradigm of progressive chic and now felt mortally betrayed to see him fraternising with Piers Morgan in *The Sun* and playing heavy rock with the lads. Thus it was that with every roaring vocal mannerism and power-guitar chord change, Bowie's achievements somehow seemed to be denoted a notch or two down the historical pecking order.

Brand X See Phil COLLINS

Garth Brooks

Born February 7 1962, Tulsa, Oklahoma
US No.1 album: 1991: *Ropin' the Wind* (Capitol CDESTU 2162)

The phenomenal success of Garth Brooks in 1991 ushered in a new era in country music. In America, where there has long been a rigidly institutionalised separation of country from the pop mainstream, Brooks knocked a hole in the barrier big enough to drive a bus through.

'Garth Brooks is not only the biggest country superstar since the Urban Cowboy boom of the early Eighties, but the most popular male singer of any kind in the country today,' trumpeted *Entertainment Weekly* in September 1991.

Brooks came along at a time when the *stylistic* division between country and rock had been under pressure for some time. On the one hand, various rock acts like John MELLENCAMP had been borrowing country melodies and making use of fiddles, accordions and pedal steel guitars for many years; on the other, New Country singers like Dwight Yoakam had successfully adapted a hefty backbeat and a rock'n'roll attitude to an otherwise traditional country formula.

Thus, although they never made the Top 40 or got played on rock radio, a new generation of country stars, including Clint Black, Lyle Lovett and Alan Jackson, had begun to enjoy success outside the traditional (specialist) audience for the genre. Brooks capitalised on the rising head of steam, and in much the same way that VAN HALEN and BON JOVI made heavy metal acceptable to listeners and programmers of American Top 40 radio, so Brooks became the country star that the mass rock audience learned to love. As *Billboard* editor-in-chief Timothy White observed: 'Today's generation buys Garth the way they'd buy STING or JESUS JONES or Tom PETTY, because they like him, not because he's country.'

A late starter in the music business, Brooks arrived in Nashville in 1987 with a degree in advertising and marketing obtained from Oklahoma State University, where he had studied on an athletics scholarship. His early musical tastes stretched from the classic country of George Jones and Merle Haggard to the melodic rock of Seventies bands like Kansas, Journey and Boston. Other favourites included James Taylor and Dan Fogelberg, but his most immediate inspiration was the neo-traditionalist New Country star George Strait. 'I heard . . . [Strait's] "Unwound" on my car radio, and that's the exact moment it all changed,' Garth told *People* magazine. 'I became a George wannabe and imitator for the next seven years.'

Now Brooks is the one being imitated. After a slow start, his début, *Garth Brooks* (Capitol CDP 790 897-2; 1989), eventually went on to sell three million copies and was still surfing the US Top 40 in January 1992. In the same month, the follow-up, *No Fences* (Capitol CDP 795 503-2; 1990), which has sold six million copies, was still resident in the US Top 10, and *Ropin' the Wind* (see below) was enjoying its tenth week at No.1.

While maintaining country's musical foundations, Brooks has updated its style and presentation. True, he wears a cowboy hat and has regrettable taste in shirts, but as a live performer he is more of an exhibitionist in the rock star mould – throwing water over his band or climbing a rope ladder up into the lighting gantries – than the typically static, face-in-front-of-a-microphone type.

His graphic promotional video for 'The Thunder Rolls' (from *No Fences*), a song about marital infidelity and domestic violence, was banned by country cable TV networks more attuned to a barnyard and haystacks style of visuals, but was nevertheless nominated as Music Video of the Year in the Country Music Association Awards.

Brooks' appeal stretches across the board, but most significantly he has a vast teenage following. As a performer he has been compared to Bruce SPRINGSTEEN and in 1991 he outsold PRINCE, HAMMER and Michael JACKSON.

Country music will never be the same again.

● *Ropin' the Wind* (Capitol CDESTU 2162) [US 1991/UK 1992]

Brooks' third album is a delightful conflation of hard country and soft rock. There is nothing especially revolutionary about the sound, and if Nashville had not become the inflexible and hide-bound musical establishment that it is, the album might not have caused the fuss that it has.

Brooks undoubtedly has an authentic country voice and lyrics about truckers stranded on a snowbound highway – 'Eighteen wheels anchored somewhere out of Dover' (from 'Cold Shoulder') – have a timeless ring. But he also has a maverick streak, and although he didn't write it himself, 'Against the Grain' spells out his credo with tailor-made precision: 'If you're gonna leave your mark/You can't follow like a bunch of sheep/You got to listen to your heart... Nothin' ventured, nothin' gained/Sometimes you've got to go against the grain.'

Thus, Brooks is not shy about tackling 'Shameless', a pop ballad written by Billy JOEL, which although tarted up with a melancholy pedal steel, has a soaring, unequivocally rock guitar solo. 'Burning Bridges' is full of homespun wisdoms, sung with that sobbing catch in the voice, but as a tune it would not be out of place on a FLEETWOOD MAC album. And so on.

The scale of *Ropin' the Wind*'s mass appeal in America took the UK record company by surprise, and rather than risk wasting its potential by leaving it to sink or swim in the pre-Christmas rush of 1991, they delayed its release until early 1992. Brooks' success in the UK was by no means a foregone conclusion, and as an incentive four extra tracks have been added to the UK version of the album – 'Alabama Clay', 'Everytime That It Rains', 'Nobody Gets Off in This Town' and 'Cowboy Bill' – all originally to be found on his first album, *Garth Brooks*.

James Brown

Born: May 3 1933, Barnwell, South Carolina
US No.2 album: 1963: *Live at the Apollo* (October 24, 1962)
(Polydor 843 479-2)

Thanks to the spread of sampling techniques, the man who wrote the book on black dance music has been co-opted as a central character in the sequel. James Brown's dynamic Sixties' rhythm section has featured (unknowingly) on a plethora of hip-hop, house, go-go and rap records. Indeed, according to one authoritative source, snatches of Brown's performances have turned up on between two and three thousand recordings since the vogue for sampling began, and not just by rap acts either. The drum part from his 1970 hit 'Funky Drummer', for instance, has been recycled endlessly, providing the basis for songs by Sinead O'Connor, George MICHAEL, Fine Young Cannibals and no doubt many others besides.

Even when the master's twitchy, grunting vocals have not been lifted directly from the original recordings, they are still an ever-present influence on the latest dance-floor hits. As a singer, dancer and showman supreme, Brown has long been acknowledged as the major influence on the current generation of multi-platinum superstars, notably Michael JACKSON, HAMMER, Bobby Brown and PRINCE.

Not a man noted for his modesty, Brown has claimed various unofficial titles during his career – The Godfather of Soul, The Hardest Working Man in Showbusiness, Soul Brother No.1, Mr Dynamite – but his right to use them has never been seriously called into question.

As an ally of successive US presidents and a confrère of black power leaders, his influence in the community at one point was such that his TV appeals for calm in the wake of the assassination of Dr Martin Luther King in 1968 played a vital part in defusing a potentially explosive situation on the streets of America's inner cities.

Yet his own volatile temperament has been less readily contained and in 1988 he was sentenced to six years' imprisonment following an incident in which he threatened two policemen with a gun, then attempted to run them over in his car while under the influence of the drug Angel Dust. He was released in March 1991 and put on parole until October 1993.

Born a few miles from the Georgia state line, Brown was shunted off to live in Augusta's 9th and Gwinnett, after his parents had separated. In that black neighbourhood of clapboard shacks, he was looked after by one 'Aunt T', when she was around, or else left to fend for himself. His school attendance was irregular, and he dropped out in his early teens. He competed in local field sports events and then trained and fought as a bantamweight boxer. He also sang with a local gospel group, The Three Swanees, and an R'n'B band called Bill Johnson and The Four Steps of Rhythm.

In 1954 he co-opted a group called The Gospel Starlighters, led by a singer and pianist friend, Bobby Byrd, and converted them into his own group, James Brown and The Famous Flames. They came to the attention of Little Richard's manager Clint Brantley, who secured a contract for them with Syd Nathan's Cincinnati-based King record label. In 1956 Brown scored a hit in the R'n'B chart with his début single 'Please Please Please'.

His early recordings, particularly ballads like 'Try Me' and 'Bewildered', took soul to new peaks of gospel-infused intensity, but success in the mainstream pop market took a while to come. Nevertheless, by 1963 he had scored his first US Top 20 single with 'Prisoner of Love', establishing a beach-head in the popular marketplace from which he proceeded to alter the entire musical landscape.

As the American critic Dave Marsh put it, 'James Brown is entitled to every bit of his vanity, because, in 1965, he invented the rhythmic future in which we live today.' The song with which Brown performed this unlikely feat was called 'Papa's Got a Brand New Bag' (1965) and what he created was the dance-soul hybrid known as funk.

Based on a relentlessly syncopated, minimalist backing track and overlaid with Brown's intensely passionate, hump'n'grunt style of vocalese, 'Papa's Got a Brand New Bag' revolutionised black (and ultimately all popular) music. It was his first Top 10 hit in America and his first hit of any description in the UK. It marked the beginning of a golden era for Brown, as he proceeded to issue a string of classic recordings including 'I Got You (I Feel Good)', 'It's a Man's Man's Man's World' and 'Cold Sweat'.

Brown lost ground in the Seventies as soul music evolved into more of an easy-listening, up-market, crossover style, and disco, which was initially inspired by his work, gradually rendered him an unfashionable anachronism.

Brown took this reversal of fortune on the chin, kept on touring and, even when he was at his lowest ebb and without a recording contract in the mid-Eighties, never lost faith in his unassailable abilities as a performer. His confidence was vindicated when, in

1986, he swept back into the American and British Top 5 with 'Living in America', a song from the soundtrack of the Sylvester Stallone movie, *Rocky IV* (Scotti Bros CD 70272; 1976).

Authoritatively described by *Billboard* as 'black music's all-time No.1 artist' Brown is a performer of colossal and enduring influence, a dynamic inspiration to those who have followed in his footsteps and one of the most important popular music entertainers ever.

● *Live at the Apollo (October 24, 1962)* (Polydor 843 479-2) [1963]

This is the legendary recording of a show at the most hallowed of New York venues, and its success underlines Brown's phenomenal impact as a stage performer. With his band drilled to perfection – so much so that individual musicians were fined for any wrong notes or missed cues – Brown performed in his prime with the energy of an athlete and a zeal that bordered on the hysterical. He would push the microphone stand away, spin himself full circle and catch it on the rebound; he would shimmy frantically across the stage, drop to one knee, then leap up and do the splits. At the end of a performance he would affect to be overcome by emotion, and a personal assistant would lead him off the stage, a cloak wrapped round his shoulder, like a spent boxer at the end of a gruelling bout.

Despite the primitive sound quality and an absence of any major numbers from Brown's astonishing catalogue of hits (only Elvis PRESLEY, The BEATLES and Stevie WONDER have more US Top 40 entries to their names), *Live at the Apollo* captures the thrilling essence of Brown's non-stop, roller-coaster revue show and boasts peak performances of 'Think', 'I'll Go Crazy' and 'Lost Someone'. Faced with his record company's implacable opposition to the idea of a live album, Brown was forced to finance its release himself. The album eventually sold a million.

● *Star Time* (Polydor 849 108-2) [1991]
● *Sex Machine – The Very Best of James Brown* (Polydor 845 828-2) [1991]

The four-CD, 71-track, boxed set *Star Time* is very nearly the definitive James Brown collection. It incorporates every major recording from 'Please Please Please' to 1984's 'Unity, Pt.1', a collaboration with Afrika Bambaataa and the Tackhead rhythm section, but mysteriously excludes the hugely popular 'Living in America', released at the tail end of 1985.

Organised, compiled and annotated by Brown's dedicated biographer Cliff White, it is as near perfect a distillation of this performer's awesome legacy as we are likely to get. 'Funky Drummer', 'Get on the Good Foot', 'Try Me', 'Funky President', 'Bewildered', 'Say It Loud – I'm Black and I'm Proud', 'Prisoner of Love', 'Give It Up or Turnit a Loose', 'Papa's Got a Brand New Bag', 'The Payback', 'It Got You (I Feel Good)', 'It's a Man's Man's Man's World', 'Cold Sweat' and 'Get Up (I Feel Like Being a Sex Machine)' are just the tip of the iceberg.

For those without the necessary £35 to lash out on *Star Time*, there is *Sex Machine – The Very Best of James Brown*, a one-disc, 20-track compilation which skims off the cream of that epic collection *and* includes the errant 'Living in America'. Take it to the bridge!

Kate Bush

Born: Catherine Bush, July 30 1958, Kent
UK No.1 albums: 1980: *Never for Ever* (EMI CZ 360)
                1985: *Hounds of Love* (EMI CZ 361)
                1986: *The Whole Story* (EMI CDP 746414
                2)

When Kate Bush swept to the top of the chart in 1978 with her first single, 'Wuthering Heights', opinion was polarised, to put it mildly. To many she was, and still is, an artist of pure, idiosyncratic talent, a fragile beauty, possibly a genius. To others her ululating singing style, and the eccentric displays of amateur theatrics which accompany it, are about as comforting as the feel of silver paper on a newly filled tooth.

Something of a child prodigy, she was 'discovered' by PINK FLOYD guitarist David Gilmour and signed to EMI at the tender age of 17. Her open-ended contract allowed her to develop her material at her own speed, essential to begin with, but a habit which has yielded less impressive results in later years.

Now in her thirties, Bush has become an introverted writer

who applies the language of an adult to a romanticised, fantasy world view that does not seem to have altered significantly since she was 12 years old.

- *The Kick Inside* (Fame CDP 746012-2) [1978]

Her first album, this encompasses all those qualities for which she is still either loved or loathed today. The title track, about a girl on the verge of committing suicide having been impregnated by her brother, establishes an emotional tenor as shrill as her voice.

- *Hounds of Love* (EMI CZ 361) [1985]

A huge commercial success and Bush's most satisfying album to date. The best songs – 'Running Up That Hill', 'Hounds of Love', 'The Big Sky' – still have a tang as sharp as fresh lemon on the palate. And who can forget all that wind-machine hanky-panky with Donald Sutherland in the video of 'Cloudbusting'? Classic Bush.

- *The Whole Story* (EMI CDP 746414 2) [1986]

This mid-career retrospective neatly encapsulates her 12 best single releases from the epochal 'Wuthering Heights' up to 'Experiment IV' in 1986.

- *The Sensual World* (EMI CDEMD 1010) [1989]

It took four years of working in her home recording studio to come up with this sluggish affair which, despite its painstaking attention to detail, suggests an artist increasingly beset by cabin fever.

- *This Woman's Work* (Anthology 1979–1990) (EMI CDKBBX 1) [1990]

For Bush completists making the switch to CD, this massive, limited edition boxed set is the perfect collection, incorporating *all* her albums released to date (except the compilation *The Whole Story*) along with two extra volumes of otherwise unavailable 'rarities'. EMI has no copies left, but some shops may still have it in stock. Expect to pay around £100.

The Byrds

Convened: 1964, Los Angeles, California. Split up: 1973
Gene Clark (f) – vocals/tambourine; Michael Clarke (f) – drums; David Crosby (f) – guitar/vocals; Chris Hillman (f) – bass/vocals; Roger (né Jim) McGuinn (f) – guitar/vocals
US No.6 albums: 1965: *Mr Tambourine Man* (Columbia 465 566-2)
1967: *The Byrds' Greatest Hits* (Columbia 467 843-2)

The Byrds set out to forge the missing link between the lyric-intensive folk of Bob DYLAN and the energised harmony pop of The BEATLES. Certainly there were powerful elements of both those acts in their music, especially the phenomenally successful début single 'Mr Tambourine Man', speaking of which Roger McGuinn later recalled, 'I tried to make my voice sound like a cross between DYLAN's and John LENNON's.' The song sailed to No.1 in Britain and America in 1965.

But the group is actually best remembered for its extraordinarily distinctive guitar sound, a resonant chiming noise which emanated from McGuinn's electric 12-string Rickenbacker, and which owed nothing to either the moptop leaders of the British invasion or the freewheelin' Voice Of A Generation. A gorgeous, rich mesh of swirling arpeggios, laced with shimmering harmonic overtones, if ever a guitar has been heard ringing down the years like Chuck BERRY's proverbial bell, then this is it.

Ironically, it is a sound that has its origins in folk, since the 12-string guitar is not an instrument primarily associated with rock. In its more common, non-electric guise, it is primarily used as a strummed accompaniment for voices in an acoustic setting. Its double complement of strings makes it ideal for filling out the sound with big, full chords in situations where there is no amplification, but physically difficult to play as a lead instrument.

McGuinn cleverly turned convention on its head. He transplanted the 12-string to a rock group setting, then, instead of strumming it, he either picked out intricate motifs or else sallied forth on melodic flights of fancy, as on the pealing intro to 'So You Want to be a Rock'n'Roll Star' or the remarkable free-form, jazz-influenced solo in 'Eight Miles High'.

The key to the Byrds is that none of the original line-up came from a rock background. Instead, they bought into rock using the currency of folk, traditional harmony singing and, later, elements of country, jazz and bluegrass. It was a bold and original contribution which enriched the stock of popular music immeasurably.

The Byrds themselves were history by the start of the Seventies, and their relevance had been pretty doubtful since the 1968 album *Sweetheart of the Rodeo* (Edsel EDCD 234), a country-influenced set featuring vocalist Gram Parsons (died 19.9.73). But first Tom PETTY forged a career out of his love for their blend of harmony and rock textures, then gradually a host of other disciples of *that* guitar sound, led by R.E.M., emerged on the American college gig/radio network.

In Britain the example of the Byrds filtered down through the work of James Honeyman-Scott of the PRETENDERS to a new generation of guitarists – such as Johnny Marr of The SMITHS – whose 'jangly' sound came to define a strand of Eighties indie rock. Whether they know it or not, bands like Ride, The House of Love and The STONE ROSES all owe a stylistic debt to The Byrds, while The Charlatans actually lifted a quote from 'Everybody's Been Burned' on their 1990 hit 'The Only One I Know'.

● *Greatest Hits* (Columbia 467 843-2) [1967]

After 'Mr Tambourine Man', the Byrds enjoyed a heady rush of hits, so much so that this compilation was originally in the shops just a little more than two years later. By then, both Gene Clark and David Crosby had left, and McGuinn was left to preside over the patchy output of a group which was buffeted by constant personnel upheavals for the rest of its days.

So, allowing for the absence of one or two later gems, such as 'Chestnut Mare', these 11 tracks represent the very core of The Byrds legend. Four of them were written by DYLAN – 'Mr Tambourine Man', 'All I Really Want to Do', 'Chimes of Freedom' and 'My Back Pages' – and two by folk singer Pete Seeger – 'The

Bells of Rhymney' and 'Turn! Turn! Turn!' (adapted by Seeger from the Book of Ecclesiastes) – which supports the impression that the band was functioning at its best when it was working squarely on the cusp of folk and rock.

● *The Byrds* (Columbia 467 611-2) [1990]

Strangely, given The Byrds' continuing influence and appeal, most of their recorded legacy was unavailable on CD until this lavishly presented 4-CD boxed set, unofficially called *The Ultimate Collection*, was released at the tail end of 1990. It is the fruit of sessions supervised by McGuinn, during which the entire Byrds back catalogue was thoroughly sifted through and 90 tracks selected and carefully remastered.

As well as all the career highlights, the collection incorporates 17 previously unreleased songs, including live versions of 'Turn! Turn! Turn!' and 'Mr Tambourine Man', recorded at a Roy Orbison tribute held in 1990. The accompanying booklet is a mine of information, with a detailed appreciation of the band by *Rolling Stone* journalist David Fricke, a Byrds family tree and recollections from many of the key players.

A wonderful package by any standards, its desirability is further enhanced by the continuing paucity of other available Byrds material.

Johnny Cash

Born: February 26 1932, Kingsland, Arkansas
US No.1 album: 1969: *Johnny Cash at San Quentin*
(unavailable)

A maverick performer of immense artistic stature, Johnny Cash is the original country singer who appeals to young rock'n'rollers, conventional folkies, people who 'don't like country' and hard-core fans alike.

Born into a poor sharecropping family, Cash learnt the meaning of hardship early on and at first hand. He was hauling water for a road gang when he was 10 and hefting huge sacks of cotton by the age of 12. Two of his six siblings died when they were still children. In later life he has never forsaken the cause of the underdog either as a subject for his songs or as the object of whatever practical assistance he may be able to render.

Blessed with a bass voice of extraordinary depth and roundness, and forever tagged as 'the man in black', Cash often casts himself in the role of the outlaw cowboy, the chain-gang prisoner, or a man facing some other sort of desperate plight with dignity rather than despair. He makes regular fund-raising appearances for a variety of causes, notably educational programmes designed to help the Amerindians.

His musical career began in earnest in 1956 when he was signed to Sam Phillips' Sun records, the independent label that had launched Elvis PRESLEY. Cash proved an immediate success in the specialist country market, and before the year was out he was high in the pop chart too with his own million-selling composition 'I Walk The Line'.

In 1957, he gave the first of the prison concerts that became a regular feature of his touring work, and by the time of his two live 'prison' albums – *Johnny Cash at Folsom Prison* (1968; unavailable) and *Johnny Cash at San Quentin* (see above) – he had established a near-mystical rapport with his rowdy, captive audiences.

The magic of those performances are such that they must rank as two of the best albums Cash has ever recorded. Both are certified multi-million sellers, yet neither is available in CD format in the UK. The two albums are combined on one magnificent disc, *Johnny Cash at Folsom Prison and San Quentin* (import Columbia CGK 33639), but only as an American import; hardly ideal, but still not bad value at a retail price of approximately £17.

The pressures of stardom led Cash into a damaging cycle of drug dependency which was to creep up on him at various stages of his life. In October 1965, when he was arrested in El Paso attempting to cross the Mexican border with a guitar case full of pep pills, most observers assumed he was a write off.

'I took all the drugs there are to take, and I drank,' Cash told author Peter McCabe in 1973. 'Everybody said that Johnny Cash was through 'cause I was walkin' around town, 150 pounds. I looked like walking death . . .'

However in 1968 he kicked the habit, took up religion and married country singer June Carter (who, with Merle Kilgore, had co-written Cash's 1963 hit 'Ring of Fire'). A period of happiness, stability and success followed. In the wake of his prison album triumphs he became a show-business personality, hosting his own *Johnny Cash Show* on ABC-TV, and developing an acting career, notably playing opposite Kirk Douglas in *The Gunfight* (1970).

He has maintained a steady touring and recording schedule right through to the present, and although he has never matched the work of his golden era in the Fifties and Sixties, his influence on a succeeding generation of performers is plain. He was elected to the Country Music Association's Hall of Fame in 1980.

Cash has cheated death many times. In 1983 he underwent abdominal surgery at Nashville's Baptist Hospital to correct the effects of prolonged amphetamine abuse. Afterwards he attended the Betty Ford clinic in California, and subsequently campaigned against the misuse of drugs. He underwent open-heart surgery in 1989, but was back on the road within months, a craggy monolith who seems as enduring as the reprobate characters in his songs.

- **Johnny Cash Collection** (Castle Collector Series CCSCD 146) [1988]

Cash has a habit of re-recording his old hits whenever he changes his record label so that the new company can repromote the songs for which he is best known, even though the original performances remain the property of the old company. The most recent batch to be put out in this way goes under the banner *Classic Cash* (Mercury 834 526-2; 1988). But although these new versions are perfectly listenable, and indeed technically superior recordings, the originals, cut when the man was in his prime, are better performances in 95% of cases.

For an efficient compilation of the original recordings from the Sun era (1956–58), the *Johnny Cash Collection* is recommended. It incorporates his first single, 'Cry Cry Cry', along with the ground-breaking crossover hits 'I Walk the Line', 'Ballad of a Teenage Queen' and 'The Ways of a Woman in Love', plus many others.

- **The CBS Years 1958–1986** (Columbia 4504662) [1987]

Cash moved from Sun records to Columbia (CBS as it was known until recently) in 1958 and proceeded to record a string of excellent albums – *Ride This Train* (1960), *Blood, Sweat and Tears* (1963), *Bitter Tears* (1964) and *Orange Blossom Special* (1965) – none of them available on CD.

However, his primary work from this period is gathered up on *The CBS Years 1958–1986*. Sung in the dark, hard drawl that has done so much to shape the course of modern country music, numbers like 'Five Feet High and Rising' (a hit in 1959), 'Ring of Fire' (1963) and 'Folsom Prison Blues' (1968) remain among the most plangent themes that the singing cowboy genre has to offer. Among these and other gems such as 'Ballad of Ira Hayes', 'Orange Blossom Special' and 'Highway Patrolman' (a duet with Bruce SPRINGSTEEN), the album includes 'A Boy Named Sue', the cheerful piece of knockabout nonsense that in 1969 became his biggest hit single ever.

Ray Charles

Born: Ray Charles Robinson, September 23 1930, Albany, Georgia
US No.1 album: 1962: ***Modern Sounds in Country and Western Music*** (unavailable)

A musician of transcendental ability, Ray Charles is fluent in all three of the basic musical forms of black America: jazz, blues and gospel. In the Fifties he welded them into a new, coherent whole, thereby creating soul music. That taken care of, he turned his attention in the Sixties to the traditionally closed world of country which he cracked open with the most commercially successful album of his career, the remarkable *Modern Sounds in Country and Western Music* (see above).

Glaucoma rendered Charles blind at the age of six, though not soon enough to spare him the trauma of seeing his younger brother drown in a wash-tub accident the year before. At seven he was sent to Florida's State School for the Deaf and Blind in St Augustine. While there he developed a keen interest in music, consolidating an early skill on the piano and learning to play the clarinet, saxophone and trumpet as well as how to read and write music in braille.

Orphaned by the age of 15, Charles struck out from school and home with the intention of making a living as a musician. 'Times and me got leaner and leaner,' he recalled, 'but anything beats getting a cane and a cup and picking out a street corner.'

After various cross-country swings he moved to Los Angeles in 1949, where, with mixed results, he made his first recordings, adopting the professional name of Ray Charles in order to avoid confusion with the boxer Sugar Ray Robinson.

Having secured a contract with Atlantic in 1952, he went on to dominate the R'n'B charts for most of the Fifties before cracking the American pop Top 10 with his call and response classic 'What'd I Say' in 1959. After this watershed, he changed record labels to ABC and enjoyed a long stretch of spectacular mainstream success.

The towering authority of his rough-hewn, R'n'B vocal style was to have an immense impact on the rock singers of the Sixties – Joe Cocker and Eric Burdon of the Animals were two of many who cited him as a formative influence – while his songs were recorded by artists like The ROLLING STONES ('I'm Movin' On'), John Mayall's Bluesbreakers with Eric CLAPTON ('What'd I Say') and, more recently, Van MORRISON ('I Can't Stop Loving You').

A man of protean talents, Charles recognised no musical boundaries. In 1961, on the eve of his success as a 'country star', he recorded the swinging big band blast of *Genius + Soul = Jazz* (Essential ESSCD 009), a collaboration with The Count Basie Orchestra (minus Basie), produced by Quincy Jones.

Alas, like so many supremely gifted musicians, Charles saddled himself with a thoroughgoing heroin addiction and on December 3 1966 he was convicted on charges of possessing heroin and marijuana and given a five-year suspended prison sentence, a $10,000 fine and put on probation for four years.

It was around this time that the magic began to fade. The tone of the American charts had been affected by the British rock invasion of the Sixties, while a new wave of soul stars, all of them influenced by Charles' example, had risen in his wake, among them Sam Cooke, Otis REDDING and the inimitable James BROWN.

Though always a highly respected performer, Charles stepped back from the cutting edge, becoming more of a mainstream cabaret-style entertainer. Even so, his versatility has remained such that in the same year that he scored a big country hit with his album *Wish You Were Here Tonight* (Collectors Choice 902 289-2;

1983), he also headlined the 30th Kool Jazz Festival in New York alongside Miles Davis and B.B. KING.

In 1985 he played a leading role, together with Michael JACKSON, Bruce SPRINGSTEEN and most of the American popular music élite, in the recording of USA For Africa's 'We are the World' – the American equivalent of Band Aid's 'Do They Know It's Christmas?'.

A millionaire with a mansion and even a private jet, Charles has become a distinguished and decorated music business veteran. Yet he continues to tour, cutting a fragile but spry figure on stages around the world. His last UK appearance was at London's Barbican Centre in November 1989, and as recently as January 1990 he was to be found riding high in both the UK and US charts with the single 'I'll be Good to You', a collaboration with Quincy Jones and Chaka Khan.

Despite some loss of strength in the upper register, the rich and expressive timbre of his voice and the perfection of his timing remain intact, testament to the towering and enduring talent of a performer who is unquestionably in a class of his own.

- *The Right Time* (Atlantic 241 119-2) [1987]

Ray Charles was the founding father and supreme exponent of soul no less than Elvis PRESLEY was the king of rock'n'roll, and here is the proof. Though it wasn't his début, the first song to telegraph the full splendour of Charles' peculiar genius was his 1954 classic 'I Got a Woman'. It is a number which finds Charles applying a searing dose of spirituality to a decidedly secular lyric, his rich, rasping voice underpinned by a jazz-blues piano motif that soaks like burning kerosene into the fabric of the song. A huge R'n'B hit, 'I Got a Woman' was both influential and controversial. 'Many people saw my work as sacrilegious,' Charles later remarked. 'They said I was taking church songs and making people dance to them in bars and nightclubs.'

After that, the floodgates opened and Charles released an epoch-making series of singles, among them 'Hallelujah, I Love Her So', 'This Little Girl of Mine', '(Night Time is) The Right Time', 'Drown in My Own Tears', 'I'm Movin' On' and 'What'd I Say', all collected on this essential compilation.

- *The Classic Years* (Essential ESBCD 144) [1991]

A minor quibble perhaps, but the truly 'classic' Ray Charles years are represented by the Atlantic recordings from 1952–1959 collected on *The Right Time* (see above). *The* (not-quite-so) *Classic Years* nevertheless captures the essence of the most prolific and commercially successful period of Charles' career, dating from 1960 to 1973 when he was signed to the ABC label in America.

A three-CD, 47-track set, it incorporates his three US No.1s – 'Georgia On My Mind', 'Hit the Road, Jack' and 'I Can't Stop Loving You', along with many more of his most fondly remembered songs: 'Your Cheating Heart', 'Take These Chains From My Heart', 'Busted', 'Crying Time' *et al.*

The lush string arrangements may suggest a supper club ambience to ears attuned to the more clamorous sounds of rock, but Charles' extraordinary vocal performances are usually sufficient to dispel any creeping blandness in the material. Such is the plangent tone of his voice and the sublime quality of his timing that even potentially hackneyed choices such as the LENNON/McCARTNEY chestnuts 'Eleanor Rigby' and 'Yesterday' are recast with a truly striking emotional fervour.

Eric Clapton

Born: Eric Patrick Clapp, March 30 1945, Ripley, Surrey
US No.1 album: 1974: *461 Ocean Boulevard* (Polydor 811 697-2)

There have been few more conspicuous figures among the rock aristocracy which emerged in the wake of Live Aid than Eric Clapton. His 1986 album *August* (Duck 925 476-2) was the most successful of his solo career. In 1987 he was officially canonised by the music industry when the BPI honoured him with an award for his 'Outstanding Contribution to British Music'. The same year a six-part Radio 1 series, *Behind the Mask*, recounted the story of his life; LWT's *The South Bank Show* followed suit with an authoritative hagiography; and a compilation *The Cream of Eric Clapton* (see below) achieved platinum sales in the UK.

1987 was also the year that he first played a run of six shows at the Albert Hall. This became an annual residency which had expanded to 24 nights in 1991, as commemorated on the double-live CD *24 Nights* (Reprise 7599-26420-2; 1991). Another 12-night stand in 1992 continued the tradition, which Clapton likes to regard as rock's equivalent of the proms.

Yet despite his celebrity, and an unquestionably distinguished record of service, Clapton is nothing like the performer he used to be. 'When you're in your mid-20s you've got something that you lose,' he told Q magazine in 1986. 'If I was a sportsman I would have retired by now. You've just got a certain amount of dynamism that you lose when you turn 30. You have to accept that, otherwise you're chasing a dream.'

Brought up by his grandparents after his parents separated, Clapton was educated at Ripley primary school and St Bede's secondary modern, after which he embarked on a course of stained glass design at Kingston Art College.

Heavily influenced by the work of the master American blues guitarists – in particular Robert JOHNSON, B.B. KING and Buddy Guy – Clapton is a self-taught musician, who began playing in his first group, The Roosters in January 1963.

His initial break came in October 1963 when he was invited to join The Yardbirds, a local band which had just taken over The ROLLING STONES' residency at the Crawdaddy club in Richmond. With his searing blues style and powerful charisma, Clapton swiftly eclipsed the singer Keith Relf as the principal focus of attention in the group. But, in what was to become a familiar pattern, he left them on the eve of their chart break-through in 1965, complaining that their music had become 'too commercial'.

His ensuing membership of John Mayall's Bluesbreakers, which he joined in April 1965, was a brief but historic engagement, and it was around this time that someone claimed to have seen a graffiti proclaiming 'Clapton is God', a wholly unsubstantiated anecdote which has become one of the more tediously over-reported aspects of Clapton lore.

He left Mayall in July 1966, the month that the *Bluesbreakers with Eric Clapton* album (see below) began a four-month residency in the chart. Together with Ginger Baker (drums) and Jack Bruce (bass/vocals) he immediately formed CREAM, the prototype 'supergroup'.

After the breakup of CREAM in November 1968 Clapton, together with Baker, Steve WINWOOD (keyboards/vocals) and Ric

Grech (bass; ex-Family; died 17.3.90) founded the ill-fated Blind Faith, another supergroup, which although it enjoyed a US and UK No.1 with its début album *Blind Faith* (Polydor 825 094-2; 1969), simply could not survive the pressure of impossibly high expectations from all quarters.

In truth, Clapton, who was still only 24 when Blind Faith split up in January 1970, had taken a battering at the hands of fame. He retreated into the ranks of a little-known American group, Delaney and Bonnie and Friends, from whose ranks he eventually recruited his own band, a low-key, laid-back aggregation which in a moment of whimsy he called Derek and The Dominos.

The Dominos broke up in 1971 and for three years Clapton did little but nurse an escalating heroin addiction. Despite a gallant attempt by Pete Townshend to pull him out of this slough of despond by organising a comeback concert at the Rainbow in 1973, it was not until he underwent a course of electronically adapted acupuncture in 1974 that Clapton finally shook off the habit.

Relinquishing the guitar hero mantle, he carved a niche for himself as a mainstream singer, but with the abrasive nihilism of punk challenging the old order, the Seventies were a hard time for acts like Clapton, especially in the UK.

By the turn of the decade the heroin had been replaced by a couple of bottles of cognac a day. The doctors who admitted him to hospital in Minnesota during his 1980 tour of America estimated that he would have had roughly 45 minutes to live if his ulcer had exploded into his pancreas as it looked likely to do at any moment.

Again Clapton recovered his grip, and with the revitalisation of the middle-aged rock market, thanks in no small part to the spread of CD technology, he took up a comfortable place as a revered elder statesman of rock.

Although possessing one of the genre's few truly original guitar voices, Clapton has recorded nothing of note as an instrumentalist since 1969. And as a performer in general he has never topped 'Layla', which he recorded in 1970. But what an astounding catalogue of ground-breaking performances he had amassed by then.

- With The Yardbirds: *Five Live Yardbirds* (Charly CDCHARLY 182) [1964]

With a line-up of Chris Dreja (guitar), Jim McCarty (drums), Keith Relf (vocals/harmonica, later of Renaissance) and Paul Samwell-Smith (bass), The Yardbirds were very much in the English R'n'B mould of The ROLLING STONES.

This is the only album Clapton cut with them and, as the title suggests, it was recorded live at London's Marquee club. Despite the primitive sound quality and some over-ambitious arrangements, there are clear indication's of Clapton's awesome potential on tracks like 'Five Long Years' and 'Smokestack Lightning'. Best of all is an amphetamined reading of Chuck BERRY's 'Too Much Monkey Business', where Relf turns BERRY's tongue-twisting lyric into a *tour de force* of incomprehensible cool.

- With John Mayall: *Bluesbreakers with Eric Clapton* (Decca 800 086-2) [1966]

This is the album which sparked off the blues boom of the Sixties and brought a new level of instrumental expertise to popular music. Indeed, there is a strong case for calling it the first *bona fide* rock album.

The line-up comprised Clapton, Mayall (vocals/keyboards/harmonica/guitar), John McVie (bass, later of FLEETWOOD MAC) and Hughie Flint (drums, later of McGuinness Flint and The Blues Band).

According to Clapton, the album was recorded in a weekend. 'We just did our club gig in the studio. I don't think we did more than one take of anything.'

Yet right from the opening bars of 'All Your Love', where Clapton's distinctive vibrato and steely tone slice through the song's central motif with the cool violence of a guillotine, this remains an album of exceptional vitality and undiminished appeal. Clapton plays a blinder throughout, sweeping the board on the album's two instrumentals – 'Hideaway' and 'Steppin' Out' – and producing solos of haunting, visceral intensity, especially on the slow blues numbers 'Double Crossing Time' and 'Have You Heard'.

Mayall's contribution is usually overlooked, but his hyena-call vocals lend the album a distinctively moody flavour, and his two voice-and-harmonica routines – 'Parchman Farm' and 'Another Man' – are superb. He was also, let's remember, the man who made the whole thing happen in the first place.

● As Derek And The Dominos: *Layla and Other Assorted Love Songs* (RSO 823 277-2) [1970]

Such was Clapton's desire to shun the limelight by the time this was released that he refused to have his name on the sleeve, and although successful in America, and subsequently renowned for its title track, this album has never charted in Britain.

Featuring Duane Allman (guitar; The Allman Brothers Band; died 29.10.71), Jim Gordon (drums), Carl Radle (bass; died 30.5.80) and Bobby Whitlock (keyboards), it is a bridge between Clapton's blues-based guitar heroics of the Sixties and his more mature work primarily as a singer during the Seventies. 'Bell Bottom Blues', 'Tell the Truth' and 'Why Does Love Got To Be So Sad' harness fluent and emotional guitar playing to a far more restrained and soulful delivery than of yore.

● *The Cream of Eric Clapton* (Polydor 833 519-2) [1987]

This compilation picks up the story from CREAM's second single, 'I Feel Free', continuing with 'Badge', 'Sunshine of Your Love', 'Strange Brew', 'White Room' and the stunning 'Crossroads'.

Although it was 'Layla' that opened Clapton's account with the mainstream rock market of the Seventies, and 'Cocaine' that inspired a thousand pub-band cover versions, his choice of Bob MARLEY's 'I Shot the Sheriff' as a single in 1974 was one of Clapton's most enduring post-CREAM contributions. At the time, 'serious' rock fans thought he was daft to meddle with such nonsense, and Clapton deserves credit both for his part in demolishing such crass barriers, and for a tasty version of the song.

After that, he put himself out to grass, though the cud was never less than stylishly chewed, as attested by 'Lay Down Sally', 'Knockin' On Heaven's Door', 'Wonderful Tonight', 'Let It Grow', 'Behind The Mask' and all the others.

● *Crossroads* (Polydor 835 261-2) [1988]

This sumptuously packaged, 73-song, four-disc, boxed collection provides the most rounded musical portrait of Clapton yet.

Presented in chronological order, with full and accurate details of the recording of each track, the collection traces his work from The Yardbirds' first studio session in 1963 – skimpy, stumbling versions of John Lee HOOKER's 'Boom Boom' and Jimmy Reed's 'Baby What's Wrong' – to the relaxed, bland largesse of tracks like 'Miss You' and 'Wanna Make Love To You' from the *August* sessions (see above).

In between, it successfully combines the roles of 'greatest hits' and 'rare moments' collections, including all the high points together with too many previously unreleased recordings to list here.

It is an especial pleasure to have all the CREAM singles (including oddities like 'Wrapping Paper' and 'Anyone for Tennis') together in one long-playing place, along with wired highlights from his stints with John Mayall's Bluesbreakers (including the long deleted 'Lonely Years' single from 1966) and Blind Faith.

Where the collection comes into its own as a historical document is in its inclusion, after 'Layla', of five previously unreleased tracks intended for the aborted second Derek and the Dominos album. As Anthony De Curtis relates in the accompanying booklet, Clapton remembers that the session 'broke down halfway through because of the paranoia and the tension.'

The last of those tracks – 'Snake Lake Blues', a soulful, bluesy instrumental – was recorded in May 1971. For Clapton, the three-year hiatus between that song and the track which follows it (the twee 'Let It Grow', recorded in May 1974) was the real crossroads in both his life and his career. Whatever troubles he resolved at that time, he also lost a distinctive attacking streak in his style.

As a star who had so nearly gone super-nova, Clapton now settled down to the humdrum business of survival, developing among other talents a fine interpretive line in soft-rock spirituals, like 'Knockin' On Heaven's Door'. But any hint of danger in his work had passed. Even the long, live work-out of Otis Rush's poignant slow blues 'Double Trouble', from 1980's *Just One Night* (RSO 800 093-2; 1980), or the rough, acoustic, mock-delta blues B-side 'Too Bad' (1984) sound in some way polite and emasculated.

The Clash

Convened: 1976, London. Split up: 1985
Mick Jones (f) – guitar/vocals; Topper Headon – drums; Paul
Simonon (f) – bass/vocals; Joe Strummer (f) – vocals/guitar
UK No.2 albums: 1978: *Give 'Em Enough Rope* (Columbia CD
32444)
1982: *Combat Rock* (Columbia CD 32787)

If there is one group, apart from The JAM, that built something of
lasting value out of the nihilistic cant that characterised the punk
era, then it was The Clash.

Musically, their calling card was a supreme sense of urgency
conveyed by the clanging sound of guitar riffs pumped out in
rapid, straight-arm jerks, and a vocal style of near-comic, breathless slobbishness.

The cake was gilded by a carefully measured commitment to
the anarcho-yob gesture politics of the time. For reasons which
now seem hard to explain, it was always the group's policy not to
appear on *Top of the Pops*, although their dislike of the 'establishment' stopped short of rejecting a lucrative recording contract
with the multi-national Columbia records (then CBS).

Organised heroism like that is the stuff of legend, and all the
signs suggest that as punk's answer to The ROLLING STONES, The
Clash could have ended up as big as U2.

As we know, they failed to make the distance.

After the split, there were high hopes for Jones' group Big
Audio Dynamite, a beatbox-rock posse which recorded a sharp
début, *This is Big Audio Dynamite* (Columbia CD 26714; 1985). But
Jones wasn't bright enough to carry it through in the long term,
and BAD gradually turned to worse. Strummer contributed one
brilliant song, 'Love Kills', to the soundtrack of the Alex Cox
movie *Sid and Nancy* (1986; deleted) and put out a pitiful solo
album, *Earthquake Weather* (1989; deleted), before taking over from
the hyper-bibulous Shane MacGowan in The POGUES. Simonon
formed the little-known Havana 3AM and Headon drove mini-
cabs.

● *The Clash* (Columbia 468783 2) [1977]

The American critic Robert Christgau's pronouncement that this was 'the greatest rock'n'roll album ever manufactured anywhere' might have made sense in the context of the punk era. Few recordings have so successfully embodied such an exhilarating, righteous fury as this album did, and tracks like 'Career Opportunities', 'London's Burning' and 'Janie Jones' are more than great songs; they defined the attitudes of an era.

But technically it is a horror show. Whereas the essential recordings which preceded punk have proved ideally suited to the enhanced audio fidelity of CD (*Dark Side of the Moon* or *Songs in the Key of Life*, for instance), punk's spontaneous, anti-corporatist, DIY ethic necessarily threw up a body of work that was better tailored to the vinyl single; something to be played to death for a month or two and then dumped.

The Clash was produced by the band's 'live soundman' (i.e. roadie) Micky Foote, a man of very limited studio experience, though not as limited as the members of the group themselves. Strummer's vocals are pasted uncomfortably on top of the mix, the drums sound like paper bags, and really there is not a lot to be gained from hearing it all a great deal more clearly than before.

If it had existed at the time, CD would have been very non-punk. *The Clash* is one of the few great albums which the digital technology signally fails to accommodate.

● *Give 'Em Enough Rope* (Columbia CD 32444) [1978]

This got a critical pasting at the time, on the grounds that the band had drifted away from its punk moorings by hiring a proper producer (Sandy Pearlman) and producing a moderately sophisticated rock band sound. In fact rough and tumbles like 'Tommy Gun' and 'English Civil War' have weathered remarkably well.

● *London Calling* (Columbia 460114 2) [1979]

The Clash's magnum opus, without a doubt, but was it the best album of the Eighties? Most certainly, according to *Rolling Stone*, which described it as the album with which The Clash 'stormed the gates of rock convention and single-handedly set the agenda – musically, politically and emotionally – for the decade to come.'

It remains a rich, passionate and powerful set of songs, tapping into a broad range of influences from the rockabilly strut of 'Brand

New Cadillac' to the loping reggae of 'The Guns of Brixton'. With its martial beat and apocalyptic imagery, the title track – a direct descendant of The Yardbirds' classic 'Shapes of Things' – stands as one of the most fully realised songs The Clash ever committed to disc.

In the same way as The BEATLES' *Revolver* signalled the end of an era of innocence in the Sixties, so songs like 'Clampdown', 'Spanish Bombs', 'Koka Kola' and 'Lost in the Supermarket' pointed the way forward from the parochial posturing that had given punk its initial impetus into a new era of internationally inspired music and politicking.

- **Combat Rock** (Columbia CD 32787) [1982]

'Should I stay or should I go?' sang Jones on this, their biggest selling album, to which Strummer and Simonon responded by giving him the elbow. One of the few overtly anti-American albums to sell a million copies in that land, other highlights include 'Straight to Hell' and 'Rock the Casbah'.

Simonon and Strummer recruited a couple of yes-men, and a new Clash line-up stumbled on for one more album – *Cut the Crap* (Columbia 465110 2; 1985) – but *Combat Rock* was the true and fitting swansong of this mighty group.

- **The Story of The Clash Volume 1** (Columbia 460244 2) [1988]

This 28-track, two-disc compilation incorporates most of The Clash's finest moments and will thus prove a severe headache to compilers of the subsequent volume(s) implied by the title.

The early stuff still sounds unbelievably rough, but the exhilarating rush of those first adrenaline-powered months is recalled by a host of glottal battle-cries, among them 'London's Burning', 'White Riot', 'Career Opportunities', 'Complete Control', 'Janie Jones', and 'Capital Radio'.

Behind the Cro-Magnon leather-boy look, there were shrewd ears and agile minds at work. The quartet took on board the emergent Jamaican/American techniques of rap and dub ('The Magnificent Seven', 'This is Radio Clash'), while retaining the longstanding passion for reggae which prompted '(White Man) In Hammersmith Palais'. None of which eclipsed their ability to rock out when the occasion demanded, as on 'Clampdown' and 'London's Calling'.

An essential compilation, this has a tremendous spirit of energy and discovery stretching right the way through.

● *The Singles* (Columbia 468946 2) [1991]

This is a functional, chronological, but incomplete sweep through The Clash's singles from 'White Riot' to 'Should I Stay or Should I Go', the song from 1982 which rose to No.1 in 1991 thanks to its use as the soundtrack to the 'pool hall' advertisement for Levi's jeans. It is hard to think of a clearer cut case of 'turning rebellion into money' than those ads, and the band which once shunned the commercial forum of *Top of the Pops* had finally, if posthumously, accepted the industry's shilling. A jolly good ad it was too.

Further exploitation of the legend was quick to follow, in the form of this 18-track compilation which duplicates no less than 14 of the tracks on *The Story of the Clash* (see above). The four 'different' tracks are of minor significance – 'Remote Control', 'The Call Up', 'Hitsville UK' and 'Know Your Rights' – and frankly, the most enlightening thing about this package is the accompanying lyric sheet, which unravels many of the mysteries thrown up by Strummer's impossible diction.

Phil Collins

Born: January 31 1951, London
UK/US No.1 albums: 1985: *No Jacket Required* (Virgin CDV 2345)
1989: *... But Seriously* (Virgin CDV 2620)
UK No.1 album: 1981: *Face Value* (Virgin CDV 2185)

Phil Collins is not like other superstars. He has remained one of the likely lads; a man without pretension, artifice or even a suit that fits, who makes the business of creating multi-million-selling records seem routine. He will happily talk to anyone, press or punter, or turn up at any awards ceremony, and over the years has applied his protean talents to everything from playing drums in the esoteric jazz-rock ensemble Brand X (see below) to producing a solo album for Frida Lyngstad of Abba.

The idea of cultivating a glamorous mystique is anathema to him. Before the start of his Albert Hall shows in 1990, he personally made the five-minutes-to-showtime announcement over the house PA, jovially informing the audience that '. . . if you haven't been to the bathroom it's time to go.'

Collins first made his mark as drummer with GENESIS, later taking over as vocalist without so much as a hiccough when Peter GABRIEL left the fold in 1976. Given the group's high-flown pretensions and traditionally earnest demeanour, it came as something of a surprise to discover that Collins was also blessed with a sharp ear for pop and a nose for what makes it sell. So successful was his solo début *Face Value* (see below) that for a while his work with GENESIS was completely eclipsed.

A man of phenomenal energy, Collins always has something on the go. His list of production credits includes albums by Eric CLAPTON, John Martyn, Adam Ant, Philip Bailey and Howard Jones. He has recorded with Brian Eno and Robert Plant, and worked as drummer in both CLAPTON's and Martyn's backing bands. He has acted in the TV series *Miami Vice* and took the starring role in *Buster*, a film about the Great Train robber Buster Edwards. The *Buster* soundtrack (Virgin CDV 2544; 1988) spawned Collins' UK No.1 hit 'A Groovy Kind of Love'. He was the only person to perform at both the London and Philadelphia end of Live Aid, though exactly *why* he did so has never been fully explained.

While there seems to be no limit to the scope of Collins' abilities, one inevitably wonders at the level of his commitment to any of the myriad strings to his bow. If Peter GABRIEL had written 'Another Day in Paradise' (a No.2 hit for Collins in 1989), it would have been hailed as a searing indictment of Thatcher's Britain, but all Collins got were snide comments about the size of his bank balance.

Along with DIRE STRAITS, Collins is a pillar of the CD-era/adult rock establishment, a man for whom rock is more about quality of cut than about depth of material. Adored for his uncomplicated style and straight-guy personality, he is a modern song-and-dance man with the platinum touch.

- *Face Value* (Virgin CDV 2185) [1981]

The album which launched Collins' solo career was written and recorded during the break-up of his marriage. A nation of romantic souls succumbed without a murmur to the straightforward charm of songs that were supposedly about a real relationship as opposed to the more usual showbiz displays of fictional emotion. 'I Missed Again' and 'If Leaving Me is Easy' are plainly stated missives from the heart of a genuine, vulnerable bloke, someone you could take at, yes, face value. Over the years 'In the Air Tonight', an atmospheric piece known for the dramatic moment when the drums come in three minutes late, has grown into a fire-breathing monster that can only be placated by constant exposure to inert audiences at charity concert galas.

- *No Jacket Required* (Virgin CDV 2345) [1985]

The melodic pop-rock formula was refined but essentially unchanged for this astoundingly successful album. Not a glamorous enough sound to be the latest teenybop sensation and not a 'relevant' enough message for the chattering classes, *No Jacket Required* addressed itself directly to the huge mass of ordinary men and women happily ensconced in the middle ground. Highly emotional and calmly professional in roughly equal measure, its stand-out songs include 'Sussudio', 'One More Night' and 'Take me Home'.

- *. . . But Seriously* (Virgin CDV 2620) [1991]

Here Collins strives for a little more gravity than of yore with lyrics that broach various issues of social concern, for instance the plight of London's homeless on 'Another Day in Paradise'.

Otherwise the statutory ingredients are present and correct as usual: the light, meticulously crisp production; the hyperactive horn section, so tight that it sounds like a synthesiser; guest appearances by the usual cronies (CLAPTON, Steve WINWOOD and others); a neatly organised portfolio of fizzy Motown pastiches, delicate ballads and upfront pop-rockers; and rising above it all Collins' clean, disciplined, slightly brittle English voice.

Brand X

Convened: 1975, London. Split up: 1982
Phil Collins (f) – drums/vocals; John Goodsall (f) – guitar;
Percy Jones (f) – bass; Rob Lumley (f) – keyboards
UK No.37 album: 1977: *Moroccan Roll* (Charisma CASCD
1126)

'I'm only a drummer that sings a bit,' Collins said in a rather small
voice as he was about to take the stage at a charity concert in 1991
sandwiched between two of the classical music greats, Jessye
Norman and Placido Domingo. He was being modest, as well he
might in such company, but nevertheless truthful. For the plain
fact is that for all his multifarious talents as singer, actor, pianist,
writer, producer and percussionist, it is as a drummer that Collins
most truly excels.

Brand X was a loose jazz-rock aggregation that Collins helped
to develop as a sideline to his work in GENESIS. Its line-up was
variable, with personnel drifting in and out of the ranks between
albums and sometimes even between tracks, but Collins was
featured as drummer (and occasional vocalist) on at least some
part of six of the group's seven albums.

● *Unorthodox Behaviour* (Charisma CASCD 1117) [1976]

The group's début provided the blue-print for all that followed.
The musicians with whom Collins is featured (Lumley, Goodsall
and Jones) are superlative players, and the level of technical
expertise required by some of these pieces is on a par with that of
top jazz-rock fusionists like Weather Report and Mahavishnu
Orchestra. Nevertheless Collins is completely at home with the
complex arrangements, and breezes through the outrageously
swift twists of 'Euthanasia Waltz' and 'Born Ugly'. He turns in a
particularly devastating display at the end of 'Nuclear Burn', the
sort of spectacular performance for which you could forgive him
a dozen 'Groovy Kind of Love's.

● *Do They Hurt?* (Charisma CASCD 1151) [1980]

Brand X's best album, although, as it happens, Collins does not
feature very much on it. Guitarist John Goodsall is on cracking

75

form throughout and Percy Jones takes the art of fretless bass playing to a new dimension. 'Cambodia', a Goodsall composition featuring the immense drumming of Michael Clarke, is the outstanding track. Jones' bass lines writhe and glower across a melody of majestic foreboding while Clarke rains down blows on his kit like a piston gunning a heavy industrial pump.

Ry Cooder

Born: March 15 1947, Los Angeles, California
UK No.18 album: 1982: *The Slide Area* (Warner Bros K2 56976)

Ry Cooder is rock's original student of vanishing folk styles. Long before it became fashionable to fuse rock with everything from township jive to salsa, he was already juggling an impressive array of traditional influences in his music. As well as his trademark use of bluesy slide guitar, gospel harmony vocals and southern swamp-funk rhythms, he has laced his albums with the regional flavours of Tex-Mex, cajun, Hawaiian, country and even reggae music.

But although he laid the foundations for the surge of interest in ethnically diverse music in the Eighties – paving the way for Los Lobos to enjoy spectacular success with their recreation of Ritchie Valens' Spanish-language hit 'La Bamba', for instance – Cooder has not reaped much in the way of rewards for himself. 'Timing seems to be a real key factor,' he remarked ruefully in 1988. 'If your timing is off in the entertainment business, it's like you never existed.'

Cooder's career has been a mixture of good and bad timing. As an introverted only child with a consuming enthusiasm for playing guitar, it was his good fortune to grow up in Los Angeles in the Sixties.

'That whole BEATLES explosion made it possible to have a job in music,' he later recalled. 'Before then, the musicians I knew were broke, hungry, dead, scuffling and totally out of the mainstream economics. I'm talking about blues singers, jazz musicians, country musicians, hillbillies, Texas-Mexicans, Cajuns, you name it. They were on the periphery for ever. After The BEATLES there was a lot of activity. All the record companies, night-club owners and agencies were rabidly looking round for what the hell was gonna happen next. It all started to erupt and I got work. I was at high school and all of a sudden I was earning money by playing the guitar. It was the damnedest thing.'

Towards the end of the Sixties Cooder played with Taj Mahal in a group called The Rising Sons, and as a member of Captain Beefheart's Magic Band in 1967 his radically traumatised country blues technique was a prominent feature of the underground classic *Safe as Milk* (released with *Mirror Man* on That's Original TFOCD 11).

As a session man he has one of the most august CVs in rock. Yet despite his telling contributions to albums by The ROLLING STONES, Johnny CASH, Little Feat, The Doobie Brothers and Van MORRISON, to name just a few, he looks back on such work with little satisfaction.

'I didn't prosper as a session man. I was in it for the education, but it gets to be a grind, and nowadays it's become highly technical as well. You have to really be good and tricked out with synthesisers and all the latest gear. I couldn't play on a modern record. I wouldn't know how.'

He secured his first and only solo recording contract in 1970, and although he has fared indifferently in America, during the Seventies he built up a strong following in Europe and particularly in Britain. As part of his 1982 European tour he played an impressive eight consecutive nights at the 3,600-capacity Hammersmith Odeon, and in 1988 he played two nights with his Moula-Banda Rhythm Aces at the (then) 10,000-capacity Wembley Arena.

After the 1982 tour Cooder returned to his home in Santa Monica and spent the next five years working in the movie soundtrack business. His earlier collaborations with directors Walter Hill (*The Long Riders*; 1980; unavailable) and Tony Richardson (*The Border*; 1982; unavailable) led to him writing and/or recording soundtracks for a succession of films including another of Hill's, *Crossroads* (1986; unavailable) and Wim Wenders' celebrated marathon *Paris, Texas* (1985; unavailable), where Cooder's lugubrious slide guitar motifs instantly conjure visions of tumbleweed clumps blowing fitfully across desert landscapes. So far, his only soundtrack on CD is *Johnny Handsome* (WEA 925 996-2; 1989).

Despite conspicuous success on the live circuit, Cooder has never converted his cult status into the mass-market appeal that he obviously desires. He surfaced in 1992 as a member of Little Village, a sort of roots-rock 'supergroup' comprising Cooder, John Hiatt (vocals/ guitar); Jim Keltner (drums) and Nick Lowe (bass/ vocals).

● *Paradise and Lunch* (WEA 244 260-2) [1973]

From the acoustic finger-picking and lazy J.J.Cale-style drawl of 'Tamp 'Em Up Solid' to the country-funk à la Little Feat of 'Married Man's a Fool', and even a quasi-reggae harmony version of 'It's All Over Now', this is vintage Cooder at his best. The album abounds with immaculate harmonies, relaxed, sensual grooves and a sense of rhythmic adventure unrivalled in this neck of the musical woods.

● *Chicken Skin Music* (WEA 254 083) [1976]

A Cooder classic, this is where his languid, dust-bowl blues guitar hitches up with the celebrated Tex-Mex accordionist Flaco Jiminez, Hawaiian steel-guitarist Gabby Pahinui and gospel singer Bobby King to create a wonderful rootsy stew of cross-cultural syncopations. Check the funky brass band in 'I Got Mine'; the Salvation Army meets The NEVILLE BROTHERS?

● *Bop Till You Drop* (Warner Bros 256 691) [1979]

This was Cooder's bid for a bigger slice of the market, and it almost came off. Performed in a more straight ahead R'n'B style, with little in the way of exotic instrumentation beyond a touch of mandolin on 'Look at Granny Run Run', it features Chaka Khan on a couple of tracks ('Down in Hollywood' and 'Don't You Mess Up a Good Thing') and boasts the nearest thing Cooder has had to a hit single, a sprightly version of the Pomus/Shuman song 'Little Sister'.

● *Why Don't You Try Me Tonight?* (Warner Bros 240 864-2) [1986]

The lack of hits makes this 'Best of . . .' compilation a subjective affair, as well as underlining how little of his most familiar material has been written by Cooder himself.

Still, no one would argue with the inclusion of 'Little Sister', 'How Can a Poor Man Stand Such Times and Live?' and the gorgeous instrumental versions of 'I Think it's Gonna Work Out Fine' and 'Dark End of the Street'.

Interestingly, there's not one track from *The Slide Area* (see above), which although it was his highest placed chart entry, is not one of his more distinguished offerings.

● *Get Rhythm* (Warner Bros 925 639-2) [1987]

A sturdy effort, this, but one which offers no new angles. The Johnny CASH square bash of the title is given a whooping neo-gospel treatment, and there are gritty, roots-to-the-fore versions of an obscure Chuck BERRY song, '13 Question Method', the Blackwell/PRESLEY standard 'All Shook Up' and even a re-run of 'Across The Border Line', co-written with John Hiatt. If you liked it before, here's more of the same.

Elvis Costello

Born: Declan McManus, August 25 1955, London
UK No.2 albums: 1979: *Armed Forces* (Demon FIENDCD 21)
1980: *Get Happy!!* (Demon FIENDCD 24)

Cherished as something of a deity by the chattering class of rock enthusiasts, Elvis Costello has come to resemble a sandwich-board man parading an old message. It's not just the got-10p-for-a-cup-of-tea-mate image which he has sprouted his way of keeping in step with the go-ahead Nineties; it's the overwrought style and consumptive grumpiness which he has brought to bear to an ever greater degree on his work since the mid-Eighties.

'I have no position in pop now, I resigned my post,' the singer declared, somewhat cryptically, in 1986, just around the time that the angry young man started turning into a misanthropic old bore. From that point on it was as if all the twitchy energy and snappy wit that informed his early work dissipated, leaving only concentrated doses of venom and ire gnawing at the heart of his songs like rats on a bone.

It all started so promisingly, too. If anyone could claim to have been the British New Wave's equivalent to Bob DYLAN then it was Costello: all those words, tumbling out in a poetic profusion that was light years away from the glottal angst purveyed by The SEX PISTOLS and The CLASH. Yet for all his skilful way with a lyric, and the casual excellence of his backing group The Attractions, Costello was no less angry or iconoclastic than the boot-boys of punk. If anything the little geek who had dared to appropriate the name of the very King of Rock'n'Roll was even hotter under the collar than his spikier peers. It was just that he wasted none of his energy on gestures, preferring to plough every ounce of effort that his wiry frame had to offer into writing and playing his music.

- *My Aim is True* (Demon FIENDCD 13) [1977]

Recorded with a minuscule budget for the fledgling independent Stiff label, Costello's début is a bustling, mercurial foretaste of things to come. The limitations of a workmanlike production job are exposed by the digital format, but the album transcends any technical shortcomings by dint of Costello's extraordinarily fecund songwriting. An impressive strike rate includes 'Welcome to the Working Week', 'Miracle Man', 'Alison' and 'Angels Wanna Wear My Red Shoes'.

- *This Year's Model* (Demon FIENDCD 18) [1978]

The first album to feature The Attractions, this is Costello on sizzling form, lashing out at everything in his path with caustic wit and a savage, reckless excellence. A special commendation is due to drummer Pete Thomas for his thunderously rapid drum motif on 'Lipstick Vogue', but they are all playing like men possessed; and Costello clearly *is* possessed. 'Pump It Up' and '(I Don't Want to Go to) Chelsea' were the hits.

• *Get Happy!!* (Demon FIENDCD 24) [1980]

Costello discovers soul. 'Each song I could go through and tell you which band we were being,' he said of this album. 'Al Green on one, The Four Tops on another. . . .' Not to mention Sam and Dave on the superlative version of their song 'I Can't Stand Up for Falling Down', which Costello here makes his own for ever more.

• *The Best of Elvis Costello – The Man* (Demon FIENDCD 52) [1985]

A cracking compilation, crammed with instant classics: 'Watching the Detectives', 'Alison', 'Accidents Will Happen', 'Good Year for the Roses', 'I Wanna Be Loved', 'Shipbuilding' and many others. Culled from the era when he still knew when to hit the self-edit switch, this is the essential Costello CD primer.

The Robert Cray Band

Convened: 1974, Eugene, Oregon
Robert Cray (f) (born: August 1 1953, Columbus, Georgia) – vocals/guitar; Kevin Hayes – drums; Tim Kaihatsu – guitar; Jimmy Pugh – keyboards; Karl Sevareid – bass
UK No.13 album: 1988: *Don't Be Afraid of the Dark* (Mercury 834 923-2)
US No.13 album: 1986: *Strong Persuader* (Mercury 830 568-2)

Robert Cray is not only the most important and innovative black blues artist since the first generation of electric greats like Muddy WATERS and John Lee HOOKER, he is also the most successful.

He was resident in Virginia when he started his first high school band in the mid-Sixties, using a $69 Harmony guitar his mother had bought for him while his army quartermaster father was serving in Vietnam.

Cray recalls that living in Virginia he heard 'the coolest music. There was a whole Southern soul scene on the radio – the Stax/ Volt stuff, the Atlantic sound: "Tell It Like It Is" by Aaron Neville, "I'm Your Puppet" by James and Bobby Purify, "Soul Man" by Sam and Dave. Then along came Jimi HENDRIX and CREAM and I got swept up by all these new electric sounds.'

Cray first saw Albert Collins at a rock festival in 1969 and became a disciple of the ice-picker's 'cool' blues guitar playing. The same year he met bassist Richard Cousins, who remained his partner in The Robert Cray Band until 1991.

After 15 years of scuffling in relative anonymity round the blues circuit of the Pacific North-West, Cray was eventually welcomed into the upper echelons of the rock world virtually overnight, sharing stages with Eric CLAPTON, Tina TURNER and Huey Lewis, and appearing on film with Keith Richards and Chuck BERRY to name a few.

The situations and characters in his songs draw from the wellspring of crude emotion that has forever inspired the blues: failed love affairs and eternal triangles, the cheating, lying and sadnesses that attend personal relationships. But Cray has brought the persona of the bluesman bang up to date. In one song, he complains about his woman having made off, not with his last dime, but with his credit cards, if you please.

There has been no shortage of musicians willing to plunder the blues for their own ends, but instead of borrowing further from the depleted original stock, Cray has contributed a new body of possibilities to the form.

● *Bad Influence* (Demon FIENDCD 23) [1984]

The dry, low-budget production of Cray's second album, far from being a disadvantage, highlights the telling economy of his approach and emphasises the wondrous cohesion of his band, which at this point comprised Cousins, Peter Boe (keyboards) and David Olson (drums). Produced by Bruce Bromberg and Dennis Walker (as all Cray's albums have been), *Bad Influence* was the first collection properly to showcase Cray's winning combination of soulful vocal style, astringent guitar tone and tightly focused songs.

Both 'Phone Booth' and 'Bad Influence' (later recorded by Eric CLAPTON) are major planks in the Cray legacy and remain in his live set to the present. In Britain *Bad Influence* became the first blues album to top the independent chart, and despite some lesser material lurking towards the end, this *is* the disc which opened a new chapter in the story of the blues.

● *False Accusations* (Demon FIENDCD 43) [1985]

Bromberg and Walker's crisp, uncluttered production continues
to chime perfectly with Cray's fastidious style of playing on the
follow-up to *Bad Influence*, which develops the same basic themes
but turns up the heat by several degrees, notably on the searing,
slow ballad 'The Last Time' and the perky strut of 'S.O.F.T.
(Change of Heart, Change of Mind)'. Although still recording for
a small independent label, the same team were now able to
marshal greater resources and expertise, and if this had been
Cray's major label début it would have been a massive hit.

● *Strong Persuader* (Mercury 830 568-2) [1986]

While Cray's roots have remained securely bedded in the hard soil
of his blues and soul heritage, his musical branches were now
reaching well into the contemporary rock marketplace. Led by the
US hit single 'Smoking Gun', this became a million-seller, which
meant that Cray had outstripped every conventional expectation
of the career curve of a blues performer.

It was the first Cray album to feature the 'legendary' Memphis
Horns (Wayne Jackson – trumpet/trombone; Andrew Love –
tenor saxophone) who later became a full-time appendage to the
Cray Band.

● *Don't Be Afraid of the Dark* (Mercury 834 923-2) [1988]

Here The Memphis Horns are increasingly in evidence: shoring
up the tuneful groove of the title track, rising above the choppy
minor chords of 'Your Secret's Safe With Me', leading the way on
a gorgeous, achingly slow, sub-Otis REDDING soul lament, 'At Last',
and generally investing the bright, precise sound that is Cray's
hallmark with bold shades of authentic Southern soul.

Perhaps not one of Cray's strongest sets of songs overall, it is
still a delight to hear him loosen up on the relaxed, old-style
shuffle, 'Across The Line', while the darkly emotional content of
the lyrics forestall any hint of a diluted vision.

● *Midnight Stroll* (Mercury 846 652-4) [1990]

A stronger collection of songs than *Don't Be Afraid of the Dark*, this album provides firm evidence of Cray's increasing confidence as a singer. The high, whooping shrieks which punctuate 'These Things' and the fade of 'Bouncin' Back' make these among the most passionate and unrestrained vocal performances he has ever committed to disc.

'My Problem' and 'The Things You Do To Me' (both written by Cray) are slow, smouldering ballads cast in the Otis REDDING tradition, and it is the late flowering of Cray as a writer that is the particular joy of *Midnight Stroll*. For, apart from a couple of scorching swingers – 'Labor of Love' and 'Walk Around Time' – and producer Dennis Walker's more measured tale of woe 'The Forecast (Calls for Pain)', it is Cray's own songs which dominate, and none more so than the pulverising, down-tempo 'Move a Mountain'. The disdainful you're-out-of-my-life message of this minor-key soul-blues is dramatically underpinned by accusatory stabs of sound, as if the music were prodding the hapless victim of the lyric on the chest.

Crazy Horse See Neil YOUNG

Cream

Convened: 1966, London. Split up: 1968
Ginger Baker (f) – drums/vocals; Jack Bruce (f) – bass/vocals/harmonica/piano/cello; Eric CLAPTON (f) – guitar/vocals
UK No.1 album: 1969: *Goodbye* (Polydor 823 660-2)
US No.1 album: 1968: *Wheels of Fire* (Polydor 827 578-2)

In a career which lasted just two and a half years – less time than it takes today's bands to float their first album – Cream ushered in a new era of rock. Flaunting a highly evolved instrumental technique, all three musicians were driven by the urge to express themselves through prolonged bouts of improvisation, a familiar imperative in jazz, but a practice which had hitherto been alien to rock'n'roll.

As such, their swift and superlative success prompted a fundamental reassessment of the nature of pop, which was no longer to be thought of as a three-minute medium based on

catchy melodies and simple tunes, but now became an exploratory, guitar-led free-for-all demanding to be judged by the highest
musical standards.

Baker's background was in jazz and, though you'd never guess
it from his brutish playing with Cream, he had started out doing
sessions with acts like Acker Bilk's Paramount Jazz Band, Terry
Lightfoot and Ronnie Scott. He first played with Jack Bruce in
Alexis Korner's Blues Incorporated and subsequently took up
with The Graham Bond Organisation, where Bruce also played
bass for a time. Bruce's other engagements during this period of
flux included playing with Manfred Mann (on their 1966 No.1 hit
'Pretty Flamingo', among others) as well as a brief stint alongside
CLAPTON in John Mayall's Bluesbreakers.

In America a whole 'stadium circuit' developed in the wake of
Cream's hugely successful tours. In 1967 they were voted fourth
best group in the *Melody Maker* readers' poll, behind The BEATLES,
The ROLLING STONES and The Jimi HENDRIX EXPERIENCE, but more to
the point, CLAPTON finally dislodged Hank Marvin from top of the
Best Guitarist category.

But ego problems between Baker and Bruce and the intrinsically transient nature of things in those days of anything-goes
experimentation led to the group's demise in 1968. They marked
their departure with two farewell shows at the Albert Hall on
November 26.

Their influence bore directly on the emergence and style of LED
ZEPPELIN and the legion of 'progressive' and not so progressive
heavy rock bands which followed. Yet although Cream undoubtedly pushed out the envelope of rock, many commentators,
including CLAPTON himself, later expressed dismay at the strand of
brash, galloping heavy metal which the group's example ultimately inspired.

• *Fresh Cream* (Polydor 827 576-2) [1966]

An immensely influential début, *Fresh Cream* is a mixture of
original compositions ('N.S.U.', 'Dreaming') and radically restructured blues standards (Willie Dixon's 'Spoonful', Muddy WATERS'
'Rollin' and Tumblin'', Skip James' 'I'm So Glad' and Robert
JOHNSON's 'From Four Until Late').

A commonly unremarked treasure is 'Sweet Wine', a track

which combines a neat chorus with an otherworldly instrumental passage where CLAPTON constructs a spectacular lattice-work of rattle-and-hum feedback. It's a sequence that ranks among the most exploratory of his entire career, predating as it did the sonic wizardry of HENDRIX's *Are You Experienced* by a good six months.

Elsewhere Bruce's mighty roar of a voice, CLAPTON's hard, bluesy guitar tone and the measured rampage of Baker's drumming makes this one of the key British rock recordings of the decade.

● *Disraeli Gears* (Polydor 823 636-2) [1967]

As the summer of love took hold, Cream moved away from their blues stronghold towards the land of the spacy lyric and the radio-friendly heavy riff. This intriguing creature had been born when The KINKS recorded 'You Really Got Me' in 1964, but now, as CLAPTON and Bruce gunned their instruments into unison overdrive on 'Sunshine of Your Love' and 'Outside Woman Blues', it finally came of age. Ears pricked up around the world, and suddenly the excesses of Black Sabbath, DEEP PURPLE, Iron Butterfly and Vanilla Fudge were only a distortion unit away.

● *Wheels of Fire* (Polydor 827 578-2) [1968]

This double-CD set is fitting testament to both the ambition and hubris of Cream's jam-to-the-death credo. Half the album was studio-recorded in New York and many of those tracks – 'White Room', 'Sitting on Top of the World', 'Politician' and 'Born Under a Bad Sign' – are among the best of the band's portfolio.

The other disc, featuring just four numbers in all, was recorded live at the Fillmore West auditorium in San Francisco. Of these, the opening version of Robert JOHNSON's 'Crossroads', arranged and sung by CLAPTON, ranks as one of the finest examples of his guitar work ever captured on disc. Playing with incisive clarity against a thunderous Bruce/Baker backdrop, CLAPTON pulls out all the stops on a high, keening sequence that moves in tight, sweeping arcs across the beat like a scythe cutting through a field of corn.

Less engaging are the ensuing marathons of 'Spoonful', probably the definitive recorded example of extended rock improvisation, but not a track which bears repeated listening; 'Traintime' featuring Bruce tootling on his harmonica with much breathless, but ultimately pointless, bravado; and Baker's notorious drum solo 'Toad', a 15-minute percussive frenzy during which the superhuman sticksman takes his art to the limit – and some distance beyond, as far as most people are concerned.

Crosby, Stills and Nash/Crosby, Stills, Nash and Young See Neil YOUNG

The Cure

Convened: 1976, Crawley, Sussex
Perry Bamonte – keyboards; Simon Gallup – bass; Robert Smith (f) – vocals/guitar; Porl Thompson – guitar; Boris Williams – drums
UK No.3 album: 1989: *Disintegration* (Polydor 839 353-2)

It would have taken a supremely athletic leap of the imagination to spot an arena-rock colossus in the making when a wan trio comprising Robert Smith, Michael Dempsey (bass) and Lol Tolhurst (drums) released their début single as The Cure in 1978. The song was called 'Killing an Arab' and with its comically naff, dustbin-lid cymbal splashes and coy literary references (to Albert Camus' *L'Etranger*), it augured a career on the art-rock wing of the New Wave, where acts like Wire and XTC have traditionally languished well away from the heart of rock's body politic.

However, Smith has proved a much shrewder judge of popular mood than anyone who has met him could reasonably have guessed. While maintaining his carefully cultivated air of fagged out eccentricity, he presided over an expanding line-up. Dempsey was replaced by Gallup in 1980, Tolhurst switched to keyboards in 1982 and by the time Thompson and Williams had both slotted into place in 1986, the group had become prime exponents of what was eventually called Gothic rock. Indeed, the drony, post-punk mutation of psychedelia which characterised *The Top* (Fiction 821 136-2; 1984) made that album one of the key staging posts in the establishment of the Gothic genre.

By the end of the Eighties Tolhurst had been forced out amid great acrimony and replaced by Bamonte, making Smith the only founder member left. Despite certain outré visual trademarks – the electric-shock hairstyles, Smith's unpleasantly smudged lipstick – the group's static live shows, notable for their astounding collages of light and rolling banks of dry ice, were by now reminiscent of none other than PINK FLOYD. Despite their manifest influence on a new generation of indie bands (Blur, Slowdive, Chapterhouse *et al*) The Cure had become the very kind of dinosaur act that Smith and others of his ilk had so roundly condemned when starting out in that brave new dawn in the aftermath of punk.

- *Staring at the Sea* (Fiction 829 239-2) [1986]

Over the years, The Cure have enjoyed a string of upbeat, neo-vaudevillian hit singles which have balanced a portfolio otherwise weighed down with the gloomy mantras of their album tracks. *Staring at the Sea* is a compilation that stretches from 'Killing an Arab' through to 'Close to Me'. It includes 'The Walk', 'The Love Cats', 'The Caterpillar', 'In Between Days' and 'Jumping Someone Else's Train', but many of their best hits have been recorded since this album was made.

- *Kiss Me Kiss Me Kiss Me* (Fiction 832 130-2) [1987]

All songs on this 18-track marathon are five-way group compositions, which goes some way towards explaining their long instrumental sequences and messy, organic growth patterns. The results are at least unpredictable, with moments of chaotic despondency – such as the melodramatic 'Torture' and the doomy wah-wah intro to 'The Kiss' – suddenly giving way to bright, left-field pop songs like 'The Perfect Girl', 'Catch' and 'Why Can't I Be You'. With its restless, vaguely anarchic quality, this is The Cure at their arch and rambling best.

- *Disintegration* (Polydor 839 353-2) [1989]

More or less a re-run of *Kiss Me Kiss Me Kiss Me* (see above), this sounds as if The Cure are doomed forever to wander listlessly along corridors flooded with mist and the murky rays of oil lanterns. Each song starts with a long, mordant intro eventually interrupted by Smith's quavering voice rising in a pale, cadaverous moan, singing about being eaten by a spider or whatever. When he's finished there is a leisurely, drifting outro, which fades into the distance just in time for the next ponderous, clanking introduction.

Typical is the slow, menacing tone of 'The Same Deep Water as You', which unfurls at roughly the pace of autumn leaves dropping from a tree. It drags you in like the glint of a hypnotist's watch, so much so that Smith's airy vocals, pasted carelessly on top, are almost a distraction. The album has a musty, enigmatic grandeur about it, but a far bigger mystery is how music this draggy could have become so perennially popular.

The Spencer Davis Group See Steve WINWOOD

Deep Purple

Convened: 1968, Hertfordshire. Split up: 1976. Reconvened 1984
Ritchie Blackmore (f) – guitar; Roger Glover – bass; Jon Lord (f) – keyboards; Ian Paice (f) – drums; Joe Lynn Turner – vocals
UK No.1 albums: 1971: *Fireball* (EMI CDP 746240 2)
1972: *Machine Head* (Fame CDFA 3158)
1980: *Deepest Purple* (Fame CDFA 3239)

Although they eventually became the premier, no-nonsense head-banging band, Deep Purple initially harboured high-flying, pseudo-classical aspirations. They performed Jon Lord's preposterous *Concerto for Group and Orchestra* (EMI CDP 794 886-2; 1970) with the Royal Philharmonic Orchestra at the Albert Hall in 1969, but soon succumbed to the basest of musical drives, honing a whiplash heavy-rock formula to thrusting perfection. By 1975 they had secured a listing in the *Guinness Book of Records* as the 'world's loudest band'.

Like so many prime movers of the genre, their fiery musical chemistry depended on the friction generated by warring factions within the group. In Purple's case a trio of technically adept regular blokes – Glover, Paice and Lord – acted as buffers between the bombastic polarities of guitar wizard Ritchie Blackmore and their best known vocalist, the shrieking Ian Gillan.

Blackmore's mega-decibel histrionics earned him a place (alongside Jimmy Page and Rory Gallagher) at the forefront of the second wave of rock-guitar virtuosos. Lord perfected a graphic organ-bashing routine. And Gillan was so often shunted off stage to make way for his colleagues' lengthy bouts of instrumental extemporisation that he kept on quitting the band in a huff.

Deep Purple split up at the end of a UK tour in 1976. The line-up at that point comprised David Coverdale (vocals, later of WHITESNAKE), Tommy Bolin (guitar, died 4.12.76), Glenn Hughes (bass), Lord and Paice. In their absence the group acquired the sort of mythical status which LED ZEPPELIN now enjoys, but they blew it by reforming, initially with the classic line-up of Blackmore, Gillan, Glover, Lord and Paice in 1984. History repeated itself when Gillan walked out again, and like an old fighter returning to the ring, the band's stock has diminished steadily ever since.

- *Deep Purple in Rock* (Harvest CDP 746032 2) [1970]

Described somewhat optimistically by the *Penguin Encyclopedia of Popular Music* as 'arguably [the] most influential UK hard-rock album ever', this is the mighty, roaring slab of turbo-powered proto-metal that established Deep Purple as a first division force, and inspired a lot of guitarists still at the bedroom-mirror stage of their careers to start getting some seriously heavy chops organised. Highlights include 'Speed King', 'Into the Fire', 'Hard Lovin' Man' and the famed shriek-a-long-a-Gillan 'ballad' 'Child in Time'.

- *Machine Head* (Fame CDFA 3158) [1972]

In much the same vein as 'In Rock' but melodically stronger, this is the collection which spawned 'Smoke on the Water', the most widely disseminated song Deep Purple ever recorded. In the late Seventies some of the hipper musical equipment shops inaugurated a system of fines for patrons who played certain intolerably over-familiar riffs when trying out guitars. By far the most overworked sequence was the intro to 'Smoke on the Water', which duly earned its practitioners the stiffest penalty of all.

• *Deepest Purple* (Fame CDFA 3239) [1980]

The best of several available 'greatest hits' compilations, although it omits the band's first US hit, 'Hush'. A chance to thrill again to the inimitable, bucking rifferama of 'Black Night', 'Strange Kind of Woman', 'Smoke on the Water', 'Woman From Tokyo' *et al.*

Def Leppard

Convened: 1977, Sheffield, Yorkshire
Rick Allen (f) – drums; Steve Clark (f) (died 8.1.91) – guitar; Phil Collen – guitar; Joe Elliott (f) – vocals; Rick Savage (f) – bass
UK/US No.1 album: 1987: *Hysteria* (Bludgeon-Riffola 830 675-2)

Of the acts featured in this book, none can rival Def Leppard in their obsessive quest for perfection and corresponding paucity of output: just four albums released in 15 years of trading. These are *On Through the Night* (Vertigo 822 533-2; 1980), *High 'n' Dry* (Vertigo 818 836-2; 1981), *Pyromania* (see below) and *Hysteria* (see below), all of which have sold a million. The latter three were produced by Mutt Lange – also renowned for his work with AC/DC and Foreigner – and *Pyromania* and *Hysteria* have registered sales in excess of ten million copies each.

Although sounding initially like a poor boy's Thin Lizzy, and lumbered with a name devised as an obscure pastiche of LED ZEPPELIN, the Sheffield school chums made respectable inroads on the UK market as front runners in the so-called New Wave of British Heavy Metal (along with Saxon, Iron Maiden and others). But Lange and manager Peter Mensch – a formidable New Yorker whose other clients include METALLICA – spotted a vast potential for the band in America. In a classic coals-to-Newcastle job, they first cracked the US mass market with *Pyromania*, then returned to clean up in Britain.

Guitarist and founder member Pete Willis was sacked in 1982 for being drunk on the job during the recording sessions of *Pyromania*. Yet although Def Leppard ostensibly subscribed to the clean-living lifestyle of the New Rock Professional, the band was curiously subject to the sort of mishaps associated with living the old-fashioned rock'n'roll high life. While driving his Corvette Stingray on a stretch of the A57 on New Year's Eve 1984, Allen was tempted into a race with an Alfa Romeo. The drummer lost his left arm in the resulting crash, but was courageous and ingenious enough to harness electronic drum technology in such a way as to use a foot-pedal with his left leg to do the job of the missing limb.

A more final catastrophe befell guitarist Steve Clark, who died in 1991 of the traditional cocktail of booze and drugs. The band has yet to announce his replacement or to set a release date for the next album.

- **Pyromania** (Mercury 810 308-2) [1983]

By coolly harnessing Leppard's stadium-sized instrumental clout to a collection of MTV and radio-friendly melodies – notably 'Photograph', 'Rock of Ages' and 'Foolin'' – producer Mutt Lange fashioned a laundered but particularly virulent strain of commercial hard rock. This is the album which ushered in the era of heavy metal's dominance of the American rock mainstream. Jon BON JOVI, whose band released its début the following year, was a confessed Def Leppard/Joe Elliott fan and there is no doubt that BON JOVI's magnum opus of 1986, *Slippery When Wet*, was influenced by *Pyromania*.

- **Hysteria** (Bludgeon-Riffola 830 675-2) [1987]

The AOR, bubblegum-metal formula was rigorously refined and applied to even more devastating effect on *Hysteria*, which produced six chart singles in the UK and four Top 10 hits in the US: 'Hysteria', 'Pour Some Sugar on Me', 'Love Bites' and 'Armageddon It'.

Dire Straits

Convened: 1977, London
Alan Clark – keyboards; Guy Fletcher – keyboards; John Illsley (f) – bass; Mark Knopfler (f) – vocals/guitar

With additional touring line-up 1991–93: Danny Cummings
– percussion; Paul Franklin – pedal steel guitar/dobro; Phil
Palmer – guitar; Chris White – saxophone/flute; Chris
Whitten – drums.

UK/US No.1 album: 1985: *Brothers in Arms* (Vertigo 824
                                   499-2)

UK No.1 albums: 1982: *Love Over Gold* (Vertigo 800
                                   088-2)

                     1988: *Money For Nothing* (Vertigo 836
                                   419-2)

                     1991: *On Every Street* (Vertigo 510
                                   160-2)

It is impossible to overstate the hostility of the environment in
which the fledgling Dire Straits found themselves in the closing
months of 1977. The London pub circuit where they played their
first gigs was so utterly in thrall to the smash and clatter of punk
that much longer established groups than Dire Straits were
falling by the wayside – Racing Cars and Meal Ticket spring to
mind, and there were many others.

It was a time when 'laid back' was one of the most insulting
descriptions in the critical lexicon; a time when *The Old Grey
Whistle Test* presenter Bob Harris was physically assaulted in a club
by a gang led by Sid Vicious, for no better reason than that he was
a prominent old hippy, a figurehead of the reviled *ancien régime*.

Enter the Straits, at that time comprising Knopfler and Illsley
together with Knopfler's brother David (guitar) and Pick Withers
(drums). These quiet, staid, polite dudes led by a virtuoso
guitarist/mumbling singer with a receding hairline were touting
gruff, bluesy serenades closer in spirit to the work of old-timers
like Bob DYLAN and Richard THOMPSON than to the 'anarchic'
orthodoxy of The SEX PISTOLS or The CLASH.

Early dates supporting acts like TALKING HEADS and Slaughter
and The Dogs were a trial, but Dire Straits sailed through,
supremely confident in both their abilities and their vision.
Having swum so easily against such a fearfully rough tide, their
immunity to the vagaries of fashion was guaranteed for ever
more. The critics, of course, never forgave them.

But the story didn't end there. With their emphasis on
meticulous production values, and their uniquely well-defined

appeal to the mature, discerning and affluent section of the rock market which emerged in the mid-Eighties, Dire Straits turned out to be the group above all others that turned a generation of music lovers on to CD.

- *Dire Straits* (Vertigo 800 051-2) [1978]

The album which introduced the world to the group's laconic charms is a simple production, recorded for the modest sum of £12,500 at Basing Street Studios, near Notting Hill Gate in London. The sounds may be cheap, but the clarity of exposition remains exemplary, with Knopfler's clear, ringing tones contributing a plaintive, lyrical quality to songs including 'Down to the Waterline', 'Wild West End' and the eternally revered 'Sultans of Swing'.

- *Brothers in Arms* (Vertigo 824 499-2) [1985]

According to Philips, manufacturers of compact disc hardware and sponsors of Dire Straits' 1991–93 world tour, *Brothers in Arms* was 'the key album in transforming CD from a new-fangled curiosity into a mass-market music carrier', and they should know. It was estimated that in the early stages of the marketing of compact-disc technology there was a point at which everyone who owned a CD player had a copy of this disc. It topped the charts in at least 25 countries and recent sales figures put total sales to date in excess of 20 million copies. In the UK it is the biggest selling album of all time, eclipsing even Michael JACKSON's *Thriller*.

Quite why this should be is difficult to explain. Naturally it was boosted by the success of the singles 'Walk of Life' and 'Money for Nothing' (a US No.1, featuring STING). Nor has the album's commercial potential been hindered by the conventional wisdom among hi-fi dealers that few pieces of rock music demonstrate the superior sound quality of CD better than the opening section of 'Money for Nothing'.

But beyond the fact of its superior fidelity, it is one of those rare albums that captured exactly the right spirit at the right time. Its haunting melodies and reflective mood chimed perfectly with the adult rock *Weltanschauung* of the late Eighties. Elegantly combining bold themes with a notable lack of clamour, numbers like 'So Far Away', 'Your Latest Trick' and the epic title track are part of a soundtrack which somehow pulls together the prime elements favoured by a post-Live Aid, CD-owning, *Q*-magazine-reading, MTV-watching generation and turns them into a comfortable and cohesive whole. Whatever your views on Dire Straits' music, this is no mean feat when you think about it.

- *Money For Nothing* (Vertigo 836 419-2) [1988]

An aptly titled compilation which offers little beyond a straight-forward repackaging of 'Sultans of Swing', 'Romeo and Juliet', 'Walk of Life', 'Private Investigations', 'Brothers in Arms' *et al*. As a bonus there are live versions of 'Portobello Belle' and 'Telegraph Road', the latter a 12-minute epic from *Love Over Gold* (see above) which remains Knopfler's most obvious attempt to emulate Bruce SPRINGSTEEN.

- *On Every Street* (Vertigo 510 160-2) [1991]

Although in many ways another masterful achievement, this is an album which carries too many numbers, like 'Calling Elvis' and 'When It Comes to You', that sound like J.J. Cale turning over in his sleep. The impression of Knopfler as an old codger before his time is not merely reinforced, it becomes inescapable.

Yet some of his performances are stunning. During the coda of the slow, bluesy 'You and Your Friend' he uses his regular electric guitar in one side of the mix and a National Steel played with a slide in the other to set up a dialogue of unearthly sadness.

'Heavy Fuel' is the album's 'Money for Nothing', based on an easy-riding groove that ZZ TOP would be proud of. Knopfler adopts the first person singular to poke gentle fun at the cliché of the hard-drinking, rabble-rousing lifestyle. The narrative is inspired by John Self, a character in Martin Amis' novel *Money*. Knopfler pulls the same trick on 'My Parties', taking on the persona of a smug, middle-American suburbanite trotting out a well-rehearsed repertoire of banalities for every social occasion.

These tableaux are so splendidly observed that it is not hard to detect that small but significant element of love which the best satirists reserve for their subjects. It is an empathy which partly explains Knopfler's unerring ability to strike such a resonant chord with the very people he lampoons. The protagonist of 'My Parties' boasts about his 'party cart' and the 'brass toilet-tissue holder with its own telephone' and Knopfler invites us all to snigger knowingly. But you can be sure that were this same, not-so-perfect host to invite you to check out his CD collection, you would find a copy of *Brothers in Arms* not very far from the top of the pile.

The Doors

Convened: 1965, Los Angeles, California. Split up: 1972
John Densmore (f) – drums; Robby Krieger (f) – guitar; Ray Manzarek (f) – keyboards; Jim Morrison (f) (died 3.7.71) – vocals
US No.1 album: 1968: *Waiting for the Sun* (Elektra 974 024-2)

'Death makes angels of us all,' intoned Jim Morrison with eerie prescience on 'The Severed Garden (Adagio)', one of his poetry readings set posthumously to music on *An American Prayer* (1978, unavailable). As a victim of relentless, self-inflicted, Dionysian excess, Morrison's status was far from angelic by the time of his tawdry demise at the age of 27. Drunk, bloated and dissipated, his fate embodied the nightmarish downside of the hippy dream.

Yet such is the perverse logic by which rock's icons are judged that he has been lionised ever since. Certainly, The Doors are about the only group from that era whose music has never gone out of fashion. Oliver Stone's movie *The Doors* (Soundtrack: Elektra 7559-61047-2), starring Val Kilmer in the rôle of Morrison, produced a Doors jamboree in 1991, and no less than four of the band's titles appeared in the Top 10 of back catalogue albums sold during the first half of the year.

But their work also sold consistently well throughout the Eighties and their stock even remained buoyant during the punk era, partly because of Francis Ford Coppola's use of 'The End' in the magnificent opening sequence of *Apocalypse Now* in 1979, but mostly because, as a hit and run phenomenon, The Doors had clearly outpunked punk.

Morrison's extreme performances and unruly behaviour had got the group banned from venues before they had even secured a record deal, and the fame and fortune which brought him unlimited access to alcohol did not exactly quieten him down. Unfortunately, by the time he was arrested in 1969 for waving his cock at an audience in a Miami concert hall, the sinister Adonis was rapidly turning into an oafish sot.

● *The Doors* (Elektra 974 007-2) [1967]

While most of the rock world luxuriated in the good vibes and enhanced cultural freedoms that became available during the summer of love, *The Doors* offered an altogether darker prescription. Morrison's twin obsessions with sex and death imbued the band's music with a languid, sensual menace, whether it be the radio-friendly 'Break on Through' and 'Light my Fire' (an edited version of which became a US No.1 single) or the murky, apocalyptic visions of the 11-minute opus 'The End'.

Their début album was recorded in two weeks, virtually live, and still retains an extraordinary vitality. Even so, Manzarek's Vox Continental organ (a museum piece by today's standards) now sounds incredibly quaint, and the group's quirk of not employing a bass player (Manzarek took care of the bottom end on a Fender Rhodes piano bass) leaves Densmore's clattery drumming over-exposed and makes for a rather tinny sound quality overall.

No matter. What the band did here was to amalgamate the traditions of southern blues (Howlin' Wolf's 'Back Door Man'), European baroque (Weill/Brecht's 'Alabama Song'), poetic licence and radical free-form extemporisation into a subversive yet broadly popular package that eventually proved more influential than anyone would have believed possible at the time.

● *Strange Days* (Elektra 974 014-2) [1967]

Here the band began to evolve a more experimental sound, larding tracks like 'Strange Days' and 'I Can't See Your Face in my Mind', with odd touches of studio trickery. But they got a bit carried away with the cacophonous mumbo jumbo of 'Horse Latitudes', the first number to expose the self-indulgent streak in their music that was to become more pronounced in future years.

The jewel in the crown is another 11-minute epic, 'When the Music's Over', a table-banging manifesto of startling passion. Manzarek's relaxed, jazzy groove is counterpointed first by Krieger's dive-bombing guitar intro, then vandalised by a loopy, Alice-in-Wonderland multi-tracked solo. Morrison's voice, drawling and lazy to begin with, rises eventually to a crescendo of rage as he vents his impatience and frustration. 'We're getting tired of hanging around. . . . We want the world and we want it *now*.' Right on.

- *Waiting for the Sun* (Elektra 974 024-2) [1968]

The making of *Waiting for the Sun* was by all accounts a trying affair, and there are several tracks that attest to the rushed and chaotic nature of its writing and recording. Even so, it emerged with sufficient dashes of inspiration to carry the day, and is best remembered for the relaxed charm of 'Love Street' and the hippy machismo of 'Hello, I Love You', a US No.1 which remains the pithiest definition of free love yet recorded.

The fiercely anti-militaristic theme of 'The Unknown Soldier' chimed with the escalating national mood of opposition to the Vietnam war, but the trashy sensationalism of the accompanying promotional film (a blindfolded Morrison being shot, spewing blood, etc) was symptomatic of an ego rapidly spiralling out of control.

- *L.A. Woman* (Elektra 975 011-2) [1971]

After a series of lack-lustre albums, Morrison seemed to pull himself together enough to make one last effort at capturing the spirit of the group's earlier work. The result was *L.A. Woman*, which *Rolling Stone* implausibly described as 'The Doors' greatest album (including their first).' Completed shortly before and released shortly after Morrison's death, it included songs like 'Been Down So Long' and a version of John Lee HOOKER's 'Crawling King Snake' which marked a return to the bluesy moorings of the group's early work. With its faltering twang and ghostly tinkling piano, 'Riders on the Storm' and the motoring voodoo of the title track were the last great songs to emerge from the band.

- *Best of The Doors* (Elektra 960 345-2) [1973]

Re-issued in 1991, this old compilation is still the definitive Doors primer, incorporating all the major hits together with a sensible cross-section of such other favourites as 'Roadhouse Blues', 'The Crystal Ship' and 'Love Me Two Times'.

- *In Concert* (Elektra 7559-61082-2) [1991]

There have been three live albums by The Doors: *Absolutely Live* (Elektra K 262 005; 1970), *Alive She Cried* (Elektra 960 269-2; 1983) and *Live at the Hollywood Bowl* (Elektra 960 741-2; 1987). *In Concert* is a double-CD which incorporates the best of all three – in effect, most of *Absolutely Live* and bits of the other two – together with a previously unreleased 16-minute version of 'The End'.

Whatever their status as a studio band or in the charts, once they got themselves up on a stage The Doors were little short of incendiary, and this album chronicles the sort of rock'n'roll show which simply doesn't happen any more. Naive, unpredictable and self-indulgent (Morrison spends his time between numbers reciting poetry, demanding marijuana from the audience and threatening to pull down his trousers), they nevertheless tap into some unholy magic when they finally get the charabanc rolling.

From the bullish swagger of 'Roadhouse Blues' to the 15-minute conceptual melodrama of 'The Celebration of the Lizard' there is an unassailable sense of occasion underpinning the overwrought grandeur of the performances. The sexual drama of 'You Make Me Real' and 'Texas Radio and the Big Beat' is fuelled by Morrison's extremes of not-always-poetic licence, while the shattering crescendo of 'The End' is the ultimate, unrefined testament to what The Doors were really all about.

Bob Dylan

Born: Robert Allen Zimmerman, May 24 1941, Duluth, Minnesota
UK No.1 albums: 1963: *The Freewheelin' Bob Dylan* (Columbia CD 32390)
1965: *Bringing It All Back Home* (Columbia CD 32344)

1968: *John Wesley Harding* (Columbia 463 359-2)

1969: *Nashville Skyline* (Columbia CD 63601)

1970: *Self Portrait* (Columbia 460 112-2)

1970: *New Morning* (Columbia CD 32267)

US No.1 albums: 1974: *Planet Waves* (Columbia CD 32154)

1975: *Blood on the Tracks* (Columbia CD 69097)

1976: *Desire* (Columbia CD 32470)

Bob Dylan not only gave rock its primary voice, he also gave it something to say. At a time when the sentiments of most lyrics were dictated by the excesses of youthful hormones, he introduced poetic virtues and injected the higher-minded tenets of folk and protest music into the veins of the delinquent rock'n'roll corpus.

The effect of his nasal, stylised drawl and acute yet magnificently embroidered word play has been all-pervasive, his influence plainly extending from the work of John LENNON, Keith Richards and Jimi HENDRIX to that of Elvis COSTELLO, Mark Knopfler, Bruce SPRINGSTEEN and beyond.

The product of a middle-class Jewish family, Robert Zimmerman enrolled at the University of Minnesota in Minneapolis in 1959, dropped out the following year, and by 1961 had arrived in New York, bearing a new surname inspired by his admiration for the Welsh poet Dylan Thomas. Singing in the folk clubs and coffee bars of Greenwich Village, he was soon spotted by producer John Hammond and signed to Columbia records.

His sound was uniquely harsh and authentic, but his message and melodies had such lucid and universal properties that they were successfully recorded by a myriad of other acts from the mellifluous Peter, Paul and Mary ('Blowin' in the Wind') to the pioneering Jimi HENDRIX Experience ('All Along the Watchtower').

Dylan was at the peak of his powers when, on 30 July 1966, he almost lost his life in a motorcycle accident. He spent 18 months out of the public eye while he recovered from injuries, never fully detailed, but which apparently included a broken neck.

Although by the end of the Sixties, Dylan was no longer a firebrand, his premier status was confirmed by appearances as the main attraction at the first Isle of Wight Festival in 1969 and at George HARRISON's Concert for Bangla Desh in 1971.

In 1977 Dylan's stormy 12-year marriage to Sara Lowndes ended in divorce. At the same time he had to wrestle with the implications of his rapidly changing place in the scheme of things. Far from being the 'voice of a generation', Dylan was now a conspicuous member of rock's old guard, and as such a target of (frequently vicious) censure by the young turks of the punk movement who considered him out of date and irrelevant.

Dylan's response to these upheavals was not the drink and drugs that (temporarily) inured so many of his peers, but work and religion. He embarked on a world tour in 1978 that took in several nights at London's Earls Court arena and a massive outdoor show at the Blackbushe Aerodrome. A succession of tiresome albums with a pronounced Bible-bashing streak ensued.

Dylan retained his place on the top table throughout the Eighties, while frequently giving the impression that he did not much care for the enormous authority which was invested in him by others. Given the unique opportunity of closing the Live Aid concert in 1985, he shambled on stage in front of millions of TV viewers and busked his way with dire results through a couple of songs which his accompanists – Keith Richards and Ron Wood of The ROLLING STONES – had never heard before, let alone rehearsed. Between numbers he mumbled something about helping the farmers of the mid-West and, as if by royal edict, the Farm Aid charity was born.

In 1988 he teamed up with Jeff Lynne, George HARRISON, Tom Petty and the late Roy Orbison in the Traveling Wilburys (see under George HARRISON), a whimsical but good-natured distraction. He also found time to tour with The GRATEFUL DEAD, another historic liaison but yielding a live album – *Dylan and The Dead* (Columbia 463 381-2; 1989) – that was embarrassing.

Indeed, most of his recent albums have been mediocre at best, but whatever his latterday circumstances, nothing can detract from Dylan's status as the most intellectually significant godhead of the Sixties rock revolution.

- *The Freewheelin' Bob Dylan* (Columbia CD 32390) [1963]/*The Times They Are A-Changin'* (Columbia CD 32021) [1964]/*Another Side of Bob Dylan* (Columbia CD 32034) [1964] (three-disc CD set Columbia 467 390-2) [1990]

Dylan initially won international acclaim with his second album, *The Freewheelin' Bob Dylan*, which boasts a raft of songs combining social commentary with a brutal critique of the ways of the (old) world. 'Blowin' in the Wind', 'Don't Think Twice, It's All Right', 'A Hard Rain's A-Gonna Fall', 'Talking World War III Blues' and 'Masters of War' are songs which provided a rallying cry for a new generation of idealistic and disaffected youth, and reflected the profound cultural and political changes that were sweeping through Western societies during the Sixties.

With a title track which has since become ingrained on the fabric of popular culture, the follow-up, *The Times They Are A-Changin'*, elaborated on the themes of social revolution and misplaced patriotism ('With God On Our Side').

Another Side of Bob Dylan drew a line under the first stage in Dylan's development as the folk troubadour with a far-reaching resonance in rock'n'roll circles. Three of its songs were covered by The BYRDS – 'Chimes of Freedom', 'My Back Pages' and 'All I Really Want To Do' (which was also covered by Sonny and Cher).

These three epoch-making albums have been collected together into a single handsome set, but also remain available as individual items.

- *Bringing It All Back Home* (Columbia CD 32344) [1965]

It seems difficult to believe in these days of constant musical cross-pollination, but Dylan's decision to 'go electric' was so controversial that he was actually booed off stage when he appeared at the Newport Folk Festival in 1965, backed for the first time by the Paul Butterfield Band instead of his lone acoustic guitar. It didn't deter him from taking to the road with a full-time electric backing band initially known as The Hawks, later rechristened The BAND.

Yet whatever the folk purists thought about it at the time, this was the period of Dylan's greatest artistic potency, and *Bringing It All Back Home* started a run of extraordinary excellence. Recorded at the cusp of his 'conversion' from folk to rock, it is divided into an acoustic half, including 'Mr Tambourine Man' and 'It's All Over

Now, Baby Blue' and an electric (band) half featuring 'Subterranean Homesick Blues' and 'Maggie's Farm'.

- *Highway 61 Revisited* (Columbia 460 953-2) [1965]

Released just five months after *Bringing It All Back Home*, this
astonishing album remains the crowning glory of Dylan's career.
It opens with 'Like a Rolling Stone', a song that redefined the
parameters of the hit single. Its quintessentially ramshackle, bare-
boned arrangement – reedy harmonica, Hammond organ, rough
acoustic and electric guitar – provides a rugged vehicle for the
tumbling stream of words, their sour, vindictive tone shored up
by the effortless, poetic fluency and arrestingly idiosyncratic
phrasing of Dylan's delivery.

Less specific, but even more menacing is the brooding paranoia
which infuses 'Ballad of a Thin Man' with its bad-dream lyric
ending in the repeated taunt of 'You know something is
happening here, but you don't know what it is, do you, Mr Jones?'

Time and again Dylan displays his formidable mastery of mood,
metre and melody in numbers including 'Queen Jane Approximately', 'Tombstone Blues', 'Highway 61 Revisited' and the
bitterly elegiac finale of 'Desolation Row'.

- *Blonde on Blonde* (Columbia CD 22130) [1966]

Reputedly the first double record (of new material) ever released
by a popular music act – and now a single CD – *Blonde on Blonde* was
recorded in Nashville, and prefaced Dylan's resolve to move on
from his folk origins to explore the country roots of rock. Another
collection of astounding breadth and depth, the material ranges
from the yearning 'I Want You' to the bawdy 'Rainy Day Women
12 & 35', with a strong romantic flavour to the despairing
'Visions of Johanna' and the reflective 'Sad Eyed Lady of the
Lowlands'. The album had been out for two months when Dylan
suffered his motorbike crash.

- *Greatest Hits* (Columbia 460 907-2) [1967]
- *More Bob Dylan's Greatest Hits* (Columbia CD 67239) [1971]

Although Dylan hasn't been within sniffing distance of a hit single
since the Seventies, and the ambitious scope of his best work has

always steered him primarily towards the album-buying sector of the market, he nevertheless competed with the best of the three-minute pop icons of the Sixties. Indeed, no star of that era could have achieved such pre-eminence without featuring strongly in what used to be called the hit parade.

In Britain Dylan enjoyed four Top 10 hits in 1965 alone – 'Subterranean Homesick Blues', 'Like a Rolling Stone', 'The Times They Are A-Changin'' and 'Positively Fourth Street', all included on *Greatest Hits* along with 'Rainy Day Women # 12 & 35', 'I Want You', 'Mr Tambourine Man' and others.

More Bob Dylan Greatest Hits is a double CD which inevitably includes many not-such-great hits, even though most of them are pretty good songs just the same. Along with one or two later chart entries ('Watching the River Flow', 'Lay Lady Lay') and several tracks that were missed from the early period ('Maggie's Farm', 'All I Really Want To Do', 'My Back Pages'), it also showcases numbers written by Dylan but popularised elsewhere, notably 'All Along the Watchtower' (Jimi HENDRIX) and 'Mighty Quinn' (a hit in the UK for Manfred Mann).

● *John Wesley Harding* (Columbia 463 359-2) [1968]

The first album to be released after Dylan's recovery from his accident, this was again recorded in Nashville, and bears a noticeably mellower sound than its predecessors. Songs like 'I'll Be Your Baby Tonight' are cast in a louche country vein, while others such as 'Ballad of Frankie Lee and Judas Priest' and 'I Dreamed I Saw St Augustine' feature a liberal (and ominous) sprinkling of biblical references.

● *Nashville Skyline* (Columbia CD 63601) [1969]

This full-blown country album confirmed the direction in which Dylan had been heading for several years. Along with the soulful romanticism of 'Tonight I'll Be Staying Here With You' and 'Lay Lady Lay' it incorporates a notable duet with Johnny CASH on 'Girl from the North Country' where the harmonies wobble and roll like ships on a high sea.

Virtually unrecognisable as the work of the angry young man who had sung 'Highway 61 Revisited', it was around this time that cranky rumours that Dylan had died in the motorbike crash and been replaced by a lookalike began to circulate. The album was nevertheless a resounding commercial success.

- *Planet Waves* (Columbia CD 32154) [1974]
- *Before the Flood* (Columbia CD 22137) [1974]
- *The Basement Tapes* (Columbia 466 137-2) [1975]

Dylan had spent much of the time during his extended convalescence playing and recording with The BAND at a house called Big Pink. Much of the music he made during that period (1967–68) surfaced seven years later on *The Basement Tapes*, an album of mythical status, which captures Dylan in a relaxed and sometimes surreal mood on tracks like 'Clothes Line Saga' and 'Open the Door, Homer', and seething with anger and anguish on 'Tears of Rage', 'This Wheel's on Fire' and 'Too Much of Nothing'.

Dylan and The BAND drifted apart thereafter, but reunited to record the excellent *Planet Waves*. It yielded no hits, but the album stayed at the top of the US chart for four weeks, and songs like 'Forever Young' and 'The Wedding Song' restored both Dylan and The BAND to critical favour after a lean period during the early Seventies.

On a winning roll, they undertook a substantial tour of America which resulted in the superlative live album *Before the Flood*. With its wonderfully loose, fresh versions of 'It Ain't Me, Babe', 'Ballad of a Thin Man', 'The Night They Drove Old Dixie Down', 'Like a Rolling Stone', 'Blowin' in the Wind' and many others, this is the best officially available live Dylan recording, and *de facto* a hard-to-beat collection of greatest hits.

- *Blood on the Tracks* (Columbia CD 69097) [1975]

Dylan's most assured album of the Seventies, *Blood on the Tracks* is a bleak, cathartic affair with songs like 'Idiot Wind' and 'Shelter from the Storm' coming as close as any of his later material does to the raging, sneering glory of his prime. The sparse arrangements provide simple, effective backdrops for the needle-sharp word play of 'Tangled Up in Blue' and 'Simple Twist of Fate'. This is the last Dylan album to rank among his masterpieces.

- **Oh Mercy** (Columbia 465 800-2) [1989]

Just when the critics had come to the end of their tether, and his audience seemed to have dwindled to a core of ageing die-hards, Dylan effected a remarkable, if overdue, renaissance with this album. Produced by man-of-the-moment Daniel Lanois in New Orleans, it features the witty 'Everything is Broken', the scathing 'Political World' and the sinister 'Man in a Long Black Coat' among its many charms. It was too little too late (to borrow a cliché from the political pundits), but *Oh Mercy* still ranks as easily Dylan's best work of the Eighties.

- **Biograph** (Columbia CD 66509) [1985]
- **The Bootleg Series Volumes 1–3** (Rare & Unreleased) 1961–1991 (Columbia 468086 2) [1991]

The fanatical completist fervour which grips his hard-core followers coupled with his profligate creative nature has made Dylan a natural candidate for the CD boxed set. *Biograph* opened the account: a highly desirable, three-disc, 53-song compilation of his recording career from 1962 to 1981, which includes 18 previously unreleased tracks and indispensable sleeve notes by journalist Cameron Crowe.

But there was much more to come and, as England's foremost Dylan authority John Bauldie underlines in his copious accompanying text to the award-winning boxed-set *The Bootleg Series Volumes 1–3 (Rare & Unreleased) 1961–1991*, Dylan produced a vast amount of material that was surplus to his recording needs during the early stages of his career, much of it as good as anything that found its way on to the official releases of the time.

There are 58 tracks on *The Bootleg Series*, many of them previously unreleased, spread roughly chronologically over three discs. The bulk of the goodies are on Volume 1, which provides a fascinating insight into the folk roots of Dylan's art.

Of the many gems here, 'Talkin' John Birch Paranoid Blues' demonstrates his often overlooked humour and underlines the political protest dimension of his early work; 'Who Killed Davey Moore?' is a searing anti-boxing diatribe; and 'Moonshiner' illustrates the great subtlety of expression of which Dylan used to be capable.

Such revelations need to be balanced against less-than-essential alternate takes of 'Subterranean Homesick Blues', 'Like a Rolling Stone' and others which start to creep in during Volume 2, and the inevitably less distinguished more recent material of Volume 3, but certainly Volume 1 knocks Dylan's official releases during the Eighties into a cocked hat.

Electronic See The SMITHS

EMF

Convened: 1989, Forest of Dean, Gloucestershire
James Atkin (f) – vocals; Derry Brownson (f) – samples; Mark Decloedt (f) – drums; Ian Dench (f) – keyboards/guitar; Zac Foley (f) – bass
UK No.3 album: 1991: *Schubert Dip* (Parlophone CDPCS 7353)

Younger than HAPPY MONDAYS, snappier than Inspiral Carpets and considerably more visible throughout 1991 than The STONE ROSES, EMF are the most recent in a succession of bands which have welded the trappings of rap and dance culture on to a basic rock group chassis. The resulting vehicle is a souped-up racer, designed to be driven hard for short bursts.

They came roaring out of the stocks with a début single, 'Unbelievable', which sailed out of nowhere to No.3 in the UK chart in the autumn of 1990 and went straight to No.1 in the American chart in July the following year. With JESUS JONES' single 'Right Here Right Now' at No.3 in the US the same week, talk was rife on both sides of the Atlantic of another 'British invasion' of America (the third?).

In Britain EMF (standing for Epsom Mad Funkers, Ecstasy MotherFuckers, Eat More Fruit and other permutations depending on mood and circumstance) had erroneously been perceived as a transient pop phenomenon, a yobbish version of New Kids On The Block. In truth they are more in the tradition of bands like The SMITHS and Echo and The Bunnymen – a serious rock act with broad commercial appeal – which is how the Americans see them.

• *Schubert Dip* (Parlophone CDPCS 7353) [1991]

While not possessed of quite the same melodic flair, EMF's most obvious spiritual link is with JESUS JONES. The opening salvo of 'Children', 'Long Summer Days' and 'When You're Mine' establishes a formula built on the foundations of Decloedt's pile-driving drum motifs and overlaid with gaudy, shrieking layers of keyboard, guitar and Brownson's sampled effects. Over this elegant cacophony the unmistakably English whine of Atkins' vocals are frequently reminiscent of Terry Hall (of The Specials and Fun Boy Three).

They ran into trouble with Yoko Ono over the use on 'Lies' of a sample of the voice of John LENNON's killer Mark Chapman, in his prison cell, reciting the lyric of LENNON's 'Watching the Wheels'. The band settled out of court for $15,000 and the offending voice was removed from subsequent pressings. Other snatches of 'found' sound, including Kermit the Frog and a Radio 3 announcer reading from T.S. Eliot, have so far proved less troublesome.

Very much the rapid-fire sound of the moment, they have time on their side and may do great things yet.

Eurythmics

Convened: 1980, London
Annie Lennox (f) – vocals; Dave Stewart (f) – keyboards/guitar/vocals
UK No.1 albums: 1983: *Touch* (RCA PD 70109)
1989: *We Too Are One* (RCA PD 74251)
1991: *Greatest Hits* (RCA PD 74856)

Although Annie Lennox and Dave Stewart have yet to work together as Eurythmics in the Nineties, they were, without doubt, one of the most striking partnerships of the Eighties. Perhaps uniquely in pop, they personified the spirit of a decade that bore witness to technological innovation and musical retrenchment in roughly equal part. A marriage of opposites, their continuing appeal is based on the musical and visual tension between the sleek, androgynous, icy-voiced Lennox and the rumpled, rock'n-'roll recidivist Stewart.

The odd couple met in 1976 and became lovers soon afterwards, a romance that lasted for four years. During that time they founded The Tourists, a post-punk power-pop group with 'serious' rock band pretensions. Their biggest hit was a version of Dusty Springfield's 'I Only Want to Be With You', a song which eventually became a credibility-destroying millstone round their necks.

If nothing else, the cruel critical drubbing which the music press inflicted on The Tourists (none of whose three albums has been transferred to CD) alerted Lennox and Stewart to the pitfalls of innocently rocking out, and when they regrouped as a duo in 1980, adopting the name Eurythmics, they took great care to make their pop modish and to keep their image both flexible and mysterious.

As well as her classically trained musicianship, Lennox provided a strikingly ambiguous visual persona, ideal material for the new video format that was already becoming such an important factor in the marketing of rock, while Stewart shrewdly applied his traditional 'backroom' skills as musician and producer to the new synthesiser technology.

- *Eurythmics Box Set* (RCA ND 74384) [1990]
  Three-disc set incorporating: *Sweet Dreams (Are Made of This)* [1982]/*Touch* [1983]/*Be Yourself Tonight* [1985]

The three essential early Eurythmics albums are available either individually or gathered together in this handy boxed-set package for approximately £23.

It was their second album, *Sweet Dreams (Are Made of This)*, which marked the initial break-through. Recorded on eight-track equipment in a flat in Chalk Farm, North London, this album, with its cool, clean melody lines and novel use of keyboard and drum-machine techno-trickery played a pivotal role in the emerging synth-pop revolution. It proved that with the right tunes it was possible to make massive hit records (something that punk had generally failed to do) without either going on the road for years on end or spending a fortune on 'professional' studio time. The title track was an enormous worldwide success (a US No.1), and has retained a special place in the duo's live shows ever since.

With *Touch* they developed the formula, this time doing the recording on 24-track in a disused church in Crouch End, North London, and producing another string of elegantly crafted hits, notably 'Who's That Girl?', 'Right by Your Side' and 'Here Comes the Rain Again'.

With *Be Yourself Tonight*, Stewart's true colours began to show and the emphasis shifted slightly but perceptibly away from cool, sophisticated synth-pop towards power-chord raunch on numbers like 'Would I Lie to You?'. The album became a hit-making machine, providing their first UK No.1, 'There Must Be an Angel (Playing With My Heart)', and further successes with 'Be Yourself Tonight', 'It's Alright (Baby's Coming Back)' and 'Sisters are Doin' It for Themselves', a sparky duet between Lennox and veteran soul diva Aretha FRANKLIN.

- **We Too Are One** (RCA PD 74251) [1989]

The frosty clarity of Lennox's vocal delivery has rarely sounded more chilling than it does on 'Don't Ask Me Why' or the rather baldly stated lyric of 'I Hate You' (chorus: 'You hurt me, I hate you/ You hurt me, I hate you', and so on for several repeats). Stewart, meanwhile, indulges his by-now fully revealed penchant for hoary bump'n'grind guitar riffs on the single 'Revival', to which Lennox applies a vocal punctuated by a range of surly grunts which sound as if they are inspired by the work of heavy-breathing WHITESNAKE crooner David Coverdale.

In between these extremes there is an excursion into neo-BEATLES chamber-pop on 'Sylvia', an eerie, rumbling funk-up called 'How Long' and a pleasingly cathartic ballad, 'When the Day Goes Down', which winds up the set. An alert production, courtesy of Stewart and Jimmy Iovine but, unusually for Eurythmics, the album failed to produce a Top 20 hit and, for the moment, marks the last time that Lennox and Stewart recorded together.

- **Greatest Hits** (RCA PD 74856) [1991]

With Lennox celebrating the birth of her first child, and Stewart at large with his facsimile of a rock'n'roll band, The Spiritual Cowboys, the time was ripe for a stop-gap collection that couldn't and didn't fail. *Greatest Hits* is just that, boasting nine ex-Top 10 titles and several more besides. There are some worthwhile inclusions on CD that purchasers of the vinyl format have to make do without, namely 'Angel', 'Would I Lie to You?', 'Missionary Man', 'I Need a Man' and 'The Miracle of Love'.

The Faces See Rod STEWART

Fairport Convention

Convened: 1967, London. Split up: 1979. Reconvened annually since 1980
Sandy Denny – vocals; Ashley Hutchings (f) – bass; Dave Mattacks – drums; Simon Nicol (f) – guitar/vocals; Dave Swarbrick – fiddle/vocals; Richard THOMPSON (f) – guitar/vocals
UK No.8 album: 1971: *Angel Delight* (unavailable)

Until Fairport Convention, it was simply taken for granted that the foundations of British rock were built out of raw musical materials imported from America, specifically the blues. From The ROLLING STONES, who started out by plotting the co-ordinates of 'Route 66', to CREAM, who ended up standing at Robert JOHNSON's 'Crossroads', the musical revolution of the Sixties ushered in a singing and playing style, together with a set of lyrical preoccupations that were steeped, both consciously and unconsciously, in the trappings of Americana. (When Joe Strummer eventually sang, 'I'm so bored with the USA' in 1977, it was like a slap in the face to an entire generation of older musicians, some of whom responded as if they had just been woken from a deep slumber.)

Fairport Convention were the exception. They looked instead to their local heritage for inspiration and introduced the little-used vocabulary of English folk to the language of electric rock. Their working practices also differed from those of their more conventional rock brethren. In the matter of personnel (constantly changing) and initial rate of production they behaved more like a jazz band. Their second, third and fourth albums were all released in 1969, the same year that the group's van crashed on a motorway, killing their original drummer Martin Lamble.

The classic line-up, as listed above, only existed for three months between September and December 1969, but it is those six people, some of them in it from the beginning, some of them still in it today, who did most to fashion the sound and personality of a group that seemed to take on a quasi-mystical life of its own. After recording the definitive folk-rock album *Liege and Lief*, Sandy Denny left to form Fotheringay (*Fotheringay* Hannibal HNCD 4426); Ashley Hutchings took off to found Steeleye Span (*Best of Steeleye Span* Chrysalis CCD 1467); and two months later Richard THOMPSON embarked on a solo career.

The band recruited bassist/vocalist Dave Pegg and set off on another eight-year stretch of serpentine personnel changes and mediocre albums. They eventually split up, but the band never died and, after many annual get-togethers at their own Cropredy Festival in Oxfordshire, a semi-permanent line-up incorporating Pegg and Nicol eventually re-emerged towards the end of the Eighties.

Although the popular climate was as favourable as it had ever been, with groups like The POGUES and All About Eve capitalising, in part, on their legacy, Fairport Convention had by then declined to the level of a friendly pub band. Nevertheless, there are few groups who in their day stamped such an indelible mark on the margins of English rock culture.

- **What We Did on Our Holidays** (Island IMCD 97) [1969]

Although at this stage the band still included vocalist Ian Matthews – who as leader of Matthews' Southern Comfort subsequently enjoyed a UK No.1 hit with 'Woodstock' – it is Sandy Denny, with a voice like the purest cut crystal, who dominates this album. The band had yet to settle into its true métier, but 'Meet on the Ledge' and 'Fotheringay' are among the best numbers it ever recorded.

- **Unhalfbricking** (Island IMCD 61) [1969]

This watershed release marked the debut of fiddler Dave Swarbrick, a man with a vast knowledge of traditional folk. In a long fiddle and guitar duel, he and THOMPSON transformed the traditional folk ballad 'Sailor's Life' into a full-scale sub-psychedelic rampage. Here, at last, was an innovatory English response to the progressive noodlings of American bands like Jefferson Airplane,

Quicksilver Messenger Service and It's A Beautiful Day.

The album also includes Denny's touching 'Who Knows Where the Time Goes' and the group's only hit single 'Si Tu Dois Partir', a French-language arrangement of Dylan's 'If You Gotta Go', replete with squeeze-box, fiddle and washboard.

● *Liege and Lief* (Island IMCD 60) [1969]

Here they reached the apogee of the folk-rock fusion, with songs like 'Crazy Man Michael' and 'Matty Groves', the latter an extended version of a traditional song that became one of the all-time Fairport favourites.

● *The History of Fairport Convention* (Island IMCD 128) [1972]

A strong mid-price collection of material from the essential Fairport era which underlines just how pivotal THOMPSON's contribution was to the group's groundbreaking music.

The early material like 'Meet on the Ledge', 'Sailor's Life', 'Now be Thankful' and 'Sloth' is still spine-tingling stuff; austere, poignant, driven music. Can it be mere coincidence that selections like 'Angel Delight' and 'Breakfast in Mayfair', culled from the period after THOMPSON's departure in January 1971, now sound rather soft and twee by comparison?

Bryan Ferry See ROXY MUSIC

Fleetwood Mac

Convened: 1967, London
Billy Burnette – guitar/vocals; Mick Fleetwood (f) – drums;
Stevie Nicks – vocals; Christine McVie – keyboards/vocals;
John McVie (f) – bass; Rick Vito – guitar/vocals
UK/US No.1 album: 1977: *Rumours* (Warner Bros 256 344)
UK No.1 albums: 1979: *Tusk* (Warner Bros 266 088)
                    1987: *Tango in the Night* (Warner Bros
                    925 471-2)
                    1990: *Behind the Mask* (Warner Bros
                    7599 26206-2)

US No.1 albums: 1975: *Fleetwood Mac* (Warner Bros 254
                          043)
                    1982: *Mirage* (Warner Bros 256 952)

No other group has suffered quite the range of domestic
upheavals that have beset Fleetwood Mac. In making the unlikely
transition from scuffling British blues band to a sanctuary for
diamanté Californian soft-rock celebrities, their story reads more
like a Hollywood soap than the history of a rock act.

The group was founded by guitarist and vocalist Peter Green,
who first made a name for himself as successor to Eric CLAPTON in
John Mayall's Bluesbreakers, with whom he recorded one glorious album *A Hard Road* (London 820 474-2; 1967). Green
recruited a line-up comprising two of his cronies from The
Bluesbreakers – John McVie (bass) and Mick Fleetwood (drums) –
together with the untested talent of Jeremy Spencer (guitar/
piano/vocals).

If Green had decided to call his group something other than a
composite of the names of its drummer and bass player, the
tenuous air of continuity might well have vanished altogether as
an endless succession of musicians passed through the ranks,
leaving that same rhythm section partnership as the only
constant factor in a long and bumpy process of evolution.

In May 1970 Green quit to go quietly mad and in February 1971
Spencer was whisked off to join some loony religious cult. After
five lean years of debilitating personnel changes and a relocation
to Los Angeles, a line-up eventually emerged that included
McVie's wife, Christine (née Perfect, ex-Chicken Shack), and the
romantically linked Californian singing/songwriting duo of Stevie
Nicks and Lindsay Buckingham.

The music mutated to match the change of era and locale.
Instead of gutsy Elmore James and plaintive Robert JOHNSON licks,
they were now creating popular music of sophisticated gentility
for which the rubric adult oriented rock might well have been
coined.

Indeed, while it is Eighties acts like DIRE STRAITS and Phil COLLINS
that sold the concept of CD to the more mature and discerning
rock fan, it was Fleetwood Mac who in the mid-Seventies first
identified that audience and started catering for it, well before CD
had even been invented.

The personal and personnel upheavals continued. The McVies were divorced in the late Seventies, but neither of them left the band; Fleetwood married and divorced his wife twice and, thanks to some stupendously maladroit dabbling in real estate, was declared bankrupt in 1984; Buckingham announced his decision to leave the group on the eve of their 1988 world tour and was literally chased out of the house by his former lover Nicks, and so on.

By this time, no matter how turbulent their private lives, the band's songwriting had become about as exciting as one of those *Lifestyles of the Rich and Famous* commentaries. Like all good soap, no matter what the developments or where the storyline goes, there is a guiding sleight of hand at work in Fleetwood Mac's music to ensure that everything always returns to exactly the same predictable point of equilibrium in the end.

● *Rumours* (Warner Bros 256 344) [1977]

This album, which supposedly documents the ceaseless emotional tumult within and surrounding the band, is one of the biggest-selling recordings in the history of rock – well past the 20 million mark at the last count. They pulled off this achievement by being the first act successfully to harness traditional rock band instrumentation to the sort of misty, drifting, soft-centred material that sounds chic, adult and recognisably like rock music, but which does not impinge on conversation at the dinner table.

With various combinations of Christine Perfect's glacé vocals, Stevie Nicks' bitter-sweet quaver and Lindsay Buckingham's chundering vocal and guitar work-outs to the fore, any cracks in the structure are smoothly papered over by the bass and drums of Fleetwood and McVie, whose musical rapport is based on a hand-in-glove understanding of the need to keep reliable, basic time.

● *Greatest Hits* (Warner Bros WX 221) [1988]

This is a straightforward canter through the best known bits of the Californian-era Mac's enduringly bankable legacy, a fine collection for those wishing to recap on the comforting resonances of 'Little Lies', 'Seven Wonders' and 'Everywhere' from *Tango In The Night* (see above); 'Sara' and 'Tusk' from *Tusk* (see above);

'Go Your Own Way' and 'Don't Stop' from *Rumours* (see above); and Nicks' *tour de force* of gypsy-fied romanticism 'Rhiannon' from *Fleetwood Mac* (see above).

● *The Blues Years* (Essential ESBCD 138) [1990]

Among their other accomplishments, Fleetwood Mac's early albums redefined the limits of how many times Elmore James' 'Dust My Broom' slide guitar lick could be shoehorned into songs with different titles. It rings out like a clarion call within the first seconds of this three-disc set, introducing 'My Heart Beat Like a Hammer', and pops up again in virtually identical shape on 'Coming Home', 'Dust My Broom', 'Doctor Brown', 'Need Your Love Tonight', 'I Believe My Time Ain't Long', 'I Can't Hold Out' and 'I'm Worried'. This was the work of Jeremy Spencer, the group's principal roustabout, obsessive blues purist, and something of a one-dimensional talent.

But Spencer's repetitively ebullient contributions serve as the perfect counterpoint to the true genius of Peter Green, a man who could use a guitar to communicate an air of such sweet and unutterable melancholia it is almost too painful to bear.

The Blues Years incorporates the first two Fleetwood Mac albums – *Fleetwood Mac* (1967; unavailable) and *Mr Wonderful* (Essential ESSCD 010; 1967) together with singles such as 'Black Magic Woman', 'Albatross' and 'Man of the World' and rare early material – some of it great, some less so – all at the very reasonable price of about £22.

No amount of digital cleaning up could ever alter a sound that is (thankfully) still as hard and grimy as the windows in some of the under-the-arches dives the band was playing at the time. This set is a reminder of why today's airbrushed soft rock phenomenon was once considered one of the most authentic-sounding bands to emerge from the British blues boom of the Sixties.

Aretha Franklin

Born: March 25 1942, Memphis, Tennessee
US No.2 albums: 1967: *I Never Loved a Man the Way I Love*
                    You (unavailable)
                1968: *Lady Soul* (Atlantic 781818-2)

'If you want to know the truth, Aretha never left the church,' explained her father, the Rev C.L. Franklin, perhaps the most celebrated Baptist minister of his day. In other words the thrilling, whooping, unearthly singing voice which earned its owner the undisputed sobriquets Lady Soul and the Queen of Soul was always a sanctified instrument. Unfortunately, the superb double live album *Amazing Grace*, released in 1972, which features Franklin making an emotional return to the gospel standards which she sang as a child, is unavailable on CD. Indeed, a huge swathe of Franklin's back catalogue, including practically all the classic material from the Sixties and early Seventies, has yet to surface in the digital format.

It is her righteous application of the gospel spirit to the more earthbound specifics of soul that has made Franklin one of the most revered and influential singers of the last 30 years. After a five-year spell at Columbia that yielded just one minor hit, she signed to Atlantic records in 1967. There, under the aegis of producer Jerry Wexler, she was suddenly propelled to the highest peaks of popular acclaim, enjoying a barrage of chart successes unrivalled by any female performer of that era. Even today, the only woman with more American Top 10 hits to her name is MADONNA.

Additionally, Franklin can claim 15 Grammy awards, the distinction of being the first woman to be inducted to the Rock'n'Roll Hall of Fame, several honorary doctorates, the keys to a dozen American cities and a voice which has officially been designated one of Michigan state's 'natural resources'. People tend to forget she is also an accomplished pianist.

● *Lady Soul* (Atlantic 781818-2) [1968]

Her third album on Atlantic remains a singularly impressive monument to a supreme talent. Virtually a hits collection by default, it hosts 'Chain of Fools', 'People Get Ready', '(You Make

Me Feel Like) A Natural Woman' and 'Since You've Been Gone (Sweet Sweet Baby)'. These are the songs and performances of her prime, and they demonstrate a range and passion that is little short of divine.

- *Who's Zoomin' Who?* (Arista 259053) [1985]

Having spent several reclusive years nursing her ailing father, who died in 1984, this was the comeback album which re-established Franklin as a major international presence in the Eighties. Produced by Narada Michael Walden, it was easily her biggest success for fifteen years and earned Franklin her first platinum long-playing disc (for formally recognised sales in excess of one million copies). In America the album produced no less than four hit singles: 'Freeway of Love', 'Who's Zoomin' Who?', 'Another Night' and 'Sisters are Doin' It for Themselves', an unimpeachably right-on duet with Annie Lennox of EURYTHMICS.

- *20 Greatest Hits* (Atlantic 241135-2) [1987]

In attempting to identify the 1001 'greatest singles ever made' for his book *The Heart of Rock and Soul*, American rock critic Dave Marsh finished up with a list that comprised more entries by Aretha Franklin than by any other artist. Here, on one great compilation, is the reason why. It includes 'Respect', 'I Say a Little Prayer', 'Chain of Fools', 'Think', 'Baby I Love You', 'Natural Woman', 'Don't Play That Song', 'Do Right Woman, Do Right Man'.

Free

Convened: 1968, London. Split up: 1973
Andy Fraser (f) – bass/keyboards; Simon Kirke (f) – drums; Paul Kossoff (f) (died 19.3.76) – guitar; Paul Rodgers (f) – vocals/guitar
UK No.2 albums: 1970: *Fire and Water* (Island IMCD 80)
1974: *The Free Story* (Island CID 9945)

At a time when CREAM and Jimi HENDRIX were pioneering ever-wilder extremes of virtuoso improvisation, and The WHO were engaged in the construction of their first rock opera, Free invented a stark, minimalist blues-rock style built on a slow, strutting tempo, and despatched with all the cool sense of purpose of a stalking cat.

Kossoff and Kirke, who had both been playing in a London group known as Black Cat Bones, headhunted Rodgers from a blues band called Brown Sugar. Fraser, who had recently been fired from John Mayall's Bluesbreakers, was recommended as a suitable bass player and the four musicians made their first appearance as Free on April 19 1968 at the Nag's Head in Battersea.

The band was helped initially by Alexis Korner (died 1.1.84), a guru of the English R'n'B scene in the Sixties. Korner used his influence to get them gigs, and bent the ear of recording mogul Chris Blackwell, who swiftly signed the group to Island Records.

● *Tons of Sobs* (Island IMCD 62) [1968]

Free's début was in the shops just six months after their first gig. Kirke was 19, Kossoff and Rodgers 18 and Fraser a mere 16 years old when it was released. Produced by the late, great Guy Stevens, *Tons of Sobs* is a patchy affair which nevertheless won the approval of the hard core of devotees which the band had already attracted on the live circuit. It yielded no hits, but 'The Hunter', a Booker T and the MG's composition, became one of the group's most enduring stage favourites.

● *Free* (Island IMCD 64) [1969]

Thanks to incessant touring, the group had evolved its extraordinarily taut, muscular style by the time of its self-titled second release. Rodgers later complained that the album was 'underproduced', but 'I'll Be Creepin'', 'Free Me' and 'Songs of Yesterday' remain unspoilt examples of just about the leanest, most austere rock-group sound ever recorded.

● *Fire and Water* (Island IMCD 80) [1970]

A slow, searing masterpiece, this is the album which threw up the million-selling 'All Right Now', one of a handful of rock songs which seem to exist in a state of eternal grace. Like 'Layla' and 'Stairway to Heaven' it's a number of such classic stature and enduring popularity that it transcends words of explanation, adulation or criticism. It was a hit in 1970, 1973, 1978, 1982 and 1991 and doubtless we haven't heard the last of it yet.

The fabric of other songs like 'Fire and Water' and 'Mr Big' is stretched in similar push-and-pull patterns that weave themselves around thin air with the tensile strength of wire fencing. Yet on the ballads 'Oh I Wept' and 'Don't Say You Love Me' there is also harmonic sophistication and a surprising degree of tenderness.

- *Highway* (Island IMCD 63) [1971]

Highway concentrates on the gentler, more sophisticated side of the group. 'Be My Friend', 'Bodie' and 'Love You So' are great songs which emphasise the poignant, reflective aspect of Free's musical nature. But while the band was happy to reveal the vulnerable flipside of their rampant macho man image, the majority of the fans evidently preferred a cruder emotion. The album was a flop, even though it came straight after the internationally successful *Fire and Water*.

- *Free Live!* (Island IMCD 73) [1971]

This is a rough, untreated production which nevertheless captures the group on spellbinding form. Kossoff's guitar keeps cutting out and they are all over the shop during 'All Right Now', but nothing can detract from the highly charged atmosphere and sheer nerve of their outlandishly slow versions of 'Fire and Water', 'Mr Big', 'The Hunter' and 'I'm a Mover'. A lone studio song, 'Get Where I Belong', tagged on at the end, is among the most poignant and overlooked recordings the band ever made.

- *Free at Last* (Island IMCD 82) [1972]
- *Heartbreaker* (Island IMCD 81) [1973]

After personality clashes and a drug-related deterioration in Kossoff's health, Free split for seven months. When they got back together the magic had gone and these two albums, although successful, make a disappointing swansong to a career which promised so much more.

Free at Last includes the hit 'Little Bit of Love', but is otherwise flabby and unremarkable. *Heartbreaker* was patched together after Fraser had quit in July 1972 (for the second time), using various outside help and only part-time contributions from the ailing Kossoff. It is entirely forgettable, apart from its only hit, 'Wishing Well'.

- *The Free Story* (Island CID 9945) [1974]
- *All Right Now* (Island CIDTV 2) [1991]

All Right Now, a compilation album, was released to cash in on the use of 'All Right Now', the single, as the soundtrack of an ad for Wrigleys chewing gum. It sounds great, since all the tracks on it have been digitally remastered, but as a selection of songs it is beaten hands down by the much older compilation, *The Free Story*. As well as the obvious stuff – 'My Brother Jake', 'Wishing Well' and the inevitable 'All Right Now' – *The Free Story* gathers up less celebrated highlights such as 'I'm a Mover', 'I'll Be Creepin'' and 'Get Where I Belong', making it the more attractive investment of the two.

Bad Company

Convened: 1973, London
Boz Burrell (f) – bass; Simon Kirke (f) – drums/vocals; Mick Ralphs (f) – guitar/vocals; Paul Rodgers (f) – vocals/guitar
US No.1 album: 1974: *Bad Company* (unavailable)

Bad Company was effectively a stadium-sized version of Free. Joining Rodgers and Kirke after the demise of Free were ex-Mott The Hoople guitarist Mick Ralphs and ex-King Crimson bassist Boz Burrell. Sharing management and record label with LED ZEPPELIN, they enjoyed instant success and bestrode America like a colossus throughout the Seventies with a mighty succession of albums, of which only *Straight Shooter* (Swan Song SS 8502-2; 1975) and *Run With the Pack* (Swan Song SS 8503-2; 1976) are available on CD.

Despite healthy sales, and one or two UK hits, British fans never took the band to their hearts in the way they had done with Free. Whereas Bad Company had the temperament to chart a steady course at the highest international level, they lacked the fire in the veins that made Free's music such an affecting experience.

Bad Company petered out for a while during the Eighties. Rodgers formed The Firm with ex-LED ZEPPELIN guitarist Jimmy Page, a dream ticket in theory, but in reality a group with so much heavyweight musical muscle it could barely walk. After two moderately successful albums – *The Firm* (Atlantic 781 239-2; 1985) and *Mean Business* (Atlantic 781 628-2; 1986) both deleted – the receivers were quietly called in.

Bad Company was denied a decent burial when Kirke, Burrell and Ralphs reunited with ex-Ted Nugent vocalist Brian Howe replacing Rodgers. Although latterly a pale shadow of its former self, the band continues to do sensible business in America.

● *10 From 6* (Atlantic 781 625-2) [1986]

A sturdy collection, comprising ten of the best tracks from the six best Bad Company albums, this includes 'Can't Get Enough', 'Feel Like Makin' Love', 'Bad Company', 'Run With the Pack' and 'Shooting Star'.

Peter Gabriel

Born: February 13 1950, Woking, Surrey
UK No.1 albums: 1980: *Peter Gabriel* (Charisma PGCD 3)
1986: *So* (Charisma PGCD 5)

1977 was not the best of times for an ageing hippy vocalist with a tendency to look like a sunflower to release his first solo recordings, but the die had been cast for Peter Gabriel two years earlier when he quit his post as singer of GENESIS for 'personal reasons'.

Luckily, he scored an early hit with his début single 'Solsbury Hill', a beguiling song which kept his stock buoyant during the early stages of a career which took several years to get properly established.

But as soon as he was established, Gabriel became involved in a variety of projects which have had a profound effect, not only on him and his work, but on the whole of the contemporary music environment. His contribution to the introducing of World Music as a strand of popular culture in Britain is second to none. He financed the initial World of Music and Dance (WOMAD) festival at Shepton Mallet in 1982, the first time that anyone had flown in artists from Africa, Indonesia, China and elsewhere to share equal billing with acts like SIMPLE MINDS and Echo and The Bunnymen. Gabriel lost a fortune on the promotion, but it was an idea whose time was not long in coming.

His growing political idealism led him to play an integral part in organising Amnesty International's Conspiracy of Hope tour in 1986, along with Bono, STING and Joan Baez, and to follow it up with the more ambitious Amnesty world tour in 1987 which featured Gabriel, Bruce SPRINGSTEEN, Tracy Chapman, Youssou N'Dour and STING.

More recently, in partnership with WOMAD, he has set up his Real World label (through Virgin), and has campaigned on behalf of Greenpeace.

- *Peter Gabriel* (Charisma PGCD 3) [1980]

With its 'melting face' cover, the third of Gabriel's four eponymously titled albums (this one unofficially known as *Melt*) is an educated, assertive work that explores the minds of a succession of psychotic characters with a chilling, mordant intensity. The menacing ambience, particularly gripping on 'Intruder', 'No Self Control' and 'I Don't Remember', is a function both of the mugwumping sound of Tony Levin's stick playing and a ban on all cymbals that was imposed on drummers Phil COLLINS and Jerry Marotta by Gabriel and producer Steve Lillywhite. With all the messy highs eliminated, the mix is thus screwed to a very severe torque.

The album yielded a big international hit in the caustic 'Games Without Frontiers', and at least one classic in the desperately moving 'Biko', a dignified expression of rage and sorrow at the murder of the South African activist Steve Biko, delivered some time before eulogies to the victims of political oppression became fashionable in the rock world.

Gabriel has never muddied his trail with anything but the most painstakingly considered and stringently controlled recording projects, but on this third album he also hits a peak of stark, creative excellence.

● *So* (Charisma PGCD 5) [1986]

Flagged by its video-award-winning, US No.1 single 'Sledgehammer', *So* converted Gabriel into an international superstar. His fascination with African-tinged polyrhythms was by now much in evidence. 'Red Rain' mixes funk with tribal percussive patterns, while brooding thundercloud piano chords underpin the passionate vocal with its familiar yodelling nuances.

In 'Big Time' the swagger of the Hammond and horns perfectly complements the braggadocio of the song's lyric about a rising star whose head is growing to match the size of his fame and bank account. Yet the album balances such brassy bashes with moments of deep reflective insight. The tension of 'Mercy Street', for instance, is sustained by Djalma Korrea's shimmering triangle rhythm, and the music glistens quietly like water tumbling along a brook.

Contrasting with the measured bombast of 'Sledgehammer', there is the austere delicacy of 'Don't Give Up', on which Kate BUSH contributes a vocal counterpoint of outstanding grace and sympathy.

● *Shaking the Tree* (Virgin PGTVD 6) [1990]

Sub-titled *Sixteen Golden Greats*, this is a necessarily lopsided compilation of favourites from Gabriel's back catalogue. With five tracks (including 'Sledgehammer' and 'Big Time') taken from his magnum opus *So* (see above), and four songs (including 'Games Without Frontiers' and 'Biko') lifted from the desolate soundscape of his third *Peter Gabriel* album (see above), the collection accurately reflects the high concentration of excellence on those two releases. The picture is rounded out with a couple of hits from other albums – 'Shock the Monkey' and the perennial 'Solsbury Hill' – and the generous inclusion of a song by his Senegalese protégé Youssou N'Dour as the title track.

Marvin Gaye

Born: April 2 1939, Washington DC. Died: April 1 1984
US No.2 album: 1973: *Let's Get It On* (Motown WD 72085)

It is often said that Marvin Gaye suffered from a split personality.
He was a performer of consummate grace, one of the most
eminent stars in the Motown galaxy and a devoutly religious,
married man capable of immense charm. But spin the coin and
there was an arrogant tyrant, a personality warped by insecurity,
bouts of depression and, as he freely admitted, a debilitating
intake of drugs: 'Grass since I was a kid . . . alcohol, cigarettes,
uppers and downers, heroin, cocaine. . . . I dug all of them.'

Gaye's voice was no less schizoid. Motown biographer Nelson
George identified a three-way split: 'A harsh, impassioned, rough
'rock' sound; a resilient, firm, undeniably masculine falsetto or
high tenor, often used to dramatise key words in a lyric; and a
smooth, cool midrange that was closest in texture to his own
delicate, gentle, speaking voice.'

His versatility as a singer, combined with the sheer breadth of
his talent as a writer, producer and multi-instrumentalist, enabled
Gaye to play a critical role in steering soul music from its rough
and ready R'n'B beginnings through the complex machinations of
the Motown charm school and into the urbane, hi-tech gloss of
the Eighties.

The son of a Pentecostal minister, Gaye learnt his trade singing
and playing organ in the church choir. He joined the US Air Force
at the age of 16, but didn't take well to the discipline. By 1957 he
was back in Washington singing doo-wop in a group called The
Marquees.

He moved to Detroit in 1960 and found work as a session
drummer and backing vocalist before signing as a solo artist to
Berry Gordy's fledgling Motown label in 1961. He further
cemented relations with the label when he married Gordy's sister
Anna the same year.

Gaye enjoyed his first hit with 'Stubborn Kind of Fellow' in
1962. His subsequent rise to the top coincided with (and
contributed towards) the period of explosive growth which
Motown sustained over the next eight years. He was certainly the
label's top male singer of the decade, his most notable success
being the incomparable 'I Heard It Through the Grapevine', a

transatlantic No.1 in 1968. American critic Dave Marsh put 'Grapevine' at the top of his list of 'The 1001 Greatest Singles Ever Made', describing it as an 'essay on salvaging the human spirit', and a song which 'distils four hundred years of paranoia and talking-drum gossip into three minutes and fifteen seconds of anguished soul-searching.'

Gaye held his place at centre stage during the upheavals that beset Motown during the Seventies, and indeed produced the best albums of his career at that time. But his private life was a mess. He was divorced and remarried in 1977, then divorced again in 1978. In 1979, embroiled with hard drugs and pursued by the Internal Revenue for an unpaid tax bill of two million dollars, he fled to Hawaii, where he took up residence in a trailer.

Gaye spent 1981 dividing his time between London and Ostend in Belgium, while he recorded *Midnight Love* (see below). The album was a huge success, but Gaye's problems persisted and in November 1983 he moved into his parents' house in Los Angeles. A few months later, in what was clearly the mother of domestic disputes, his father shot him dead at home.

- *What's Going On* (Motown WD 72611) [1971]

Gaye's masterpiece, this was an album which effectively redefined the parameters of soul. Having bucked the ailing Motown 'production line' system by producing and writing the bulk of the material himself, Gaye created a lavishly orchestrated cycle of songs that captured the spirit of the times and kick-started the development of a social conscience in black music. 'Mercy Mercy Me (The Ecology)' (a UK hit for Robert PALMER in 1991), 'Inner City Blues (Make Me Wanna Holler)' and 'What's Going On' were all US Top 10 hits, and the album had a profound influence on artists from Curtis Mayfield to Stevie WONDER.

- *Let's Get It On* (Motown WD 72085) [1973]

Here Gaye transfers his attention from the affairs of the world to those of the bedroom, instigating one of the most unabashed celebrations of sex in the popular music canon. 'Let's Get It On', 'Keep Gettin' It On' and 'You Sure Love to Ball' may sound like titles from a Lenny Henry interlude, but Gaye consistently balances his libidinal message with acute sensitivity.

Good as the album still is, the total running time of 30 minutes is rather short shrift for a CD these days. It used to be available together with *What's Going On* (35 minutes) on a single 'two for one' disc, but it didn't take Motown's accountants long to figure out the financial ramifications of such an attractive offer, and the configuration was deleted in November 1990.

- *Midnight Love* (Columbia CD 85977) [1982]

After a lean patch culminating in his departure from Motown in 1981, Gaye came back as strong as ever with yet another album on his favourite subject. The flagship single, 'Sexual Healing', was a worldwide platinum success, and *Midnight Love* was an important example of how synthesiser technology and third-world rhythms could be adapted to produce hi-tech urban soul with an irresistible dance-floor groove – the sort of thing later made commonplace by producers like Jimmy Jam and Terry Lewis. Clearly, Gaye still had much to offer; sadly, this was his last chance to do so.

- *Anthology* (Motown WD 72534) [1986]

An almost definitive compilation, the 47 tracks include the immortal 'I Heard It Through the Grapevine', 'Too Busy Thinking 'Bout my Baby', 'How Sweet It Is (To Be Loved by You)', 'Let's Get It On' and 'Ain't No Mountain High Enough', the latter being one of many searing duets with his adored partner Tammi Terrell. An essential item even though there is nothing from the 'Sexual Healing'/*Midnight Love*, post-Motown period.

Genesis

Convened: 1967, Godalming, Surrey
Tony Banks (f) – keyboards; Phil COLLINS – vocals/drums; Mike Rutherford (f) – guitar/bass/vocals
UK No.1 albums: 1980: *Duke* (Charisma CBRCD 101)
    1981: *Abacab* (Charisma 800 044-2)
    1983: *Genesis* (Charisma GENCD 1)

1986: *Invisible Touch* (Charisma GENCD
2)
1991: *We Can't Dance* (Virgin GENCD 3)

From not-so-humble beginnings as a group of Charterhouse
public school boys with Peter GABRIEL as their featured vocalist,
Genesis has weathered upheavals that would have thrown most
bands off the rails completely. Not only that, they have inspired
successive generations of fans with devotional brand loyalty to a
portfolio which, over the years, has run the gamut from complex
pomp-rock to catchy three-minute pop.

The original line-up of Banks, Rutherford, GABRIEL, Anthony
Phillips (guitar/vocals) and Chris Stewart (drums) were signed to
Decca records by another Charterhouse old boy, Jonathan King.

After a change of drummer they produced a derivative,
directionless début, *From Genesis to Revelation* (Razor MACHK 11;
1969), that sold little more than 600 copies when it was first
released. Another change of drummer and they immersed
themselves in the gloom of the English underground, where they
nurtured a communal enthusiasm for intractable, neo-symphonic
compositions, which began to manifest itself on *Trespass* (Charisma CASCD 1020; 1970).

Guitarist Steve Hackett and COLLINS joined in August 1970,
considerably bolstering the group's musical firepower on the third
album *Nursery Cryme* (Charisma CASCD 1052; 1971). GABRIEL
meanwhile lent their live shows an increasingly theatrical flair by
indulging to the hilt his penchant for performing in bizarre
costumes and masks.

Slowly they pushed their way into the public consciousness,
achieving their first chart entry with *Foxtrot* (Charisma CASCD
1058; 1972) and a Top 10 placing with *Genesis Live* (Charisma
CLACD 1; 1973) a concert recording of variable quality, originally
intended for an American radio show broadcast.

● *Selling England by the Pound* (Charisma CASCD 1074) [1973]

As the title suggests, this album celebrates the group's peculiarly
English heritage, both in the quaint lyrics and the occasional
snatches of folk-derived harmonies thrown into 'The Battle of
Epping Forest' and elsewhere. The studied eccentricity of 'I Know

What I Like (In Your Wardrobe)' furnished an unlikely first hit single.

- **The Lamb Lies Down on Broadway** (Charisma CGSCD 1) [1974]

This double-disc 'concept' album about a Puerto Rican street kid called Rael on a transcendental search for his soul is the weightiest monument to the earnest and unnecessarily convoluted formula which defines the early-Seventies vintage Genesis.

A work which eventually inspired a legion of copyists – of which only Eighties' band Marillion lasted any distance – the fans loved it while the critics gave it a panning. Depending on your viewpoint, it stands either as a masterpiece or as one of the most fatuous releases of the decade.

As with all previous albums, the composing and arranging credits were shared throughout by the whole group. Listening to it now, it sounds as if the idea was for each of the contributors to try and cram as much of their own bits as possible into every nook and cranny of every song. In reaching for such unwieldy extremes of inventiveness, they betrayed their immaturity as much as they demonstrated their grasp of advanced musical technique.

- *A Trick of the Tail* (Charisma CDSCD 4001) [1976]
- *Wind and Wuthering* (Charisma CDSCD 4005) [1976]

When GABRIEL left in 1975, Genesis' demise was not so much predicted as assumed. But, after the rest of the group had auditioned many unsuitable candidates, they finally allowed COLLINS to have a go at the lead vocal on 'Squonk'. Apart from sounding uncannily like GABRIEL, it turned out that COLLINS had the drive, personality and ambition to become a frontman who would make Genesis twice as successful as it had been with GABRIEL.

The shake-up seemed to focus the group's mind, and coming after the baroque extremes of *Broadway*, the first album featuring COLLINS on vocals, *A Trick of the Tail*, is a straightforward collection of songs fashioned to an altogether simpler and more direct design.

The writing credits are broken down for the first time, with the main beneficiary being Banks, whose name appears against every title. The arrangements are powerful and uncluttered, the production strong, and the epic finale, 'Los Endos', has remained a stirring part of the live show right up to their last UK performances in 1987.

After this, the pastoral noodling of *Wind and Wuthering*, with its literary and historical references and long drowsy instrumental track 'Unquiet Slumbers for the Sleepers . . . in that Quiet Earth' sounds like a bad case of treading water.

● *Seconds Out* (Charisma GECD 2001) [1977]

An impressive live album which draws a neat line under the band's first, 'progressive' era, this was recorded in Paris at the end of a six-month tour in 1976. It features peak performances of 'Squonk', 'Supper's Ready', 'Cinema Show', 'I Know What I Like' and 'The Lamb Lies Down on Broadway' and was the last time that guitarist Steve Hackett featured in the band.

● *. . . And Then There Were Three . . .* (Charisma CDSCD 4010) [1978]

'Three too many' as one reviewer put it, memorably summing up the continuing critical antipathy towards the band. As when GABRIEL left, so the departure of Hackett prompted a shake-up in working practices, which entailed a further streamlining of the group's writing and performing style. Having reached the furthest limits of cult celebrity, Genesis now took their first tentative steps into the mainstream.

Here the songs are shorter, catchier and in the case of 'Follow You, Follow Me', destined for *Top of the Pops*. Most people (including their fans) were aghast when, the year after punk had supposedly wiped the slate clean, it became the first Genesis single to reach the UK Top 10. But there were plenty more where that came from.

● *Duke* (Charisma CBRCD 101) [1980]
● *Abacab* (Charisma 800 044-2) [1981]
● *Genesis* (Charisma GENCD 1) [1983]

There was no stopping them once the ball had started rolling, and by the turn of the Eighties Genesis had metamorphosised into a radio-friendly, transatlantic, chart-singles band.

There was a succession of spin-off hits from each of these albums: 'Turn it on Again' from *Duke*; the title track from *Abacab*; 'Mama', 'Illegal Alien' and 'That's All' from *Genesis*.

Despite vestiges of the group's progressive roots, notably in Banks' keyboard mini-symphonies such as 'Duke' and 'Duke's End', it was COLLINS' less complicated, populist instincts which gradually came to dominate their output over the course of these three albums.

Apart from his distinctive vocal tone and landslide drum breaks, COLLINS brought his chirpy, down-to-earth approach to bear on the band's music, steering it away from the extremes of romantic whimsy and navel-gazing to which it had typically been prone in the past.

Although Banks had released a solo album in 1979 (*A Curious Feeling* [Charisma CASCD 1148]), with Rutherford following suit in 1980 (*Smallcreep's Day* [Charisma CASCD 1149]), neither of them enjoyed more than fleeting success. It was, of course, a different story when COLLINS, the last member of Genesis to release a solo album, put out his *Face Value* début in 1981.

Rutherford eventually had his moment of glory when, under the alias of Mike and The Mechanics, he enjoyed a significant hit with *The Living Years* (WEA 256 004-2; 1988), a dreary, middle-of-the-road collection, with a sentimental title track which became a US No.1. Poor old Banks was left to fume.

- *Invisible Touch* (Charisma GENCD 2) [1986]

Having finally and wisely consigned the rambling, progressive rock arrangements to the dustbin of history, Genesis now adopted a soul-tinged, pop-rock approach which made them sound more like the Phil COLLINS Band than ever before, especially on numbers like 'Anything She Does' with its swift, crisp beat and synthesiser horn sounds, and 'The Last Domino', which romps along to a Seventies neo-disco beat.

Yet even by this point they had alienated surprisingly few of their original fans and still held considerable clout as a serious live attraction, able to sell four consecutive nights at the 72,000-capacity Wembley Stadium on their 1987 world tour, a record accomplishment at that time.

● *We Can't Dance* (Virgin GEN CD3) [1991]

Overall this is one of the better Genesis albums, boasting among its wittier moments the hit single 'I Can't Dance', a pastiche of all those macho rock'n'roll songs that have been used to sell jeans in TV ads, and 'Living Forever', a timely rebuttal of the health fascists.

'Driving the Last Spike' is a long and heartfelt paean to those staunch working men who built the British railways and 'Dreaming While You Sleep' is a grippingly mordant piece about the psychology of a hit-and-run driver, which recalls some of GABRIEL's early solo work.

The set is marred, however, by several drippy ballads with rhymes like 'time to change/. . . chance to rearrange', and a really soggy piece of coffee-morning philosophy called 'Way of the World'.

Grateful Dead

Convened: 1965, San Francisco, California
Jerry Garcia (f) – vocals/guitar; Mickey Hart – drums; Bill Kreutzmann (f) – drums; Phil Lesh (f) – bass; Bob Weir (f) – vocals/guitar; Vince Welnick – keyboards
US No.6 album: 1987: *In the Dark* (Arista 261145)

Grateful Dead began life in the hippy forcing-house of Haight-Ashbury, at the epicentre of the counter cultural explosion of the Sixties. The original line-up of Garcia, Kreutzmann, Lesh, Weir and Ron 'Pigpen' McKernan (vocals/keyboards/harmonica; died 8.3.73) became the house band for Ken Kesey's notorious 'Acid Test' happenings in 1965–6, at which copious quantities of the then-legal drug LSD were distributed freely to band and audience alike.

By all reasonable expectations they should have gone the way of their more fragile contemporaries – bands like Quicksilver Messenger Service and Moby Grape – but Grateful Dead first endured and then flourished by turning the norms of rock working practices on their head.

A group with a vast repertoire and an unrivalled appetite for extended onstage improvisation, no two of their shows are ever alike, which is one reason they have attracted a uniquely dedicated base of hard-core fans – the so-called Deadheads – who seem to be prepared to follow the band anywhere on earth.

By the same token the group has never been entirely at ease in the recording studio, where they are unable to recreate the spontaneous magic of their concert performances. Thus in the course of their lengthy career they have released no less than seven live albums of variable quality (six double and one triple, most of them unavailable) without ever having minted an entirely satisfactory studio album.

Indeed, it was estimated that, until their first big hit with *In the Dark* in 1987, 98% of the Dead's income came from the profits generated by their live performances.

* **Workingman's Dead** (WEA K2 46049) [1970]
* **American Beauty** (WEA K2 46074) [1970]

In 1970 the band reached a productive apogee, releasing their first live album, the oxymoronic *Live Dead* (unavailable) in February, then two of their best-loved studio collections in August and December.

Drawing on a wide-ranging mixture of country, R'n'B, folk, rock and jazz, the Dead's music has always had a light, trippy quality that is somewhat at odds with their forbidding name and corporate artwork, but *Workingman's Dead* was the first album to present it in a readily digestible form and to gain general recognition beyond the inbred community of 'Heads'.

In its own ragged way, 'Uncle John's Band' recalls the free-spirited harmony folk-rock which Crosby, Stills and Nash championed at their peak, while the good-natured country-rock of 'Casey Jones' manages to warn against the perils of the high life while still sounding as if it hasn't got a care in the world: 'Drivin' that train/High on cocaine/Casey Jones you better watch your speed'. Yes, indeed!

American Beauty is in much the same mildly psychedelic country-rock vein. 'Truckin'', a loose-rolling boogie, is a classic road song, cramming in more American town name-checks per verse than anything since 'Route 66', while a rich seam of spirituality (alternative style) is mined on numbers like 'Friend of the Devil' and 'Ripple'.

- *Skeletons from the Closet* (Thunderbolt CDTB 018) [1987]

Since the Dead have hardly had any hits to speak of, no two people ever agree on precisely which songs constitute the 'best' of their vast legacy. However, certain titles keep on cropping up, among them 'Sugar Magnolia', 'Uncle John's Band', 'One More Saturday Night' and 'The Golden Road', all included here.

This compilation is a repackaged version of the original WEA album *The Best of Grateful Dead* (released in 1974), with newly added sleeve notes.

- *In the Dark* (Arista 261145) [1987]

This was the Dead's first new studio album for seven years, and it broke on an unsuspecting American market with the quiet yet irresistible momentum of a seventh wave. No one expected it to do much better (or worse) than any of their previous releases, but something about it touched a chord with a post-Live Aid generation of ageing baby-boomers *and* their teenage offspring, all of whom had suddenly become respectful of and receptive to acts with a long history of service.

Thanks in part to the wonderfully jokey video which promoted the single 'Touch of Grey' (a group of funky skeletons playing their instruments on stage at a gig), that song became the Dead's first (and only) US hit, helping to make *In the Dark* their most successful album ever.

'While the public's tastes go up and down in cycles, we're just like the median line that's running right through that,' Lesh said, tacitly acknowledging that such sudden mass acceptance was nothing to do with any change of formula or revolution in the group's music.

Indeed *In the Dark* is as dyed-in-the-wool as any of their work, a collection of gentle country-boogie-rock songs like 'Hell in a Bucket' and 'When Push Comes to Shove', informed by good-natured sentiments about surviving to enjoy the ride.

Even when they get their teeth into something a bit more hip, such as the folky 'Throwing Stones' with its African-sounding chants towards the end, they manage to preserve a cosy and unthreatening air of familiarity; easy listening for dopeheads, current and retired alike.

• **Built to Last** (Arista 260326) [1989]

Despite the revisionist overtones of the title (it would be hard to think of a band that was *less* built to last) the Dead roam their traditional territory, tackling cheerful, inconsequential country-rock tunes like 'Foolish Heart' and 'Just a Little Light' with exactly the right degree of airy sangfroid. However, Weir's song 'Victim or the Crime', which poses some hard, overdue questions concerning the junkie's precise relationship with society and his drug, finds the band in a more adventurous mood, rocking out with a spacy extended coda, pregnant with eerie atmospherics.

That particular song took on an especially poignant air when keyboard player/vocalist Brent Mydland died of a presumed overdose on July 26 1990. Mydland, who joined the band in 1979 as replacement for Keith Godchaux (keyboards; died 23.7.80), had become integral to the group, to the point where four of the nine titles on this album are (principally) his compositions.

Even so, his death did not cause so much as a hiccup in the group's touring schedule (Bruce Hornsby filled in until a full-time replacement could be found) and like so many establishment rock acts – one thinks of PINK FLOYD, AC/DC, FLEETWOOD MAC, The ROLLING STONES, GENESIS – Grateful Dead has built up a collective momentum that is strangely impervious to even the most shattering of events for the individuals involved. It's not so much that any of these groups were intentionally 'built to last'; just that having reached a certain point, like rock itself, it now seems that they can carry on for ever.

• **Without a Net** (Arista 353935) [1990]

Their most recent live album suggests that far from tailing off, the Dead have never been stronger. The musicians read each other like an orchestra reads the dots, and they improvise at times like the instruments in a Dixieland band, all blowing away at full tilt, yet meshing together to create a glorious mélange of counterpointed parts.

On the country funk of 'Althea' or the relaxed honky-tonk of 'Mississippi Half-Step Uptown Toodeloo' and 'Walkin' Blues', they play with no overbearing heroics, just a gorgeously flowing groove. On the longer work-outs, 'Bird Song' or 'Let it Grow' for instance, they improvise in a way that carries the music through a variety of moods and changes while avoiding the aimless vamping and repetition that is the bane of so much of what passes for extemporisation in rock.

It is music from a different zone of time and space, and the Dead remain one of the furthest out wonders of the rock cosmos.

Guns N' Roses

Convened: 1985, Los Angeles, California
Gilby Clarke – guitar; Duff McKagan (f) – bass; Dizzy Reed – piano; W. Axl Rose (f) – vocals/keyboards; Slash (f) – guitar/vocals; Matt Sorum – drums
UK/US No.1 album: 1991: *Use Your Illusion II* (Geffen GEFD 24420)
US No.1 album: 1987: *Appetite for Destruction* (Geffen GEFD 24148)

Even by the inflated standards of the rock world, the hype surrounding Guns N' Roses has been extreme. They have sold a vast quantity of albums – 16 million copies of their début, *Appetite for Destruction* (see below), alone – but their true mission has been to revive the delinquent tendency in rock.

From the start of their world tour in May 1991, there was a relentless stream of reports of debauchery and violent incident, most of them centred on the antics of vocalist Axl Rose. A rock'n'roll version of Caligula, Rose rules the G N' R roost by means of whimsical dictat, refusing even to rehearse with the rest of the band, according to one popular myth.

At a concert at the 19,000-capacity Riverport Performing Arts Centre in St Louis, Missouri, on July 2 1991, Rose leapt from the stage to remonstrate with a member of the audience who was taking photographs of the band. A riot ensued during which an estimated $200,000 worth of damage was caused and more than 60 people were injured. Rose was duly arrested on four counts of assault and one of property damage and may yet face a prison sentence if he is eventually found guilty as charged.

It is such unruly behaviour rather than their music which has earned Guns N' Roses a reputation as 'the most dangerous band in the world', a title coined by *Kerrang!* writer Mick Wall (the group returned the compliment by vilifying Wall and other named journalists in their song 'Get in the Ring'). From living a life of unbelievably wasted squalor in a blitzed suburban bungalow known as the Hellhouse in West Hollywood, they have swiftly graduated to a world of cocooned unreality, attended by a ménage of bodyguards, personal masseuses, acquiescent groupies and fawning management personnel. Yet strangely, Slash still can't seem to keep himself in shirts.

So far the casualties have been relatively light. Founding member Izzy Stradlin (guitar, vocals and light songwriting duties) threw in the towel at the end of their European tour in 1991. The group's original drummer, Stephen Adler, was dismissed after *Appetite for Destruction*, allegedly because he could no longer keep in time. And lesser mortals, such as those in the road crew, have been sacked on the spot for minor indiscretions.

On a more serious note there was the tragedy of the two fans who were crushed to death in front of the stage during Guns N' Roses' set at Castle Donington in 1988, hardly the group's fault but typical of the karma that has won them such colossal notoriety.

- *Appetite for Destruction* (Geffen GEFD 24148) [1987]

As Slash pointed out to Simon Garfield of *The Independent on Sunday*, 'Music journalists . . . don't write much about our music.' So what, after wading through the hype, is there to write about? At the end of the day the Guns N' Roses début is a hotch-potch of Seventies-derived bad-boy rock'n'roll. 'Welcome to the Jungle' and 'Nightrain' combine the boozy, cowbell-driven chug of The ROLLING STONES with the high-voltage vocal shriek of AC/DC's Brian Johnson. 'Paradise City' and 'Sweet Child O' Mine' are straightforward pop-rock songs that anyone from QUEEN to Joan Jett might have turned out. The 12 songs on this album are tackled with a fair degree of bravado, but 16 million copies sold or not, it all sounds rather second-hand. Vanilla Ice has sold a lot of records too.

- *Use Your Illusion I* (Geffen GEFD 24415) [1991]
- *Use Your Illusion II* (Geffen GEFD 24420) [1991]

Having spent a leisurely four years assembling and recording material for *Use Your Illusion*, the boys unsurprisingly found themselves with a surplus of songs. Instead of weeding out the weaker numbers they opted to release the lot – 30 songs in all. In CD terms the running time could be accommodated on two discs, but the vinyl equivalent was a quadruple album. This was deemed too unwieldy and too expensive to market as a single item and so they released it as two separate volumes on the same day: September 16.

They claimed such an exercise was without precedent, although in fact John Mayall had pulled exactly the same trick in 1968 with his *Diary of a Band Vol.1* and *Vol.2* (both unavailable).

While both the *Illusions* are peppered with flashes of brilliance at the extremes, they get bogged down with a lot of sludge in the middle ground. Full-tilt rockers like 'Coma', 'Garden of Eden' and 'Double Talkin' Jive' resound with a driven, manic energy, while the best moments are provided by several reflective ballads, in particular the hit single 'Don't Cry', and the acoustic, blues-tinted 'You Ain't the First'.

Less inspired are the pseudo-metal versions of Paul McCARTNEY's 'Live and Let Die' and Bob DYLAN's 'Knocking on Heaven's Door'. Then there are the routinely offensive put-downs – 'Back Off Bitch', 'Pretty Tied Up' – and bringing up the rear a whole slew of in-between stuff, like the lazy 'Dust and Bones' and the unimaginative 'Shotgun Blues', that should either have been tightened up or discarded.

Hammer

Born: Stanley Kirk Burrel, March 30 1962, Oakland, California
US No.1 album: 1990: *Please Hammer Don't Hurt 'Em* (Capitol CDP 792 857-2)

With or without his disappearing M.C. prefix, Hammer is the most successful rapper in the brief history of the genre. Having exorcised the militant fury and pervasive bad language that is one of the commercially limiting hallmarks of hard-core acts like

PUBLIC ENEMY and NWA, he was the first to convert the traditionally minimalist presentation of rap into a properly choreographed, high-energy revue. In so doing Hammer has harnessed modern rap music to a tradition of entertainment that extends all the way back to the celebrated song-and-dance routines of his hero James BROWN and up to the stadium pop of Michael JACKSON.

In his rise to global superstardom, Hammer has thus elevated rap to a new level, enabling it to transcend for the first time boundaries of race, class and nationality. There are those who wish he hadn't bothered.

The radical critique, often voiced by less emollient rappers such as 3rd Bass (whose 'Gas Face' was a not exactly fulsome commentary on the Hammer phenomenon), is that Hammer has de-fanged rap, softening up the language of urban deprivation in order to play to the white gallery. At the opposite end of the spectrum, the more staid sort of mainstream rock fans complain about the amount of material Hammer has lifted from old records and point out that while the man is undoubtedly an impressive dance machine, he can't sing a note.

One of six children, brought up in trying conditions, Hammer almost took up a career as a baseball player before undertaking a stint in the Marines. It is a background which has imbued him with a sense of competitiveness and discipline bordering on the fanatical. Members of his 30-strong troupe (singers, dancers, musicians, DJs) were fined for any instances of bad behaviour or poor workmanship, while clocking up a gruelling 200-plus shows in 1990.

The hardest working man in showbusiness? His show is certainly one of the busiest, and his career is built on the twin pillars of phenomenal energy and a confident feel for the mainstream pulse. A respectful Christian and anti-drug campaigner who has built up his career on sound show-business principles, Hammer looks like staying the course where others have quickly slipped from grace. It's a worrying thought, but could he be the Cliff RICHARD of rap?

- *Please Hammer Don't Hurt 'Em* (Capitol CDP 792 857-2) [1990]

At the time of writing, sales of this historic album have passed the 13 million mark, making it far and away the most widely disseminated rap recording ever. The best bits of it are other people's: the razor-sharp funk riff of 'U Can't Touch This' comes from Rick James' 1981 hit 'Superfreak' (James was furious); 'Have You Seen Her?' is The Chi-Lites' old hit lifted whole (the group was delighted); the essence of 'Pray' was supplied by PRINCE (no comment); and 'Help the Children' is bolstered by a segment of Marvin GAYE's 'Mercy Mercy Me'.

Does it matter? The plagiarism issue in rap has become ridiculously overworked. Hammer gives proper credits on the disc and pays songwriting royalties to these people just as he would if he had sung their songs. How many times have rock groups used Chuck BERRY's songs and riffs with or (more often) without crediting him? Elvis PRESLEY never wrote a significant song in his life, yet Hammer has composed roughly half the tracks on this album (the duff half admittedly). Does that make Hammer better than Elvis?

The question is whether or not Hammer has made a good job of it artistically, and the verdict is – a patchy success at best. Hammer's voice has no immediately distinguishing features and his style of rhyming possesses no distinctive or unusual reson-ance. The slower stuff, like 'Have You Seen Her?' is dull, but when his dancer's instincts take over he consistently selects the sort of infectious, fleet-footed grooves that render most forms of resistance useless. And wasn't the video of 'U Can't Touch This' absolutely ace?

- *Too Legit to Quit* (Capitol CDP 798151 2) [1991]

While boasting more variety than *Please Hammer Don't Hurt 'Em*, the follow-up is a long-winded and verbose affair that finds Hammer expounding his relentlessly earnest humanitarian philosophy, often at considerable expense to the cut and thrust of the beats.

Happy Mondays

Convened: 1984, Manchester
Mark 'Bez' Berry (f) – dance/percussion; Paul Davis (f) – keyboards; Mark Day (f) – guitar; Paul Ryder (f) – bass;

Shaun Ryder (f) – vocals; Gary Whelan (f) – drums
UK No.4 album: 1990: ***Thrills 'n' Pills and Bellyaches*** (Factory
FACD 320)

Of the slew of bands to emerge from the 'Madchester' dance-rock
explosion of the late Eighties, only The Stone Roses could boast a
more powerful cachet of fashionable notoriety than that of yobbo
hipsters Happy Mondays. With shambling vocalist Shaun Ryder –
a man with the fashion sense of a roadie – at the helm, and the
ludicrous but persistent presence of 'dancer' (i.e. mascot) Bez, the
band traded on an image of slobbish indifference tinged with
outlaw daring.

Shaun Ryder likes to boast that he originally financed the band
with the proceeds of drug-pushing and tends to write lyrics that
are preoccupied with 'drinkin' and sleepin' and smokin' and
whorin'' as he put it on 'Little Matchstick Owen' from the group's
eccentrically titled first album, *Squirrel and G-Man Twenty-Four Hour
Party People Plastic Face Carnt Smile (White Out)* (Factory FACD 170;
1987).

All in all it was not an especially edifying spectacle, although
being in the right place, at the right time, with the right attitude,
they duly reaped their not inconsiderable rewards.

- ***Thrills 'n' Pills and Bellyaches*** (Factory FACD 320) [1990]

Far and away their most celebrated effort, this is an album which
comes good in spite, rather than because, of Shaun Ryder's rather
pointless warbling.

The songs are rocky dance-floor constructions, built out of odd
shreds of riffs, stolen titbits (like the 'quotes' from 'Lady
Marmalade' that liven up 'Kinky Afro') and inconsistent, half-
formed ideas, all bolted together by the unflappable rhythm
section of Gary Whelan and Paul Ryder.

Numbers like 'God's Cop' (about Chief Constable James
Anderton) and 'Donovan' (about Donovan) betray plenty of
attitude but only limited imagination. With his incisive style and
bright tone it is usually guitarist Mark Day who prods the songs
into life, and his sprightly, jagged contributions to 'Grandbag's
Funeral' and 'Holiday' are foremost among the patchy highlights.

The album also hosts the group's blissed out version of John

Kongos' 'Step On', which earlier in 1990 had become their first Top 10 single.

George Harrison

Born: February 25 1943, Liverpool
UK No.1 album: 1972: *The Concert for Bangla Desh* (Epic 468835-2)
US No.1 albums: 1970: *All Things Must Pass* (EMI CDS 746 688-8)
1973: *Living in the Material World* (Parlophone/Apple CDP 794 110-2)

With his predeliction for Eastern music and bizarre religious cults, George Harrison emerged as superficially the oddest of the ex-BEATLES, with a talent which he felt had long been stifled in the presence of LENNON and McCARTNEY. 'The usual thing was that we'd do 14 of their tunes and then they'd condescend to listen to one of mine,' he once recalled with some venom.

But for a while, after the split in 1970, it was Harrison who substantially eclipsed the tentative first efforts of the other three with his transatlantic No.1, 'My Sweet Lord' and the three-million-selling, triple-vinyl-album *All Things Must Pass* (see below). The mysteriously unavailable follow-up *Living in the Material World* (see above) was another elongated smash (triple-vinyl, triple-million). In America it was No.1 for five weeks, during which time 'Give Me Love' also topped the singles chart.

But after this early unleashing of long pent-up creativity, Harrison's solo career proceeded rather fitfully through the latter part of the Seventies, and virtually ground to a halt after his 1982 album *Gone Troppo* (unavailable) failed even to register in the UK chart.

He developed a sideline as a film producer, founding with his partner Denis O'Brien the production company HandMade Films, which backed many successful left-field projects – notably Monty Python's *Life of Brian*, *Time Bandits*, *Mona Lisa*, *Withnail and I* – and, with less success, *Shanghai Surprise* starring Sean Penn and MADONNA.

In more recent years he has thrown his weight behind the

charitable work of his wife Olivia in helping to relieve the plight of Romanian orphans, and in 1991 he announced his intention to begin touring again. Dates were scheduled to take place in Japan with his old mucker Eric CLAPTON providing the backing band.

● *All Things Must Pass* (EMI CDS 746 688-8) [1970]

A sprawling, miasmic collection, reduced from three vinyl records to two CDs, Harrison's post-Beatles début remains a deeply flawed masterwork that could have benefited immeasurably from some rigorous pruning. The hit single 'My Sweet Lord' gives fair warning of the album's intensely spiritual tone, although it later became a rather tarnished article of faith when, in 1976, an American court ruled that its melody plagiarised an old song by The Chiffons called 'He's So Fine'.

Co-produced by Harrison and Phil Spector (who Harrison later declared had been more of a liability than an asset), the album has a big, ambient sound quality that shores up any weaknesses in the vocal department and perfectly enhances the up-tempo swing of numbers like 'Wah-Wah' – a dig at Paul McCARTNEY – and 'Awaiting On You All'. Thankfully, the sitars and Eastern drones were left for later albums.

● *The Concert for Bangla Desh* (Epic 468835-2) [1972]

What with the leisurely introductions of songs and personnel, various pauses to tune up and other delays, this triple album, now a double CD, unfolds at a pace which ears attuned to today's quick-edit culture may find unacceptably slow. But what an extrordinarily influential and prescient affair it has turned out to be.

Organised by Harrison and Ravi Shankar, here was the superstar fraternity – well, DYLAN, CLAPTON, Ringo Starr, Billy Preston and, er, Leon Russell among others – going in to bat for a worthy cause 14 years before Live Aid and the ensuing frenzy of charitable rocking in the Eighties.

Then there is the incalculable influence on popular tastes of an album which begins with 17 minutes of traditional sitar music, topping the UK chart (No.2 in America) in 1972. How many

143

latter-day world music fans first had their appetites whetted by this recording?

Sadly, too, the cause remains no less relevant than it was when the original gesture was made. Certified accounts in 1990 showed a total of $14 million donated from the project so far, and proceeds from sales of the CD continue to be channelled (via Unicef) to the blighted people of Bangla Desh. The world has moved on in 20 years, but not as much as we sometimes like to think.

● *The Best of George Harrison* (Parlophone CDP 746 682-2) [1976]

A succinct summary of Harrison's best songs with The BEATLES – 'Something', 'If I Needed Someone', 'Here Comes the Sun', 'Taxman', 'While My Guitar Gently Weeps' and one or two others – together with a noticeably weaker bunch of solo tracks: 'Give Me Love (Give Me Peace on Earth)', 'Bangla Desh' and the inevitable 'My Sweet Lord'. Though it wasn't intended at the time, this compilation was to draw a neat line under Harrison's 'essential' work for at least another decade.

● *Cloud Nine* (Dark Horse 925 643-2) [1987]

Harrison effected an astonishing comeback with this album by re-focusing his sights on certain limited but secure goals. Co-produced by his future Traveling Wilbury partner Jeff Lynne, *Cloud Nine* abounds with cheerful, up-beat songs that restate the fundamentals of intelligent pop performance, notably 'Devil's Radio' and the smash hit single 'Got My Mind Set on You', an old, obscure Rudy Clark song which Harrison converted into a US No.1.

The album also neatly plugs into the lingering spirit of the BEATLES with songs like 'Fish on the Sand' (which crosses the riffs of 'No Reply' and 'I Should Have Known Better') and 'Wreck of the Hesperus', a joky tale, where he sounds like LENNON singing a McCARTNEY composition. 'When We Was Fab' is an attempt to put the BEATLES saga into perspective ('We did it all, a long time ago') with an arrangement which prompts a vague *Magical Mystery Tour déjà-vu* and even incorporates a wry, self-deprecating coda of droning sitars.

The Traveling Wilburys

Convened: 1988, Los Angeles, California
Bob DYLAN (f) (Lucky Wilbury) – vocals/guitar; George Harrison (f) (Nelson Wilbury) – vocals/guitar; Jeff Lynne (f) (Otis Wilbury) – vocals/guitar; Tom PETTY (f) (Charlie T. Wilbury Jr) – vocals/guitar; Roy Orbison (f) (Lefty Wilbury) (died 6.12.88) – vocals/guitar
US No.3 album: 1988: *The Traveling Wilburys Volume 1* (Wilbury 925 796-2)

The happy story of how DYLAN, Orbison, PETTY, Lynne (ex-Electric Light Orchestra) and Harrison convened in DYLAN's garage in 1988 to knock out a B-side for Harrison's forthcoming single 'When We Was Fab', has passed into rock folklore. The album which the five ended up recording was released under its twee collective pseudonym as a way of circumventing any contractual complications and of dampening any possibility of a 'supergroup' hype. Ironically, it was a huge success, especially in America.

Orbison died not long after its release, and by the time the other four got round to putting out a perversely titled follow-up *The Traveling Wilburys Volume 3* (Wilbury 926 324-2; 1990), the magic had begun to fade.

- *The Traveling Wilburys Volume 1* (Wilbury 925 796-2) [1988]

Although a light-hearted, essentially throwaway effort, a number of commentators felt that *Volume 1* showcased some of the participants' best work (DYLAN's in particular) for many a long year.

The ten songs, mostly of a light, pop-R'n'B hue, are all credited to The Wilburys. 'Handle With Care' was a modest hit single, while 'Lonely No More' remains an intriguing sequel to Orbison's big 1960 hit 'Only the Lonely'.

The best song on the album is DYLAN's 'Tweeter and the Monkey Man', a long, low-life narrative about a drug dealer and an undercover police agent. But it is also DYLAN whose awful ensemble singing makes 'Congratulations' and other chorus sequences sound like performances by Spitting Image.

The Heartbreakers See TOM PETTY AND THE HEARTBREAKERS

Jimi Hendrix

Born: John Allen Hendrix, November 27 1942, Seattle, Washington. Renamed (age 4): James Marshall Hendrix. Died: September 18, 1970

Experience

Convened: 1966, London. Split up: 1969
Mitch Mitchell (f) – drums; Noel Redding (f) – bass/vocals
US No.1 album: 1968: *Electric Ladyland* (Polydor 823 359-2)

It is difficult in retrospect to convey the impact of Jimi Hendrix's appearance in Britain in 1966. Like Elvis PRESLEY, he was a performer without precedent.

On an immediate level there was his wild, illicit, vaguely stoned look, which acted like a magnet on anyone in tune with Sixties youth, while simultaneously provoking incredulous revulsion in the adult world at large. Then, from an upside-down Stratocaster, slung with deceptive nonchalance around his skinny shoulders, the ex-US Airborne paratrooper summoned an awesomely powerful and original range of sounds. He fused elements of blues, soul, R'n'B, psychedelia and jazz with a shot of some unearthly voodoo well beyond the grasp of mere mortals.

When he first arrived in London the local guitar mafia – Eric CLAPTON, Jeff BECK, Pete Townshend and the rest – were sent reeling. For it was as if Hendrix had stepped straight in from another dimension, bringing with him a pair of jump-leads clipped to some supernatural supply of juice. While everyone else was still fumbling for the ignition keys, Hendrix simply kick-started the motor and took off on one of the most souped-up rides in the history of rock.

In a recording career that lasted only four years he introduced a system of ideas and technical innovations that revolutionised the playing of the primary instrument of rock'n'roll, and contributed a body of work that profoundly influenced the subsequent course of popular music.

He learned to play guitar at the age of 11. Inspired by the sounds of Howlin' Wolf, Muddy WATERS and B.B. KING on the radio, he began playing in R'n'B groups while still at school, then served an exacting apprenticeship as a backing musician on the so-called 'chitlin' circuit of black clubs, bars and theatres which sustained acts like Sam Cooke, Jackie Wilson, B.B. KING and Ike and Tina TURNER. His most prestigious job during this period was as a member of Little Richard's band, but as had happened on a number of occasions, Hendrix began to upstage the star of the show and was eventually sacked for his pains.

He was playing in his own group, called Jimmy James and The Blue Flames, in the Cafe Wha, Greenwich Village, in 1966 when Chas Chandler, former bassist of The Animals, spotted him. Taking over as his manager, Chandler took Hendrix to London, where he swiftly recruited two English musicians to form a group. Bassist Noel Redding was a novice, but drummer Mitch Mitchell proved to be a major, if unsung, talent in his own right. A devotee of jazz virtuoso Elvin Jones, Mitchell adhered to a clattering, lunatic, free-form style of drumming that made him the perfect sparring partner for Hendrix. After three days of rehearsal The Jimi Hendrix Experience débuted at Evreux, France, on October 13 1966.

Acclaim was swift and monumental, and for two years Hendrix rode a rollercoaster of success and excess. Problems began when, after a gruelling American tour in 1968, he decamped to New York. There he drifted into a twilight world of non-stop partying intertwined with long, frequently unproductive bouts of recording at the Record Plant studio. Chandler dropped out of the picture. There were arguments between Hendrix and Redding. The Experience began to lose its shine.

1969 was a year of frustration and inaction. Hendrix was busted for possession of heroin in Canada, but got off at the trial. After sporadic gigging in America, The Experience split up in June. In August Hendrix appeared at the Woodstock festival with Mitchell, bassist Billy Cox and some other odd dudes, calling themselves The Electric Sky Church. It was a noble, if chaotic, performance, some of it filmed for posterity. Hendrix's erratic new manager, Mike Jeffery, issued a raft of contradictory statements to the press and in return irked journalists at *Rolling Stone* awarded Hendrix the No News Is Big News Award in its review of the year.

In December 1969 Hendrix got together with Cox and drummer Buddy Miles to form Band Of Gypsys, and on New

Year's Eve recorded a performance at the Fillmore East, later released as a lack-lustre album in order to fulfil an old contractual obligation. The band lasted no more than a couple of further dates, after which Hendrix retained the services of Cox, but recalled Mitchell on drums.

The joyride was rapidly turning into a nightmare as Hendrix's life gradually slipped out of his control and he found himself in the classic star trap of being simultaneously surrounded by people he couldn't trust and beyond the reach of those, such as Chandler, who might have been able to help him.

He was hemmed in, too, by his audience's expectations. The recording of his last British concert at the Isle of Wight in August 1970 is a strange, sad affair. 'You all want to hear those old songs, man? Damn, we were trying to get some other things together,' he says in a break between numbers. Battling against weariness and rebellious equipment he played like a titan beset by a host of demons.

He died the following month in an ambulance racing him to hospital from the Notting Hill flat of a girlfriend, Monika Danneman. The coroner's verdict was death due to inhalation of vomit following barbiturate intoxication.

As Charles Shaar Murray argues with eloquent and informed conviction in his book *Crosstown Traffic: Jimi Hendrix and Post-War Pop*, the influence of Hendrix's work reaches to the very heart of subsequent developments not only in rock, but also in jazz, blues and soul. Certainly Hendrix was a genius, if not *the* genius of rock. But he had no idea of the power that he wielded. Not a fusser or a brooder by nature, he whacked into life with energetic glee, chopping down mountains with the edge of his hand and shifting the rock world on its axis sometime between getting up and breakfast. Sadly, for all his immense talent, the forces he unleashed were ultimately beyond his ability to control.

● *Are You Experienced* (Polydor 825 416-2) [1967]

Released on May 20 1967, a week before *Sergeant Pepper's Lonely Hearts Club Band*, Hendrix's début is an embarrassment of riches which redefined the parameters of what was possible in rock, far more so than The BEATLES' magnum opus.

From the first trilling, hammered-on sequence of notes gradually subsumed by a rising wash of feedback that introduces 'Foxy Lady', to the last clanging coda of 'Are You Experienced' with its swarm of fading, backwards-taped effects, the album is an exploding kaleidoscope of technical innovation and savage, unbridled splendour. There are great songs, among them the left-field lullaby 'May This Be Love', the frenetic rocker 'Fire' and the pseudo-soul missive 'Remember', but in retrospect it is Hendrix's extraordinary use of atonal sonic textures and howling electronic noise that is the album's most astounding feature.

The jazzy instrumental '3rd Stone From the Sun' conjures all the majesty and menace of a Jules Verne-style alien visitation; 'Love or Confusion' bowls along in a kind of spacy limbo before breaking out into a section of wailing, gnashing guitar sounds guided by what can only be described as a mutant rumba rhythm from Mitchell; and during 'I Don't Live Today' the structure of the song is eventually razed to the ground in an apocalyptic aural blitz of hurtling dive-bomb effects and disembodied off-mike comments. Even today, this kind of onslaught makes the supposedly radical dissonance of pretenders like Sonic Youth and The Jesus and Mary Chain sound very limp indeed.

Are You Experienced was to electric guitar technique what the splitting of the atom was to nuclear physics. Nothing was ever the same again.

- **Axis: Bold as Love** (Polydor 813 572-2) [1967]

There was a change of emphasis on Hendrix's second album, which showcases his gentler side with a profusion of dreamy love songs – 'Little Wing', 'Castles Made of Sand', 'Bold as Love' – that seemed to tumble from his imagination with effortless fluency. Here the roguish, 'wild man' image which so caught the popular imagination is belied by Hendrix's intuitive command of harmony and his child-like sensitivity as a songwriter, once all the superstud blarney is stripped away.

Because at that time it still wasn't the done thing to include singles on albums, and Hendrix only rarely featured a few of these songs in his live shows, there is a cache of material on *Axis* that has not become over-exposed by the posthumous repackaging and relentless recycling of the Hendrix canon. An often overlooked album, but a real gem.

- **Electric Ladyland** (Polydor 823 359-2) [1968]

A sprawling double-disc set of intermittent genius, this includes his immortal reading of DYLAN's 'All Along the Watchtower', which was a major international hit in 1968, 'Voodoo Chile (Slight Return)', which became a posthumous UK No.1 single in 1970, and a slowed down, remixed version of 'Burning of the Midnight Lamp', a UK hit single in 1967. For the first time Hendrix drafted in outside musicians, including Steve WINWOOD, who contributed organ to 'Voodoo Chile', a rambling, but in parts superlative, studio jam. Here, also, is the original home of 'Crosstown Traffic', possibly better known to a younger generation as the soundtrack of a self-consciously street-cred TV ad for Wranglers jeans.

- **Smash Hits** (Polydor 825 255-2) [1968]
- **The Singles Album** (Polydor 827 369-2) [1983]

Although the title is something of a misnomer, Smash Hits is a handy collection which incorporates the first four Hendrix singles ('Hey Joe', 'Purple Haze', 'The Wind Cries Mary' and 'The Burning of the Midnight Lamp') together with their B-sides (the magnificent 'Stone Free', '51st Anniversary', 'Highway Chile' and 'The Stars That Play with Laughing Sam's Dice'), with ballast supplied by four numbers from Are You Experienced.

A far more comprehensive compilation is The Singles Album, which collects together all the tracks ever issued as Hendrix singles and B-sides in an assiduously researched and documented package. The roll call runs from 'Hey Joe' right the way through to a rare live version of 'Gloria', which appeared as a one-sided 33-and-a-third RPM single, originally available only in the long-deleted Hendrix Box Set.

- **Jimi Plays Monterey** (Polydor 827 990-2) [1986]

Arguably the best of the many live albums that have surfaced since Hendrix's death, this is a recording of The Experience's historic performance at the Monterey Festival on June 16 1967. It was Hendrix's first gig in America since going off and becoming a star in Britain, and he rose to the occasion with a vengeance. Much to the horror of the boss of his American record company, and to the delight of 50,000 curious onlookers, he concluded his set by torching and demolishing his guitar during an anarchic finale of 'Wild Thing'. By the time he walked off the stage he was a star in America too.

The album presents this epic performance in full and in sequence, and includes 'Killing Floor', 'The Wind Cries Mary' (very rarely heard live), 'Can You See Me' (ditto) and 'Rock Me Baby', along with the more familiar 'Hey Joe', 'Purple Haze' and 'Foxy Lady'. But the track which makes the collection a must is the unique interpretation of DYLAN's 'Like a Rolling Stone', which Hendrix handles with supreme panache, interspersing the tumbling poetry of the lyric with little guitar flourishes of unearthly grace.

John Lee Hooker

Born: August 22 1920, Clarksdale, Mississippi
UK No.3 album: 1991: *Mr Lucky* (Silvertone ORECD 519)

John Lee Hooker is the last of the original blues masters who migrated from the rural American South to the urban North in the Forties, a man who, as Van MORRISON put it, is 'a window into another age'.

Although all the reference books and even his passport put his age at 75, Hooker has lately taken to disputing this, claiming that when still a teenager, he lied about his birth date in order to get round the lower age limit of 21 for joining the army. 'I was born on 22 August 1920,' he now says unequivocally. 'A lot of things you read tell a different story to the truth.'

Caveat emptor, we know that he was taught to play acoustic guitar by his stepfather, a popular Delta blues guitarist called Will Moore, who imparted a harsh, idiosyncratic boogie style to his protégés playing. During his teens Hooker drifted north to Memphis, Cincinnati and finally Detroit, where he settled in 1943. He was given his first electric guitar by the revered Texan bluesman T-Bone Walker in 1947.

Working as a janitor or in the car factory by day, he performed by night in the clubs around Hastings Street, the notorious area known as the Black Bottom (after which the dance was named).

Gradually he carved a reputation for himself which paralleled those of the legendary Chicago players, Muddy WATERS, Sonny Boy Williamson, Howlin' Wolf and the rest. 'I never did like Chicago,' Hooker always says in answer to the inevitable question as to why he alone of all the greats preferred to live in Detroit. 'Too many other blues guitarists there.'

Hooker's first single, 'Boogie Chillun', released in 1948, went straight to the top of the 'race' chart, as it was then known, and eventually sold more than a million copies, a feat which he repeated in 1951 with the song 'I'm in the Mood'.

Like many a blues musician of his time, Hooker was profligate with his talent, recording a vast amount of material in one-take sessions for anyone willing to pay the tab. The small matter of contractual obligations was circumvented by the use of a dozen or more pseudonyms ranging from geographical favourites like Texas Slim and Birmingham Sam to more transparent variations such as John Lee Booker, John Lee Cooker or even his French alias John L'Hooker.

'Dimples', released in 1964, remains his only UK hit single, but Hooker's impact on those musicians who picked up the blues baton and converted it into rock'n'roll has been pervasive. The first wave of English rock groups, including The Animals, The Yardbirds, The WHO, The Small Faces and especially The ROLLING STONES, recorded his songs and drew significant inspiration from his hard, guttural vocal mannerisms. In America his influence has been no less profound on later superstars from ZZ TOP – whose boogie *tour de force*, 'La Grange', is built on a distinctive Hooker motif – to Bruce SPRINGSTEEN, who included 'Boom Boom' in his repertoire for the *Tunnel of Love* tour of 1988.

Hooker faded from popular view during the Seventies, but came back stronger than ever towards the end of the Eighties. In 1989 he was featured in the title role of Pete Townshend's musical *The Iron Man* (Virgin CDV 2592), singing 'I Eat Heavy Metal', a departure from his normal style which he carried off with aplomb. In 1990 he teamed up with Miles Davis to record the original soundtrack to Dennis Hopper's acclaimed movie *The Hot Spot* (Antilles ANCD 8755).

Hooker still tours regularly – he played dates in England in 1988 and 1990 – and far from fading away gracefully he has become more in demand as the years roll by. *The Healer* (see below) introduced him to yet another generation of fans. He was featured in a series of US TV commercials for the Burger King chain and was seen on UK TV tapping out the heartbeat of the world in a rather fanciful ad for ICI which was given saturation exposure in 1991.

● *Boogie Chillun* (Charly CDCHARLY 4) [1986]

A grand collection of Hooker's recordings for the Vee-Jay label with which he signed in 1956, following a five-year spell on the Modern label. During his first session for Vee-Jay, in March 1956, he recorded his most famous number, 'Dimples', and then, during a 1959 session, he made new recordings of his most successful tracks from the Modern era: 'I'm in the Mood', 'Boogie Chillun', 'Hobo Blues' and 'Crawlin' Kingsnake', all included here. Hooker's playing is loosely structured and instinctive, his singing a brooding, guttural call. This music is the bedrock of the blues.

● *The Healer* (Silvertone ORECD 508) [1989]

This is the album which finally broke Hooker into the mainstream rock market; when it peaked at No.63 in the UK chart (No.5 in the UK independent chart) and No.62 in the US chart, it was considered an amazing feat for a blues singer of Hooker's authentic style and vintage.

He is joined on the album by a stellar roster of guest performers including Carlos SANTANA (whose energised Latin rock rather overwhelms Hooker on the title track), Bonnie Raitt (an exquisite grammy-winning re-recording of 'I'm in the Mood' with Raitt's lugubrious slide guitar weaving in and out of Hooker's blunt vamps), Robert CRAY (a sympathetic 'Cuttin Out'), Los Lobos (a thrilling rollercoaster boogie entitled 'Think Twice Before You Go'), Canned Heat, George Thorogood and Charlie Musselwhite.

Most of the songs were completed, in Hooker's time-honoured fashion, in only one or two takes, and the album, produced by Roy Rogers, has a rough, spontaneous sparkle unusual in a modern studio recording.

According to Hooker, the project came about because these musicians 'all live in the area [San Francisco] and they're all great admirers of me and my music.'

- **The Detroit Lion** (Demon FIENDCD 154) [1990]

Released in the wake of the success of *The Healer*, this is the definitive CD collection of the original Modern label recordings which made Hooker's name. The earthy magic of those earliest cuts is resurrected on 'Boogie Chillun' (recorded 3.11.48), 'I'm in the Mood' (7.8.51), 'House Rent Boogie' (16.11.51) and others.

- **That's My Story** [1960]/**The Folk Blues of John Lee Hooker** [Also known as **The Country Blues of John Lee Hooker**; 1959] (Ace CDCHD 927; 1990)

This two-albums-on-one-CD set focuses on Hooker's acoustic roots. *The Folk Blues of* . . . is the old blues that Hooker learnt to play back in Mississippi and Texas, items like the talking blues 'Tupelo Blues', the chain-gang work song 'Water Boy' and the ribald 'Black Snake' and 'Wobblin' Baby'. On *That's My Story*, where he is accompanied by Sam Jones (bass) and Lou Hayes (drums), Hooker essays his more recent experiences of Northern urban life on numbers including the socio-political commentary of 'Democrat Man' and the self-explanatory 'I Need Some Money'.

- **Mr Lucky** (Silvertone ORECD 519) [1991]

The success of this album was stunning. In Britain its No.3 placing made it the highest charting *bona fide* blues album ever, while at the age of 71, Hooker became the oldest artist ever to reach the UK Top 5. Proceeding along much the same lines as *The Healer*, it is another collection of celebrity duets, but this time featuring better material and a generally more coherent set of performances.

Among the stars who come out to play Hooker's songs (both old and new) are Keith Richards ('Crawlin' Kingsnake'), The ROBERT CRAY BAND ('Mr Lucky'), Johnny Winter ('Suzie') and Van MORRISON ('I Cover the Waterfront').

The stand-out tracks are a lurching 'This is Hip' featuring the gut-bucket twang of Ry COODER, and an eerie slice of jazz-funk titled 'Stripped Me Naked', which finds Hooker mumbling and moaning like a man possessed while Carlos SANTANA embarks on a wailing *tour de force* of guitar flagellation.

Best of all is a rollicking boogie with an odd time count, 'I Want to Hug You', peppered with the barrel-house piano of Chuck BERRY's former sidekick Johnnie Johnson. Like the vintage Buick on the cover, some things evidently do improve with age.

● *The Complete Chess Folk Blues Sessions* (MCA MCD-18335) [1991]

Yet more reissues of early Hooker recordings materialised in the wake of *Mr Lucky*. This set comprises some variable performances with an unidentified backing band recorded in May 1966 in the Chess studios. Half of it was released in October 1966 as *The Real Folk Blues* and the other half – nine tracks including 'Mustang and GTO' and 'This Land is Nobody's Land' – has remained unissued until now. Hooker's singing is particularly magnificent on 'Let's Go Out Tonight', where he sounds strangely redolent of Tom WAITS (whose voice had probably not long broken when this was being recorded).

● *Introducing . . . John Lee Hooker* (MCA MCD-10364) [1991]

A neat John Lee Hooker primer which catches the man at various stages of his career, this includes the version of 'Baby Please Don't Go' which inspired the Sixties hit version by Irish R'n'B roustabouts Them, and comes full circle with a 1971 duet with (ex-Them vocalist) Van MORRISON on 'Never Get Out of These Blues Alive'. Sleeve notes by the always entertaining Charles Shaar Murray are a welcome bonus.

Whitney Houston

Born: August 9 1963, New Jersey
UK/US No.1 album: 1987: **Whitney** (Arista 258141)
US No.1 album: 1985: **Whitney Houston** (Arista 610359)

A wondrous singing talent bent in the service of second division material remains the strongest impression of Whitney Houston. She should care. *Whitney Houston* (see below) is probably still the best-selling début album of all time (although its only rival, *Appetite for Destruction* by GUNS N' ROSES, may have overtaken it by now) and her run of seven consecutive US No.1 singles between 1985 and

1988 is a feat which has never been equalled.

As the daughter of Cissy Houston, niece of Dionne Warwick and family friend of Aretha FRANKLIN, Houston has had ample opportunity to inherit and absorb the finest gospel and soul singing traditions, and time and again, over the years, she has demonstrated the fluency and sheer prowess of her vocal technique. But she seems more a graduate of the Shirley Bassey school of show-business glitz than she does an heir to the spiritualised R'n'B traditions which informed the best work of her forebears.

She was thrust into the spotlight at a tender age, having backed artists like Chaka Khan and Lou Rawls and sung in concert with her mother by the time she was 17. By 20 she had been signed to Arista records by the Svengali-like figure of president Clive Davis, who has taken a hands-on interest in her career ever since.

Aggressively marketed as an air-brushed symbol of the MTV age, she has emerged, for all her talent, as a triumph of packaging over personality.

- **Whitney Houston** (Arista 610359) [1985]

The stratospheric success of the diva's début does little to allay reservations about its soapy production and the cloying sentimentality of the material. Masterminded by 'executive producer' Clive Davis, whose mission was to create the 'perfect' album, *Whitney Houston* was assembled by a team of crack producers, including Narada Michael Walden, Michael Masser and Kashif.

Between them these men have managed to iron out every crinkle in a voice which still plainly possesses extreme qualities of gentle expressiveness and window-rattling power. The hits come thick and fast – 'You Give Good Love', 'Saving All My Love For You', 'How Will I Know', 'Greatest Love of All' – but she always sounds more intent on manipulating her voice than losing herself in the lyrics.

- **Whitney** (Arista 258141) [1987]

Another set of soggy, off-the-peg material, produced in the main by Narada Michael Walden. Either she goes for the bubbly, Kids from *Fame* work-out as in 'Love Will Save the Day' and 'Love is a

Contact Sport' (surely a refugee title from a Laurie Anderson album) or she treads the well-worn path of the schmaltzy ballad, with stuff like 'You're Still My Man' and 'Just the Lonely Talking' where Walden plays 'brushes on the kit of life'.

Although the choruses of the big, slow ballad 'Didn't We Almost Have It All?' and the nearly-rock song 'So Emotional' are rendered with gale-force sorties of perfectly pitched vocal intensity, the album is tiresomely predictable in its quest for the middle-of-the-road common denominator. Another multi-platinum success, naturally.

The Human League

Convened: 1977, Sheffield
Joanne Catherall – vocals; Phil Oakey (f) – vocals; Suzanne Sulley – vocals
UK No.1 album: 1981: *Dare* (Virgin CDV 2192)

The Human League were the first synth-pop superstars, soaring to the top of the chart with *Dare* well before EURYTHMICS, Depeche Mode, Yello or The Thompson Twins made their various marks.

Like so many acts which started out in the late Seventies, The Human League was inspired by the mood of naive self-confidence which was abroad at the height of the punk revolution. The group was founded by two computer operators – Ian Marsh and Martyn Ware – who were undaunted by their complete lack of relevant experience.

'We're not musicians, and we can't play guitars or anything like that, but we approach synthesisers using maths and logic,' was how they explained their philosophy. They recruited Phil Oakey, a man with a preposterously lop-sided haircut who worked as a hospital porter in a plastic surgery ward, to be their singer. And they hired Adrian Wright in the non-musical role of 'visual director', his job being to 'illustrate' the songs on stage. This he did with a series of 700 or more constantly changing slides and various film clips.

David BOWIE said some nice things about them, and they almost got to tour with TALKING HEADS until the promoter discovered that The League planned to use a taped performance to accompany

Wright's visuals, thus freeing the other members of the group from the burdensome task of actually having to appear on stage.

But otherwise The Human League was clearly destined to remain a cult phenomenon; until, that is, Marsh and Ware suddenly left on the eve of a European tour in 1980. The pair went on to found the British Electric Foundation, a production umbrella for several projects, the first of which was their own Heaven 17.

Oakey, meanwhile, proved a canny, if eccentric, strategist. He invited Joanne Catherall and Suzanne Sulley, whom he met in a Sheffield club where they were working as cocktail waitresses, to join the group before he had heard any evidence of their ability to sing. He also recruited the more seasoned Ian Burden and Jo Callis (ex-guitarist with The Rezillos) as replacement synthesiser operatives. And in less than a year the revitalised group was topping music charts worldwide.

- *Dare* (Virgin CDV 2192) [1981]

The quintessential Human League album, *Dare* revolutionised the way in which pop was conceived and recorded. Apart from the voices of Oakey, Catherall and Sulley, the music was created entirely by means of synthesisers and computers. But far from the cold, mechanistic feel of 'traditional' synthesiser groups like Kraftwerk and Tangerine Dream, The Human League's songs were bright, hummable affairs that mixed electronic dance-beats with pop choruses in such a way as to appeal to club groovers and housewives alike. Credit for this feat must go to producer Martin Rushent as much as to the group itself. The hits from the album were 'The Sound of the Crowd', 'Love Action', 'Open Your Heart' and 'Don't You Want Me?', which was the biggest selling UK single of 1981 and a US No.1 in 1982.

- *Dare* [1981]/*Hysteria* [1984]/*Crash* [1986] (Virgin TPAK 3)

The three albums which comprise the heart of The Human League's legacy are still available individually, but this limited-edition triple-CD set, released in October 1990, collects them together for the princely sum of £26 or thereabouts. *Dare* was a hard act to follow and although *Hysteria*, produced by Hugh Padgham, yielded the hits 'Louise', 'The Lebanon' and 'Life on

Your Own', the formula of catchy hooks, single-note synthesiser lines and nagging electronic drum patterns was beginning to lose its shine.

Callis and Wright dropped out of the picture during the protracted sessions that eventually led to the release of the Jimmy Jam/Terry Lewis-produced *Crash*. The Minneapolitan dance-mix maestros took a dictatorial line with Oakey and Co., apparently drafting in session singers to replace the vocals of Catherall and Sulley after the girls had gone home. The result is an album for party animals that is cast as much in its producers' image as in that of The Human League.

- *Greatest Hits* (Virgin HLCD 1) [1988]

This is a tidy collection of all the group's Top 20 hits together with the less successful 'Love is All That Matters' and the Giorgio Moroder/Phil Oakey collaboration 'Together in Electric Dreams'. It draws a neat line under the League's achievements to date, but given the lameness of their most recent offering – *Romantic?* (Virgin CDV 2624; 1990) – also raises the question of whether there is anything more to come. Now down to a *ménage à trois*, Oakey, Catherall and Sulley need to find dramatically new inspiration if they are to do more than trade on the achievements of the past.

INXS

Convened: 1977, Sydney, Australia
Garry Beers (f) – bass/vocals; Andrew Farriss (f) – keyboards; Jon Farriss (f) – drums; Tim Farriss (f) – guitar; Michael Hutchence (f) – vocals; Kirk Pengilly (f) – guitar/saxophone/vocals
UK No.2 album: 1990: X (Mercury 846668-2)

Australasian groups tend to be diligent muckers who swiftly amass a vast following at home and then spend years chiselling away at the northern hemisphere markets until resistance eventually crumbles. AC/DC, Midnight Oil and Crowded House have all kept at it for years with varying degrees of success.

INXS is no exception to the pattern, and following a début antipodean hit 'Just Keep Walking' in 1980, the band doggedly expanded its operations, touring virtually anywhere that would have them, and releasing a succession of so-so albums, enlivened by the odd memorable tune: 'Original Sin' from *The Swing* (Mercury 818553-2; 1984) or 'Kiss the Dirt (Falling Down the Mountain)' from *Listen Like Thieves* (Mercury 824957-2; 1986).

Their principal asset is Michael Hutchence, an archetypal rock'n'roll narcissus in the Jagger/Geldof tradition, whose preening, bounding, look-at-me-everybody-I'm-a-star mannerisms lend a vital sense of occasion to the group's otherwise workaday performances. Their continued success is a triumph of application over inspiration.

- *Kick* (Mercury 832721-2) [1987]

There is a certain sort of rock music which works best on prime-time TV and in big venues, and by the time they came to record *Kick*, INXS had figured out exactly how best to play it. Songs like 'What You Need', 'Mystify' and their biggest hit 'Need You Tonight' are built on big, simple blocks of sound: terse chunks of rhythm guitar with gaps filled by telegraphic bursts of lyric, working up to choruses that spell out the song titles like billboard slogans.

Although X charted higher, *Kick* broke them in America and remains by far their biggest album – 1.4 million sales registered in the UK alone. The accompanying world tour lasted for a debilitating 16 months, during which time they performed to close on two million people.

- X (Mercury 846668-2) [1990]

Having grafted their way to the top, INXS continue to produce quality rock by numbers. Like a gambler who has evolved a fail-safe system, they stick to their musical methodology with undeviating determination.

But few of these songs have any substance. 'Suicide Blonde', the album's big hit, is typical: a patchwork of familiar-sounding riffs and yelped vocal bits that coalesces into a neat, danceable groove. Derivative, repetitive and manipulative, their music is good value for a party, or a disco, or doing the vacuuming perhaps, but not much use for sitting down and listening to.

Joe Jackson

Born: August 11 1954, Burton Upon Trent, Staffordshire
UK No.3 album: 1982: *Night and Day* (A&M CDA 64906)

'My ambitions are artistic as opposed to material ones. I want to be able to do better and more interesting and unique work over the years and hopefully have it appreciated by as large an audience as I can get without having to be something I'm not.' [1991.] There is the Joe Jackson manifesto in a nutshell. Unfortunately, the more interesting and unique his work has become, the more his audience has dwindled.

A formal training at the Royal Academy of Music in London (where he was in the same year as Annie Lennox of EURYTHMICS) and his subsequent experience as musical director of cabaret acts in his home town of Portsmouth set him on a maverick course from the outset, and during a wildly variegated career he has added vivid shades of jazz, Latin and classical music to a palette otherwise dominated by the bold primary colours of the rock singer-songwriter.

Always a spiky customer, he refused for many years to make promotional videos for fear of vulgarising his art, and at his most wilful he has thrown himself into projects, such as the entirely instrumental, quasi-classical *Will Power* (A&M CDA 3908; 1987), which have had no earthly chance of reaping significant commercial rewards.

● *Look Sharp!* (A&M CDMID 115) [1979]

Jackson rode in on the tail end of the British New Wave with an image that was more dodgy spiv than angry punk, and a songwriting eloquence that quickly drew comparisons with the already established Elvis COSTELLO and Graham Parker. His début remains a minor masterpiece of intelligent pop craftmanship, with up-tempo rockers like 'One More Time' and 'Got the Time' (later covered by thrash-metal barons Anthrax) balanced by the more severe mood of 'Fools in Love' and the prickly humour of his first hit 'Is She Really Going Out With Him?'. The production now sounds unbelievably austere, with no over-dubs or extraneous clutter to impede the stark but imaginative arrangements of bass, drums, guitar, piano and voice.

● *Night and Day* (A&M CDA 64906) [1982]

Of the widely differing musical currents that Jackson has plugged into over the years, none has suited his sophisticated style and melancholy temperament quite so well as the strain of Latin-tinged pop which he came up with on *Night and Day*. By far his most successful album, it hosts his biggest hit, 'Steppin' Out', along with the painfully emotional 'Breaking Us in Two', some sobering thoughts on the essence of New Manhood in 'Real Men', and the epic finale 'A Slow Song', which became one of the most potent numbers in his live performances.

● *Blaze of Glory* (A&M CDA 5249) [1989]

Most of Jackson's earlier fans had been put off the scent by the time he inaugurated a belated purple patch with *Blaze of Glory*. 'I'm really interested in what happens to artists beyond the age of 30,' he said at the time, and Jackson has become one of the very few songwriters seriously to grapple with the notion of rock as an 'adult' phenomenon, becoming a spokesman, as it were, for a generation that once worshipped the idea of youth and is now having to get used to the reality of middle age.

Loosely organised as an autobiographical trek through Jackson's formative years, songs like 'Me and You (Against the World)' and 'Down to London' essay the trials and joys of growing up in the pop culture of the Sixties and Seventies with typical verve and wry wit. Other high points of this excellent but predictably overlooked album include the insanely brilliant instrumental 'Acropolis Now' and the sad but funny tale of the ageing rocker who dreams of being 'Nineteen Forever'.

● *Stepping Out – The Very Best of Joe Jackson* (A&M 397 052-2) [1990]

A sensible collection of high points, from 'Is She Really Going Out With Him?' to 'Nineteen Forever'. It's interesting to note how cohesive the collection is, despite Jackson's gadfly reputation. But then his three instrumental albums are not represented at all, and only one track apiece is taken from the reggae-inspired *Beat Crazy* (A&M CDA 3241; 1980), the 1940s swing-era syncopations of *Jumpin' Jive* (A&M CDMID 116; 1981) and the double-disc *Live 1980/86* (A&M CDA 6706; 1988).

● *Laughter and Lust* (Virgin America CDVUS 34) [1991]

Another fine and varied collection that gives a menopausal twist to some otherwise conventional rock themes. 'My House' finds Jackson empathising with the middle-aged executive dreading his nightly return to the cloying tedium of suburban family life. In 'The Old Songs' he simultaneously rails against the unrealistic expectations of eternal youth fostered by the rock'n'roll myth, and bemoans the wave of nostalgia that has engulfed his generation: 'The hopes and dreams of twenty years ago/They're all over the bloody radio.'

A mixture of intelligent, up-beat rock leavened on several tracks by hot-blooded latino rhythms, this is one of the most accessible and heartfelt albums Jackson has produced since his earliest work.

Michael Jackson

Born: August 29 1958, Gary, Indiana
UK/US No.1 albums: 1982: *Thriller* (Epic CD 85930)
1987: *Bad* (Epic 450 290-2)
1991: *Dangerous* (Epic 465802 2)

It was in 1987 that Michael Jackson swept the board in the annual *Rolling Stone* readers' poll, winning every category in which he appeared. These were: Worst Male Singer, Hype of the Year, Worst Video ('Bad'), Worst Album Cover (*Bad*), Most Unwelcome Comeback and Worst-Dressed Male Rock Artist. The magazine's writers (who, of course, know better) later judged Thriller to have been the 7th *best* album of the Eighties, and the public at large voted with their wallets to make it the biggest-selling recording of all time with estimates ranging from 38 million to 45 million copies sold at the last count.

The key to Jackson's transcendental success, and part of the explanation for the hostility it arouses in a certain breed of dyed-in-the-wool rock fan, is a background steeped in the old-fashioned (pre-rock'n'roll) virtues of show business. Instead of hanging out with the guys in the neighbourhood, Jackson misspent his youth (when he wasn't performing himself) watching other artists – some great, some less so – from the wings of theatres on the American chitlin' circuit. As he observes in his autobiography, *Moonwalk*, published in 1988: 'Some musicians – SPRINGSTEEN and U2 for example – may feel they got their education from the streets. I'm a performer at heart. I got mine from the stage.'

When Jackson's producer, Quincy Jones, was asked which artists had most influenced his client, he responded without hesitation: James BROWN, Walt Disney, Gene Kelly and Fred Astaire.

Jackson was 11 when he first saw his own little face on the cover of *Rolling Stone*. In 1971, two years after The Jackson 5 (see below) had scored its first hit, Jackson (then 13) was signed separately to Tamla Motown as a solo act and immediately sallied forth with a string of his own hits – 'Got to be There', 'Rockin' Robin', 'Ben' (a US No.1 in 1972) and others – which were released in tandem with his work as a member of the group.

Jackson's success as a solo star rapidly overtook and eventually dwarfed the achievements of The 5. Indeed, he became the single most significant popular music act of the Eighties. Yet he was no great innovator, like Elvis PRESLEY or Bob DYLAN, nor was he ever a rôle model for a generation as The BEATLES or The ROLLING STONES had been before him. He simply emerged as a tremendous all-rounder at a time when rock music was taking over as the world's primary mainstream entertainment. He is as good a dancer as he is a singer and he has employed the new technology to make videos that are as full of stylish impact as his music. The appeal of his slick, pneumatic song-and-dance routines cuts across barriers of age, race, class and nationality.

Above all, Jackson is a stringent perfectionist. He explained why it had taken five years to release *Bad*, the follow-up to *Thriller*: 'Quincy and I decided that this album should be as close to perfect as humanly possible. A perfectionist has to take his time . . . He can't let it go before he's satisfied, he can't. When it's as perfect as you can make it, you put it out there . . . That's the difference between a No.30 record and a No.1 record that stays No.1 for weeks.'

Jackson has not reacted well to the relentless barrage of (frequently prurient) media attention which success on such a grand scale has generated. As he has become an increasingly reclusive and secretive figure, so reports of his eccentricities have grown ever more lurid and fantastic. In Britain *The Sun* newspaper posed the question that came to dominate popular reportage of his private life: 'Is Jacko Wacko?'

He is known to have kept snakes and a pet chimpanzee called Bubbles who, apparently, sleeps in the same room as him. He attempted to buy the bones of John Merrick, the so-called Elephant Man, after seeing the movie starring John Hurt. He has been photographed wearing a face mask to ward off germs, and sleeping in an oxygen chamber, a practice which he apparently believes will help to prolong his life to 150.

He is known to have had a nose job and a cleft put in his chin, but Jackson categorically denies persistent allegations that he has had his whole face restructured and his skin tinted a shade lighter than its natural tone.

And so it goes on. When his *Bad* tour reached England in 1988, Jackson's constant companion was the American TV child actor Jimmy Safechuck. In London the pair paid an after-hours visit to the huge toy shop, Hamley's. It seems as if Jackson, having started his career so young, has been forced to stretch his childhood well into adult life. 'I believe I'm one of the loneliest people in the world,' he wrote, in what became the most frequently quoted remark from *Moonwalk*.

● *Off the Wall* (Epic CD 83468) [1979]

Off The Wall marked the start of Jackson's passage to the superleague. Although less subject to the triumphal bandying of statistics – it has sold but a trifling 17 million copies – it is, arguably, the most satisfying of his solo albums. Said to be producer Quincy Jones' favourite Jackson album, it has a warmth and soulfulness on tracks like 'She's Out of My Life', 'Don't Stop Till You Get Enough' and 'Rock With You' that was later lost in the neurotic quest for dance nirvana that is the essential hallmark of both *Thriller* and *Bad*.

- *Thriller* (Epic CD 85930) [1982]

Again produced by Jones, this has become one of the certified wonders of the rock world, more a phenomenon than a collection of songs. Lasting a mere 43 minutes, *Thriller* furnished an incredible tally of seven Top 10 hit singles in America, a better strike rate than many acts achieve on the 'greatest hits' retrospectives which span their entire careers.

Retailers reported that *Thriller*'s attraction reached far beyond the normal strata of album buyers, appealing to people who had never previously visited a record shop in their lives. Even the documentary *The Making of Michael Jackson's Thriller* (1984) became, for a time, the best-selling music video ever released.

Thriller was also a vital staging post in the evolution of the pop-soul genre and much of the black dance music that followed – in particular the work of the Jimmy Jam/Terry Lewis production axis – took its cue from the sound and ambience of *Thriller*.

The title track, 'Billie Jean' and 'Beat It' – the last incorporating Eddie VAN HALEN's celebrated heavy metal guitar solo – are songs that have fired the imagination of the pop industry while simultaneously catching the ear of the most casual consumer. Slick, bright and honed to perfection, this album is part of the fabric of popular music legend.

- *Bad* (Epic 450 290-2) [1987]

The *Thriller* formula was further refined and the same mega-successful result obtained, with sales of 25 million logged by 1991. 'Smooth Criminal', 'Just Good Friends' and 'Bad' vibrate to the clipped, inhumanly precise sound of electronic drums, accurately tracking the pulse of modern urban life itself, while the ballads 'I Just Can't Stop Loving You' (a duet with Seidah Garrett) and 'Liberian Girl' provide a more exotic setting for Jackson's high, emasculated tenor.

Once again the accompanying videos were memorably graced by several impossibly sharp dance routines, with Jackson this time togged up like a cross between a street gladiator and a bondage fetishist's rag-doll.

● *Dangerous* (Epic 465 802-2) [1991]

No longer in touch with the latest trends, but under heavy pressure to match the achievements of the past, Jackson here produced an expensive botch. The 11-minute video – made at a staggering cost of $6 million – to promote the first single 'Black or White' was an obvious attempt to emulate his landmark video for 'Thriller'. But like the album itself, it has no coherent thread and, despite some superb feats of technical wizardry, offers nothing new.

Co-written and co-produced principally with Teddy Riley of swing-beat dance trio Guy, the album achieves a tough, focused, synthesised dance sound on its best numbers, 'Jam', 'She Drives Me Wild' and 'Why You Wanna Trip on Me?'.

But the platitudinous ballads 'Heal the World' and 'Gone Too Soon' underline a dull and predictable streak and for all his crotch-grabbing antics Jackson now sounds about as dangerous as a teddy bear.

The Jacksons [née The Jackson 5]

Convened: 1964, Gary, Indiana. Split up: 1984
Jackie Jackson (f) – vocals; Jermaine Jackson (f) – vocals;
Marlon Jackson (f) – vocals; Michael Jackson (f) – vocals; Tito
Jackson (f) – vocals
UK No.1 album: 1983: *18 Greatest Hits* (Motown WD
72629)

Joe Jackson used to be a steel-mill worker who played guitar in a local R'n'B group called The Falcons. His wife Katherine, a devout Jehovah's Witness who plays clarinet, piano and sings, used to work as an assistant in a department store. Their nine children – in order of birth Rebbie, Jackie, Tito, Jermaine, LaToya, Marlon, Michael, Randy and Janet – have become the most celebrated family of performers in the history of popular music.

Under Joe's strict tutelage and with encouragement and support from Katherine, five of the brothers formed The Jackson 5 with Michael, still only six years old, as the lead singer. The sixth brother, Randy, joined the line-up much later on, while all three sisters – Rebbie, LaToya and Janet – performed with the group in a temporary capacity at various times. Janet went on to became a significant star in her own right, enjoying two US No.1 albums:

Control (A&M CDA 5106; 1986) and *Rhythm Nation 1814* (A&M CDA 3920; 1989).

Jackson senior steered The Jackson 5 from talent competitions and a residency in the local striptease parlour to a recording contract with Tamla Motown records, signed in 1969 reputedly for a dismal 2.7% cut of the royalties.

Success with Motown was instantaneous and spectacular as the group's first four singles – 'I Want You Back', 'ABC', 'The Love You Save' and 'I'll Be There' – all went to the top of the American chart, each title registering sales in excess of a million copies.

In 1975 four of The 5 joined the exodus of acts from the by-then ailing label. Changing their name to The Jacksons for contractual reasons, they signed to Epic, where they teamed up with the celebrated writing and production team of Kenny Gamble and Leon Huff. The results were mixed. The single 'Show Me the Way to Go' was the group's first and only UK No.1 in 1977, but the album *Goin' Places* (unavailable), released later the same year, failed even to breach the US Top 60.

● *Anthology* (Motown ZD 72529) [1976]

The Jackson 5 joined Motown at a crucial time in the label's evolution. The first wave of Sixties acts such as The Temptations, Smokey Robinson and The Miracles, and The Four Tops were running out of steam. With hits like 'ABC', 'Mama's Pearl', 'Lookin' Through the Windows' and 'Little Bitty Pretty One', The Jacksons remoulded the Motown sound and introduced it to a new, younger generation of teenyboppers.

Although never much of an albums band, they scored enough hits to justify this double-disc compilation, which also includes a selection of Michael's early solo hits like 'Rockin' Robin' and 'Ben'.

The Jam

Convened: 1975, Woking, Surrey. Split up: 1982
Rick Buckler (f) – drums; Bruce Foxton (f) – bass/vocals; Paul Weller (f) – vocals/guitar
UK No.1 album: 1982: *The Gift* (Polydor 823 285-2)

With a terse musical style forged during the punk upheavals of 1976, The Jam channelled a furious energy into songs that were a perfect reflection of their times. The trio's immaculately severe mod look, like their music, was that much smarter than the ripped and safety-pinned chic of their contemporaries, and they rapidly transcended their punk origins in a way that groups like The Buzzcocks and The Damned never could.

The Jam's initial stylistic debt to The WHO gradually gave way to a harsh but distinctive sound that reaped both critical acclaim and escalating commercial success. By 1982 they were probably the biggest band in Britain, at which point, with their third No.1 single 'A Town Called Malice'/'Precious' and a No.1 album not long behind them, Weller decided to call it a day.

'The longer a group continues, the more frightening the thought of ever ending it becomes,' he explained. 'That is why so many of them carry on until they become meaningless. I've never wanted to get to this stage.'

Such rigorous prescience was cold comfort to Foxton and Buckler, for whom a lifetime of obscurity beckoned. Nor did the prescription seem to apply when considering the fate of Weller's next project, The Style Council, a group which virtually redefined the concept of carrying on to the point of meaninglessness, and indeed some distance beyond.

- *All Mod Cons* (Polydor 823 282-2) [1978]

Singles were never a problem, but it took The Jam until this, their third album, to master the requirements of the long-playing format. Here the cold anger and vivid imagery of songs like 'A-Bomb in Wardour Street' and 'Down in the Tube Station at Midnight' are balanced by the more delicate emotions of 'English Rose' and 'The Place I Love'. A hard, clipped version of 'David Watts' – Ray Davies' ambiguous paean to the trials and tribulations of schoolboy hero-worship – bounds along with typically unbridled zest.

- *Setting Sons* (Polydor 831 314-2) [1979]

Weller's moodiest moment, full of dark, simmering rage that boils over into numbers like 'Private Hell', 'Thick as Thieves', 'Burning

Sky' and the incandescent 'Eton Rifles'. Not an essential Jam item, perhaps, but one of the most revealing.

• *Greatest Hits* (Polydor 849 554-2) [1991]

There was something of a Jam renaissance at the start of the Nineties. Morrissey recorded a striking version of 'That's Entertainment', and with the help of a TV advertising campaign, this repackaged collection reached No.2 in July 1991.

Comprising in chronological order all The Jam's 17 official singles plus the two album tracks that charted as import singles – 'That's Entertainment' and 'Just Who is the Five O'Clock Hero?' – this definitive compilation underlines the group's consummate skill in negotiating the demands of the three-minute medium.

The opening volley of 'In the City', 'The Modern World' and 'News of the World' is a classic succession of short, sharp shocks. Weller surrendered none of his flinty resolve as the group's ambition broadened and they moved into a purple patch with 'Going Underground', 'Start!' (both No.1 hits) and the deranged 'Funeral Pyre', a song of such extreme sentiments and violent momentum that it is a wonder that it ever earned a place in the UK Top 5.

Then something snapped, and for all the subsequent popularity of 'Absolute Beginners', 'A Town Called Malice' and 'Beat Surrender', the wiry tension on which the best Jam material depended had gone. In its place we got the first stirrings of Weller's born-again soul-boy routine (most obviously on 'Beat Surrender') which led to the eventual embarrassment of The Style Council.

The Style Council

Convened: 1983, London, England. Split up: 1990
Mick Talbot (f) – keyboards; Paul Weller (f) – vocals/guitar
UK No.1 album: 1985: *Our Favourite Shop* (Polydor 825 700-2)

Weller founded The Style Council with Mick Talbot, a stocky East London mod who had previously done time with The Merton Parkas and Dexys Midnight Runners. A dreary musical collective,

The Council provided an outlet for Weller's painfully self-conscious soul influences and a platform for his increasingly strident party political views.

Unlike The Jam, interest in The Style Council peaked early and then simply fizzled out from all quarters. The group was eventually forced to call it a day after Polydor declined to release what would have been its final album.

Weller resurfaced at the helm of The Paul Weller Movement in 1991 and immediately recaptured some of the old magic with a hit single 'Into Tomorrow' (Freedom High FHPC1), a ravishing song with a beguiling hint of retro-psychedelia that was as good as anything that reached the UK chart all year.

- *The Singular Adventures of The Style Council* (Polydor 837 896-2)

The Style Council never made a satisfying album, and this collection of singles remains the principal fruit of their recorded legacy: 'My Ever Changing Moods', 'Have You Ever Had It Blue?', 'Solid Bond in Your Heart' are cool, melodious tunes, and about as soulful as a visit to Pizza Hut.

Jesus Jones

Convened: 1988, London
Barry D (f) – keyboards/samples; Jerry De Borg (f) – guitar/vocals; Mike Edwards – vocals/guitar; Gen (f) – drums; Al Jaworski (f) – bass/vocals
UK No.1 album: 1991: *Doubt* (Food FOODCD 5)

With their strange haircuts, bright, buzzy music and frantic stage show, Jesus Jones dragged rock, kicking and screaming, into the Nineties. The group is the brainchild of Mike Edwards, their songwriter, producer, spokesman and leader, and he doesn't hang about. Within months of getting together, they recorded their first single, reputedly for just £125, and watched it climb with little difficulty to No.42 in the UK chart.

Their trick has been to recast in a high-energy, rock group context the sampling techniques on which the acid house and rap movements were founded. Such a technologically adventurous approach has made them one of the few forward-looking bands to emerge from the retro-fixated Eighties, and they have forged the vital link between pioneers of the hip hop-rock coalition (hip rock?) like Pop Will Eat Itself and a new generation of hi-tech indie-pop stars such as EMF.

The Americans love it and in 1991 Jesus Jones and EMF spent two weeks vying with each other in the Top 3 of the US singles chart (with 'Right Here Right Now' and 'Unbelievable' respectively).

- *Liquidizer* (Food FOODCD 3) [1989]

The band's influential début welds an alarmingly disparate array of ingredients into a coherent musical formula. What at first listen sounds like an undifferentiated tidal wave of noise, loaded with hyperactive squawks of treble and a kind of cement-mixer effect clanking around in the mid-range, is in fact a sophisticated combination of psychedelic drones, rap-culture funk-dance rhythms, neat harmony vocals and hi-tech acid-house gizmology, all pieced together like a highly complex jigsaw. 'I've got a great knowledge of rock music,' Edwards told *The Independent*, 'and like to use different elements, as opposed to the Stalinism of house music, which is exactly the same as the Stalinism of punk music – the attitude that nothing existed before.' It's a rather exhausting experience, just the same.

- *Doubt* (Food FOODCD 5) [1991]

Keeping up with the Joneses is like bowling along in a fairground dodgem as they take their odd amalgam of techno-bleep and hardcore-thrash to even further extremes on their second album. It is best at its crudest; the riot of noise which underpins 'Stripped', for instance, recalls the adrenaline-rush effect of the best PUBLIC ENEMY soundtracks. Yet the album also houses no less than four hit singles – 'Real Real Real', 'Right Here Right Now', 'International Bright Young Thing' and 'Who? Where? Why?' – all of them endowed with a cute melodic touch that suggests a cool strategist's brain at work behind all the bluster.

Billy Joel

Born: May 9 1949, The Bronx, New York
US No.1 albums: 1978: *52nd Street* (Columbia CD 83181)
                    1980: *Glass Houses* (Columbia 450 087-2)
                    1989: *Storm Front* (Columbia 465 658-2)

Part of Billy Joel's peculiar appeal is that he has never decided what to do with the embarrassing amount of talent at his disposal. Like a bee that wants to pollinate every flower in the field, part of him likes to bend his classical piano training in the service of heavy, techno-flash rock; another part likes to pretend that he is Ray CHARLES; and yet another that he is a purveyor of straightforward, high-class pop like his biggest UK hit 'Uptown Girl', a joyous homage to the glory days of The Four Seasons, which sailed to No.1 in 1983. His problem, if you could call it that, is how to convince people such as the *Rolling Stone* critic who described him as 'a vaudevillian piano man and mimic', that he is genuine.

Graduating from a life of adolescent petty crime and a short-lived amateur boxing career, Joel took his first steps into the pop world as a member of local Long Island band, The Echoes. His next group, The Hassles, recorded two albums in the late Sixties and he then set up a heavy rock duo called Attila, which released one album in 1970.

Eventually, in 1972, Joel put out his first solo release, *Cold Spring Harbor* (Pickwick 982 637-2), the initial success of which can be gauged from the fact that he spent much of the next year working as a lounge-bar performer under the pseudonym of Bill Martin.

He put the experience to practical use as inspiration for the title track of his next album, *Piano Man* (Columbia CD 80719; 1973), his first significant success.

- *The Stranger* (Columbia 450 914-2) [1977]

The multi-platinum album that transformed Joel into an act of major international standing, *The Stranger* boasts the million-selling single 'Just the Way You Are'. This cabaret-style ballad became a cocktail-lounge standard, and once it had been covered by Frank Sinatra, among others, Joel's popular image as something of an MOR crooner was cemented.

Joel has never sought to deny this side of his work – 'My show business is genuine, it's not phony,' he told *Q* magazine – yet much of the other material here, in particular the complex 'Scenes from an Italian Restaurant', 'She's Always a Woman' and the title track, are clearly numbers which tap the lodestone of a deeper level of inspiration.

● *Greatest Hits Volume I & Volume II* (Columbia CD 88666) [1985]

Thanks in part to the 'Piano Man' image, Joel is frequently described as an American equivalent of Elton JOHN. But while he has tended to enjoy his greatest commercial success with songs that mirror JOHN's mainstream pop sensibility – for example the boppy 'Tell Her About It' or indeed 'Just the Way You Are' – Joel's music actually has far more gravity than JOHN's.

'Allentown', from *Nylon Curtain* (Columbia CD 85959; 1982), is a stirring and contemplative song about the anguish of large-scale unemployment. 'Goodnight Saigon', from the same album, describes the horror of the Vietnam war from the perspective of the young American marines who were dumped in a steamy swamp in a distant land to fight an enemy they couldn't see for a cause they didn't understand. Replete with thunderous helicopter noises at beginning and end, the powerful resonance of a piece like this gives the lie to the notion of Joel as an empty-headed song-and-dance man.

Elsewhere there is the sub-metal of 'Big Shot', the neo-Chuck BERRY rifferama of 'You May Be Right' and more obvious favourites including 'The Stranger', 'It's Still Rock and Roll to Me' and of course 'Uptown Girl'. In all, a fitting tribute to Joel's protean talent.

● *Storm Front* (Columbia 465 658-2) [1989]

Not since the days when DYLAN still had full command of his faculties has such a mass of detail been crammed into such an intelligent and palatable pop form, as it is on Joel's brilliant hit single 'We Didn't Start the Fire'. And much of the other material on *Storm Front* is informed by a similar degree of musical literacy and intellectual coherence.

Joel's trademark remains the seemingly effortless appropriation of whatever elements a given song needs from a wide range of musical genres. I defy anyone who did not know that it was a Billy Joel song to identify the voice as even being that of a white singer on the delightfully up-beat, *nouveau*-Stax arrangement of 'When in Rome'.

The only reservation is that Joel can be too clever for his own good. When he plays the heavy rock manqué – as on 'That's Not Her Style' – the performance lacks that indefinable quality of authenticity needed to turn a neat song into a credible whole. Versatile certainly, but like that most notorious of dilettantes, Robert PALMER, you get the nagging impression that Joel never likes to get his hands *too* soiled with the nitty gritty of any particular style.

Elton John

Born: Reginald Kenneth Dwight, March 25 1947, Pinner, Middlesex

UK/US No.1 albums:	1973:	***Don't Shoot Me, I'm Only the Piano Player*** (DJM 827 690-2)
	1973:	***Goodbye Yellow Brick Road*** (DJM 821 747-2)
	1974:	***Caribou*** (DJM 825 488-2)
	1974:	***Elton John's Greatest Hits*** (DJM DJMCD 3)
UK No.1 albums:	1989:	***Sleeping With the Past*** (Rocket 838 839-2)
	1990:	***The Very Best of Elton John*** (Rocket 846 947-2)
US No.1 albums:	1972:	***Honky Chateau*** (DJM 829 249-2)
	1975:	***Captain Fantastic and the Brown Dirt Cowboy*** (DJM 821 746-2)
	1975:	***Rock of the Westies*** (DJM 832 018-2)

One of rock's most decorated veterans, Elton John is a songwriter with a rare gift for conjuring melodies of timeless and universal appeal. All the rest – the preposterous costumes, the outrageous showmanship, the gaudy buffoonery and the fake American singing accent – is mere window-dressing.

Unfortunately, there have been long stretches when the core material has barely been visible among the ephemera and even John's sympathisers would have to admit that during the latter half of the Eighties his extra-curricular activities were more noteworthy than his musical achievements.

There was the long and painful legal battle with his publishers Dick James Music (DJM), which ended in 1985 with both sides claiming victory; there was the break-up with his bride of just three years, Renate Blauer, in 1987; there was his abortive attempt to sell Watford football club to Robert Maxwell the same year; there was the auction in 1988 of personal memorabilia at Sotheby's, realising a total of £14.8 million in four days; and there was his libel action against *The Sun* newspaper in 1988, which netted him one million pounds in compensation for some of the most lurid and damaging stories ever written about any major rock star, true or false, living or dead.

John's distraction during these trying times was evident from the paucity of new hits and the general impression of a career in free fall. In August 1989 when asked by Terry Wogan to comment on the fact that he had never enjoyed a UK No.1 single (apart from his 1976 duet with Kiki Dee 'Don't Go Breaking My Heart'), John said, 'It would have been nice, but it doesn't bother me. I don't suppose I ever will have one now.'

He was wrong, as it turned out. In less than a year, the double-sided single 'Sacrifice'/'Healing Hands' was No.1 in the UK and an astonishing renaissance in John's fortunes was underway. Like Eric CLAPTON in 1987, he emerged from a long lean period to be canonised by pundits and public alike. Among a host of ensuing successes and tributes there were two UK No.1 albums, a BRITS Award for Best British Male Artist, a couple of books, a TV documentary and a lavish boxed set, *To Be Continued. . . .* (see below).

But perhaps the most telling homage was *Two Rooms – Celebrating the Songs of Elton John and Bernie Taupin* (Mercury 845 749-2; 1991), an album of interpretations of the duo's songs by various artists including Kate BUSH, STING, The WHO, Rod STEWART, Sinead O'Connor, Phil COLLINS, The BEACH BOYS, Eric CLAPTON and George MICHAEL.

Apart from underlining the respect which John commands among so many of his most distinguished peers, the album draws attention to the enduring and highly traditional qualities of the songs he wrote with Taupin. Their methods invite comparison with the pre-rock'n'roll working practices of Tin Pan Alley. Not only does John play the piano – as opposed to the more ubiquitous rock composers' tool, the guitar – but there is a strict demarcation of functions within the partnership, John writing the music and Taupin independently supplying the lyrics (hence the 'two rooms' in which the songs are created).

The pair began composing to order, as staff writers at DJM in 1968, which may account, in part, for the unashamedly vacuous streak that their music has always exhibited. Along with the many pop standards they have minted, there has also been a persistent quota of populist dross. One of their early compositions, 'I Can't Go On Living Without You', was very nearly selected as the British entry for the Eurovision song contest to be sung by Lulu in 1969, but lost out in the end to 'Boom Bang A Bang'.

'To me a song's like a postage stamp,' John once said. 'You lick it, stick it on an envelope and that's the last you ever see of it.'

- *Elton John* (DJM 827 689-2) [1970]

For many a die-hard Elton fan, the eponymous second album remains his best. There is a degree of openness and vulnerability about Taupin's lyrics – especially on the much-covered stand-out track 'Our Song' – which John matches with unfussy arrangements and compellingly direct performances. From the cod-gospelese of 'Border Song' to the unforgettable hook of 'Take Me to the Pilot', it remains the most beguiling and poetic of John's early albums.

- *Tumbleweed Connection* (DJM 829 248-2) [1971]
- *Honky Chateau* (DJM 829 249-2) [1972]

There is a stirring undertow to much of *Tumbleweed Connection* (1971) which rejoices in a wealth of country, blues and gospel connotations, particularly 'Burn Down the Mission'. Taupin was going through his Wild West phase and most of the songs are larded with implausible lyrics about cowboys and guns.

With *Honky Chateau* John began an incredible run of seven consecutive US No.1 albums, a feat unrivalled to this day; it prompted his biographer Philip Norman to describe him as 'the definitive rock star of the Seventies . . . bigger than any solo artist before or since, with the single exception of Elvis PRESLEY.'

Apart from 'Rocket Man', which became a huge hit, and the funky 'Honky Cat', the album is an undistinguished though popular collection with a predominantly country feel.

- *Don't Shoot Me, I'm Only the Piano Player* (DJM 827 690-2) [1973]
- *Goodbye Yellow Brick Road* (DJM 821 747-2) [1973]

John was cruising at a phenomenally high altitude when he released two of his best and biggest-selling albums in the same calendar year. *Don't Shoot Me, I'm Only the Piano Player* was trailed by its two enormous and stylistically contrasting hits: the plaintive 'Daniel' and the mock-revivalist bobby-soxer stomp 'Crocodile Rock' – John and Taupin at their 'postage stamp' best.

Goodbye Yellow Brick Road is John's *pièce de résistance*. A colossal international success, it boasts a string of his classics, including the title track, 'Bennie and the Jets', 'Saturday Night's Alright for Fighting' and the enduring 'Candle in the Wind'. Originally a double vinyl album, it is accommodated in all its ritzy glory on a single CD.

- *The Very Best of Elton John* (Rocket 846 947-2) [1990]
- *To Be Continued. . . .* (Rocket 848 236-4) [US 1990/UK 1991]

For most people, familiarity with the many hit singles that have graced John's career has come about by a process of osmosis. 'Philadelphia Freedom', 'The Bitch is Back', 'Don't Let The Sun Go Down on Me' and 'Song for Guy' are numbers that have been unconsciously absorbed as part of the aural scenery by anyone who has listened to pop radio, gone to a college dance or sat in a restaurant over the last 20 years or so. Perhaps that is one reason why the sound quality seems to be so fantastically enhanced on these two collections, both of which incorporate most of John's hits down the ages.

That explanation is not intended to detract from the commendable (if anonymous) remastering job that has been done in transferring these and other titles from John's illustrious history on to compact disc. Hats off also to Gus Dudgeon and Chris

Thomas, who between them take the lion's share of the production credits, underlining John's knack of finding a winning team and sticking with it.

The Very Best of Elton John is a two-disc compilation which sticks to the basic 'greatest hits' format – 30 tracks from 'Your Song' to 'You Gotta Love Someone' – while *To Be Continued. . . .* is an exquisitely boxed four-disc set, which goes the extra mile by including rarities such as an early demo version of 'Your Song' and odd B-sides, along with all the major hits.

Robert Johnson

Born: May 8 1911, Jackson, Mississippi. Died: August 16 1938

Probably the most influential blues singer of all time, Robert Johnson was certainly the most mysterious. A dapper itinerant, with unnaturally long fingers, he was widely believed to have made a pact with the devil in order to acquire his haunting voice and prescient guitar-playing skills. He died at the age of 27 (on the same date that Elvis PRESLEY was to die 39 years later), apparently poisoned by the jealous husband of one of his legion of women friends.

● *The Complete Recordings* (Columbia 467 246-2) [1990]

Johnson's recorded legacy – a mere 29 songs together with 12 alternate takes, making 41 tracks in all – was assembled in its entirety for the first time in 1990. The release of *The Complete Recordings*, on CD and cassette only, coincided with the publication of a remarkable essay, *Searching for Robert Johnson*, by American blues authority Peter Guralnick.

'Johnson's music remains the touchstone against which the achievement of the blues is measured,' says Guralnick, and certainly Johnson's mordant yelp and clipped acoustic guitar style had an unimaginable influence on the development of the blues and its miscreant musical baby, rock'n'roll.

The songs on this indispensable album later became standards among Chicago originals like Muddy WATERS ('Sweet Home

Chicago') and Elmore James, who based his much-imitated bottleneck style around Johnson's 'I Believe I'll Dust my Broom'.

The effect of his material on the key players in the British rock explosion was similarly profound. While with Cream, Eric CLAPTON covered 'From Four Till Late' and 'Cross Road Blues' (calling it 'Crossroads'). The ROLLING STONES popularised 'Love in Vain' and 'Stop Breakin' Down Blues'; FLEETWOOD MAC recorded 'Hellhound on my Trail' and others; while LED ZEPPELIN, having ripped off the central verse of 'Traveling Riverside Blues', shamelessly claimed composer credits for a number which they now said was called 'The Lemon Song'.

The crude technical quality of these recordings, Johnson's inspired but approximate guitar phrasing and the keening edge of desperation in his haunted vocals conspire to make this a collection that could not be more out of step with the pristine values of the CD medium. The fact that Johnson's work is finally receiving more widespread attention than at any time in the past bears witness to the truism that no matter how sophisticated the technology becomes, it is the inherent quality of the music that counts.

B.B. King

Born: Riley B. King, September 16 1925, Indianola, Mississippi
US No.25 album: 1971: *Live in Cook County Jail* (unavailable)

A figure of towering authority and seemingly boundless goodwill, B.B. King initiated a blues style that became a cornerstone of rock guitar playing. His intuitive way of placing high, arching notes held on with extreme left-hand vibrato, followed by swiftly dancing clusters of notes and heavy, half-vamped clunks was a paramount influence on the playing style of Eric CLAPTON, and hence virtually every blues-based rock guitarist that followed.

Yet, as a young man living in the heart of the Mississippi delta, the chances of King even owning an electric guitar were remote. He worked picking cotton for a wage of $22.50 a week, and the prospect of buying one of the $200–$300 guitars he saw in the Sears & Roebuck catalogues was not enhanced by the fact that there was no electricity in his part of town.

Striking out in 1946, King moved north to Memphis in search of work as a musician. Initially none was forthcoming, but in 1948 he won a regular ten-minute slot on a black music radio station, WDIA, and word of his highly charged performances in the Beale Street blues clubs began to spread. He cut his first record in 1949, and has maintained an intensive recording and touring schedule ever since, releasing more than 70 albums and averaging close to 300 one-nighters per year since the early Fifties.

King regards himself as a worldwide ambassador of the blues, a task which he performs with messianic zeal. As well as regular visits to the established markets of Europe, Japan and Australasia, he has in recent years taken his band to Africa, Israel, South America and the Soviet Union.

He is renowned for his benefit work, including regular concerts at prisons. At the last count he had three honorary doctorates, one of them from Yale. He returns each year to his old neighbourhood, where he puts on a weekend of free concerts and catches up with childhood friends, some of whom still work on the same plantation.

Like his blues-playing contemporary John Lee HOOKER, King has provided invaluable inspiration to the architects of rock, and has, in return, received sporadic endorsements by sundry celebs. On *Indianola Mississippi Seeds* (Castle Communications CLACD 141; 1970) he is joined by Joe Walsh, Leon Russell and Carole King.

More recently, U2 recruited him to provide lead vocals and a succession of stinging guitar breaks on their song 'When Love Comes to Town' (from the album *Rattle and Hum*). Released as a single in 1989, 'When Love Comes to Town' reached No.6 in the UK, introducing King, at a stroke, to a vast new audience.

- *Live at the Regal* (unavailable) [1964]
- *Live in Cook County Jail* (unavailable) [1971]

Despite his prolific output, King is one of those road-hardened performers who never does full justice to his art in the studio, and quite frankly, he's knocked out too many long players too indiscriminately for anyone to expect that he should (roughly two a year for forty years, while maintaining a non-stop touring itinerary). His best albums have invariably been live recordings and although the most celebrated of these have not had the benefit of a CD release in this country, they are usually obtainable, at a price, as US imports.

Live at the Regal (MCA [USA] 31106) catches King on peak form in a Chicago theatre playing material which was to form the backbone of his set for many years to come, notably 'Everyday I Have the Blues' 'How Blue Can You Get' and 'It's My Own Fault'.

Live in Cook County Jail (MCA [USA] 31080) is a similarly barnstorming affair, with the jovial King entertaining a captive audience in rafter-raising mood. The set-list includes 'Worry Worry', 'Three O'Clock Blues' and 'The Thrill is Gone', King's only (US) Top 20 single.

Wouldn't it be great if MCA could be persuaded to stick both of these albums on to one CD and give it a mid-price UK release?

- **Best of B.B. King** (MCA CMCAD 31040) [1973]

So far there has been no sensible CD anthology of B.B. King. This old collection from his days with the ABC label in America is still the one which most neatly sums up the essence of this expansive man's portfolio. 'Caldonia', 'Ain't Nobody Home', 'Nobody Loves Me But My Mother' and the studio version of 'The Thrill is Gone' are among its treasures.

- **Midnight Believer** (MCA DMCL 1802) [1978]

In the later stages of his career, King has tended to make albums in a plush, soul-funk idiom, which upsets the purists, but provides a fine setting for his wonderfully soulful yet frequently over-looked singing. Every album is accompanied by a press release or sleeve note quote from King saying 'This is the best album I've ever made', a statement that is nearly always a triumph of hope over experience.

However, *Midnight Believer*, recorded with The Crusaders, is certainly his best in this latter-day style. Foremost among several strong tracks is the relaxed gait of 'When It All Comes Down' and the delicate, unforced pathos of 'Hold On', one of his most profoundly stirring performances in this or any other vein.

Kool and The Gang

Convened: 1969, Jersey City, New Jersey
Robert 'Kool' Bell (f) – bass; Ronald Bell (f) – saxophone/
keyboards; George Brown (f) – drums; James 'J.T.' Taylor –
vocals; Claydes Smith – guitar; Curtis 'Fitz' Williams –
keyboards
UK No.4 album: 1983: *Twice as Kool* (unavailable)

For a group with such a disproportionately low profile, Kool and
The Gang maintained a phenomenal strike rate throughout the
Eighties. In Britain they notched up 22 hit singles between 1979
and 1989 and were the only American act to feature on Bob
Geldof's superstar Band Aid single 'Do They Know It's Christmas?'. In America their platinum No.1 single 'Celebration'
redefined the concept of 'crossover' when it became the officially
endorsed soundtrack to the 1981 Superbowl, the winning of the
Democratic presidential nomination by Walter Mondale and the
greeting of the hostages returning from the American embassy
siege in Iran in 1981.

Yet thanks to an anonymously collective image, several
changes of line-up and the rather generic quality of their party-
time soul music, Kool and The Gang are still not as well known as
faded contemporaries such as Chic, The Commodores and Earth
Wind And Fire, let alone more current big names like Lionel Richie
and George Benson.

Roughly speaking the FLEETWOOD MAC of soul, Kool and The
Gang is led from the rear by a rhythm section that has held
together since 1964, anchoring a front line that has changed to
match the prevailing stylistic trends of the day. The Bell brothers,
bassist Robert (aka 'Kool') and saxophonist Ronald, started out
playing with drummer George Brown and various others, in a
fusion band called The Jazziacs in 1964. The group evolved from
its jazz roots, undergoing a series of name and personnel
changes before emerging as Kool and The Gang, a street-funk
band operating in the musical tradition of SLY AND THE FAMILY
STONE and James BROWN, but without the vocal theatrics at the
front.

Their early US hits – 'Funky Stuff' (1973) and 'Jungle Boogie'
(1974) – were sketchy, horn-led instrumentals, punctuated by
chunky rhythm guitar and in-your-face bass licks. However, the

band was quick to compromise with the disco revolution of the late Seventies, smoothing out their sound to fit 'Open Sesame' on to the colossally successful soundtrack of *Saturday Night Fever* (RSO 800 068-2; 1977) – 30 million copies sold at the last count.

In 1978 they switched direction completely, recruiting James 'J.T.' Taylor as the group's first featured vocalist, and immediately a golden run of hits began. The first album to feature Taylor, *Ladies Night* (De-Lite 822 737-2; 1979, deleted March 1990) was a US Top 10 hit, and the single 'Ladies Night' finally opened their account in the UK, where it peaked at No.9.

The floodgates opened, and in the next five years Kool and The Gang enjoyed more US hits than any other act, their nearest competitors being Michael JACKSON, PRINCE and DIRE STRAITS. Their popularity was consolidated by a spectacular stage show which married the special effects flavour of a Stephen Spielberg movie to the sweat and grind of a Sixties soul revue.

But in 1986 James Taylor departed to pursue a solo career and the spell was broken. The band recruited three vocalists to replace him – Gary Brown, Skip Martin and Odeen Mays – but the post-Taylor material has failed to recapture the magic.

● *The Singles Collection* (De-Lite 836 636-2) [1988]

With a dearth of new songs to match the glories of their back catalogue, Kool and The Gang went on a recycling binge. This is the best of several retrospective compilations that appeared towards the end of the Eighties, and incorporates all the biggest hits: 'Ladies Night', 'Celebration', 'Get Down On It', 'Ooh La La La (Let's Go Dancin')', 'Joanna', '(When You Say You Love Somebody) In the Heart', 'Cherish' and the rest.

● *Great and Remixed '91* (Mercury 848 604-2) [1991]

A bunch of the best known Kool and The Gang songs surfaces again, this time remixed and remodelled by three of the hottest producers of the day, Ben Liebrand, Oliver Momm and Youth.

'Ladies Night', 'Get Down On It' and the inevitable 'Celebration' are bolstered by some of the really old material, including the first two US hits, 'Funky Stuff' and 'Jungle Boogie'. This throws an illuminating perspective on the two very distinct phases of Kool and The Gang's career, the early material boasting lots of raucous chants, choppy bass-drum kicks and crisp horn-section motifs, while the later stuff is guided by a metronomic pulse, smooth washes of keyboards and the slick soul vocals of James Taylor.

Hearing it all strung together and spruced up like this, it is nevertheless obvious that the two styles are simply different sides of the same coin. As if to prove the point, the final track, 'The Megamix', is a seamlessly remixed medley of 'Funky Stuff'/'Get Down On It'/'Ladies Night' and all the others, overlaid with a sprinkling of electronic percussion and a little street-wise rapping of unidentified provenance. Not only do all the elements blend together into a perfectly homogenous cocktail, it also sounds ridiculously modern for a band which started out as jazz-funk fusionists more than two decades ago.

Lenny Kravitz

Born: May 26 1964, New York
UK No.8 album: 1991: *Mama Said* (Virgin America 261326)

Lenny Kravitz bowled into view in 1989 touting an image and a sound that was so far out it quickly became in. Like his flared jeans, hippy-length dreadlocks and Carnaby Street chic, his music originates in another era, yet has carved an impressive contemporary niche. In a Nineties pop scene that resembles a vast extension of *All Our Yesterdays*, Kravitz is the perfect yesterday man.

Of mixed Russian Jewish and black Bahamian parentage, Kravitz moved as a teenager from New York to Los Angeles where he joined the California Boys Choir. Having taught himself from an early age to play piano and guitar (and later drums and bass), he learned music theory and eventually sang with the Metropolitan Opera Company of New York, while writing and recording the rock music demos that eventually won him a recording contract.

Blessed with great reserves of energy and a quixotic charm, Kravitz quickly became the new darling of the rock élite. MADONNA asked him to write her a song and the result was her 1991 hit 'Justify my Love'. Yoko Ono recruited him for her ill-fated concert

tribute to John LENNON, staged in Liverpool in 1990. And together
with Sean Lennon (John and Yoko's son), Kravitz presided over
the Band Aid-style charity recording of 'Give Peace a Chance'
which was released, ironically, on the day war started in the Gulf
in 1991.

● *Let Love Rule* (Virgin America CDVUS 10) [1989]

This exciting début established Kravitz as a maverick talent with
a quaint obsession for psychedelic pop garnished with raw funk
trimmings. Veering from the magical-mystery-tour cadences of 'I
Build This Garden for You' to the pumped-up beat-pop of 'Mr
Cab Driver' and 'Flower Child', it is a lot of not-so-innocent fun
that indicates pretty clearly where Kravitz is coming from. The
musical flavours are redolent of The BEATLES, Jimi HENDRIX and
PRINCE, while Kravitz also cites Curtis Mayfield, Bob MARLEY and
John LENNON's solo work as primary among his influences.

Produced and almost entirely performed by Kravitz himself,
the album has a robust, primitive vitality. Ever the technological
refusenik, Kravitz chose to use outdated analogue recording
equipment, Sixties microphones and even 12-year-old master
tape to record the album. 'It just sounds better,' he said.

● *Mama Said* (Virgin America 261326) [1991]

In the wake of Kravitz's escalating worldwide popularity, this was
a much bigger commercial success than *Let Love Rule*, but it covers
no new ground and by the time of its release Kravitz's whole retro
stance was becoming rather self-conscious. The sound on this disc
is dreadful – as if you were listening to vinyl with a big wodge of
fluff on the needle – but that is apparently what Kravitz was
aiming for.

'My whole reason for going back isn't to be cute or retro, it's to
return to when the tape sounded good,' he told *Q* magazine. 'You
put on a record like *Led Zeppelin I*, T. Rex, Stevie WONDER's
Innervisions, *Let it Bleed*, Bob MARLEY, all the great recordings from
that era from the late Sixties to the early Seventies. Man . . . the
sound never got any better than that. It started to get worse. All
those digital reverbs, digital mixing desks, that *noo* equipment all

sounds like shit to me. It doesn't make the music sound pure or natural or true.'

A moot point, but on disc, Kravitz's attempts to turn the clock back can sound uncomfortably contrived. A case in point is the highly stylised 'Philly sound' pastiche, 'It Ain't Over 'Til It's Over', an untypical track that turned out to be his biggest hit single in both Britain and America.

Led Zeppelin

Convened: 1968, London. Split up: 1980. Reconvened 1985 (Live Aid), 1988 (Atlantic Records 40th Anniversary)
John Bonham (f) (died 25.9.80) – drums/vocals; John Paul Jones (f) – bass/keyboards/vocals; Jimmy Page (f) – guitar/vocals; Robert Plant (f) – vocals/harmonica

UK/US No.1 albums:	1969: *Led Zeppelin II* (Atlantic 240 037)
	1970: *Led Zeppelin III* (Atlantic 250 002)
	1973: *Houses of the Holy* (Atlantic 19130-2)
	1975: *Physical Graffiti* (Swan Song 289 400)
	1976: *Presence* (Swan Song 259 402)
	1979: *In Through the Out Door* (Swan Song 259 410)
UK No.1 albums:	1971: *Untitled (Four Symbols)* (Atlantic 250 008)
	1976: *The Song Remains the Same* (Swan Song 289 402)

While The BEATLES steered rock through its infancy during the Sixties, Led Zeppelin took over the reins some time after puberty in the Seventies, transforming a precocious child into a pan-global Goliath. Under the maverick managership of Peter Grant they flouted pop conventions, disdaining to appear on television and never issuing singles in the UK – even their most famous song 'Stairway to Heaven' was only ever available on the group's untitled fourth album (see below).

Instead they toured their way to superstardom, blazing a trail on the emergent American stadium circuit and creating a word-of-mouth legend that eventually became bigger than the band itself ever was.

Although born of the Sixties' blues boom, they replaced the hippy ideals of peace and love with darker shades of mysticism and sexual braggadocio. Jimmy Page's violently aggressive, heavy-duty riffing combined with John Bonham's primeval back-beat and Robert Plant's penile shriek to create a formula which spawned a legion of imitators and unwittingly sparked off the heavy metal genre.

Rising from the ashes of Sixties psyhco-blues-rock band The Yardbirds, in whose ranks Page had replaced Jeff BECK, Led Zeppelin became rôle models for a style of rock whose distinguishing trait was excess in all areas. As an adjunct to the untold millions of records sold, they pursued a hedonistic, hotel-wrecking, partying-all-hours lifestyle to which Bonham eventually succumbed, the victim of alcohol poisoning after a prodigious bout of lunchtime drinking.

Key players in the creation of modern rock mythology, Zeppelin's memory remains one of the wildest wonders of contemporary popular music.

- *Led Zeppelin* (Atlantic 240 031) [1969]
- *Led Zeppelin II* (Atlantic 240 037) [1969]

The Led Zeppelin début established an awesomely muscular, blues-derived formula that extended from a souped up version of Willie Dixon's divine slow blues 'I Can't Quit You Baby' to the 2.26-minute proto-thrash of 'Communication Breakdown'. The mordant, pile-driving riff of 'Dazed and Confused' with its nebulous, orgasmic interlude was a prelude to the extremes in store.

On the staggeringly successful follow-up, *Led Zeppelin II*, released just eight months later, the fireworks began in earnest with the definitive power-chord riff and explosive aural sex sequence of 'Whole Lotta Love'. Other highlights on an album which sometimes seems a little too upfront for its own good, include Page's defiantly ragged, unaccompanied solo break in 'Heartbreaker' and Plant's ineffably salacious, hormones-a-go-go delivery of 'The Lemon Song', a thinly disguised rip-off of Howlin

Wolf's song 'Killing Floor', still brazenly credited here to Page/Plant/Jones/Bonham.

- *Led Zeppelin III* (Atlantic 250 002) [1970]

By way of contrast to its predecessor, here was the pastoral, acoustic side of the band. There are rockers – notably 'Immigrant Song' – but the flavour is better defined by the folk textures of 'Gallows Pole' and the rootsy acoustic-slide guitar interjections of 'Hats Off to (Roy) Harper'.

- [Untitled] (Atlantic 250 008) [1971]

The untitled fourth album houses the elegaic masterpiece 'Stairway To Heaven', Zeppelin's most celebrated song, along with 'Black Dog', 'Rock and Roll' and 'When the Levee Breaks'. A gilt-edged, monster-selling Zeppelin album, although curiously one of the few which failed to top the US chart.

- *Physical Graffiti* (Swan Song 289 400) [1975]

Perhaps the last great Zeppelin album in the classic mould, this double set is divided into one weighty disc ('In My Time of Dying', 'Trampled Underfoot', 'Kashmir') and one not-so-essential disc ('The Wanton Song', 'Boogie with Stu').

- *In Through the Out Door* (Swan Song 259 410) [1979]

Reviled by the punk generation and unsure of their place in the scheme of things, Zeppelin nevertheless came back with no little panache with what was to be their last album of new recordings. The guitar-hero angle was played down, and Jones was given free rein to make this by far the most keyboard-orientated of their albums. In producing a fine set of songs, including 'In the Evening', 'Carouselambra' and 'All My Love', they did not pander to expectations or fall back on the old routines. Truly, a dignified exit.

- *Led Zeppelin (Box Set)* (Atlantic 7567-82144-2) [1990]
- *Remasters* (7567-80415-2; deleted) [1990]

Despite and probably even because of their megalithic popularity, the hip response to Led Zeppelin was, for many years, that of implacable disdain for their old-school power riffs and macho posturing. 'I don't even have to listen to their music,' said Paul Simonon of punk visionaries The CLASH. 'Just looking at one of their album covers makes me want to vomit.'

A reappraisal of the band began gathering momentum in the mid-Eighties when the influence of Zeppelin's omnipotent musical presence during the preceding decade began to make itself felt in fields as diverse as hip hop and hardcore. After James BROWN, Led Zeppelin has become one of the most frequently sampled acts of the Seventies. Bonham's drum intro to 'When the Levee Breaks' (from the fourth album) is always showing up in odd places, but the most brazen steal was probably that of The Beastie Boys, who lifted the riff of 'The Ocean' (from *Houses of the Holy*) for their song 'She's Crafty'.

But, in the fullness of time, it is the essential integrity of Zeppelin's music which has emerged most clearly. Thanks to Grant's astute management and stringent quality control, their legacy has remained just ten great albums (eight of them UK No.1s) with no messy compilations or cheap-shot repackages to tarnish the purity of their reputation.

The posthumous silence was eventually broken, but the tradition of excellence maintained, by the snappily titled *Led Zeppelin*, a handsome four-CD boxed set comprising 54 of the best tracks from the group's catalogue, selected and ordered by the three surviving members of the band and painstakingly remastered by Jimmy Page himself. A condensed, double-CD version entitled *Remasters* was deleted soon after its release, and the boxed set has latterly become unofficially (and very confusingly) known as *Remasters*.

The idea for the compilation was initiated by Page, who was dissatisfied with the sound of the existing Zeppelin CDs. 'I didn't think the quality was very good on them,' he said. 'I really wanted to have a crack at improving the overall sound spectrum.'

The vexed question of the variable sound quality of CDs where old analogue tape recordings have been transferred on to the new digital format without being remastered is discussed in the introduction of this book. Comparing the remastered versions of Zeppelin's material with the CD originals, there can be no doubt that, even on standard domestic hi-fi equipment, the remastered versions have greater clarity and presence. The dense mesh of interlocking guitar lines on 'Celebration Day', for instance, is much more readily disentangled; the remorseless thump of Bonham's kit in 'Kashmir' just that shade punchier.

But let's not get things out of perspective. Page presumably heard the old Zeppelin CDs on state-of-the-art equipment. Having produced the albums himself he would have been aware of minute variations in bias and equalisation, and he was in a position to call for improvements.

Consider, however, the review of Zeppelin's back catalogue on CD by Paul Du Noyer in the September 1987 edition of *Q* magazine, the rock CD-buyer's Bible. Du Noyer, an experienced reviewer who went on to become *Q*'s editor, had no complaints about the quality of the sound on those original CDs – quite the reverse. 'In fact we can hear it [Led Zeppelin's music] more distinctly now than ever before,' he wrote. 'Thanks to modern technology, it has become possible to experience rock music's closest approximation to a medieval bloodbath ... in complete sonic fidelity, within the comfort and privacy of your own home.'

Of course, the subsequently remastered material *is* superior, but don't feel you have to chuck your old CDs in the bin just yet.

Actually, the most striking overall feature of the remastered anthology is the sheer breadth of Zeppelin's musical portfolio. I liked them best when they were doing their sub-metal deconstructions of the blues – stuff like 'Since I've Been Loving You' and the epic 'I Can't Quit you Baby' the version here recorded (unbelievably) off the cuff at a sound check in 1970.

But as numbers like 'Bron-Y-Aur Stomp' underline, they also took their acoustic side seriously, and it was the seamless combination of folky lyricism and heavy rock which provided their most ubiquitous anthem, 'Stairway to Heaven'.

Later, as Jones extended his interest in keyboards, they took on board the synthesiser revolution without missing a step and, if nothing else, this astounding compilation should lay to rest the fallacious idea that Led Zeppelin was simply a mouth and trousers heavy metal prototype.

Robert Plant

Born: August 20 1948, West Bromwich, West Midlands
UK No.2 album: 1982: *Pictures at Eleven* (Swan Song SK 259418)

Jimmy Page may have been the dark soul of Led Zeppelin, but it was Robert Plant who actually got off his arse and built a solo career of any note after the group's demise.

Plant earned success and commanded respect partly by going with the musical grain of his past while not attempting either to recreate or compete with it, and partly by sticking to the job in hand.

While John Paul Jones noodled around doing film soundtracks and earning himself the odd producer credit with bands like The Mission, and Page co-founded with vocalist Paul Rodgers a short-lived metal supergroup called The Firm (see under FREE), Plant has turned out a series of elegantly poised albums with just enough power and bite to remind you where he's from, but none of the naff old blarney that so frequently besets the work of superannuated heavy rockers like Ozzy Osbourne.

- *Now and Zen* (Es Paranza 790 863-2) [1988]
- *Manic Nirvana* (Es Paranza 7567-91336-2) [1990]

By the time of his fourth and fifth albums Plant was producing songs of a calibre streets ahead of anything a revamped Led Zeppelin might hope to achieve. With strong support from the same young, agile band on both these albums, he plays to his strengths with alert good humour.

The strangulated yells and sweeping glissandos of his glory days have been superseded on *Now and Zen* by a cooler, more reflective delivery, heard to especially good effect on the ballad 'Ship of Fools' and the haunting 'The Way I Feel', a song of measured grandeur that winds up with a sparkling guitar hook.

Manic Nirvana is mostly given over to the subject of the leonine raver's rampant libido, with tracks including 'Nirvana' ('The loin [sic] sleeps tonight'), 'Big Love' ('She loves to go down. . . .'), 'S S S & Q' ('I'll kiss your flower anywhere'), which speak for themselves.

John Lennon

Born: October 9 1940, Liverpool. Died: December 8 1980
UK/US No.1 albums: 1971: *Imagine* (EMI CDP 746 641-2)
1980: *Double Fantasy* (Capitol CDP 791 425-2)
UK No.1 album: 1982: *The John Lennon Collection* (Parlophone CDP 791 516-2)
US No.1 album: 1974: *Walls and Bridges* (Parlophone CDP 746 768-2)

'Part of me suspects that I'm a loser and the other part of me thinks I'm God Almighty,' John Lennon told *Playboy* magazine the year he died. This was the kind of contradiction which mirrored the progress of his solo career, a frustrating, stop-start affair impelled by an awkward combination of truculence, indolence and erratic bursts of genius.

By far the most complex personality of the four ex-BEATLES, Lennon's status as the group's supposed genius-in-residence meant that more was expected of him as a solo artist than of the other three. But while his enquiring mind and spirit of adventure led him to places that the rest of the group would never have ventured, his grasp of melody was never as firm as McCARTNEY's.

True, McCARTNEY's post-BEATLES work tended to be lighter than Aero (and almost as consistent), but did Lennon really achieve a great deal more? Egged on by the ever-present Yoko Ono, he spent much of his time, when he wasn't transposing political slogans into disposable musical statements, tramping around the darker recesses of his soul in a pair of lead boots, before retiring for five years to become a 'house-husband'.

The hard truth is that Lennon was admired as a solo act for what he represented much more than for what he achieved.

• *John Lennon/Plastic Ono Band* (EMI CDP 746 770-2) [1970]

A rough-hewn gem, this album was recorded mostly at Lennon's home studio at his Georgian manor in Ascot. Lennon played all the guitar parts and some piano, while the so-called Plastic Ono Band – not a real band so much as an all-purpose rubric which Lennon coined to describe whichever supporting musicians were involved in any of his or Yoko's projects – comprised on this occasion Ringo Starr (drums), Klaus Voorman (bass) and Billy Preston (keyboards).

It was his first solo album since the break-up of The BEATLES, and Lennon took the opportunity to offload a ton of highly personal angst in lyrics which Robert Christgau memorably described as 'crude psychotherapeutic clichés'. Most notable in this regard are 'Mother' and 'My Mummy's Dead', which give full vent to the neuroses Lennon had apparently acquired in childhood because of his mother's indifferent manner and premature death.

'God' is a trenchant renunciation of idols, both the religious and the rock'n'roll variety, in which he expresses the simple article of faith by which his post-BEATLE life was to be guided: 'I just believe in me, Yoko and me/That's reality.'

But it is 'Working Class Hero' which, despite its rather self-pitying tone, rams home the feelings of bitterness and alienation that fuelled Lennon's unreliable muse, and that it seemed no amount of wealth or fame could eradicate. This song is, arguably, the most powerful and unequivocal statement of his entire solo career.

With its sparse, rugged sound, the album was a modest success, but garnered nothing like the sales or acclaim which Lennon had enjoyed as a matter of course with The BEATLES.

● *Imagine* (EMI CDP 746 641-2) [1971]

'Now I understand what you have to do,' said Lennon once *Imagine* had achieved the huge transatlantic success which had eluded the preceding *Plastic Ono Band* album. 'Put your political message across with a little honey.'

With soul-baring songs like 'Jealous Guy' and 'Oh My Love', the implausibly anti-materialist title track and the mean-spirited McCARTNEY put-downs 'How Do You Sleep?' and 'Crippled Inside', this remains Lennon's best known and most fondly remembered work. Produced with little flair by the fading Phil Spector and featuring George HARRISON on guitar, it is a strangely dour collection with no real spring in its step.

● *Rock'n'Roll* (Parlophone CDP 746 707-2) [1975]

After the dismal pseudo-politico peregrinations of *Mind Games*

(Parlophone CDP 746 769-2; 1973) and *Walls and Bridges* (see above), it was a relief to hear Lennon tackling a collection of covers from his teddy-boy past with something approaching the raucous conviction of his youth. The peculiarly harsh timbre of his runtish, white-rock voice – with its simultaneously snappy and vulnerable cast – is showcased on unselfconscious readings of numbers such as Gene Vincent's 'Be Bop a Lula', Ben E. King's 'Stand By Me', Chuck BERRY's 'Sweet Little Sixteen' and Buddy Holly's 'Peggy Sue'.

Here, then, was a timely reminder of the great music that had got him into the whole millionaire rock'n'roll star mess in the first place. It was also the last anyone was to hear of him for five years, barring a compilation of singles bearing the mysterious title of *Shaved Fish* (EMI CDP746 642-2; 1975).

• *Double Fantasy* (Capitol CDP 791 425-2) [1980]

The tragedy of Lennon's violent and premature death hoisted his comeback album (released the previous month) to the top of the charts, while obscuring its rather patchy quality. Comprising seven tracks by Lennon and seven by Yoko, it undoubtedly boasts flashes of the old magic with 'Watching the Wheels' and the poignant '(Just Like) Starting Over'. But 'Woman' is Lennon at his most bathetic, while the rest of his tracks are unmemorable, to put it kindly. The less said about Yoko's contribution the better.

• *The John Lennon Collection* (Parlophone CDP 791 516-2) [1982]

With the exception of *John Lennon/Plastic Ono Band* (see above), this greatest hits compilation is the only essential John Lennon album. From the living hell of 'Cold Turkey' to the feel-good sloganeering and knockabout chants of 'Give Peace a Chance' and 'Merry Xmas (War is Over)', Lennon has always had his heart, if not his music, in the right place. This harvests the best of the crop, including 'Imagine', 'Jealous Guy', 'Mind Games' and 'Instant Karma' among other perennials.

Level 42

Convened: 1980, London
Gary Husband – drums/vocals; Mark King (f) – vocals/bass;
Mike Lindup (f) – keyboards/vocals
UK No.2 albums: 1987: *Running in the Family* (Polydor 831
593-2)
1988: *Staring at the Sun* (Polydor 837 247-
2)

The foundations of Level 42's success seem to be as unshakable as
they are unlikely. On the one hand they are revered among the
serious 'muso' fraternity for their technical expertise: Mark King
is *always* voted Best Bassist by the readers of technical magazines
like *Making Music* and *International Musician*. Yet they are also
adored by a mass of soft-core pop fans who go for their shopping-
mall soul melodies and homely, boy-girl lyrics. Somewhere in
between is the Ford Cortina crowd with their fluffy dice and bass-
heavy woofers, who find Level 42's slick funk overdrive the
perfect accompaniment to life in the fast-to-middling lane.

The group's original line-up of King, Lindup and the brothers
Boon and Phil Gould (guitar and drums respectively) got together
in London, although King and the Goulds all came from the Isle of
Wight. Initially an instrumental jazz-rock band, it wasn't long
before the thumb-thwacking King developed a smooth line in
vocal appliqué and they gained access to the charts via the disco
dance-floor.

It was pure coincidence that they came to prominence during
the brief era of glamorous pop stars like Boy George and Duran
Duran, since Level 42 never had much in the way of looks or
image to help them. They depended instead on the old-fashioned
virtues of superior musicianship and hard work. Indeed, their
output was almost as rapid as King's overheated bass-playing: in
just four years from August 1981 they released eight albums
(including a solo project by King).

Perhaps it was not surprising that in December 1987 the Gould
brothers retired, Boon suffering from an ulcer and Phil from
nervous exhaustion. They were replaced by Gary Husband (ex-
Allan Holdsworth's band) and guitarist Alan Murphy (ex-Go
West; died 19.10.89).

The group fell out with Polydor over their album *Guaranteed*

(RCA PD 75055; 1991). The record company insisted that improvements be made before it was released. They had a point; it is a strangely lacklustre set, but Level 42 took umbrage, then legal advice, and are now signed to a different company.

Since Murphy's demise from pneumonia with complications related to AIDS, the remaining trio has hired in the guitar-playing services of Jakko Jakszyk and techno-jazz genius Allan Holdsworth, according to requirement and availability.

● *World Machine* (Polydor 827 487-2) [1985]

After a slow start in the autumn of 1985, *World Machine* took up residence in the UK chart for the whole of 1986. Produced by Paris-based keyboardist Wally Badarou, it extended the group's appeal to the heart of the pop market, while maintaining their hard core fan base intact. This was crossover with a vengeance and Level 42's tensile jazz-funk sound was ubiquitous throughout 1986 in the singles, albums, dance, soul and CD charts, as well as boutiques, restaurants, clubs and concert halls around the world. The hits were 'Leaving Me Now' and 'Something About You', the latter being the group's only release to breach the US Top 10.

● *Running in the Family* (Polydor 831 593-2) [1987]

This was the one where it all came together. With the unique combination of slap-happy, disco-funk rhythms and killer pop choruses having been further refined, *Running in the Family* produced significant hits with the title track, 'Children Say', 'It's Over', 'To Be With You Again' and the high-stepping 'Lessons in Love', possibly their finest song and certainly one of King's best bass lines.

Also notable is the frantic fusion of 'Fashion Fever' and the exceptional but strangely overlooked melody of 'Two Solitudes'. King keeps his restless thumb more firmly in the pocket than on previous excursions and the grooves are generally ridden with a modest panache.

● *Level Best* (Polydor 841 399-2) [1989]

There was no shortage of material when it came to compiling a greatest hits collection. As well as the obvious inclusions, the album reprises early favourites, such as the breezy 'Starchild', 'Love Games', 'The Chinese Way' and the perennial live set-piece 'Hot Water', all songs which underline the remarkably consistent flavour which the band has maintained during an unusually industrious innings.

Madonna

Born: Madonna Louise Ciccone, August 16 1959, Detroit, Michigan

UK/US No.1 albums: 1984: *Like a Virgin* (Sire 925 181-2)
                    1986: *True Blue* (Sire 241 049-2)
                    1989: *Like a Prayer* (Sire 925 844-2)
UK No.1 album: 1990: *The Immaculate Collection* (Sire 7599-26440-2)

She is the biggest-selling female recording artist of all time. As far as her former beau Warren Beatty is concerned she has no private life left to live, so completely has she sacrificed her personality on the altar of self-publicity. She has the clout to bring the entire Cannes Film Festival, the world's press and Terry Wogan to worship at her feet.

On stage she simulates masturbation beneath a huge gold cross, then dresses in a cleric's costume and seduces a 'priest', a routine which so impressed a Vatican official that he described her act as 'one of the most satanic shows in the history of humanity'.

But who knows what really makes Madonna tick? The corps of armchair psychologists disguised as the world's rock press have been quick to point to her traumatised childhood. The eldest daughter of Catholic-Italian parents, Madonna was six when her mother died of breast cancer. Her father remarried, but even so, a lot of adult responsibilities came her way early in life. 'I feel like all my adolescence was spent taking care of babies,' she told reporter Denise Worrell in 1985. 'I saw myself as the quintessential Cinderella. You know, I have this stepmother and I have all this work and I never go out and I don't have pretty dresses.'

She took piano lessons until she could persuade her father to spend the money on dance classes instead, and later won a dance scholarship to the University of Michigan, where she stayed for one and a half years before cutting loose to seek her fortune in New York City. Although she arrived there homeless and, so the story goes, with $35 in her back pocket, she quickly became established with the drifting fraternity of musicians, learning to play drums and guitar along the way, and eventually securing a recording contract in 1982.

The whole of Madonna's subsequent, astonishing, worldwide success has certainly been greater than the sum of the musical parts would suggest, given a portfolio bulging with neat, disco-orientated, pop tunes, sung in a capable if undistinguished voice. 'I couldn't be a success without also being a sex symbol,' was her ambiguous comment in *Spin* magazine on the matter of her brash yet remote sexual-fantasy image.

Over the years, the fish-net tights and severely cut corsetry may have intrigued the boys, but at the outset it was the teenage girls who found her provocative *décolletage* irresistibly enthralling. To them Madonna was a daring anti-authority rôle model, powerful enough to flaunt herself as she pleases without having to answer to the affronted morality of either conservative parents or feminist elder sisters. It is a measure of her strength as an icon that those teenagers and Madonna have grown up together, leaving the rest of the adult rock establishment little choice but to fall into line behind them.

Among all the controversy, one thing is clear: Madonna is not a manipulated idol. She co-writes the majority of her songs, and has co-produced all her albums since *True Blue* in 1986. On stage her strong, muscular body reflects a poise and physical confidence that could not be further removed from notions of weakness or compliance. The constant factor in all her *outré* costume changes are her practical, low-heeled boots which enable her to move with a sure, cat-like agility, using her sex only as blatantly and in the same dominant way as many a male rock star from PRESLEY onwards has done. She says 'Fuck' whether or not she is being broadcast live by the BBC.

Her fans used to be personified as aspirant 'wanna be' types, but it is more of a 'can do' philosophy which has seen Madonna emerge as the woman on top in the Nineties: light on soul, an uncomfortable mixture of traditional and modern values, but always uncompromisingly of the moment.

● *Like a Prayer* (Sire 925 844-2) [1989]

A carefully written and meticulously produced batch of modern pop songs that ache a little, bounce a lot and promise nothing more than they can ultimately deliver, this was the collection that finally brought Madonna the credibility she had long desired.

But it is still difficult to judge how much of her music is the product of real feelings and how much of it is a coolly calculated exercise in line with the latest marketing strategies. The mildly titillating mixture of religious and sexual imagery that propelled the title track to No.1 and led to its being banned in Italy of all places (where TV broadcasting norms are reputedly the most permissive in the world) is a good case in point.

The best art reflects life, but there is an unhealthy neatness about the way in which the melodrama of the real-life break-up of Madonna's marriage to Sean Penn provides romantic lyrical fodder for 'Till Death Do Us Part', which is delivered in a robotic, semi-rap style reminiscent of Blondie's 'Rapture': 'He takes a drink, she goes inside/He starts to scream, the vases fly'.

Elsewhere the delights are mixed. The all-purpose funk/pop of 'Express Yourself' is one of those superficial neo-soul singalongs with roots in Motown and feet of clay, while 'Cherish' is bobby-socks pop of a sort to give the younger generation of Kylies a run for their money.

But there *is* a new-found maturity in material like 'Love Song', a lascivious, slow funk work-out co-written with Prince, and 'Keep it Together', a hot-blooded up-tempo dance track in which Madonna explores her thoughts about family ties.

The epilogue is an intriguing throwaway collage of atmospherics called 'Act of Contrition' where a wildly distorted taped-in-reverse guitar provides the backdrop to Madonna's voice, solemnly reciting a prayer, then suddenly bawling out a hotel receptionist about a room reservation. It all sounds wantonly bizarre and marvellously subversive.

● *The Immaculate Collection* (Sire 7599-26440-2) [1990]

It is easy to forget that Madonna used to be the Kylie of her day. The excitable sleeve notes of this, her only 'greatest hits' retrospective, describe her early records as music that 'literally shook the world'. However, listening again to the pert pop arrangements of 'Holiday', 'Borderline', 'Material Girl' and 'Crazy For You', they sound more like songs that were designed to shake the teeny-bop money tree, and in that regard every bit as calculated as anything that Stock, Aitken and Waterman subsequently came up with.

Nevertheless, Madonna began seriously to buck the system around the time of her 1986 album *True Blue* (see above), which was when she took a grip on the songwriting and production reins, and broadened her market with the brazen controversy of 'Papa Don't Preach' and the lush, romantic lilt of 'La Isla Bonita'.

With several notable omissions ('Who's That Girl?', 'True Blue', 'Causing a Commotion' and others), *The Immaculate Collection* is a tidy summary of events up to 1990's ode to posing, 'Vogue', and the steamy funk-up of 'Justify My Love' (written by Lenny KRAVITZ), music of a significantly greater specific gravity than that of the chirpy fare with which Madonna launched herself.

Bob Marley and The Wailers

Convened [as The Wailing Wailers]: 1964, Kingston, Jamaica. Split up: 1981
Bob Marley (Born: February 6 1945, St. Ann's, Jamaica. Died: May 11 1981) (f) – vocals/guitar; Aston 'Family Man' Barrett – bass; Carlton Barrett (died 17.4.87) – drums; Peter Tosh (f) (died 11.9.87) – vocals/guitar; Bunny Wailer (né Livingstone) (f) - vocals/percussion
UK No.1 album: 1984: *Legend* (Tuff Gong BMWCD 1)

The baton lies where it fell, and more than a decade after his death from lung cancer and a brain tumour, Bob Marley remains the greatest – indeed, in many people's minds, the only – reggae star of all time. With his group The Wailers, he transformed the world of popular music by transporting the languid Jamaican reggae beat from the fringes of specialist import shops and skinhead dance halls to the centre of the international stage, becoming in the process the first Third World musician to acquire superstar status in the West.

Brought up in the slum neighbourhood of Trenchtown in

Kingston, Marley's eventual influence on the course of rock was incalculable. Prior to his break-through, so little was known about reggae among the rock fraternity that when Eric CLAPTON boldly took his version of Marley's 'I Shot the Sheriff' to the top of the US chart in 1974 it caused a sensation. Suddenly, all eyes were on Marley himself and he proceeded to alert the world to a history of melodic and rhythmic riches derived from the early syncopations of ska and bluebeat, all emanating from that one small island in the Caribbean. The effect on the next wave of rock groups was profound, with The POLICE and The CLASH foremost among the acts which made extensive use of reggae rhythms and recording techniques.

Marley's music was interwoven with the philosophy of rastafarianism, a pseudo-religious cult which espouses the belief that Haile Selassie, the former emperor of Ethiopia (otherwise known as Ras Tafari) is God, even though he died in 1975. As Marley's fame grew, he became as much of a cultural ambassador as he was a musician, often called upon to explain his dreadlocked appearance and to defend aspects of the rasta creed, such as the unshakable belief in the benign properties of ganja, a point of particular interest to police and customs officials wherever he travelled.

In Jamaica he became a figure of extraordinary influence. The former prime minister Michael Manley, talking to Robin Denselow of *The Guardian*, described Marley as 'one of the most articulate troubadours of the ghetto, its suffering and its pressures', adding on a more personal note, 'When he became a millionaire I wondered if he would become soft or gimmicky, but he never compromised. His concern was the same, but his range of interests grew, so he sang of Zimbabwe as well as Trenchtown.'

- [Billed as The Wailers]: *Catch a Fire* (Tuff Gong 846 201-2) [1973]
- [Billed as The Wailers]: *Burnin'* (Tuff Gong 846 200-2) [1973]

The Wailers began life as a straight vocal group, and the experience stood them in good stead by the time they eventually evolved into Jamaica's premier vocal *and* instrumental band and won a contract with Chris Blackwell's Island label. Their début recording for Blackwell was *Catch a Fire* and the keening, gospel-tinged harmonies on the chorus of 'Slave Driver' highlight the melody of the song and the anguish of the lyric, while on 'Stir It Up' (a Marley composition that had been a UK hit for Johnny Nash the year before) the gorgeous, mellifluous harmonies gild the irresistible tug of one of reggae's all-time classic bass lines. Marley's often unremarked sense of humour surfaces in 'Kinky Reggae', which rejoices in the opening lines 'I went downtown/I saw Miss Brown/She had brown sugar/All over 'er booga-wooga'.

Burnin' is much the same formula, with a more militant tone infusing the lyrics of numbers like 'Burnin' and Lootin'', 'Rasta Man Chant' and the timeless anthem of underclass pride 'Get Up, Stand Up'. It's also the album on which 'I Shot the Sheriff' made its first appearance.

- **Natty Dread** (Tuff Gong 846 204-2) [1974]

The clear emergence of Marley as the group's leader, which prompted the departure of founder members Tosh and Wailer, made for a sharper focus in both playing and presentation, and this album – a personal favourite of Marley's, owing not least to the adventurous guitar playing of new recruit Al Anderson – is certainly one of the key collections in the Wailers canon. 'Lively Up Yourself', 'No Woman, No Cry', 'Them Belly Full (But We Hungry)' and the lonesome 'Talkin' Blues' are songs which essay the troubles of the poor and the dispossessed with as much dignity as any musician has ever mustered.

- **Rastaman Vibration** (Tuff Gong TGLCD 5) [1976]
- **Exodus** (Tuff Gong TGLCD 6) [1977]
- **Kaya** (Tuff Gong TGLCD 7) [1978]

Although *Rastaman Vibration* was Marley's only album to reach the US Top 10, it is not exactly bristling with memorable songs. 'Roots, Rock, Reggae' was a minor US hit, but the number which attracted most attention was 'War', in which the group set extracts from one of Haile Selassie's speeches to music.

Exodus also charted strongly in Britain (No.8) and America (No.20), and is still a strong and enjoyable collection, while *Kaya*, a set of love songs including the sublime 'Is This Love?', is probably the most melodic, non-political album Marley ever put out.

● *Live at the Lyceum* [formerly *Live*] (Tuff Gong CID 9376) [1975]

The few thousand people privileged to have witnessed Marley's two concerts at London's Lyceum in July 1975 have never stopped speaking in hushed tones about the magical atmosphere of those events. Certainly there is an almost tangible aura of excitement and joy captured on this exceptional live recording, which includes definitive versions of 'I Shot The Sheriff', 'Get Up Stand Up' and the achingly poignant 'No Woman, No Cry', one of Marley's finest vocal performances ever. It is an album which still stands as the most vivid testament to his uncanny ability to articulate a universal spiritual truth through his music.

● *Legend* (Tuff Gong BMWCD 1) [1984]

Of the several 'Best of' and 'Greatest Hits' compilations, this posthumous tribute is the most even collection of hits and good bits, including 'Jamming', 'Stir It Up', 'Is This Love?' and the full-length, live version of 'No Woman, No Cry' among many others.

Paul McCartney

Born: June 18 1942, Liverpool
UK/US No.1 album: 1982: *Tug of War*
UK No.1 albums: 1971: *Paul and Linda McCartney* Ram (EMI CZ 29)
1980: *McCartney II* (Fame CDM 752 024-2)
1984: *Give My Regards to Broad Street* (Parlophone CZ 395)
1989: *Flowers in the Dirt* (Parlophone CDPCSD 106)

A musician and writer of immense and enduring talent, Paul McCartney has turned out to be far and away the most prolific and successful ex-BEATLE. As long ago as 1979 he was awarded a unique rhodium disc in recognition of his sales of 200 million albums.

But he is also given to inordinate lapses of judgement and taste. For every gem like 'Maybe I'm Amazed', 'Band on the Run' or

'Figure of Eight' there is an embarrassment like 'Mary had a Little Lamb', 'Wonderful Christmastime' or the Frog-Chorus-assisted 'We All Stand Together'.

The majority of his work falls somewhere between the two extremes: elegantly written, competently sung pop ditties that argue the case for McCartney as a seasoned rock variety performer whose solo achievements have acquired none of the resonance that distinguished his contributions to The BEATLES. (Where is the McCartney/Wings song to rival 'Let It Be' or 'Yesterday' or 'Eleanor Rigby'?) His biggest post-BEATLES success, 'Mull of Kintyre', has the melodic characteristics of a nursery rhyme.

But at least that is what he is good at, and what people like. Where McCartney has tended to come unstuck is in allowing unrealistic assumptions about the scope of his talent to lead him into projects beyond his competence, notably his benighted movie *Give My Regards to Broad Street* (see above) and his dreary *Liverpool Oratorio* (EMI Classics CDS 754 371-2; 1991) written with the American conductor Carl Davis to accompany the celebrations marking the fifteenth anniversary of the Royal Liverpool Philharmonic Society in 1990.

Such grandiose follies have not dented his popularity in the long run, and McCartney remains one of rock's evergreens. His famous question 'Will you still need me/Will you still feed me/When I'm 64?' sounds increasingly rhetorical with every passing year.

● *Tug of War* (1982)

Although his best post-BEATLES work has been presented in a group format, McCartney got a second wind after the demise of Wings, and this George-Martin-produced album, recorded with contributions from Ringo Starr, Carl Perkins, Stevie WONDER, Denny Laine and Andy Mackay of ROXY MUSIC, remains one of his more convincing efforts. Highlights include 'Take It Away', 'Tug of War' and the nostalgic 'Ballroom Dancing'.

● *All the Best* (Parlophone CDP 748 507-2) [1987]

A scintillating cross-section of hits from both solo and Wings-era

McCartney that combines the craftsmanlike appeal of 'No More Lonely Nights', 'Live and Let Die', 'Say Say Say' and 'Jet' with the silly 'Silly Love Songs', the bathetic 'Pipes of Peace' and the platitudinous 'Ebony and Ivory', the latter a duet with Stevie WONDER. The inevitable 'Mull of Kintyre' and 'Band on the Run' are in there somewhere too.

- *Flowers in the Dirt* (Parlophone PCSD 106) [1989]

Despite his heart-stopping (and microphone-stopping) appearance at the grand finale of the UK Live Aid, and his strange compulsion for appearing on practically any TV or radio chat show that could be bothered to issue an invitation, the Eighties were overall a relatively lean period for McCartney.

Flowers in the Dirt signalled something of a renaissance, thanks in particular to four songs which McCartney co-wrote with Elvis COSTELLO. On 'That Day is Done', 'Don't Be Careless Love', 'My Brave Face' and 'You Want Her Too' COSTELLO provides the aggressive, intellectual yang that McCartney's trite, good-blokeish yin has been lacking for so long.

It was also the album which coincided with McCartney's decision to tour for the first time since the demise of Wings. Having constructed a show that celebrated The BEATLES' heritage as much as it did his own post-BEATLES career, McCartney took a six-piece band on a ten-month hike around the world, selling three and a half million copies of *Flowers in the Dirt* in the process.

Wings

Convened: 1971, Machrihanish, Nr. Campbeltown, Strathclyde. Split up: 1980
Denny Laine (f) – guitar/vocals/keyboards; Linda McCartney (f) – keyboards/vocals; Paul McCartney (f) – vocals/bass/guitar/keyboards/drums

UK/US No.1 albums:	1973:	*Band on the Run* (Parlophone CDP 746 055-2)
	1975:	*Venus and Mars* (Fame CDP 746 984-2)
US No.1 albums:	1973:	*Red Rose Speedway* (Fame CDM 752 026-2)

1976: **Wings at the Speed of Sound** (Parlophone CDP 748 199-2)
1976: **Wings Over America** (Parlophone CDS 746 715-8)

With such a forceful and celebrated personality as McCartney, it's easy to overlook the fact that the cream of his 'solo' work has actually been recorded and performed in a group environment. Wings provided a settled context in which Linda could make her contribution and gave McCartney the chance to draw a firm line under his life as one of The BEATLES (the 'this is a new group, not a reliving of past glories' syndrome).

McCartney still wrote all the best songs, naturally took the lion's share of the royalties and exercised his due proprietorial rights in any policy decisions that had to be taken. Despite the subsequent whinging of ex-members of the group, it seems doubtful whether Denny Laine (ex-Moody Blues) and others who passed through the ranks - notably the guitarists Henry McCullough (ex-Joe Cocker's Grease Band) and Jimmy McCulloch (ex-Thunderclap Newman; died 27.9.79) - made any appreciable difference to the final outcome.

- **Band on the Run** (Parlophone CDP 746 055-2) [1973]

Recorded in Lagos by the core line-up of Laine and the McCartneys, *Band on the Run* remains McCartney's best post-BEATLES album. It sold more than six million copies and yielded a series of transatlantic hits: 'Helen Wheels', 'Jet' and the title track, along with the moody LENNON pastiche 'Let Me Roll It' and the eccentric 'Picasso's Last Words'.

- **Wings Over America** (Parlophone CDS 746 715-8) [1976]

The most positive aspect for McCartney of being technically 'in a band' was that it gave him the impetus to get out and perform. In 1972, when The BEATLES were still rock divinities (whether together or as individuals), Wings took off on a tour of universities and colleges, which it would have been unthinkable for McCartney to undertake as a solo act.

Three years later, with Jimmy McCulloch on guitar and Joe English on drums, the group embarked on what was declared at the time to be the most comprehensive world tour in the history of rock – from September 1975 until October 1976.

Although rough and ready by today's standards, *Wings Over America*, a double-live set, captures some of the raw excitement of those shows, with notably sparky versions of 'Jet', 'Lady Madonna' and 'Let Me Roll It' among many others.

Meat Loaf

Born: Marvin Lee Aday, September 27 1947, Dallas, Texas
UK No.1 album: 1981: *Dead Ringer* (Epic CD 83645)

A juvenile misfit who was especially shy with girls, Marvin Aday was dubbed Meat Loaf by his school friends on account of his gross size. However, it was he who had the last laugh, eventually flaunting his derisive nickname as a badge of pride and strutting his way with bullish fervour through raunchy duets with Cher and Ellen Foley.

The passport to his success, and indeed the one towering monument to it, was *Bat Out of Hell* (see below), a rococo monstrosity of an album which enjoyed a run in the UK chart that has so far been bettered only by FLEETWOOD MAC's *Rumours*.

It was his second album, but might as well have been his début for all the attention that the preceding *Stoney and Meat Loaf* (1970; unavailable) had attracted. Disillusioned by his early lack of success, Meat had embarked on a career as an actor, winning a part in the cult movie *The Rocky Horror Picture Show* (1975) and performing with the National Lampoon Show touring company.

But then he met singer, dramatist and songwriter Jim Steinman, who heard in Meat's bellowing voice the perfect vehicle for realising his aspirations to create rock on a Wagnerian scale. Meat provided the larynx and an elephantine stage presence, while Steinman supplied the songs. Their partnership yielded just two albums, *Bat Out of Hell* and the disappointing follow-up *Dead Ringer* (see above), after which they each drifted into lengthy but essentially humdrum careers, apart.

In 1991 it was reported that the pair was back together, working on an album to be called *Bat Out of Hell II – Back Into Hell* for release in early 1992.

- **Bat Out of Hell** (Re-issued 1991 as **Bat Out of Hell Re-Vamped** Epic CDX 82419) [US 1977/UK 1978]

The enduring appeal of *Bat Out of Hell* has earned it a quasi-mythical status out of all proportion to Meat Loaf's otherwise relatively modest achievements. In 1991 it was reissued with one additional track included on the new CD (and cassette) version: 'Dead Ringer for Love', the memorable sparring match with Cher, which in 1981 had provided Meat with his biggest hit single. Although at this point the album had already logged a total of 395 weeks in the chart (more than seven and a half years), it once again went soaring back into the UK Top 20.

Originally released with no fanfare in the aftermath of punk, *Bat Out of Hell* is the archetype of everything that the spiky-haired revolutionaries were supposed to have done away with. Baroque, melodramatic and wrought on a grand, pseudo-operatic scale, its tracks are long, intricate pieces – 'Bat Out of Hell' (9:48), 'Paradise by the Dashboard Light' (8:28), 'For Crying Out Loud' (8:45) – with bombastic finales and bathetic emotional overtones.

By contemporary standards the production, by Todd Rundgren, sounds rather dry and lack-lustre, and for an album which seeks to roll the most portentous characteristics of Bruce SPRINGSTEEN, The WHO and Phil Spector into one jaw-dropping bundle of excess, its transition to CD is a bit of a disappointment.

Locked into a Seventies time-warp, it remains something of an aberration and certainly doesn't boast the timeless quality that comparable long-runners such as *Dark Side of the Moon*, *Rumours* and *Bridge Over Troubled Water* can claim.

John Mellencamp

Born: October 7 1951, Seymour, Indiana
US No.1 album: 1982: *American Fool* (Riva 814 993-2)

The second of five children, John Mellencamp was born in a town with a population of roughly 12–14,000. According to Mellencamp, 'It's the kind of place where everybody knows everybody's business. They're big on religion. Drunk on Saturday night, but they're all in church tithing on Sunday. Very few people leave town that don't come back.'

Mellencamp now lives in Bloomington, another small town about an hour's drive from Seymour. Despite his multi-millionaire status he still likes to think of himself as a regular chip off the Seymour block. If he wasn't a rock star he figures he would be a construction worker. He's proud that his best friends are still ordinary guys with ordinary families and ordinary jobs.

These are the values which permeate his music: straight-ahead, essentially conservative songs, written from personal experience in the blue-collar, SPRINGSTEEN/Seeger/PETTY tradition of Adult-Rock-with-Sincerity.

Mellencamp married at 18, becoming a father before he was even out of college. At around the same time he met guitarist Larry Crane and together they formed a group called Trash. 'We were absolutely the worst band in the world,' Mellencamp reminisced in 1988. 'Trash did "Search and Destroy", "I Wanna Be Your Dog", all the most garagy stuff. . . .' Even so, Crane ended up playing in Mellencamp's band right up until the late Eighties.

Ironically, for a man whose career and music have been built on such 'regular guy' credentials, Mellencamp has twice lent his name to disastrously inappropriate hype campaigns. His first manager, Tony DeFries, set about marketing him in 1976 as some sort of bizarre, post-glitter sensation. Renaming the fledgling Mellencamp 'Johnny Cougar', DeFries (formerly David BOWIE's manager) declared Cougar to be the star that would provide the missing link between BOWIE and SPRINGSTEEN. Later, in London, where Mellencamp lived for eight months in 1977–78, his next manager Billy Gaff (also Rod STEWART's manager) launched a massive poster campaign which, in terms of both overkill and negative response, rivalled Columbia's 'Is the world ready for Bruce SPRINGSTEEN?' farrago of 1975.

Mellencamp pulled through in the end, regardless, relegating Cougar to a middle name which he had dropped altogether by the time of his 1991 album *Whenever We Wanted* (see below).

The Eighties' farming crisis directly affected many of his friends and extended family, and he became a key figure in setting up and performing at the three Farm Aid concerts (1985/6/7). Curiously, he turned down an invitation to play at Live Aid in 1985, stating that 'concerts that just raise money aren't a good idea.'

- *American Fool* (Riva 814 993-2) [1982]

After all the false starts and ill-fated attempts to shoe-horn Mellencamp's image and music into other people's ideas of what it should be, the quality that he finally tapped to such striking effect on *American Fool* was old-fashioned, no-frills honesty. Now billed as John Cougar, he at last came good with what was reputedly the year's biggest-selling album in the US.

Housing two enormous US hits, 'Hurts So Good' and 'Jack and Diane', this is an album with a pronounced sense of time and place, and although it struck a big emotional chord in America, it managed only a meagre showing at No.37 in the UK chart. Mellencamp has always been rather disdainful of overseas markets and has never made the slightest effort to tour Britain or promote his albums here. The single 'Jack and Diane', which made it all the way to No.25, remains his highest UK chart placing.

- *Uh-Huh* (Riva 814 485-2) [1983]
- *Scarecrow* (Riva 824 865-2) [1985]

With their singer now billing himself as John Cougar Mellencamp (or Little Bastard on the co-production credit of *Scarecrow*), both these albums sold in excess of four million copies, and even had the critics eating some of the harsh words which had greeted the initial populist success of *American Fool*. *Uh-Huh* produced the classic 'Pink Houses', one of those ambivalent anthems of loyal protest that only Americans seem capable of writing, while on *Scarecrow* the financial plight of the small farmers was unequivocally condemned. With songs like 'Small Town', 'Rumbleseat', and 'Face of the Nation', Mellencamp simultaneously bemoans the plight and salutes the integrity of the people and places of his rural Midwestern background. It remains the most consistently mature material he has recorded to date.

- *Whenever We Wanted* (Mercury 510 151-2) [1991]

A convincing, back-to-basics album; chock-full of lyrics with attitude – 'I Ain't Ever Satisfied', 'Crazy Ones', 'They're So Tough' – loosely drawled around itchy guitar and cowbell riffs, super-hardened for maximum impact.

The logic of the switch to hell-raising raunch from the relatively mellow roots-rock material of his preceding two albums – *Big Daddy* (Mercury 838 220-2; 1989) and *The Lonesome Jubilee* (Mercury 832 465-2; 1987) – might seem perverse, given that the album was released on Mellencamp's fortieth birthday, but there are no quibbles about the execution.

The key to its success is the devastating guitar playing of David Grissom, whom Mellencamp has borrowed (not for the first time) from Joe Ely's band. A player who manages to combine melodic precision with immense power, Grissom provides strong and graceful binding for Mellencamp's concise, neatly parcelled songs.

The only shadow is the absence of Mellencamp's long-standing partner, guitarist Larry Crane, whose name has quietly disappeared from the credits, with an almost Orwellian lack of explanation.

Metallica

Convened: 1981, San Francisco, California
Kirk Hammett (f) – guitar; James Hetfield (f) – vocals/guitar;
Jason Newsted – bass; Lars Ulrich (f) – drums
UK/US No.1 album: 1991: *Metallica* (Vertigo 510 022-2)

In the mid Eighties, at about the time that BON JOVI was demonstrating that heavy metal could be fashioned into high quality pop, darker forces were at work on the other wing of the genre. Here lurked the hard cases. They came on stage wielding their axes like superhuman psychopaths and their goal was to produce ever more extreme songs about medieval torturers and imminent global destruction.

In their search for the ultimate power-assisted buzz, these new wild men of rock picked up on the punk-minimalist idea that the faster they played, the better the chances of reaching nirvana. Thus was born thrash metal, an unholy, numbing noise revered for its unequivocally primeval qualities but mostly for its insane *speed*.

A slew of bands grew up around this ideal – Anthrax, Slayer, Megadeth and many besides – but the true trailblazers, and ultimately the most successful of them all, were Metallica.

Lars Ulrich and James Hetfield founded the group as a reaction against the melodic soft rock that was becoming increasingly dominant at the turn of the decade. Their anti-image was a studied mess of T-shirts, tattered jeans and long, unkempt hair, while on stage they played at such awe-inspiring speed and volume that their performances verged on caricature: The Ramones of heavy metal.

Having quickly established a fanatical cult following, they moved to New York and recorded their début album *Kill 'Em All* (Vertigo 838 142-2; 1983), released initially on the fledgling independent label Music For Nations.

As well as their obvious grass-roots appeal, Metallica (and the thrash bands which followed in their slipstream) won street credibility and a measure of critical acclaim previously unheard of for an act operating in the milieu of heavy metal, a style which since the Seventies has been second only to country music as the pariah of popular music genres.

As they toured America supporting Ozzy Osbourne, and then Europe in their own right, their noisy third album *Master of Puppets* (Vertigo 838 141-2; 1986) quietly sold a million. Sadly it was that same year, on September 27, that their original bassist Cliff Burton was killed on tour in Scandinavia, when the band's tour bus careered off the road.

Burton's super-manic style of head-banging, which involved a continuous flailing of his vast mane of hair (from roughly floor to ceiling level in some of the small clubs where they started out), was a visual tag which the band has never replaced. But otherwise they hardly missed a beat, pausing only to recruit Jason Newsted (ex-Flotsam And Jetsam) before returning to complete the interrupted tour.

Despite their ragged, fierce personae, these speed-obsessed idiot savants revealed themselves, when off stage, to be fairly ordinary lads, with no perceptibly greater history of psychological disorder than those of their fans. And in fact, as celebrations of chaos go, thrash is a highly disciplined and streamlined affair.

Stark, exciting and unremitting, thrash has become absorbed into and reflects the strange tribal rituals of an increasingly broad section of rebelliously minded youth. There are elements of the thrash ethic to be found in computer spaceship games, video nasties, horror comics and the junk cultures that surround motorbiking and skateboarding, all thrill-based activities where short, sharp shocks prompt a generous flow of adrenaline. What it all means, of course, is anybody's guess.

● . . . *And Justice For All* (Vertigo 836 062-2) [1988]

Initially taken as evidence that Metallica were beginning to soften up, this long and complex album marked a watershed in the band's musical aspirations. For in among the hurtling overkill which naturally predominates, there is the odd gently melodic passage, and even one or two reflective moments of sub-Wishbone Ash double lead guitar.

The lyrical preoccupations are much the same as ever – pain, death, dementia and, er, the generation gap – but there are song structures and some highly complex arrangements that are a marked development from the one-speed-fits-all blueprint with which the band started out. An intriguing, difficult album that is way removed from the usual heavy rock stereotypes; perhaps 'progressive metal' would be a suitable tag.

● *Metallica* (Vertigo 510 022-2) [1991]

The all-black cover of this, their fifth long player, may be reminiscent of Spinal Tap's magnum opus, but the music is no joke. Built from guitar riffs and drum motifs of preternatural gravity, the collection has about it the terrible, leisurely beauty of an atomic explosion.

Hetfield's vaguely libertarian lyrics advocate a noble, unforgiving barbarism – 'In wildness is the preservation of the world' – but there is nothing disorganised or remotely undisciplined about this assortment of songs. On the contrary, like LED ZEPPELIN before them, Metallica have recognised the value of delicate acoustic interludes, appealing harmonic progressions and an elegant precision of design as essential components of any album where the ultimate aim is the delivery of a juddering, megaton-riff payload.

Metallica appeals to that part of the psyche that finds the violent certainties and casual cruelty of an Arnold Schwarzenegger movie beguiling. As a cultural experience it has its limitations, but as an exercise in musical *force majeure* this is little short of perfection.

George Michael

Born: Georgios Kyriacos Panayiotou, June 25 1963, London
UK/US No.1 album: 1987: *Faith* (Epic 460 000-2)
UK No.1 album: 1990: *Listen Without Prejudice Volume 1*
(Epic 467 295-2)

Elton JOHN called him 'the greatest songwriter of his generation', which is going it a bit when you consider that few if any of his songs have been covered by other acts. But there is no doubt that George Michael has the voice to carry a pleasant tune and, as the Nineties get into gear, that he ranks as the only British presence in the international nouveau-pop super-league that comprises the likes of PRINCE, MADONNA and Michael JACKSON.

Although the selling of Michael has tended to turn on an image of him as a cross between a stubbly teddy bear and a randy, cartoon stud, his biography, *Bare*, written by Tony Parsons, portrays a well-meaning if rather earnest character much given to long and tedious bouts of public self-analysis. As a performer his style is firmly rooted in the conservative pop tradition of English household names like Cliff RICHARD and Michael's childhood hero Elton JOHN.

Within two years of Wham!'s demise (see below), Michael had already forged a spectacular, internationally successful solo career, particularly in America, where he graduated effortlessly from teen idol to critically acclaimed, 'adult-audience' performer.

● *Faith* (Epic 460 000-2) [1987]

Written, arranged and produced by Michael himself, his solo début is a stylistically varied collection which carries off the fine balancing act between soft rock and variety-turn pop with some aplomb. A capable if rather characterless singer, Michael's vocal mannerisms are redolent of Freddie Mercury on the title track, while the single 'I Want Your Sex', with its provocative title and torrid video, managed to stir up a mild storm-in-a-teacup controversy in the PRINCE vein.

The elements of social realism which crop up in a trio of songs – the sad 'Hand To Mouth', a half-baked R'n'B chug called 'Look At Your Hands' and the neurotic-sounding 'Monkey' – sound awkward in such a shamelessly commercial setting, but Michael has never been one to turn down the brownie points he gets for trying. The late-night pseudo-jazz-noir swing of 'Kissing A Fool' makes you wonder what happened to Sade.

A pleasant enough album in a lightweight pop vein, but who would have predicted it would sell a staggering 14 million copies?

● *Listen Without Prejudice Volume 1* (Epic 467 295-2) [1990]

As the release date for this album neared you could rarely switch on the TV or open a newspaper without being confronted by Michael. One thing he made clear throughout this barrage of media exposure was his intention to get off the promotional treadmill, just as soon as he'd finished the next interview. The other point he reiterated, time without number, was his ambition to be remembered as a songwriter of lasting merit rather than as a transient pop star.

Yet Michael's strength is patently his ability to deliver a song with pleasing conviction and to filter his ideas through a variety of contemporary pop styles. He is clearly not a writer of substance and there is nothing in the way of original or memorable material on offer here. The best track by far is the haunting, cod-gospel chant, 'They Won't Go When I Go', which was written by Stevie WONDER. More typical is the slushy, predictable chord progression of 'Praying For Time', one of several songs with about as much resonance as high-class airport music.

Wham!

Convened: 1981, London. Split up: 1986
George Michael (f) – vocals; Andrew Ridgeley (f) – vocals/ guitar
UK/US No.1 album: 1984: *Make It Big* (Epic CD 86311)
UK No.1 album: 1983: *Fantastic* (Inner Vision CD 25328)

In four years Wham! went from making a home-produced demo hymning the joys of being young, unemployed and optimistic, to announcing their retirement. The same duo which hired a £20 Portastudio to record 'Wham! Rap' had become rather less carefree millionaires by the time they bid their farewells in front of an audience of 72,000 at Wembley Stadium.

Although they made a nice couple to look at, the imbalance between the contributions of George Michael and Andrew Ridgeley, his former school friend from Bushey Meads Comprehensive in Hertfordshire, was obvious from the start. Michael was in charge of musical direction, and took the lead in writing and producing; he was the principal singer and by far the more dominating personality on stage. Ridgeley was left to deal with matters of style and image, and although he usually had a guitar in his hand it was difficult to tell whether or not it was plugged in.

Having harnessed the outrageous managerial chutzpah of Simon Napier-Bell (a veteran of acts including The Yardbirds and T. Rex and author of the most hilarious rock'n'roll memoirs yet published), Wham! swept all before them during a necessarily brief period of teeny-bop glory.

Their most memorable exploit was a junket to China in 1985, when they played the 10,000-seater Workers' Gymnasium in Peking. At the time much play was made of the broader significance of the visit, but Napier-Bell was soon boasting that it had all been a huge hype to get exposure for Wham! on the American news networks and thus break *Make It Big* (see above) in the States, which it did. Michael later described the visit as 'supposedly some kind of cultural milestone, in retrospect a sham'.

- *The Final* (Epic CD 88681) [1986]

All you'll ever need to know about Wham! and a bit besides is incorporated in this ace hits collection with everything from the weeny-rap sloganeering of 'Young Guns Go For It' and 'Wham! Rap' right through to the sophisticated crooning of 'Last Christmas' and 'The Edge of Heaven'. 'Wake Me Up Before You Go Go' remains, effortlessly, their supreme contribution. What a nice pair of boys they were.

Joni Mitchell

Born: Roberta Joan Anderson, November 7 1943, Alberta, Canada
US No.2 albums: 1974: *Court and Spark* (Asylum 253 002-2)
1974: *Miles of Aisles* (unavailable)

Musician, songwriter, photographer, artist, painter; Joni Mitchell is every inch the modern Renaissance woman. She has personally illustrated all of her 16 album covers and her abstract acrylics have been known to fetch as much as $60,000.

In the summer of 1990, she travelled with her camera and her husband, jazz bass player Larry Klein, through the Canadian locales of her itinerant childhood – the small towns of Fort Macleod, Calgary, Maidstone, North Battleford and Saskatoon, blips on the map amid the vast prairie lands of Alberta and Saskatchewan.

'I photographed the lakes of my childhood; the farm machinery; the grain elevators, which we call prairie skyscrapers – tall wooden structures, painted bright greens and oranges and burgundys with yellow roofs.' Then she 'sandwiched' the images to a series of self-portraits. 'You get a buff of trees in the eyes and it looks like heavy eye make-up, or a road going up my nose, and there's a field of wheat with my husband standing where my nose is and my eye becomes a moon; oh, there's some really profound stuff.'

Quite so. But it is in her primary rôle as the *grande dame* of rock's singer-songwriter tendency that she has long been famed for her ability to come up with the 'really profound stuff'. One of the more wholesome torch-bearers of Sixties hippydom, she wrote the 'Woodstock' anthem (a hit for Crosby, Stills, Nash and Young, and Matthew's Southern Comfort) without actually attending the festival. She has never relied on either a militant or a decorous image, although she did stick a picture of her naked bottom on the cover of *For the Roses* (see below), an image which was discreetly removed from later pressings.

Instead she has exploited her femininity in other ways, writing about intensely personal relationships from a woman's perspective, but shunning the drippy love song conventions. If her openness has left her vulnerable, she is still nobody's victim. Experimental, bold, intelligent and original, she transported her folk textures to a jazz environment with a series of albums starting with *Court and Spark* (see below) and culminating in the live *Shadows and Light* (unavailable; 1980). Along the way she released *Mingus* (1979; unavailable), a disappointing collaboration with, and tribute to, the ailing jazz bassist, Charles Mingus, who died soon after it was recorded (5.1.79). *Don Juan's Reckless Daughter* (Asylum 263 003; 1977) was a more inventive project in a similar vein, for which she was joined by jazz fusionists Jaco Pastorius (bass; died 22.9.87) and Wayne Shorter (saxophone) of Weather Report.

It was a change of direction which she now believes lost her a large chunk of her audience. 'I've pretty much been stricken from the history of rock'n'roll in America,' she says ruefully. 'However, I am being written up in some classical music textbooks. They include me along with Stevie WONDER, Duke Ellington and others as twentieth century composers. I am one of the pioneers of music with a broader harmonic sense than rock'n'roll, but I don't fit into any of the handy pigeon-holes. That's why it's taken 20 years for me to spawn imitators, and even they have a hard time getting started, the poor dears.'

● *Ladies of the Canyon* (Geffen K 244 085) [1970]

Mitchell's third album marks the point at which she began to break free of the traditional folk-singer mould. It also reflects the profound changes that had taken place in her life since leaving Canada with her first husband, Chuck Mitchell, in the mid-Sixties. The marriage had ended soon afterwards and the country girl from the Canadian prairie lands was now living with Graham Nash (of Crosby, Stills and Nash) in Laurel Canyon, and experiencing life at the hub of the Los Angeles rock-star community.

The yearning for a return to a more pastoral (if highly idealised) existence gave rise to her hippie magnum opus 'Woodstock', while 'Big Yellow Taxi' may have been the first certifiably eco-friendly pop song, and remains her only single to have charted in the UK. Other highlights include 'For Free' and 'The Circle Game', a song of hers which had previously been recorded by Tom Rush.

● *Blue* (Reprise K 244 128) [1971]

Mitchell reached an apogee of rigorous self-analysis with her fourth album, *Blue*, a ravaging emotional critique of the post-Aquarian age which set the course for a succeeding generation of bohemian chanteuses from Suzanne Vega to Tracy Chapman, Michelle Shocked and beyond. The brilliant lustre of songs like 'California', 'This Flight Tonight' and 'Carey' offers a stark yet loving appraisal of the heartaches and neuroses lurking just below the surface of the freewheeling California lifestyle.

- *For The Roses* ((WEA 253 007) [1972]
- *Court and Spark* (Asylum 253 002-2) [1974]

With *For the Roses* came the first stirrings of a musical ambition far broader than the familiar voice and acoustic guitar formula. Switching from guitar to piano for most numbers, Mitchell wrote the album during a period of intense self-examination, yet songs like 'You Turn Me On I'm a Radio' and 'Cold Blue Steel' have a flamboyant appeal. Bobby Notkoff provides a chamber string section while band-leader Tom Scott furnishes horn and woodwind arrangements.

Court and Spark, Mitchell's only million-seller, remains by far the most commercially successful release of her distinguished career. The choice of Tom Scott's jazz-orientated LA Express as her first proper backing band confirmed her intention to move away from the folk nexus of her previous work. So too did the inclusion of 'Twisted', written by jazz chanteuse Annie Ross – the first non-original song to grace a Joni Mitchell album.

With its glorious vocal glissandos, 'Raised on Robbery' is typical of the increasingly ebullient mood, while 'Help Me' and 'Free Man in Paris' both provided significant US hits.

- *The Hissing of Summer Lawns* (WEA 253 018) [1975]

Arguably her last album of genius, this yielded nothing in the way of hits, but contains some of her most complex and ambitious work ever. Its underlying theme is the tension between jungle and metropolis. Which will win out? The battle is fought via the imagery of the cover illustration – a trio of Amazon Indians carrying their god, the anaconda snake, dwarfed by a big city skyline – and the choice of instrumentation, which matches off synthesisers against the warrior drums of Burundi, as featured on 'The Jungle Line'. 'Don't Interrupt the Sorrow' and 'The Boho Dance' are among the high points of an album which PRINCE once declared to be his all-time favourite.

• *Night Ride Home* (Geffen GEFD 24302) [1991]

Her most recent album is less of a bid to win new converts, more an updated restatement of first principles. 'Cherokee Louise' and 'The Windfall' are in her classic folk-tinged mould, while there is a chirpy quality to songs like 'The Only Joy in Town' and 'Ray's Dad's Cadillac' which recall the lightness of touch she brought to her old hit 'Big Yellow Taxi'. A darker force is evoked on 'Slouching Towards Bethlehem', her intriguing musical adaptation of W.B. Yeats' apocalyptic poem, 'The Second Coming'.

Van Morrison

Born: George Ivan, August 31 1945, Belfast
UK No.4 album: 1990: *The Best of Van Morrison* (Polydor 841
970-2)

In 1991 a simple ceremony took place in an East Belfast back street as a mark of respect to one of the city's most distinguished sons. A tasteful commemorative plaque, commissioned by the Belfast Blues Appreciation Society, was placed by the door of 125 Hyndford Street bearing the legend 'Singer songwriter Van Morrison lived here from 1945 to 1961'.

The plaque was unveiled by the American blues veteran Buddy Guy and among those present was one of Morrison's uncles, as well as old neighbours and musician friends such as Eric Bell (ex-Thin Lizzy). No one was expecting Morrison to turn up himself, of course, but doubtless the old buzzard would feel a touch of pride to know that he had been thus honoured.

Morrison's response was, in fact, swift and terse. Communicating through his solicitors he demanded that the plaque be removed. 'Our client was not consulted nor asked for permission for use of his name in this matter.'

Such eccentric and mean-spirited behaviour is strangely typical of a performer who has consistently produced music of transcendental beauty and grace, and many are the tales of journalists who have been forced to abandon interviews in the face of his curt, dismissive manner or his demands to the right of editorial veto over what is subsequently printed.

Brought up as a Jehovah's Witness, Morrison started out playing harmonica, guitar and saxophone with several local bands while still at school. He first came to international prominence as the singer with Them, a Belfast-based, hard-core rhythm and blues group whose brief career is summed up on the album *Them* (Decca 820 563-2). Singing in an aggressive, biting style that was easily a match for Mick Jagger's raucous sneer, Morrison steered the band through two UK hits with 'Baby Please Don't Go' and 'Here Comes the Night', before leaving in 1967 and travelling to New York to begin a solo career.

With his harsh timbre, nonchalant timing and impossible enunciation, he has since matured into one of the most expressive and distinctive singers the UK has ever produced.

● *Astral Weeks* (Warner Bros K 246 024) [1968]

Much has been made of the bold streak of Celtic mysticism which informs Morrison's work, and nowhere is it more evident than on this masterly solo début, which prompted critical superlatives and public indifference in roughly equal measure at the time.

Although The BEATLES had already used a variety of non-guitar/drums/keyboards instrumentation on *Revolver* and *Sergeant Pepper's Lonely Hearts Club Band*, there were still formidable barriers blocking the use of vibes, flute and string sections in rock music. Morrison butted straight through them, fashioning an album which journeys a long way beyond the traditional haunts of rock or even 'roots' music. Recorded in two days flat, the album produced no hits, but songs like 'Madame George', 'Sweet Thing' and 'Young Lovers Do' make it a beautiful if inaccessible masterpiece.

● *Moondance* (WEA 246 040) [1970]

With a tighter sound and more tightly structured material than that of *Astral Weeks*, this proved to be the commercial breakthrough for Morrison in both Britain and America. It combines elements of American roots rock on numbers like 'And It Stoned Me' (an elegant pastiche of The BAND) with the jazz swing of the title track and the spiritual introspection of 'Into the Mystic'. 'Come Running' was a US Top 40 hit.

- *St Dominic's Preview* (Polydor 839 162-2) [1972]

An album which finds Morrison exploring certain soul and jazz grooves in greater depth than before, especially on the 11-minute epic 'Listen to the Lion' and the title track. In 'Jackie Wilson Said' – a hit ten years later for Dexys Midnight Runners – Morrison pays tribute to the great R'n'B vocalist of the Fifties, while a riot of jazz horns tumble across the striding bass line.

- *Into the Music* (Mercury 800 057-2) [1979]

After a period of recuperation and transition, Morrison returned to what he does best. The range of stylistic influences which his music incorporates is staggering. A jaunty, easy-going strut like 'Bright Side of the Road' casually embraces folk-tinged fiddle, bluesy harmonica, a soul band brass section, countrified banjo picking and neo-gospel backing vocals, all jostling merrily behind Morrison's gruff, apparently throwaway delivery. Other highlights include 'Angelou' and a searing rendition of an old Cliff RICHARD hit 'It's All in the Game'.

- *Van Morrison and The Chieftains: Irish Heartbeat* (Mercury 834 496-2) [1988]

This inspired collaboration with Irish folk veterans The Chieftains is a collection of traditional songs, along with two Morrison compositions in a compatible vein, all played with sprightly grace on acoustic instruments and sung by Morrison in his clipped, truculent manner. The antecedents of Morrison's vocal style are laid bare in songs like 'Star of the County Down' and 'Marie's Wedding', where his ragged, soulful phrasing blends into the fabric of the pure Celtic folk melodies like the sea meeting the sky.

- *Avalon Sunset* (Polydor 839 262-2) [1989]

The Celtic soul master is in a peaceful and reflective mood as he makes several ringing declarations of Christian belief including 'When Will I Ever Learn to Live in God' and a surprisingly affecting duet with Cliff RICHARD on 'Whenever God Shines His Light'. On these and others, faint gospel nuances tug and flow around gorgeous, uplifting choruses.

As the song titles suggest, Morrison was by now on a full-blown Christian kick that was entirely consistent with his long-standing leaning towards quasi-religious mysticism.

The outstanding track is 'Coney Island', a richly evocative and instantly nostalgic declamation set against a lush string arrangement that finds the maverick Morrison recalling a time of childlike innocence while roaming the deepest recesses of his spiritual lair.

● *The Best of Van Morrison* (Polydor 841 970-2) [1990]

For all his unassailable merits as a performer, Morrison is not an artist one associates with a vast catalogue of hit records. The surprise of this collection is to discover how many of the songs are embedded in the consciousness, sometimes to the point of over-familiarity. The early Them recordings – 'Gloria', 'Baby Please Don't Go' and 'Here Comes the Night' – are songs that have been recycled relentlessly by any number of other acts, often rather badly.

'Moondance', 'Bright Side of the Road', 'Brown-Eyed Girl', 'Warm Love', 'Jackie Wilson Said' and 'Cleaning Windows' have all had a similarly extended shelf life for one reason or another. Some of these older productions now sound scrappy and dated, but the consummate skill of Morrison's phrasing endures unscathed, especially on a song like 'Moondance' where he flits to either side of the beat with a disdainful sureness of touch.

The collection spans virtually his entire career, although there is surprisingly only one track, 'Sweet Thing', from *Astral Weeks* (see above). Still the question remains: how can someone with such a lumpy, prosaic demeanour have created such a raft of poetic marvels?

Morrissey See The SMITHS

The Mothers of Invention See Frank ZAPPA

The Neville Brothers

Convened: 1977, New Orleans, Louisiana
Aaron Neville (f) – vocals; Art Neville (f) – keyboards/vocals;
Charles Neville (f) – saxophone; Cyril Neville (f) – percussion/
vocals
UK No.35 album: 1990: *Brother's Keeper* (A&M 395 312-2)

The Neville Brothers are one of those bands for whom touring
has become the habit of a lifetime rather than a special occasion.
Like the Mardi Gras from which their music is descended, they
always seem to turn up at a certain time of year, bringing a chunk
of their native New Orleans with them.

Their songs are the stuff of instant legend: voodoo-soul
melodies with titles like 'Mojo Hannah', 'Brother Blood' and 'Fire
on the Bayou' garnished with neo-gospel harmonies and propelled
by a restless interplay of shuffling funk syncopations. On stage,
anyone with a free hand will end up clonking a cowbell, threading
another line into the already complex weave of rhythmic patterns
created by the drums and Cyril's energetic percussion displays. In
the studio they have such an abundance of technique and practical
experience to call on, it is something of a mystery that they have
never fully captured the vivid excitement of their best live work.

As individuals, the Nevilles have been around since the dawn of
rock'n'roll. Art and Aaron's recording career began in 1954 when
as part of a vocal group The Hawkettes, they enjoyed a local hit
with Art's composition 'Mardi Gras Mambo'. Aaron enjoyed
considerable success as a solo act in 1966 when he reached No.2 in
the US chart with the ballad 'Tell It Like It Is'. Not long afterwards
he and Art were drafted into New Orleans producer Allen
Toussaint's studio house-band.

As a logical outgrowth of such work, Art founded The Meters
in 1969, a super-session group that gradually became as much of
a name act as the stars with whom it worked in the studio – a kind
of New Orleans equivalent to Memphis' nonpareil studio band,
Booker T and The MG's.

The Meters enjoyed a couple of minor instrumental hits,
'Sophisticated Cissy' (1969) and 'Cissy Strut' (1969), which had a
disproportionately significant influence on the direction of funk in
the Seventies, steering it away from the heavy grunt and stomp
of the James BROWN school, towards the more languid rhythmic

accentuations subsequently favoured by Little Feat and others.

Championed by The ROLLING STONES in the Seventies, The Meters put out their own recordings, while earning their bread and butter by working on albums by Dr John, Robert PALMER, Labelle, Paul McCARTNEY and others. Cyril, until then playing in his own band, Soul Machine, joined The Meters in 1975. When the group eventually split in 1977, it didn't take a great leap of the imagination for Art and Cyril to rope in Aaron and a fourth brother, saxophonist Charles – who had cut his teeth on the road with Bobby Bland and B.B. KING – and set up in fraternal business as The Neville Brothers.

Aaron eventually rekindled his solo career in the wake of the enormous success of his slushy duet with Linda Ronstadt, 'Don't Know Much', taken from Ronstadt's album *Cry Like a Rainstorm, Howl Like the Wind* (Elektra 960 872-2; 1989). By 1991 Aaron's solo album *Warm Your Heart* (A&M 397 148-2; 1991) was doing bigger business in America than the Nevilles' *Brother's Keeper* had managed the year before.

● *Fiyou on the Bayou* (Demon FIENDCD 65) [1981]

It was with this album that the Nevilles first consciously set out to adapt their raw Mardi-Gras-derived sound to the more broadly based needs of the mainstream rock market. Producer Joel Dorn bolstered the angelic wobble of Aaron's voice with unashamedly extravagant orchestration – the New York Philharmonic was hired for 'Mona Lisa' – while marshalling a harder sound for the dancier items. The title track bears a passing resemblance to the sort of ethnic-rock fusion which SANTANA had pioneered a decade earlier. Although, ironically, it was not a commercial success, *Fiyou on the Bayou* was a watershed album in the development of the distinctive Neville-ised sound.

● *Yellow Moon* (A&M CDA 5240) [1989]

One of the most critically applauded non-chart albums of the decade, this was the next staging post in bringing The Nevilles to the attention of that elusive 'broad' rock market, which was by now boasting an increasingly Nevilles-friendly adult demographic in the wake of the CD revolution. Produced by Daniel Lanois (of

U2, Peter GABRIEL and Bob DYLAN fame) the album's strongest feature is Aaron's singing of two DYLAN 'ballads', 'With God on Our Side' and 'The Ballad of Hollis Brown', and Sam Cooke's R'n'B standard 'A Change is Gonna Come'.

● *Brother's Keeper* (A&M 395 312-2) [1990]

After the adulation afforded to *Yellow Moon*, there was a minor backlash against the follow-up, *Brother's Keeper*, but it was the Nevilles' UK chart début and one of their best albums yet.

Half gospel, half voodoo, the Nevilles' music is at its best when the band is riding the groove rather than trying to fashion a rounded pop statement, and the centrepiece of *Brother's Keeper* is Art Neville's sinister state-of-the-nation rap 'Sons and Daughters', a detour into Gil Scott-Heron territory which is driven along by nothing more than a relentlessly spooky snare shuffle.

The harmonies are spun to perfection throughout, but it is rhythms like the in-the-pocket Southern funk of 'Brother Jake' that galvanise the ear, bringing to mind, in one or two instances, the fabled work of The Meters.

● *Legacy (A History of The Nevilles)* (Charly CDNEV1) [1990]

A sprawling retrospective set, comprising pre-Neville Brothers material. Starting with 'Mardi Gras Mambo', it collects the recorded highlights of Aaron's early solo work ('Tell It Like It Is', 'All These Things', 'Cry Me a River') and rounds up the best cuts from the first stage of The Meters' chequered career, including 'Sophisticated Cissy', 'Cissy Strut', 'Look-Ka Py Py', 'Message From The Meters', etc.

Nirvana

Convened: 1988, Aberdeen, Washington
Kurt Cobain (f) – vocals/guitar; David Grohl – drums; Chris Novoselic (f) – bass
US No.1 album: 1991: *Nevermind* (Geffen DGCD 24425)

By the start of the Nineties, the process of making and marketing rock had become tiresomely predictable. Record companies, the media, retailers and fans could all see the international blockbusters coming a mile off. Irrespective of their musical merits, new releases by Michael JACKSON, U2, METALLICA, DIRE STRAITS, GUNS N' ROSES, GENESIS and others of that ilk were the highly crafted products of an industry that functioned like a well-oiled machine.

At that stratospheric level of activity there was no room for spontaneity. The strategies involved in marketing those albums – incorporating single releases, advertising, promotion, videos, radio and TV appearances – were planned and executed like military operations. Any element of surprise had long been eliminated from the equation.

Then along came Nirvana, and suddenly it was like the Sixties again, with everyone concerned working in the dark and wondering just what had happened.

From their beginnings with the Seattle-based indie label Sub Pop, Nirvana had shown the makings of a promising cult band. Like their grunge-rock label-mates, Mudhoney and Tad, they were an instant success on the college/alternative circuit in America, and quickly found their way on to John Peel's radio show in Britain. This was a reasonable start, enough to justify an initial pressing of 40,000 copies of the group's second album, *Nevermind* (see below).

Given such a low-key start, the speed and scale of *Nevermind*'s success was unprecedented. Within four months it had sold 2.5 million copies in America alone, and changed perceptions of what constitutes mainstream heavy rock virtually overnight.

The group's stated influences are radical art-noise pioneers Sonic Youth, pop-airheads Abba and The BEATLES. Yet despite their disclaimers ('We're heavy, but we're not heavy metal'), Nirvana's appeal is as much to dyed-in-the-wool heavy rock fans as it is to their counterparts in the much trendier hard-core crowd, demolishing at a stroke a barrier at which bands like The Red Hot Chili Peppers and Faith No More have been chipping away for a while.

By the start of 1992 there was already talk of 'post-Nirvana rock', as a new school of similarly loud, aggressive, 'alternative' rock'n'roll acts stood poised on the brink of success, among them Pearl Jam, Soundgarden and Alice In Chains. A new chapter in rock has begun.

- *Bleach* (Tupelo TUPCD 006) [1989]

Nirvana's début, recorded on eight-track equipment in three days at a cost of $600, is a much rawer but perfectly logical predecessor to *Nevermind*. Featuring Cobain, Novoselic and original drummer Chad Channing, the album is a perfect introduction to that trademark sound of strafing guitars, roaring vocals and intelligent, left-field melodies. Stand-out tracks include 'School', 'Negative Creep' and an early single called 'Blew'.

- *Nevermind* (Geffen DGCD 24425) [1991]

Although their musical textures are often indistinguishable from those of any heavy rock band – overloaded guitar, piston-like drum sound, Cobain's scream-singing vocals – it is Nirvana's melodic facility that sets them apart. On numbers like 'In Bloom' and the UK Top 10 single 'Smells Like Teen Spirit' they constantly strive for unusual chord sequences and a melody good enough to justify their existence.

Then they pile on the aggression with a ferocious energy that implicitly recognises their punk heritage, most notably on 'Breed', 'Stay Away' and 'Territorial Pissings', the latter a pell-mell assault on the senses which caused Jonathan Ross much grief when they played it in place of their scheduled number on his live chat show.

'Come As You Are' recalls the style of Killing Joke, and there are echoes of PIXIES here and there, but overall the music has an indefinable quality that is Nirvana's own.

They play a neat little trick, that only works thanks to CD technology, by including an extra track 'hidden' at the end of the disc. Several minutes after the last listed song ('Something in the Way') finishes, there is another track, apparently called 'Endless Nameless', which suddenly springs out on the unsuspecting listener. According to Novoselic there was no artistic motive behind the idea; it was just a prank.

Mike Oldfield

Born: May 15 1953, Reading, Berkshire
UK No.1 albums: 1973: *Tubular Bells* (Virgin CDV 2001)
1974: *Hergest Ridge* (Virgin CDV 2013)

Mike Oldfield had the mixed fortune to scale the pinnacle of his life's achievements at the age of 20, when he released his magnum opus *Tubular Bells* (see below). Still, he had started young, working the folk-club circuit with his sister Sally at the age of 14, and playing bass as a member of Kevin Ayers and The Whole World by the time he was 17.

Tubular Bells was the first album to be released on Richard Branson's Virgin Records label, and its remarkable worldwide success – five years in the UK chart and eventual sales of more than ten million copies – bankrolled the company during its early years. It was not a repeatable achievement, even though the follow-up *Hergest Ridge* (see above) was basically *Son of Tubular Bells* with slower tempos, and rode to the top of the chart on the back of its predecessor's popularity. (*Hergest Ridge* was actually knocked off the No.1 slot by the long-running *Tubular Bells*.)

- ● **Tubular Bells** (Virgin CDV 2001) [1973]

Who can forget the grainy, archive film which *The Old Grey Whistle Test* dug up to accompany its first, and frequently repeated, TV presentations of excerpts from *Tubular Bells*? Predating the rise of the promotional video by roughly eight years, that black and white footage of dozens of little skiing figures, tumbling about in the snow, became a mnemonic for the sound of trebly guitars overdubbed into grandiose orchestral layers and iced with the tinkling chatter of bell chimes.

In America the music had more sinister (but no less memorable) connotations thanks to a section of it being used as the soundtrack to the film *The Exorcist*.

The album was the result of a year's lonely studio work by Oldfield, who created his pop 'symphony' by playing 21 instruments himself, patiently building up great wodges of sound one upon another.

With its restful instrumental textures and meandering, repetitive structure, it was a harbinger of the wallpaper music that is now called New Age, but more importantly, Oldfield's meticulous production values brought a new sophistication to contemporary popular music that had been conspicuously absent from both the frothy whirl of pop and the heavy rattle and hum of rock'n'roll.

As the prototype coffee-table rock album, *Tubular Bells* is a work which saw the CD era coming. 'I don't think you can listen to *Hergest Ridge* (see above) on anything but a very good record player,' Oldfield said of the follow-up, but he might just as well have been talking about *Tubular Bells*. Like PINK FLOYD's *Dark Side of the Moon*, it's one of those albums they play in the shop to demonstrate the crystal clarity of CD. CD buffs have long regarded *Tubular Bells* as a litmus test for advanced audio fidelity equipment.

- **The Complete Mike Oldfield** (Virgin CDMOC 1) [1985]

Although the towering achievement of *Tubular Bells* has cast a long shadow over the rest of Oldfield's career, he has subsequently enjoyed patchy success in a variety of settings. There were his Christmas hits in the Seventies – 'In Dulce Jubilo' and 'Portsmouth'. There was a string of chart entries in the Eighties featuring the bewitching soprano of Maggie Reilly including 'Five Miles Out', 'Family Man' and 'Moonlight Shadow'. And then there was his film score work for Roland Joffe's 1984 movie *The Killing Fields*, which was perhaps his true métier all along. All these bits and pieces, together with extracts from *Hergest Ridge* and the ubiquitous *Tubular Bells*, are collected together on *The Complete Mike Oldfield*, a handy compilation-cum-curriculum vitae of this reclusive chap's work.

Robert Palmer

Born: Alan Palmer, January 19 1949, Batley, Yorkshire
UK No.5 album: 1985: *Riptide* (Island IMCD 25)

Blue-eyed soul singer, brutish heavy rocker, club mix connoisseur, torch-song traditionalist and champion of 'ethnic' music styles, that's Robert Palmer, the suave, Yorkshire-born libertine with a knack for sampling genres the way most musicians would sample sounds.

Palmer's childhood was spent in Malta where his father, a surveillance operative attached to the navy, was posted. 'All the expatriate families in Malta emulated the *South Pacific* lifestyle,' recalls Palmer. 'They all had reel-to-reel tape-recorders and they recorded off the American Forces Network and they all partied each night at each other's houses. I'd be up in bed and I'd hear them blasting out Lena Horne, Peggy Lee, Nat King Cole, Frank Sinatra, Billie Holiday. To me that music was hip. When I got back to England and heard the music scene I was disgusted until I heard Otis REDDING and soul music. That was my rebel music. Otherwise, the likes of Cliff RICHARD and The Shadows sounded pretty cornball compared to Billie Holiday.'

In his teens Palmer was recruited as singer of the Alan Bown Set which he left to take up with jazz-rockers Dada. After some changes Dada mutated into Vinegar Joe, a good-time R'n'B outfit featuring Palmer as joint lead vocalist with Elkie Brooks.

Vinegar Joe hit the skids in 1973, whereupon Palmer hightailed it to the States. There he cut a series of sophisticated albums which dabbled in styles ranging from soul to Southern funk and reggae, but which enjoyed only limited commercial success.

His break-through came in the wake of a fleeting association with Duran Duran's John Taylor and Andy Taylor which produced *The Power Station* album and short-lived 'supergroup' of the same name.

Like Bryan Ferry, Palmer is a conspicuously well-turned-out member of rock's otherwise rumpled aristocracy. His videos, especially the notorious 'Addicted to Love' where he surrounded himself with an unlikely 'band' of porcelain-faced models, portray him as a rakish customer, and his wildly free-ranging musical proclivities suggest a broad dilettante streak to his character. But he has an enquiring intellect and the rigorous mind-set necessary to produce work that is consistently of the very highest standard. There is a solid base to his talent and a worldly confidence in his approach that has sustained him through many lean years and suggests he will be a major player for a long time to come.

- *Sneakin' Sally Through the Alley* (Island IMCD 20) [1974]

Having shot his bolt with the good time rock'n'rolling of Vinegar Joe, for his first solo effort Palmer turned his attention to the steamy Southern funk rhythms and blue-eyed bayou soul that had earned Little Feat such unabashed critical acclaim. Indeed, the lead-off track is a version of The Feats' 'Sailing Shoes', and Feats' mainman, the late Lowell George, together with various members of the New Orleans super-session group, The Meters, show up throughout. An audacious album which, perhaps inevitably, falls short of its ambitious target.

● *Clues* (Island IMCD 21) [1980]

On to his sixth solo album and Palmer was now in synth-pop/club mode, racking up minor UK hits with clipped electro-rhythm tracks ('Looking for Clues', the gorgeous 'Johnny and Mary') and enlisting robo-pop star Gary Numan as spiritual guide and musical partner on 'I Dream of Wires' and 'Found You Now'. Tremendously poised stuff, if occasionally lacking in warmth.

● *Riptide* (Island IMCD 25) [1985]

Palmer's *magnum opus*, *Riptide* hosts his two biggest hits, 'I Didn't Mean to Turn You On' and the colossal 'Addicted to Love' a platinum-selling US No.1 in 1986. By now Palmer had given up segregating his various musical interests between different albums and was chucking it all in at once and seeing what stuck. The result here is an outrageously varied collection marked by some heavy swings of mood: from the gentle crooning of the Forties ballad 'Riptide' to the hard-riffing heavy rock of 'Flesh Wound'; from the New Orleans syncopations of Earl King's old blues song 'Trick Bag' (harking back to the *Sneaking Sally* era) to the sleek, hard-core electro/club groove of 'I Didn't Mean to Turn You On'.

● *'Addictions' Volume 1* (Island CID 9944) [1989]

A Robert Palmer 'greatest hits' collection could not be anything other than a sweeping rollercoaster ride across stylistic boundaries, and sure enough this lurches from the lumpen rock'n'roll of 'Bad Case of Loving You (Doctor Doctor)' to the swirling African JuJu syncopations of 'Pride' in the first two tracks alone. Most of the important stuff is here – 'Addicted to Love', 'Looking for Clues', 'Some Guys Have All the Luck', 'Johnny and Mary', 'Simply Irresistible' and more – although he's already had several hits since ('She Makes My Day', 'Mercy Mercy Me/I Want You') which are presumably bound for Volume 2.

The Power Station

Convened: 1985, New York. Split up: 1985
Robert Palmer (f) – vocals; Andy Taylor (f) – guitar; John
Taylor (f) – bass; Tony Thompson (f) – drums
US No.6 album: 1985: *The Power Station* (Fame CDFA 3206)

Palmer wrote a set of lyrics for some music which John Taylor and
Andy Taylor of Duran Duran had sent him on a tape in the post.
From this small beginning, the idea developed of recording an
album, and, with Chic's powerhouse drummer Tony Thompson
on board, the Power Station was born. 'It was nuts,' says Palmer.
'We just did it at the weekend. It was like a crazy party for 48
hours. I don't know how stuff got done. Maybe that's part of the
appeal of the record, that it's so careless.'

Superficially spontaneous perhaps, but in fact there were some
carefully calculated trade-offs here. Palmer was looking for a way
to reach a young pop audience, while the Taylors were desperate
for some adult rock credibility. Both sides got what they wanted,
although Palmer baulked at the idea of actually touring with the
band. The other three recruited little known vocalist Michael Des
Barres (ex-Silverhead, ex-Detective), with whom they played at
Live Aid, and then fizzled out shortly afterwards.

• *The Power Station* (Fame CDFA 3206) [1985]

Recorded at the studio of the same name in New York, the only
Power Station album is a monument to what can be done with a
heavy rock formula when it is dressed up with a little class. Palmer
can afford to be a bit sniffy about it, but with highlights including
'Get It On', 'Some Like It Hot', 'Communication' and a brave
version of the Isley Brothers 'Harvest for the World', it remains
far and away the best thing that anyone associated with Duran
Duran has ever been involved with.

Pet Shop Boys

Convened: 1982, London
Chris Lowe (f) – keyboards; Neil Tennant (f) – vocals
UK No.2 albums: 1987: *actually* (Parlophone CDP 746
972-2)

1988: *Introspective* (Parlophone CDP 790 868-2)

1990: *Behaviour* (Parlophone CDP 794 310-2)

Pet Shop Boys have provided a memorable pop soundtrack for the Eighties, one which reflects both the glamour and the hardness of their era. But there is a disconcerting hollowness at the centre of the duo's work which not even the pithiest of their material has altogether concealed.

Their story began when Chris Lowe (born October 4 1959) and Neil Tennant (born July 10 1954) struck up a conversation in an electronics shop in the Kings Road. Lowe was studying for a degree in architecture, while Tennant, already armed with a history degree, was a staff writer at *Smash Hits*. Discovering a shared enthusiasm for dance music in general and Hi-NRG in particular, these quiet, pale creatures began writing and demoing material together.

In 1985 they won a contract with EMI, at which point Tennant felt sufficiently emboldened to quit his post at *Smash Hits*. 'West End Girls', released for the second time towards the end of the year, became a worldwide hit, eventually reaching No.1 in both the UK and the US.

Pet Shop Boys cruised through the ensuing years of stardom, barely breaking sweat as they piled up hits and awards, and graciously extended a leg-up to faded divas like Liza Minnelli (*Results* – Epic 465 511-2; 1989) and Dusty Springfield (*Reputation* – Parlophone CDP 794 401-2; 1990).

When they finally bestirred themselves to mount a tour in 1989 it was a lavish but lustreless affair involving lots of dressing up and eye-catching dance routines which failed to distract sufficient attention from a musical performance that was, at best, entirely mechanical.

• *Please* (Parlophone CDP 746 271-2) [1986]

A winsome début which finally brought the pop wing of the miserablist tendency – as established by more rock-orientated acts like The SMITHS and New Order – fully on stream. Rigid, machine-generated disco rhythms, cold synthesiser instrumentation and Tennant's expressionless, half-spoken drawl are the ingredients which lend 'West End Girls' its eerie, down-beat attraction. Other hits, including the hedonistic manifesto 'Opportunities (Let's Make Lots of Money)' and the riotous 'Suburbia' established a soulless formula which has altered little, if at all, on subsequent albums.

● *actually* (Parlophone CDP 746 972-2) [1987]

Whether wallowing in a sense of shame ('It's a Sin') or persecution ('What Have I Done to Deserve This?') the Boys' crisp, unemotional performances always evince an air of knowing detachment, an impression confirmed by the cover photograph of a yawning Tennant and a scowling Lowe. Tenant's adenoidal drone embraces more prosaic activities such as paying the rent ('Rent') and shopping ('Shopping'), with the same dry, faintly melancholic tone, while Lowe executes his one-finger synth-melodies above the metronomic drum-machine beats, like a child drawing lines in the sand. It's a tough job, but somebody's got to do it, right, lads?

● *Introspective* (Parlophone CDP 790 868-2) [1988]

Lowe and Tennant continue to capture with deadpan acuity the wistful neurosis that characterises teenage angst. In the extended club mix of 'Left to My Own Devices', even the most ordinary activity, making a cup of tea for instance, is turned into a gesture of romantic despair. Enjoyment of such peculiar and inward-looking whimsy depends in no small measure on the listener's capacity to suspend disbelief.

Other highlights on an album which musters only a measly six (long) tracks, are a remix of the Boys' chart-topping version of PRESLEY's 'Always On My Mind' and 'Domino Dancing'.

● *Behaviour* (Parlophone CDP 794 310-2) [1990]

'This Must Be the Place I Waited Years to Leave', 'How Can You Expect to be Taken Seriously?', 'My October Symphony'.... Same script, longer titles.

● *Discography* (Parlophone CDPMTV 3) [1991]

The perfect reprise of the Pet Shop Boys' not inconsiderable catalogue of hit singles, complete with snappy comments from the Boys themselves: 'It's still one of our favourites' ('Love Comes Quickly'), 'The song's lyrics tell a true story by the way' ('So Hard') and 'This is our favourite song on our fourth LP *Behaviour*' ('Being Boring').

Tom Petty and The Heartbreakers

Convened: 1975, Los Angeles, California

Tom Petty (Born: October 20 1953, Gainesville, Florida) – vocals/guitar; Mike Campbell (f) – guitar/keyboards/bass/ bouzouki/ mandolin/dulcimer; Howie Epstein – bass/vocals; Stan Lynch (f) – drums; Benmont Tench (f) – keyboards/ accordion

US No.2 album: 1979: ***Damn the Torpedoes*** (MCA DMCF 3044)

He seems to have reverted to type in recent years, but when Tom Petty first emerged like some pale rider from the mêlée of the American New Wave – alongside contenders like Television, Patti Smith and TALKING HEADS – he breathed new life into a traditional rock'n'roll guitar band formula that had fallen into conspicuous disrepute.

His long-term problem was two-fold. As a 'working-class hero', building from first principles and helping rock to rediscover its integrity, he couldn't fail to invite comparisons with Bruce SPRINGSTEEN, John MELLENCAMP and to a lesser extent Bob Seger. But Petty was unable to develop anything approaching the iconography of those acts and, to compound the situation, he had trouble sustaining the quality of his material beyond an initial burst of glory.

In truth, Petty is by inclination more of a journeyman musician than a look-at-me-everybody rock star, and his redoubtable Heartbreakers are an arena-scale bar band. It is instructive that Petty and The Heartbreakers' biggest hit single was achieved by backing Stevie Nicks on 'Stop Draggin' My Heart Around', from Nicks' album *Bella Donna* (EMI CZ 398; 1981).

Perhaps they found their true métier as Bob DYLAN's backing group, a partnership which was forged at the Farm Aid concert in

1985 and continued for the *True Confessions* tour of America, Japan and Australasia in 1986, and Europe the following year.

Due to his involvement with DYLAN and subsequently The Traveling Wilburys (see under George HARRISON), Petty has been admitted into rock's old boys' club before his time. He remains a safe pair of hands, but seems to have checked in his inspiration – and his ego – at the door.

- *Tom Petty and The Heartbreakers* (MCA DMCL 1715) [1976]
- *Damn the Torpedoes* (MCA DMCF 3044) [1979]

Petty has often talked of his early work as music that is rooted in the Fifties and Sixties but set in a contemporary context. Certainly his self-titled début conformed to that description, with street-toughened anthems like 'Anything That's Rock'n'Roll' and the haunting BYRDS sound-alike 'American Girl' rejoicing in a welcome rawness of feel, despite their coventional themes.

Petty's third album, *Damn the Torpedoes*, married credibility with choruses and marked his break-through to the big league. With rootsy, down-the-line rockers like 'Refugee' and 'Don't Do Me Like That', Petty brought unimpeachable commitment, if little mystery, to bear on a well-tried format – and reaped the dividends.

- *Let Me Up (I've Had Enough)* (MCA DMCL 1905) [1987]

Petty brings few surprises to his work, but few clichés either, even if the title track revisits that *Exile On Main St* groove so beloved of American rockers everywhere. His hallmark is brisk understatement: simple, chunky chord changes sketching an uncluttered musical backdrop to lyrics which gently explore the theme of a lifetime's relationships as so many damaged goods. With 11 new songs, including one co-written with DYLAN ('Jammin' Me'), he demonstrates that a mellow mood need not presume a bland execution.

- **Tom Petty:** *Full Moon Fever* (MCA DMCG 6034) [1989]

Never an original talent, Petty tends to absorb and be guided by what is going on around him. On *Full Moon Fever* that means DYLAN and the sounds of the past.

The DYLAN tour had just finished when Petty and another soon-to-be Traveling Wilbury, Jeff Lynne, started writing the album. It was the first to be credited to Petty without The Heartbreakers, and although Mike Campbell was also closely involved with the project, the scene of the crime is covered with Lynne/Wilbury fingerprints.

The result is heritage rock'n'roll, a modern musical equivalent of a Hovis advertisement. There are Bo Diddley beats ('A Mind With a Heart of Its Own'), Buddy Holly beats ('The Apartment Song') and a painstaking reconstruction of The BYRDS' 'Feel a Whole Lot Better', while 'Yer So Bad' sounds like a cross between The Kinks and DYLAN.

Such transparent revivalism went down a storm, especially in the States, where the album peaked at No.3 and became Petty's best-selling release since *Damn The Torpedoes* (see above).

- *Into the Great Wide Open* (MCA MCD 10317) [1991]

The trademarked Petty sound is present and correct, but this album loses its charm after prolonged exposure. Its panoramic theme is poorly served by a restrained delivery and Jeff Lynne's lightweight production. It sounds more like a weak George HARRISON album than the blue-collar rock'n'roll The Heartbreakers used to knock out with such gutsy bravado in their prime.

Pink Floyd

Convened: 1965, London
David Gilmour – vocals/guitar; Nick Mason (f) – drums; Richard Wright (f) – keyboards/vocals
UK/US No.1 album: 1975: **Wish You Were Here** (Harvest CDP 746 035-2)
UK No.1 albums: 1970: **Atom Heart Mother** (EMI CDP 746 381-2)
1983: **The Final Cut** (Harvest CDP 746 129-2)

US No.1 albums: 1973: **Dark Side of the Moon** (Harvest
                    CDP 746 001-2)
                    1979: **The Wall** (Harvest CDS 746
                    036-8)

If there is one group for which the enhanced audio medium of CD
might have been invented, it is Pink Floyd. From their earliest days
as house band at the UFO club where they rapidly became the
guiding light of England's psychedelic *avant garde*, to their latter-
day status as an international supergroup, the Floyd have never
been about personalities or attitude, let alone anything so
fleetingly trivial as rock'n'roll. The Floyd's music is about sound,
and the spectacle that such sound suggests.

● **The Piper at the Gates of Dawn** (EMI CDP 746 384-2) [1967]

Pink Floyd's début was recorded, like *Sergeant Pepper's Lonely Hearts
Club Band*, on four-track equipment at Abbey Road. The album
reflects the dominance of the group's original singer and guitarist,
Syd Barrett, an unbalanced and oddly gifted songwriter whose
talent started to turn super-nova from the day he first set foot in
a recording studio. Barrett harnessed the group's R'n'B beat-
boom roots to his acid-spiked vision of rock as a vehicle for
transcendent, inter-planetary flights of the imagination.

The opening babble of voices emerging from radio static, set
against a yammering bleeping tone emanating from some distant
corner of the cosmos, sets the tense scene for 'Astronomy
Domine'. The rest of the original group – Roger Waters (bass/
vocals), Wright and Mason – are also credited for the extended
improvisation of 'Interstellar Overdrive', the track which sign-
posted their collective interest in a textural, impressionistic
approach to rock that often dispensed with the conventional
requirements of a formal melody and an insistent beat.

Still a magnificent album, it established sufficient momentum
at the time to carry the group through the ensuing period of
nightmarish instability as Barrett, whose eccentric personality
had become aggravated both by the pressures of success and by
copious intakes of LSD, slid swiftly into insanity. He was replaced
by the more prosaic David Gilmour in 1968.

- **Ummagumma** (EMI CDP 746 404-8) [1969]

The mind-boggling Hipgnosis-designed cover – the endless mirror within a mirror photograph – was seen on many a campus coffee-bar table at the turn of the Seventies, but despite its nostalgic cachet the double CD (one disc recorded live, one in the studio) exposes a myriad of weaknesses. For the studio side, it was decided that each member of the now Barrett-less group would write one quarter of the music. As Gilmour later put it: 'I'd never written anything before. I just went into the studio and started waffling about, tacking bits and pieces together.' He wasn't the only one, by the sound of it.

- **Atom Heart Mother** (EMI CDP 746 381-2) [1970]
- **Meddle** (Harvest CDP 746 034-2) [1971]

In their different ways both these albums were evidence of an increasing coherence in the Floyd's work. The 23-minute title track of *Atom Heart Mother*, with its idiosyncratic orchestral arrangement, remains something of an oddity. But signs that the post-Barrett Floyd were beginning to find their métier are confirmed by the swirling space-boogie of 'One of These Days' which opens *Meddle* and the rampant atmospherics of its centre-piece track, 'Echoes', another 23-minute marathon that is a *tour de force* of carefully interwoven effects, gradually engulfed by wave upon wave of guitar feedback at the climax.

- **Dark Side of the Moon** (Harvest CDP 746 001-2) [1973]

This is the album which dominated the Seventies. It took Pink Floyd from the backwaters of English acid rock conceptualism into the international super-league and defined an era of album-orientated rock. It has ·enjoyed astonishing chart longevity, especially in America, where it was the group's first album to breach the Top 40. It remains a perennial presence in the CD market, and since 1987 alone (when Pink Floyd set off on the *Momentary Lapse of Reason* tour) *Dark Side of the Moon* has sold four million copies, bringing its worldwide sales tally to 23 million.

Recorded on 16-track equipment at Abbey Road studios, with the new Dolby noise-reduction system being adopted half-way through the sessions, the production, although basic by today's standards, does not sound unduly primitive. Indeed, there are later Floyd albums which sound more dated.

Not only are tracks such as 'Money', 'Time', 'Us and Them' and 'Brain Damage' powerful, concise musical statements, they also boast a cohesive thematic content. While Gilmour provides many majestic instrumental passages, Waters' lyrics bear down with stark prescience on a universal subject – the simple, often trivial pressures of daily life that can lead to insanity. There is no air of outmoded hippy optimism about this album; rather the despairing observation that with each new day '. . . you're older/Shorter of breath and one day closer to death'.

The album has been available in CD format bearing EMI's 001 catalogue number since August 1984 and it remains somewhere among the Top 10 selling CDs of all-time. With its striking audio *vérité* sound effects of chiming clocks and ringing cash tills, it is the sort of album that has traditionally appealed to the audiophile section of the rock market and has doubtless been a priority purchase for many proud investors in laser technology.

Such fans may be surprised, if not dismayed, to learn that the early CD version of the album was transferred not from the master tape, but from a standard 15 ips Dolby copy, a practice which Gilmour believes to be widespread (see also LED ZEPPELIN). 'We weren't involved initially. They just went ahead and did it. When we found out about it we had to do an investigation to find out where the real original master was, and then have that remastered, which we eventually had done.'

Dark Side of the Moon was undoubtedly a high-water mark in the Pink Floyd odyssey. 'It changed our fortunes everywhere,' Gilmour recalls. Waters, however, took a typically jaundiced view of its impact, declaring in 1987 that *Dark Side of the Moon* had 'finished the group off. Once you've cracked it, it's all over.'

Either way, the album remains a vision of rare intensity, a resonant evocation of the shadowy corners of the rock psyche. Large chunks of it still feature prominently in the live shows of both Pink Floyd and Roger Waters and it is clearly a body of work that has become part of the collective rock consciousness.

One clue to the secret of its longevity may be the curiously reductive quality which it has demonstrated over the years. As Gilmour notes wryly, 'I thought it was a very complicated album when we first made it, but when you listen to it now it's really very simple.'

- **Wish You Were Here** (Harvest CDP 746 035-2) [1975]

Although a great album, and a guaranteed transatlantic smash, *Wish You Were Here* has been overshadowed to this day by the phenomenal success of *Dark Side of the Moon*. This was the apogee of the 'classic-era' Floyd. All lyrics are written by Waters, but the songwriting benefits from a combination of contributions from Gilmour, Waters and Wright. Gilmour is on particularly striking form – witness his long, bluesy intro to 'Shine On, You Crazy Diamond' and the harsh, shimmering slide that dominates the song's reprise.

- **Animals** (Harvest CDP 746 128-2) [1977]

By the mid-seventies Pink Floyd had become a performing colossus. Their stage shows were huge theatrical spectacles incorporating vast back-projections, multiple-source quadrophonic sound projection and grand-scale gimmicks such as the model aeroplane rigged to crash and explode into the stage.

But a vicious cycle of diminishing output and questionable artistic relevance was beginning to emerge by the time of *Animals*. Gilmour and Wright had been edged out of the songwriting frame by Waters, and the music had become a more single-minded reflection of his aloof, introspective nature. The grandiose themes and Mickey Mouse symbolism of this album sit as uncomfortably now as they did in the punk-dominated environment of 1977.

- **The Wall** (Harvest CDS 746 036-8) [1979]

With its autobiographical undercurrents and bloated narrative pretensions, *The Wall* took Waters' egocentricity to new heights, but restored some of the Floyd's standing by proving the perfect vehicle for a unique stage show of tremendous dramatic power. The album sold in vast quantities, staying at No.1 for an alarming 15 weeks in America, and providing the Floyd's only UK No.1 single 'Another Brick in the Wall (Part 2)'.

As Waters' stab at a hand-me-down version of Pete Town-shend's *Tommy*, *The Wall* works well enough. But the idea of extending the 'story' into a film, starring Bob Geldof as a mildly deranged rock'n'roller called Pink, was an ill-conceived exercise in wishful thinking.

Waters' revival of the show with an all-star cast at the scene of the demolished Berlin Wall in 1990 was an embarrassment of epic proportions, both artistically and financially.

● *The Final Cut* (Harvest CDP 746 129-2) [1983]

By this stage Waters had taken over completely. Wright had been forced out of the group after the completion of *The Wall*, Gilmour had been ditched from the producer credits (though he did not relinquish his co-producer royalty points) and Mason was keeping his head down. *The Final Cut* is thus the best solo album that Waters has made yet, which isn't saying a great deal.

● *A Momentary Lapse of Reason* (EMI CDP 748 068-2) [1987]

After four years of wrangling, Gilmour and Mason reinstated Wright and recorded a new Pink Floyd album without Waters. The errant bass player, whose hubris had led him to assume firstly that such a record could not be made and, secondly, that even if it was possible it would be a hideous failure, was suddenly confronted by nemesis in the shape of *A Momentary Lapse of Reason*.

Described by a bitter and litigious Waters as 'a very facile but quite clever forgery', it is in fact a perfectly valid album which preserves standards while restating the classic Floyd values. It has sold upwards of eight million copies, which certainly makes it a very successful 'forgery'.

The truth is that Gilmour had assumed control with such impressive confidence that a new generation of rock fans, particularly in America, simply didn't notice that Waters was missing. He had forgotten the fundamental Floydian principal, intact since Syd Barrett was quietly eased out in 1968, that there are no stars in Pink Floyd that can rival the sounds (and spectacle) of the show itself.

● *Delicate Sound of Thunder* (EMI CDS 791 480-2) [1988]

Although they are a much boot-legged act, this is Pink Floyd's only official live album, apart from half of *Ummagumma* (see above). A memento of the *Momentary Lapse of Reason* tour, which turned out to be the most successful outing in the band's 21-year history, it highlights the scrupulous, fluent guitar playing of Gilmour, who also handles the vocals with considerable élan, and underlines the group's painstaking attention to musical detail even when assembling a show of such vast theatrical proportions.

A bit overloaded with tracks from *A Momentary Lapse of Reason* (five in all), it also boasts a solid cross-section of old standbys, including 'Time', 'Money', 'Another Brick In The Wall Part 2' and 'Wish You Were Here'.

Pixies

Convened: 1985, Boston, Massachusetts
Kim Deal (f) – bass/vocals; Black Francis (f) – vocals/guitar;
David Lovering (f) – drums; Joey Santiago (f) – guitar
UK No.3 album: 1990: *Bossanova* (4AD CADCD 0010)

Singer and would-be rock star Charles Michael Kitteridge Thompson IV, aka Black Francis, met guitarist Joey Santiago when the pair were both students at Amherst University, Massachusetts. They put a small ad in the Musicians Wanted section of a Boston paper: 'Band seeks bassist into Husker Du and Peter, Paul and Mary.' It attracted just the one reply, a girl from Daytona called Kim Deal, with experience as one half of a folk duo called The Breeders, but without a bass. She knew a drummer called David Lovering and in July 1986 Pixies began rehearsals in Lovering's Dad's garage.

It has been their singular· achievement to create a harsh, visceral, noisy form of rock'n'roll, with impeccable intellectual credentials, that is also unmistakably good fun. Francis' high pitched voice has a tendency to resolve into an impressively blood-curdling scream and Santiago's guitar sound usually boasts all the tonal subtlety of a concrete mixer, but the stultifying sense of alienation that is so often telegraphed by groups in this milieu is almost entirely absent from their outstanding portfolio.

- ## *Surfer Rosa* (4AD CAD 803 CD) [1988]

The critical acclaim which greeted this release, particularly in the UK, was boundless. The staff of *Melody Maker* pronounced it the best album of the year. It was produced by former Big Black and Rapeman supremo Steve Albini, a man with a finely honed understanding of the mechanics of hard-core, who coaxed and then faithfully recorded some stunning excesses from the band. Most memorable moments are the monumental thrash-out of 'Tony's Theme', and the more measured grind of 'Cactus' and 'Bone Machine', both of which buck and heave like a land-rover ploughing through a muddy field. A frighteningly good album.

- ## *Doolittle* (4AD CADCD 905) [1989]

This collection transformed Pixies from college/alternative circuit favourites to mainstream contenders, making them the biggest indie band since The SMITHS. It remains a trove of delights in a more overtly melodic vein than that of *Surfer Rosa*, but still couched in the harsh musical vocabulary of hard-core.

A truly radical departure is the delightful, dulcet-toned ballad, 'Hey', although the tuning of Santiago's guitar remains approximate enough for it not to affect their garage-band credentials.

The key to the album's success is the bewitching single 'Monkey Gone To Heaven', apparently a comment on pollution, and the band's most memorable chorus to date.

- ## *Bossanova* (4AD CAD D 0010) [1990]

Quite the best Pixies album; 14 succinct statements ranging from the surfing twang of 'Cecilia Ann' one minute to the demented shriek of 'Rock Music' the next. The band's musical approach sticks rigorously to the thrashy guitar-bass-drums format, but a good song will transcend the limitations of any idiom, and *Bossanova* is bursting with irresistible melodies and quirky little passages of improbable delight.

The best track is 'The Happening', with a chorus which initially seems to echo 'Monkey Gone to Heaven' but then takes off in a spiralling swell of falsetto voices as oddly alluring as sea sirens calling through the mist.

Black Francis' trippy nonsense lyrics are frequently redolent of Syd Barrett's early work, a typical example being their first Top 30 hit, 'Velouria' (a name made up, no doubt, to rhyme with 'I'll adore ya'). There is invariably a haunting quality to phrases where literal meaning remains deliberately opaque.

- *Trompe le Monde* (4AD CAD 1014 CD) [1991]

Here there is a sophisticated veneer but, unlike the transcendent *Bossanova*, a disappointing dearth of decent songs. The band seems belatedly to have discovered the old-fashioned maxims of punk, UK-style. The rhythm section is stiff and piston-like while Santiago's highly abrasive guitar sound seeps messily into every available crevice of the backing track, then overflows to about waist-height in the vocal mix.

Still there are odd treats here and there, and Pixies fans, together with those diehards who still hanker for the spirit of classic-era Stooges or Ramones, will enjoy rooting them out.

Robert Plant See LED ZEPPELIN

The Pogues

Convened: 1983, London
Philip Chevron – guitar/vocals; James Fearnley (f) – accordion/piano; Jem Finer (f) – banjo/saxophone/vocals; Darryl Hunt – bass/vocals; Andrew Ranken (f) – drums/vocals; Spider Stacy (f) – tin whistle/vocals; Joe Strummer – vocals/guitar; Terry Woods – cittern/concertina/banjo/vocals
UK No.3 album: 1988: *If I Should Fall From Grace With God* (Pogue Mahone 244 494-2)

With the announcement in 1991 of his retirement from The Pogues on grounds of 'ill health', Shane MacGowan joined the small but significant ranks of outstanding contributors to rock who have gone missing in action. Others include Syd Barrett (PINK FLOYD), Brian Wilson (The BEACH BOYS) and Peter Green (FLEETWOOD MAC).

No one who has seen The Pogues in the past could have been surprised by the news of MacGowan's demise. The gormless singer's alarming if entertaining portrait of drunken self-abuse could not have been sustained indefinitely, and it seems in retrospect a minor miracle that The Pogues have held together long enough to transform themselves from a novice rabble, inspired by the comic extremes of punk, to one of the top folk-rock crossover acts that Britain has produced.

The search for someone with sufficient experience, charisma and technical incompetence to fill MacGowan's shoes ended at the door of Joe Strummer, former front-man of The CLASH and a long-time collaborator with The Pogues.

History suggests that having weathered the loss of their singer and key source of inspiration, The Pogues can probably last forever and may even become more improbably successful than before. But it is now a job, not a calling, and both they and their fans must know it.

- *Rum, Sodomy and the Lash* (WEA 244 495-2) [1985]

MacGowan's muddled rasp and The Pogues' hell-for-leather approach are unlikely ever to be palatable to those for whom folk in a rock context means the gentle whimsy of Suzanne Vega or the master-craftsman approach of FAIRPORT CONVENTION. But the days when the group could be dismissed as talentless hooligans, desecrating a noble strand of their Irish heritage, had long since passed by the time of their second album *Rum, Sodomy and the Lash* (a title borrowed from Winston Churchill's memorable description of British naval tradition).

Produced by Elvis COSTELLO and featuring the original six-piece line-up of MacGowan, Finer, Fearnley, Stacy, Ranken and bassist Cait O'Riordan, it is an album placed squarely in the post-punk idiom, but drawing divine inspiration from the well of traditional Gaelic melody and folklore. Along with MacGowan originals like 'The Sick Bed of Cuchulainn' and 'The Old Main Drag', there is a fine version of Ewan MacColl's 'Dirty Old Town' and O'Riordan's touching ballad 'I'm a Man You Don't Meet Every Day'.

- *If I Should Fall From Grace With God* (Pogue Mahone 244 494-2) [1988]

After *Rum, Sodomy and the Lash*, the band recruited Chevron and

Woods, the latter a musician of immense experience whose experimental work in the Sixties and Seventies (notably with Steeleye Span) helped shape the course of Irish folk rock. An imported brass section was also on hand and the result is an album of tremendous vitality and imagination.

American visions abound, starting with 'Fairytale of New York', a duet with Kirsty MacColl which took the refrain of 'Happy Christmas your arse/I pray God it's our last' to No.2 in the UK's festive chart of 1988. An extraordinary big-band, neo-*West Side Story* instrumental, 'Metropolis', gives way to 'Thousands are Sailing', a gorgeous song, written by Chevron, on the theme of Celtic emigration.

The band is on superlative form during sustained bouts of cultural ransacking that extend as far afield as the Mediterranean for 'Turkish Song of the Damned' and beyond for 'Fiesta', with its bizarre makeshift carnival sound complete with Tijuana brass and zydeco accordion. MacGowan uses rich, vicious language in 'Birmingham Six' to describe the predicament of 'being Irish in the wrong place at the wrong time' and a slew of cheerfully obscene invective colours the up-tempo reel 'Bottle of Smoke', a breathless gallop that celebrates the day the money went on the right horse.

Elsewhere, on numbers like 'Lullabye of London' and 'The Broad Majestic Shannon', MacGowan's bronchial brogue draws out the thread of poignant melancholia that is one of the group's strongest cards.

- *Peace and Love* (Pogue Mahone 246 086-2) [1989]

Another ambitious album, but this time suffering from a lack of coherence. MacGowan's vision as a songwriter and lyricist had already outstripped his talent as a performer, and with the rest of the band blossoming in all directions, the limits of his pitifully rasping wheeze and drink-garbled diction are painfully exposed. Whether belting out 'Boat Train' at full tilt, or easing back on 'Night Train to Lorca' with its merry touches of Spanish horns, he might just as well be mumbling gibberish.

With the aid of the lyric sheet, certain over-familiar themes are detectable, still the most prevalent being the grim joys of drinking to the point of oblivion. How about this little charmer: 'First I drank the whiskey/Then I drank the gin/I tried to make the toilet/

And I broke me fuckin shin'?

Other voices were now moving in to fill the gaps. Woods sings his own traditional-sounding 'Young Ned of the Hill'; Chevron harmonises delicately with Kirsty MacColl on his BYRDS-like song 'Lorelei'; and Finer sings against a moody psychedelic drone on his song 'Tombstone'. But despite their various merits, you would be hard pushed to identify any of these songs as being by The Pogues, while a couple of splendidly weird metaphysical odysseys couched in the mystical musical vocabulary of psychedelia – 'Down All the Days' and 'USA' – only add to the confusion, even if they make sense of the album's ironic title.

● *Hell's Ditch* (Pogue Mahone 9031-72554-2) [1990]

MacGowan once again displays his gift for soaking up local colour (along with the liquor) and injecting a kaleidoscope of cosmopolitan influences into his songwriting. In the wake of a visit to Thailand, there is an Asian cast to the pretty 'Sayonara' and the soporific 'Summer in Siam'.

But his wheezy, befuddled singing is now beyond a joke and drags like a lead weight behind the sprightly performances of the rest of the band. The jaunty opener, 'Sunnyside of the Street', suffers particularly badly, but there are few tracks here that manage to rise above the destructive effects of MacGowan's state of permanent indisposition.

● *The Best of The Pogues* (Pogue Mahone 9031-75405-2) [1991]

A tidy and timely compilation drawing a neat line under the achievements of the MacGowan years. Most of the singles are here – 'Sally MacLennane', 'A Pair of Brown Eyes', 'Fairytale of New York' – along with choice album tracks such as 'The Broad Majestic Shannon' and 'Thousands are Sailing'.

The Police

Convened: 1977, London. Split up: 1986
Stewart Copeland – drums/vocals; STING – vocals/bass; Andy
Summers – guitar/vocals

UK/US No.1 album: 1983: ***Synchronicity*** (A&M CDA 63735)

UK No.1 albums: 1979: ***Regatta De Blanc*** (A&M CDMID 127)

1980: ***Zenyatta Mondatta*** (A&M CDMID 128)

1981: ***Ghost in the Machine*** (A&M CDMID 162)

1986: ***Every Breath you Take – The Singles*** (A&M EVECD 1)

The Police were the last of the old-fashioned supergroups. By the time they parted company the rock consensus had fragmented beyond repair, and never again would an act be able to boast an appeal stretching right across the board from teenage girls to ageing rock musos. The Police did it by: 1) marrying the energy of punk to the languid groove of reggae and harnessing the resulting hybrid to some of the most memorable pop melodies of recent times and 2) looking good.

'It was just a clever way of welding two things together,' Sting explained to *Q* magazine in 1987, with a typical mixture of arrogance and *sang froid*. 'I could see where the power of the punk energy lay and so we welded it to reggae, which was a much more sophisticated and seductive thing. Because we were experienced musicians we could do that. The SEX PISTOLS couldn't because they were only thrashing Bash Street Kids with instruments. It had power but no finesse so it couldn't go anywhere. It just blew up. Reggae was a closed system. They're still doing the same thing. It just goes round and round.'

For The Police, of course, things just went up and up.

The band was the brainchild of Stewart Copeland (ex-Curved Air) who met STING (ex-Last Exit) at a club in the latter's hometown of Newcastle and persuaded him to move to London with a view to starting a group. The pair recruited novice guitarist Henry Padovani, christened themselves The Police, and began playing sporadic gigs round the capital. Padovani was replaced by Andy Summers (ex-Zoot Money) at which point Copeland's brother Miles (manager of acts including Wishbone Ash) took over the reins of management.

Although inspired by the energy and attitude of punk,

Summers, Copeland and STING were all seasoned, highly skilled musicians. This caused much suspicion. Hardcore punks saw the group as too smooth and lacking in street credibility, while crustier members of the establishment viewed their approach as a cynical attempt to jump on a fashionable bandwagon. Neither critique had the slightest effect on the group's inexorable rise to the top.

• *Outlandos D'Amour* (A&M CDMID 126) [1978]

Their début introduced the musical vocabulary of reggae to the rock mainstream in much the same way as the first ROLLING STONES album co-opted American R'n'B for use in the pop culture of the Sixties. In so doing Summers, Copeland and STING may fairly lay claim to having contributed to the central core of fusions that define what rock music actually *is*. A towering achievement, the album houses the hits – 'Roxanne', 'Can't Stand Losing You' and 'So Lonely' – alongside more conventional rough-house rock like 'Next to You' and 'Born in the Fifties'.

• *Regatta De Blanc* (A&M CDMID 127) [1979]

The second album mined much the same rock-reggae vein, but with increasing self-assurance and chart-smarts. It supplied the UK No.1 hits 'Message in a Bottle' and 'Walking on the Moon'. Other stand-out tracks include 'The Bed's Too Big Without You' and the original version of 'Bring on the Night', later revived by STING as the title track of his 1986 live album.

• *Zenyatta Mondatta* (A&M CDMID 128) [1980]

The 'difficult' third album, this was recorded in some haste and suffered almost universal critical censure and even some negative comments from the band itself. Yet in retrospect it is a remarkable, raw distillation of The Police's art.

Perhaps because of the speed with which the songs were written and recorded, they tend to be concise, blunt statements. 'Shadows in the Rain' and 'Voices Inside My Head' are both neurotic, rhythmically dominated atmosphere pieces that admirably demonstrate the band's ability and willingness to experiment and extemporise.

Besides boasting the usual beguiling melodies, 'Driven to Tears' and 'When the World is Running Down You Make the Best of What's Still Around' signalled a new maturity in STING's lyrical concerns. Even coming from the pen of a young millionaire, 'Driven to Tears', which he sang at Live Aid, remains a particularly poignant comment on token reactions to colour supplement portrayals of Third World suffering: 'Seems when some innocents die/All we can offer them is a page in some magazine/Too many cameras and not enough food/This is what we've seen.'

The two singles are the rather twee 'Don't Stand So Close To Me', the Police's third UK No.1, and the curiously lambasted 'De Do Do Do, De Da Da Da', an untypically humble and precisely articulated testament to the power of words as instruments of both influence and deception.

Of The Police's bountiful back catalogue, this is the album most urgently in need of a critical reassessment.

- *Ghost in the Machine* (A&M CDMID 162) [1981]

This is a rather joyless affair, notwithstanding the nagging calypso of 'Every Little Thing She Does is Magic'. Typical of the album's grey feeling as a whole is the dour 'Invisible Sun', a single whose accompanying video, incorporating scenes from wartorn Northern Ireland, was banned from BBC television.

- *Synchronicity* (A&M CDA 63735) [1983]

Like The JAM, The Police went out at their peak, and their last recording was also their biggest seller. It houses the quietly sinister classic, 'Every Breath You Take', a single which stayed at No.1 in the American chart for two months, along with the lesser hits 'Wrapped Around Your Finger', 'Synchronicity II' and 'King of Pain'.

- *Every Breath You Take – The Singles* (A&M EVECD 1) [1986]

With the exception of the new version of their 1980 No.1, 'Don't Stand So Close To Me '86', all the songs on this incomplete collection of singles reached the UK Top 20. Apart from being the swansong of the most successful group of its era, this album also underlines the Police's uncanny ability to create a durable commercial sound from a challenging mixture of cross-cutting rhythms and oddly jigged arrangements.

Iggy Pop

Born: James Jewel Osterberg, April 21, 1947, Ann Arbor, Michigan
UK No.28 album: 1977: *Lust for Life* (Virgin CDOVD 278)

The Stooges

Convened: 1968, Detroit, Michigan. Split up: 1974
Dave Alexander (f) – bass; Ron Asheton (f) – guitar; Scott Asheton (f) – drums; Iggy Pop (f) – vocals
UK No.44 album: 1977 [first issued 1973]: *Raw Power* (Essential ESSCD 005)

The late American critic Lester Bangs took an orthodox view when he described the music of Iggy Pop and The Stooges as 'brutal, mindless, primitive, vicious, base, savage, primal, hate-filled, grungy, terrifying and above all *real*'. Pop, however, bridled at the description when interviewed in 1988:

'People used to hate our band, but you could only say that it was mindless and so on if you didn't have to go through the process of thinking the whole thing up. I was on the debate team in high school. My father taught English literature. I have speech skills. I have writing skills and I know damn well how to present my point. I'm a pro and I always was, even back then.'

Although he still prefers to be called Jim by the people around him, James Osterberg took the stage name Iggy from his first band, the Iguanas, in which he sang and played drums while still at high school. As frontman of The Stooges he won a reputation as much for his masochistic on-stage stunts as for his singing. Boasting perennial three-chord wonders like 'I Wanna Be Your Dog', '1969' and 'No Fun', the group's début, *The Stooges* (1969;

unavailable except as import, Elektra 74051-2, about £14) became the prototype for the punk revolution of the Seventies.

After the breakup of The Stooges, Pop embarked on an erratic solo career which eventually led to a spiral of diminishing returns. 'By early 1983, when I was touring *Zombie Birdhouse* (1982; unavailable), I became aware that I was a wreck. I looked 50 years old. I was getting injured on stage. I was such a miserable, vainglorious junkie. The balance of uppers and downers I was taking was leaving me about two creative minutes a day and I was not writing well any more. It was a mess. I was embarrassed. I knew I had to quit.'

Pop cleaned up, got married in 1985 and at the end of 1986 scored his first UK hit single, 'Real Wild Child'. Since then he has focused his considerable energies on producing 'good work in a condition of sobriety'. He has yet to reap the benefits commercially, but as one of the most notoriously self-destructive characters in rock he has kept on adding postscripts to a career that has long read like a succession of final chapters.

● *Iggy Pop and The Stooges: Raw Power* (Essential ESSCD 005) [1973]

The Stooges had temporarily split up in 1971 and Pop was allegedly mowing lawns to make a living when, not for the last time, David BOWIE stepped into the breach. He persuaded the group to go to London, where he oversaw the recording of their third album, *Raw Power*, an inspired collection which foreshadowed the eventual amalgamation of high-energy punk and thundering heavy metal by roughly a decade. Numbers including 'Search and Destroy' and the title track demonstrate the group's talent for organised pandemonium as well as anything else they ever released.

● *The Idiot* (Virgin CDOVD 277) [1977]
● *Lust For Life* (Virgin CDOVD 278) [1977]

This brace of David-BOWIE-produced albums remains Pop's most distinguished solo work. *The Idiot* is a glowering, mid-tempo collection of songs ranging from the neurotic metal-funk of 'Sister Midnight' to the piston-pump rhythm and discordant chorus of 'Funtime'. It also includes the original version of 'China Girl', co-written by Pop and BOWIE and later a hit for BOWIE.

Lust For Life, featuring the Tin Machine rhythm-section-to-be of Tony Sales (bass) and Hunt Sales (drums), together with BOWIE on piano, is more of a straight-ahead rock'n'roll album, but one that is blessed with a wondrous, eternal energy. To this day, 'The Passenger', with its reverberating cyclical chord sequence, and 'Lust For Life', with Hunt Sales' pounding tomtom tattoo, are among Pop's most fondly regarded signature themes.

● *Blah-Blah-Blah* (A&M 395 145-2) [1986]

Again produced by David BOWIE, this was Pop's most serious bid for major chart honours. On tracks like 'Baby It Can't Fall' and 'Shades', carefully modulated layers of synthesiser and guitar wash over a huge-sounding snare drum, while the idiosyncratic kinks and bombastic elements of Pop's volatile vocal style are neatly ironed out in favour of the lugubrious tone of a man who has not properly woken from a deep sleep. It didn't quite work, and although the single 'Real Wild Child' was a hit, the album failed to take off in quite the way that was hoped.

● *Instinct* (A&M CDA 5198) [1988]

Pop co-wrote four of the tracks with the album's featured guitarist, Steve Jones (ex-SEX PISTOLS), whose peculiarly leaden way with a power riff is something of a liability overall. Pop turns in a workmanlike vocal performance, sounding like Andrew Eldritch of The Sisters of Mercy on the attractive 'Lowdown', but sometimes betraying an uncertain finger on the melodic trigger, especially on the closing rant of 'Squarehead'.

● *Brick by Brick* (Virgin America CDVUS 19) [1990]

For those familiar with either the hyperthyroid yell or the bombed-out bass drawl, it comes as something of a shock to hear recorded evidence of Pop actually trying to sing.

The title track is a plea for balance, sanity and dignity away from the rock'n'roll rat-race. Primarily acoustic, it's one of several numbers – 'Crap Out', 'Butt Town', 'Pussy Power' – that, despite a radio-friendly ambience, did not get on to many play lists because of Pop's unguarded use of strongly 'idiomatic' language.

At least he was trying to extend his range and shake himself out of the old anarcho-punk routine that had become such a creative burden for him, and despite certain deficiencies this is an album with an odd, vibrant charm.

Elvis Presley

Born: January 8 1935, Tupelo, Mississippi. Died: August 16 1977

UK/US No.1 albums:	1960:	*G.I. Blues* (RCA ND 83735)
	1961:	*Blue Hawaii* (RCA ND 83683)
UK No.1 albums:	1960:	*Elvis is Back* (RCA ND 89013)
	1962:	*Pot Luck* (RCA ND 89098)
	1969:	*From Elvis in Memphis* (RCA ND 90548)
	1975:	*40 Greatest Hits* (unavailable)
US No.1 albums:	1956:	*Elvis Presley* (RCA ND 89046)
	1956:	*Elvis* (re-titled *Rock'n'Roll No.2* RCA ND 81382)
	1957:	*Loving You* (RCA ND 81515)
	1957:	*Elvis' Christmas Album* (RCA ND 90300)
	1961:	*Something for Everybody* (RCA ND 84116)
	1964:	*Roustabout* (unavailable)
	1973:	*Aloha from Hawaii via Satellite* (RCA PD 82642)

Unquestionably the greatest rock'n'roll star of all time, Elvis Presley was also one of the most profligate. For every exceptional song he bequeathed, there are a dozen mediocrities; for every *Jailhouse Rock* or *King Creole* at least six embarrassing movie duds; for every essential album an alarming quotient of dross. It sometimes seems as if his legacy consists of nothing but tacky memorabilia and freak-show impersonators. As the American writer Timothy White so memorably put it, 'Since his passing Elvis Presley is everywhere in evidence but nowhere in substance.'

Presley gave no proper interviews, wrote virtually no songs, played only rudimentary rhythm guitar and spent two years in the army at the most critical point of his career. Yet by the time of his death he had starred in 31 movies, sold an estimated 300 million records and shifted the world of popular music on its axis.

He did it by applying a colossal raw singing talent to a style of music that was essentially black in origin, while simultaneously transplanting the white, teenage-rebel image of James Dean from the movies to the world of pop. If he wasn't the outright creator of rock'n'roll, then he was one of its defining phenomena, and it was his towering contribution that laid the stylistic ground-rules of what has become the most pervasive art form of the twentieth century.

Brought up in a poor sharecropping family, Presley's earliest musical influences were the white gospel of the church and the black R'n'B of his neighbours. It was Sam Phillips, producer and owner of the Memphis-based independent label Sun Records, who first spotted and nurtured the saturnine hillbilly punk's incredible talent. But Phillips could not afford to keep hold of his discovery and sold Presley on to RCA in 1956. Once on a major label, success beyond anyone's wildest dreams was instantaneous.

But an arguably even more significant transaction had occurred the previous year when Presley signed over the management of his career to 'Colonel' Tom Parker, a move which ultimately cost the singer dear. For, after the triumphs of the early years with RCA, Parker's insensitive guidance set Presley on a rudderless course towards movies of an ever-declining standard ('Anybody who'll pay my boy a million dollars can make any kind of picture he wants,' said Parker) and the tasteless glitz of his blow-out years in Las Vegas.

Presley rewrote the story of contemporary music with himself in the leading role, but his recorded legacy has been of diminished relevance to the CD revolution. Presley was, after all, in his prime when the 45 rpm vinyl format had yet to become fully established, and 'Heartbreak Hotel', like all his early records, was released as a matter of course on 78 rpm for the benefit of those among the record-buying public who had yet to make the switch to 45 and 33-and-a-third rpm record-playing technology. *Plus ça change. . . .*

In the Sixties, with the advent of stereo, many of the early Presley albums were retrospectively subjected to fake 'electronically reprocessed stereo' mixes, an aural technique roughly equivalent to the latterday practice of tinting old black and white movies. Fortunately, the digital remastering that has been undertaken in transferring the material on to CD has been accompanied by a welcome return to the original mono mixes, the result being a sound quality that is far more respectful to the intent of the original productions.

- *Elvis Presley* (RCA ND 89046) [1956]

Digitally remastered in glorious mono in 1984, Presley's first album, incorporating five of the tracks recorded at Sam Phillips' Sun studios and another seven recorded in January 1956, remains one of the truly historic monuments of rock'n'roll. 'Blue Suede Shoes', 'I Love You Because', 'Tutti Frutti', 'Blue Moon', 'Money Honey' and others propelled it to the US No.1 slot where it stayed for ten consecutive weeks. You'd have to be Phil COLLINS to do that now.

- *The All Time Greatest Hits* (RCA PD 90100) [1987]

In March 1956 'Heartbreak Hotel' entered the American pop charts. An entire generation's spine tingled with a new delight as Presley's vocal, swathed in layers of mysterious echo, drawled its sultry message above Bill Black's slinky upright bass line and Scotty Moore's taut, clanging guitar riff. This revolutionary sound ushered in the golden age of both Elvis Presley and rock'n'roll. In the four years to 1960 he enjoyed more than 30 hits (13 of them US No.1s) including 'Blue Suede Shoes', 'Don't Be Cruel', 'Hound Dog', 'All Shook up', 'Love Me Tender', 'Teddy Bear', 'Are You Lonesome Tonight' *et al*.

The All Time Greatest Hits is a vast 45-track double-CD collection which boasts all of those and more: 'Good Luck Charm', 'Return to Sender' and 'Devil in Disguise' from the early Sixties, right through to later standards like 'Crying in the Chapel', 'Suspicious Minds' and 'Way Down', which in 1977 was his final UK No.1.

There are lots of Presley compilations but none that boast quite such an awesome span as this one.

- *The Complete Sun Sessions* (RCA PD 86414) [1987]
- *The Elvis Presley Sun Collection* (RCA ND89107) [1975]

The pickiest pundits still argue that Presley never bettered his first recordings, made between July 1954 and November 1955, in the Sun studios in Memphis.

The Complete Sun Sessions is the definitive collection of those recordings, and was first issued in 1987. But although Elvis completists may relish the prospect of wading through five alternate takes of 'I Love You Because', seven alternate takes of 'I'm Left, You're Right, She's Gone' and various out-takes of at least six other tunes, for people of a less fervent or academic bent, the prospect of such repetition is not so appealing.

Thankfully the out-takes and alternate takes are confined to one disc while the master takes are presented in a listenable sequence on another. Even so, *The Elvis Presley Sun Collection* – virtually the same album but without all these extra curiosities – may be a preferable option.

Either way, one of these Sun collections is an essential Elvis CD companion. For here are all the classics from that most classic Presley period: 'Mystery Train', 'Good Rockin' Tonight', 'Blue Moon of Kentucky' and of course, his first single, a souped-up version of Arthur Crudup's 'That's All Right Mama', the song which first exposed the full force of Presley's raucous, sexy, languid, explosive delivery to an incredulous Sam Phillips and set the whole ball rolling.

The Power Station See ROBERT PALMER

The Pretenders

Convened: 1978, London
Martin Chambers (f) – drums; Pete Farndon (f) (died 14.4.83) – bass; James Honeyman-Scott (f) (died 16.6.82) – guitar; Chrissie Hynde (f) – vocals/guitar
UK No.1 album: 1980: *Pretenders* (WEA 256 774-2)

Led by the waspishly anti-establishment Chrissie Hynde, The Pretenders emerged as part of the supposed new order delivered up from the wreckage of punk. They had a reputation as a bunch of drug-fuelled hard nuts, which they worked hard to maintain, with predictably tragic consequences.

But as musicians they have always been sophisticated operators who have unfailingly upheld traditional melodic virtues. Chrissie Hynde may have fraternised with Johnny Rotten and Sid Vicious at the outset of punk, and be well known for her idle talk of firebombing McDonald's while demanding that the killing of any animal be made a criminal offence. But such radical thinking has never impinged on her music.

Indeed, the first Pretenders single 'Stop Your Sobbing' (1979), an old song written by Ray Davies of The Kinks, was an unabashed slice of Sixties pop revivalism. It was Davies, along with the other stars of the first generation of English rock (The BEATLES, The ROLLING STONES, etc.) who had first inspired Hynde to be a musician. When those bands ruled the roost, she was a schoolgirl growing up in Akron, Ohio, but by the early Seventies she was living in England and already well on the road to realising her dream. While planning and setting up her band she put in a stints as a contributor to the *New Musical Express* and behind the counter at Malcolm McLaren's notorious clothes boutique called Sex.

She eventually picked up the musicians she was looking for in Honeyman-Scott, Chambers and Farndon, all from Hereford, and once they got started, press interest was not slow to follow (particularly in *NME*). They reached the UK and US Top 10 with their eponymous début, but within 27 months of the album's release two of the group's founder members were dead. It was around this time that Billy Connolly remarked darkly that they were the group that 'no one ever leaves', but in fact Farndon had already been booted out for unreliable behaviour ten months before his death.

Chambers got his marching orders sometime between *Learning to Crawl* (WEA 923 980-2; 1984) and *Get Close* (WEA 240 976-2; 1987) and The Pretenders gradually but ineluctably became nothing more than a convenient *nom de guerre* for Hynde. 'I don't think I'm interesting enough on my own to substantiate going solo,' she once protested, and that's the way it has stayed: not really a group, but not entirely a solo act either.

After her well-publicised affair with her childhood hero Ray Davies, by whom her first daughter Natalie Rae was born in 1983,

Hynde married Jim Kerr of SIMPLE MINDS in 1984. She bore him a daughter, Yasmin, in 1985, but the marriage, which seemed to be conducted primarily by telephone, did not last out the Eighties.

● *Pretenders* (WEA 256 774-2) [1980]

The group has never bettered this début which, with its resonant blend of lyrical, jangly guitars and tough-girl romanticism, provided the blueprint for all subsequent releases. From the carefully modulated quiver of 'Brass in Pocket' to the verbal pistol whipping meted out in 'Precious', Hynde's bittersweet resolve never falters. Meanwhile, a future generation of indie guitarists, alerted to Honeyman-Scott's seductive, ringing tone, started practising.

● *The Singles* (WEA 242 229-2) [1987]

With Hynde's sensual, wobbling drawl, the chiming guitar of Honeyman-Scott or subsequent clone, and the measured belt of the much-missed Chambers, The Pretenders perfected a classic chart formula while maintaining a curiously unimpeachable street cred.

All the hits are here, a remarkable run of light-with-bite tunes including 'Brass in Pocket', 'Talk of the Town', 'I Go to Sleep', 'Don't Get Me Wrong', 'Back on the Chain Gang', '2,000 Miles', 'Message of Love' and 'Thin Line Between Love and Hate', together with freshened mixes of 'Stop Your Sobbing' and 'Kid'. Also featured is the chart-topping 1985 Hynde-UB40 duet of 'I Got You Babe'.

Prince

Born: Prince Rogers Nelson, June 7 1958, Minneapolis, Minnesota
UK/US No.1 album: 1989: *Batman* (Warner Bros 925 936-2)
UK No.1 albums: 1988: *Lovesexy* (Paisley Park 925 720-2)
1990: *Graffiti Bridge* (Paisley Park 7599-274 932)

US No.1 albums: 1984: *Purple Rain* (Warner Bros 925 395-2)

1985: *Around the World in a Day* (Warner Bros 925 286-2)

Playing Hugh Hefner to Michael JACKSON's Howard Hughes, Prince triumphed as rock's Man Of The Eighties. He brought a touch of glamour, class and sex (a lot of sex, actually) to a decade which began with the decadent and superficial charms of the new romantics (Duran Duran, Culture Club, Spandau Ballet and their ilk) and ended as an ongoing celebration of *All Our Yesterdays*.

Having attended his first James BROWN show at the age of ten, Prince started playing in bands while still in junior high school, reputedly mastering more than two dozen instruments on the way. Even before leaving school at the age of 16, he had sown the seeds of a Minneapolitan music scene, in which his role was to be that of brightest star and tireless auteur.

His band at Central High School was called Grand Central (later altered to Champagne) and incorporated Morris Day (drums, later to be singer in The Time) and Andre Anderson (bass, later known as Andre Cymone, a member of Prince's backing group and solo artist). Champagne's main competitors on the Minneapolis 'Uptown' club circuit were Flyte Tyme, a group co-founded in 1974 by Jellybean Johnson (drums), Terry Lewis (bass, later one half of the Jam-Lewis production team) and Alexander O'Neal (vocals, later a solo star). Years afterwards, in 1981, Prince co-opted the entire band, rechristening them The Time, and using them as ciphers in presenting a set of his own compositions written in a harder, blacker vein than he felt comfortable putting out under his own name.

Since he signed his first recording contract in 1977 Prince has maintained a creative output verging on the profligate. Apart from 1983, he has released one new album and sometimes two every year since 1978, and still there is no live album or greatest hits compilation in sight. Of these a significant proportion have been the soundtracks of films, most of which Prince has acted in and some he has directed as well: *Purple Rain* (for which he won an oscar for Best Original Score, see below), *Parade – Music from 'Under the Cherry Moon'* (see below), *Sign o' the Times* (see below), *Batman* (see above) and *Graffiti Bridge* (see above).

Although helplessly shy and inarticulate in his occasional interviews, and self-conscious to the point of parody as an actor, Prince is a natural when it comes to the recording studio. With all the enthusiasm of a bright child let loose on a computer, he makes instinctive sense of the boundless hi-tech opportunities at his fingertips, recognising and harnessing the machine's possibilities with unmethodical, rapacious enthusiasm. His propensity for lateral thinking is astounding. He seems to have absorbed the entire history of popular music by some effortless process of osmosis, and is able to cross-reference rock, funk, soul and psychedelia before he even starts on the delicately interwoven vocal patterns and strange, skimpy arrangements that give his songs the unique sparkling quality of uncut gems.

- *1999* (Warner Bros 923 720-2) [1982]

This, his fourth album, was the one which elevated Prince to a position somewhere close to the first division. A sprawling 70-minute collection, it yielded two US Top 10 singles, 'Little Red Corvette' and 'Delirious'. The keyboard-dominated title track is typical of the album's winning formula of mainstream radio-friendly melody powered by high-octane dance-floor juice. As drummer Bobby Z explained it to *Rolling Stone*: 'I think he found his groove, and the groove never left . . . 1999 gave him the keys to a lot of doors.'

- *Purple Rain* (Warner Bros 925 395-2) [1984]

Incorporating the heads-down party rock'n'roll of 'Let's Go Crazy' (US No.1), the plaintive minimalism of 'When Doves Cry' (US No.1) and the stadium bombast of the title track (US No.2), *Purple Rain* covers all the bases and remains Prince's greatest commercial triumph: 14 million copies sold to date. It was the album which introduced his most fondly remembered backing band, The Revolution, featuring Wendy (Melvoin, guitar) and Lisa (Coleman, keyboards).

- *Parade – Music from 'Under the Cherry Moon'* (Warner Bros 925 395-2) [1986]

The film was shockingly poor and some of the pseudo-*Magical*

Mystery Tour psychedelics get a bit wearing – strings, Toytown trumpets, odd disembodied voices full of Eastern promise and so forth – but buried in the package are several slick, sparse dance songs including 'New Position' and 'Girls and Boys'.

What really makes this worthy of your attention, though, is the inclusion of 'Kiss', perhaps the song above all others – and certainly the video (featuring guitarist Wendy) – for which Prince will be most fondly remembered.

● *Sign o' the Times* (Paisley Park 925 577-2) [1987]

Having dismissed The Revolution, Prince was left to produce, arrange, compose and actually perform this lengthy album alone. It is a chaotic, recondite and frequently inspired patchwork of material with the audio ambience of an expensively crafted home-demo. Sketchy little riffs flesh out the barest of drum-machine tracks, and squeaky little harmonies momentarily pop out of the corners of the mix only to disappear again, almost immediately, without trace.

This intriguingly unorthodox technique is applied to material which is among the best Prince has recorded. The title track is one of the flintiest descriptions of American urban blight since Grandmaster Flash's landmark rap 'The Message', while 'House-quake' is Prince-style full frontal funk at its most convincing.

As well as the title track, the album produced the hits 'U Got the Look' (featuring vocals by Sheena Easton), 'I Could Never Take the Place of Your Man' and 'If I was Your Girlfriend'. The latter remains one of his most accomplished performances ever, and sums up Prince Rogers Nelson as well as any one song in his huge portfolio. A sparse, yearning and ultimately rather sad little number, it contrives to illuminate the nature of the sexual divide, while simultaneously revelling in the kind of lewd innuendo more worthy of a cheap after-shave advertisement.

● *Lovesexy* (Paisley Park 925 720-2) [1988]

Lovesexy is another jumbled collection of riches inspired by the dark libidinal forces at work in a mind overloaded with unusual musical ideas.

His continuing fascination with the workings of the female

psyche, which surfaces on the single 'Alphabet St' and the haunting 'Anna Stesia', is most plainly revealed by the cover photograph, where he poses in the nude with slender, girlie grace.

Yet despite the decidedly secular nature of the language, the title track is apparently about spiritual love 'not with a girl or boy but with the heavens above'. Frankly this seems a bit much to swallow, given the lascivious tone of his delivery.

The scope of this hyperactive masterpiece is breathtaking. From 'Glam Slam' with its swooping, mock-orchestral grandeur, to 'Dance On', a song built on little more than a frenziedly twitching skeleton of percussion, there is a wit and vitality in these recordings which Prince has not captured since.

● *Diamonds and Pearls* (Paisley Park 7599-253792-2) [1991]

The message is clear: Prince does it a lot and he would like to do it with you, please. Even on the light-hearted 'Strollin'', one of the most innocuous songs here, the lad ends up sniggering at 'some dirty magazine', while there is not even the flimsiest veil of innuendo to protect the innocent from the juvenile braggadocio of 'Insatiable', 'Gett Off' and 'Cream'.

Actually, the album is not *all* about sex. One song is about money, and the title track concerns love.

Prince's latest group of musical playmates is called The New Power Generation, and on 'Jughead', the NPG's 'lead rapper' Tony M. churns out an impenetrable spiel in a vaguely PUBLIC ENEMY vein, which sounds as if it belongs on somebody else's album.

For the most part Prince himself is in falsetto mode, peppering songs like 'Walk Don't Walk' with intricately layered harmonies to create his unique style of barber-shop soul. Ever the genre-bender, he flits from the metallic guitar soloing at the end of 'Thunder' to the township jive inflections of 'Willing and Able' with energetic glee.

A mercurial and narcissistic collection, this is streets ahead of the pneumatic monotony of the *Graffiti Bridge* and *Batman* soundtracks, even if it does not scale the twin peaks of ecstasy achieved with *Lovesexy* and *Sign o' the Times*.

Public Enemy

Convened: 1986, New York
Chuck D (f) – vocals; Flavor Flav (f) – vocals; Terminator X (f) – record decks
UK No.4 album: 1990: *Fear of a Black Planet* (Def Jam 466 281-2)
US No.4 album: 1991: *Apocalypse 91 . . . The Enemy Strikes Black* (Def Jam 468 751-2)

Shock tactics swept Public Enemy from bottom of the bill on the 1987 Def Jam tour of America and Europe (with LL Cool J and Eric B. and Rakim) to worldwide pole position among heavyweight rappers. They came onstage flanked by their four-man uniformed guard – known as S1W (Security of the First World) – whose submachine gun props and unpleasantly menacing posture rendered a chilling approximation of the rap group as paramilitary organisation. While other rappers simply bragged about how great they were with the ladies, and 'dissed' (gave disrespect to) all other rappers, Public Enemy's agenda was rather more ambitious. Against a pounding dum-dum beatbox rhythm, and a spine-chilling backdrop of 'urban reality' noises, Chuck D and Flavor Flav spelt out their goal: a new world order, no less.

As disciples of the virulent separatist leader Louis Farrakhan, Public Enemy's black power philosophy has frequently been couched in terms which the white liberal establishment finds hard to swallow, although it has made every effort to do so. The group's 'Minister of Information', Professor Griff, was generally felt to have overstepped the mark in 1989 when he made overtly and widely reported anti-Semitic statements. In America record-store chains refused to stock Public Enemy albums and the group received a series of assassination threats.

Having become a spokesman whose foot was rarely far from his mouth, Griff was eventually instructed to leave the group and was last heard of touring the American college lecture circuit in 1991, offering an intellectually stimulating programme of talks including 'The Psychological Effects of Slavery Then and Now' and 'Censorship or Censorshit'.

Public Enemy, meanwhile, continue to push back the boundaries of the rapidly evolving rap medium, notably with their ground-breaking collaboration in 1991 with heavy metal thrashers

Anthrax. However, a boldly conceived tour with Goth-rock supremos The Sisters of Mercy the same year, was a costly disaster which petered out owing to lack of ticket sales halfway through its projected 21-date itinerary.

- *It Takes a Nation of Millions To Hold Us Back* (Def Jam DEF 462 415-2) [1988]

Listening to Public Enemy's second album is like hearing a siren passing close to your window in the middle of the night; that moment when irritation, excitement and a frisson of fear chase each other like shapes flickering behind the curtain.

Much of the music here *is* the sound of sirens – and klaxons and screeching whistles and nervous semaphore blips, glued together in hypnotic anti-mantra patterns by urgent, deep funk drum rhythms and an incessant barrage of urban black patois poetry – rap to you and me.

The vitriolic message of extreme black militancy comes across loud and clear: 'Black Steel in the Hour of Chaos' urges the speedy use of guns and rioting in the event of wrongful imprisonment; 'Terminator X to the Edge of Panic' tells us that 'the federal government is the number one killer and destroyer of black leaders'; and 'Night of the Living Baseheads' insists that the US government has been scheming all along to promote crack addiction as a means of controlling the black population.

Most of this is paranoid nonsense, and much of it has the same sinister ring about it as the ravings of those fanatics who recently claimed that Jewish doctors in New York have been injecting black babies with the AIDS virus.

But there is no denying the potent rush of musical energy that such ill-contained, if poorly defined fury produces. There's not been anything quite as fundamental as this since The CLASH were out on the streets looking for a 'White Riot'.

- *Fear of a Black Planet* (Def Jam 466 281-2) [1990]

There was an all-round upping of the ante in the rap stakes during the two-year hiatus between *Nation of Millions* and *Fear of a Black Planet*. A posse of sudden-death warriors from the East Coast, led by Ice-T and NWA (Niggers With Attitude), mounted a challenge for the crown with a virulent strain of 'gangsta' rap, glorifying new extremes of manly violence and misogyny with a repetitious barrage of the most drab of undeleted expletives.

Although *Fear of a Black Planet* comes well stickered-up – 'Warning! Certain lyrics may offend – play with caution' – the album's explosive dynamism puts it in a different league to the ponderous doggerel of NWA, thankfully.

Public Enemy are none the less obsessed with issues of race and power – both physical and political – and the album is guided by the kind of tendentious reasoning that starts from the premise of a 'worldwide conspiracy to destroy the black race' and ends with assertions that even Elvis PRESLEY was a 'straight up racist' ('Fight the Power').

They ease back a touch on the sirens, klaxons and screeching whistles, but the album has all the hustling, oppressive energy of its predecessors, fuelled by an anger verging on apoplexy. The sound of gunshots, aeroplanes and a background pandemonium of milling voices create an ambience of urban paranoia, while words like 'fear', 'terror', 'knife' and 'riot' spring out of the mêlée with an intimidating force of their own.

Public Enemy have assiduously courted controversy and apart from being very good, this album remains confrontational enough to fend off challenges to the number one outlaw status in which they revel. It just seems a pity that its ultimate effect is more likely to fuel any lurking 'fear of a black planet' than to allay it.

- *Apocalypse 91 . . . The Enemy Strikes Black* (Def Jam 468 751-2) [1991]

The dentist's drill sounds are reined back yet further in favour of the more conventional sampling of rhythm tracks from old R'n'B records.

But the mean-spirited litany of complaints about their treatment at the hands of the hated whitey continues apace. Titles such as 'I Don't Wanna be Called Yo Niga', 'A Letter to the New York Post' ('America's oldest continuously published daily piece of bullshit') and 'How to Kill a Radio Consultant' are not what you would call textbook examples of how to win friends and influence media people.

The revamped version of 'Bring the Noize', recorded with thrash metal doyens Anthrax, is a logical if unexpected triumph of cross-genre co-operation between sonic extremists.

Public Image Ltd See The SEX PISTOLS

Queen

Convened: 1970, London
John Deacon (f) – bass/vocals; Brian May (f) – guitar/vocals; Freddie Mercury (f) (died 24.11.91) – vocals/piano; Roger Taylor (f) – drums/vocals

UK/US No.1 album:	1980:	*The Game* (EMI CDP 746 213-2)
UK No.1 albums:	1975:	*A Night at the Opera* (EMI CDP 746 207-2)
	1976:	*A Day at the Races* (EMI CDP 746 208-2)
	1981:	*Greatest Hits* (EMI CDP 746 033-27)
	1986:	*A Kind of Magic* (EMI CDP 746 267-2)
	1989:	*The Miracle* (Parlophone CDPCSD 107)
	1991:	*Innuendo* (Parlophone CDPCSD 115)
	1991:	*Greatest Hits II* (Parlophone CDPMTV 2)

Too clever, too rich and too absurd to be taken seriously by anyone other than their accountants, Queen have nevertheless been enjoying the last laugh at their detractors' expense for the best part of 20 years. For strip away the ornate burlesque and here is a group which has grasped the mechanics of how to achieve and maintain rock stardom more firmly than virtually any of its contemporaries.

Consider their appearance at Live Aid in 1985. There were many accolades and many memorable performances on that day – from DIRE STRAITS, U2, David BOWIE, LED ZEPPELIN, The BEACH BOYS and others – but Queen were the only act who seemed to have given serious consideration to the challenge of playing a 20-

minute set, as opposed to simply trotting out two or three of their best known hits.

They began with the opening section of 'Bohemian Rhapsody' segued into 'Radio Ga-Ga' followed by 'Crazy Little Thing Called Love' and then surged into a grand finale of 'We Will Rock You' spliced to 'We are the Champions'. No one, whatever their prejudice, could reasonably deny the breathtaking impact of that performance at that precise moment in such a highly charged emotional setting. The sight of 72,000 people doing double handclaps above their heads *exactly* the way they had all seen it in the video of 'Radio Ga-Ga' was spooky. The roar at the end of their set was unlike any audience response that I've heard before or since. On that day, in terms of sheer *power*, Queen took the art of mass-audience rock performance as far as it's ever likely to go.

Writing of Queen's appearance at Live Aid in the *Sunday Times*, Mick Brown was moved to comment on the 'awesome power of rock music to arouse'. Some of the contradictions of that power were, said Brown, 'too fantastic and too horrible to contemplate in an event such as this.'

One such 'contradiction' was that out of Bob Geldof's humanitarian gesture – possibly the greatest practical effort of charity by an individual that the world has witnessed – a new super-class of rock aristocracy was born. Queen, not surprisingly were among the principal beneficiaries. Their album Greatest Hits (see below), released four years prior to Live Aid, surged back up the chart, where it stayed for another two years.

It was the crowning glory of a career that began when Zanzibar-born Mercury (né Frederick Bulsara) recruited Taylor and May, both students at London University, to start a group. Mercury had decided in advance that they would be called Queen, a deliberately camp, attention-grabbing title which he was well equipped to embody. They recruited Deacon from the small ads, and gave their début performance at the London College of Estate Management in February 1971.

In the years that followed, the group forged a unique combination of heavy-metal thunder, complex vocal harmonies and a preposterous glam-rock image, woven into a seamless package of dramatic excess. Their most outstanding hit remains the long, elaborate set-piece 'Bohemian Rhapsody', with its celebrated cod-operatic sequence followed by a bludgeoning heavy-metal finale.

That single stayed at No.1 in Britain for nine weeks in 1975 and such was the group's popularity at the start of 1976 that all four of their albums released to that date appeared simultaneously in the Top 30.

In keeping with the grandiose splendour of their music, Queen's live shows became ever more spectacular events over the years, employing vast sets and lighting rigs. Even so, with Deacon and May both naturally retiring types and Taylor stuck behind his drums, the group depended heavily on Mercury's commanding stage presence. Prancing down multi-layered catwalks in a sequinned, skin-tight jump suit and ballet slippers, preening his way through a myriad of costume changes and singing in his majestic, slightly frayed tenor voice, Mercury always matched up to the demands of projecting the group's music and image to the four corners of the world's biggest stadiums.

Although they have continued to release albums, Queen have not played live since 1986. The group's last tour, which included two shows at Wembley Stadium, and a pioneering appearance in front of 80,000 Hungarian fans at Budapest's Nepstadion, ended with a date at the Knebworth Festival on August 9 1986.

As the group continued to avoid meeting its public, and the AIDS epidemic began to take its toll, Mercury inevitably became the target of sustained speculation. 'Yes, I did have an AIDS test and I'm fine,' he told *Woman's Own* magazine in November 1987, but rumours that he had tested HIV positive persisted. In February 1990, after Queen pulled out at the last minute from an appearance at the BRITS Awards, photographs of a very sick-looking Mercury were circulated.

But by the autumn of 1990 the group was back in the studio, recording what was to be its last new album, *Innuendo* (see above) which entered the UK chart at No.1. The last single before Mercury's death in November 1991 was 'The Show Must Go On', a song with a decidedly valedictory flavour, accompanied by a video stitched together from old footage of Queen. In a nostalgic sequence of vignettes, Mercury's enduring generosity of spirit and his arch sense of humour continued to shine through.

So widespread was the mood of sorrow when he died, that when Queen announced its plans to re-release 'Bohemian Rhapsody' in December 1991, the bookies, Ladbrokes, immediately cancelled all bets on what would be the UK Christmas No.1.

• *Sheer Heart Attack* (EMI CDP 746 206-2) [1974]

Only their third album, but Queen were already into a world of unabashed excess in all departments. At one extreme May's echo-generated 'wall of guitar' sound is the dominant feature on the convoluted 'Brighton Rock', while at the other the speedy rap and break-neck tempo of 'Stone Cold Sober' is such that it could have passed muster as a two-minute punk anthem under different circumstances.

'Killer Queen', with its enormously complex weave of harmonised guitars, vaudevillian lyrics and music-hall camperie, was the big hit single, along with the stop-start rocker 'Now I'm Here', complete with liberal quotes from Chuck BERRY in the fade. Really an embarrassment of riches.

• *News of the World* (EMI CDP 746 209-2) [1977]
• *The Game* (EMI CDP 746 213-2) [1980]

News of the World is worth recommending for May's gorgeous blues guitar playing on 'Sleeping on the Sidewalk' alone, and, as much as anything, it is that sort of unpredictable versatility that has kept Queen's stock buoyant over the years. All four musicians contribute to the songwriting, enabling them to balance gung-ho stadium anthems like 'We Will Rock You' and 'We are the Champions' from *News of the World*, against quirkier stuff like the funk forgery of 'Another One Bites the Dust' and the popabilly strut of 'Crazy Little Thing Called Love', both US No.1 hits taken from *The Game*.

• *Greatest Hits* (EMI CDP 746 033-27) [1981]

Boasting the cream of the crop from the group's first ten years, this monumental compilation stuck its ground in the UK chart for six and a half years. Its abrupt swings of mood, from the surging 'Seven Seas of Rhye' to the cloying 'You're My Best Friend' from the baroque 'Bo-Rhap' to the ludicrous 'Fat-Bottomed Girls', have only served to confirm the group's idiosyncratic appeal.

• *Greatest Hits II* (Parlophone CDPMTV 2) [1991]

Although Queen's albums since Live Aid have routinely topped the UK chart, the commercial appeal of their material is no longer balanced by the sort of musical weight that distinguishes their Seventies' portfolio. This is unlikely to cause the group too many sleepless nights, since here, right on cue, are another dozen or so major hits just ripe for a second greatest hits blockbuster. A sumptuously packaged collection of old favourites like 'Radio Ga Ga', 'Under Pressure' (with David BOWIE) and 'Friends Will Be Friends', this simply couldn't fail and it didn't.

Chris Rea

Born: March 4 1951, Middlesbrough, Cleveland
UK No.1 albums: 1989: *The Road to Hell* (WEA 2292-46285-2)
1991: *Auberge* (eastwest 9031-73580-2)

Reasonable, diligent, experienced, relaxed, highly skilled, over-weight and comfortably middle-aged, Chris Rea is very much a star for the adult-orientated, CD era, a natural choice for the emergent generation of armchair rockers. After years of craft and graft, the attributes which have earned him success are familiar enough: the gruff yet melodious singing style, the fluent, understated guitar technique, the gently evocative lyrics, the languid delivery and the pragmatic, 'anti-star' image.

A late developer, Rea was already at work in his family's ice cream parlour when in 1970, at the age of 19, he took up the guitar, inspired initially by the distinctively American playing styles of Ry COODER and Joe Walsh.

● *Whatever Happened to Benny Santini?* (Magnet 823 073-2) [1978]

Destined to be a middle-aged star, Rea peaked far too early with this début album, so titled because Benny Santini was the name his record company had initially suggested he trade under. It produced a freak American hit, 'Fool (If You Think It's Over)' – later covered by Elkie Brooks – which dragged the album into the American Top 50, but is an otherwise unmemorable collection, weighed down by several uninspiring and unfashionable ballads.

After this, Rea was faced with a long, hard slog to establish himself as a credible 'newcomer', operating at distinct odds firstly to the post-punk brigade and later to the fashion-obsessed new romantics.

● *Dancing With Strangers* (Magnet CDMAG 5071) [1987]

By the mid-Eighties, Rea had at last converted his maturity from a liability into an asset. On 'Joys of Christmas' he reels off a catalogue of social ills besetting the depressed towns of northern England. Whereas this kind of social commentary can often seem academic or sanctimonious, Rea has been around long enough to make the message stick. His sound has acquired genuine gravitas, the hard way.

His guitar playing is faultless throughout, with passages ranging from the coarse, Ry COODER/Little Feat-influenced shuffle of 'Let's Dance' to the majestic slide solo at the end of 'Que Será'.

● *The Best of Chris Rea – New Light Through Old Windows* (WEA 243 841-2) [1988]

Rea adopted a novel tack for this 'compilation', by re-recording a raft of his best known songs 'live' in the studio. The result is a satisfying return voyage round the work of a man who evidently saw the CD age coming.

His voice has grown both rougher and more expressive over the years and on the new version of 'Stainsby Girls' he sounds like a cross between Tom WAITS and Richard Butler of the Psychedelic Furs. 'Josephine', 'Shamrock Diaries', 'On the Beach', 'Let's Dance' and an extended 'Steel River' all boast the unmistakable Rea ring of quality, although certain blind spots remain, such as the gooey picture-postcard romanticism of 'Driving Home For Christmas'.

● *The Road to Hell* (WEA 2292-46285-2) [1989]

Rea's masterpiece, this was greedily sucked into the huge vacuum in the CD/adult-rock market caused by the extended absence of DIRE STRAITS (from 1986–1991), and sold one and a quarter million copies in the UK alone. Indeed, Rea sounds more than ever like Mark Knopfler, especially on the title track. Inspired by the frustration of being stuck in a traffic jam on the M4, it's one of those songs with such a wonderful symmetry that it sounds as if it must always have existed, and all Rea had to do was reach out and pluck it from the ether.

Once again there are echoes of Ry COODER's dusty guitar sound in Rea's slide playing, and on 'Looking for a Rainbow' his band musters the shuffling Dixieland funk rhythm so beloved of Little Feat.

But it is ultimately a triumph of a very personal nature. Rea wrote the entire album in four days, which, apart from being nice work if you can get it, explains the smooth flow of the collection and its thematic consistency.

Mostly he sounds off about life in the Eighties as viewed by a concerned parent living in the industrial wastelands of England's North, with media folk getting the worst hammering for upsetting his little girl with grisly news footage in the early evening ('You Must Be Evil').

Although Rea's manner remains far too affably laid-back for it to be called a 'protest' album, his points are well made and, apart from 'Tell Me There's a Heaven', a sentimental piece of guff with a frightful Mantovani-like string arrangement, this is an album which purrs along like a perfectly tuned motor.

● *Auberge* (eastwest 9031-73580-2) [1991]

With its rootsy charm and deceptively easy gait, *Auberge* is more up-beat than *The Road to Hell*, and the grim warnings of eco-disaster and industrial decay have given way to a more tranquil collection of images and themes in songs like 'Gone Fishing', 'Heaven' and 'Auberge' itself.

The consummate technical excellence which is second nature to Rea is bolstered by some new factor in Jon Kelly's production process which gives Rea's hallmarked growl a super-clear presence in the mix. The blues guitar passages which grace 'And You My Love' and 'Looking for the Summer' rank among his best recorded performances ever.

Otis Redding

Born: September 9 1941, Dawson, Georgia. Died: December
10 1967
UK No.1 album: 1968: *Dock of the Bay* (unavailable)

From a dirt-poor background, Otis Redding was thrust into a line
of work where even the strongest are drawn by the lure of excess.
Yet he remained that rarest of showbusiness animals: an artist of
supreme and expanding abilities with no drug problems, ego
disorders or self-destructive urges. His death in a plane crash at
the age of 26 was therefore a calamity of hideous proportions, the
more so since only that year he had made a triumphant
appearance at the Monterey Pop Festival, alongside Jimi HENDRIX
and The WHO, and been voted the world's Top Male Vocalist in a
Melody Maker readers' poll, dethroning Elvis PRESLEY. The phenomenon of 'crossover' had yet to be formally identified, but having
attained pre-eminence in the R'n'B market, Redding had now won
over the hippy/rock audience – the 'love crowd' as he liked to call
them – and was clearly on course for mass-market acceptance of
a sort that few soul acts of that era had ever achieved.

Having started out playing as a drummer in bands while still at
school in Macon, Georgia, Redding's scuffling years came to an
end in October 1962, when he accompanied his colleague Johnny
Jenkins to a recording session, financed by Atlantic records, which
ended prematurely. Redding, whose principal function had been
to drive Jenkins to the studio on East McLemore Avenue in
Memphis, was therefore invited to fill 40 minutes of spare studio
time by recording material of his own choosing.

The studio was that of Jim Stewart's fledgling Stax label, and
the house band which accompanied Redding that day on the
recording of two songs – 'Hey Hey Baby' and 'These Arms of
Mine' – was Booker T. and The MG's, already a celebrated force
on the Memphis scene, having just enjoyed their first hit, 'Green
Onions'.

In the five years that followed, Stax became a legend in itself,
and no act was more closely identified with the label's warm,
grainy, vintage soul sound than Redding together with Booker T.
and The MG's (Booker T. Jones – organ; Steve Cropper – guitar
and co-writer of many of Redding's songs; Donald 'Duck' Dunn –
bass; and Al Jackson – drums) and the Mar-Key horns, led by

trumpeter Wayne Jackson.

Redding was drowned in Lake Monoma near Madison, Wisconsin, along with four members of his road band The Bar-Kays, when their twin-engined Beechcraft plane, chartered to take the company to that night's show, crashed in heavy fog.

● *The Otis Redding Story* (Atlantic K 781 762-2) [1988]

Basically, Otis Redding had two songs. One is a storming, stomping soul man strut and it goes under titles such as 'Hard to Handle', 'I Can't Turn You Loose' and the classic 'Respect' (his song, but a much bigger hit for Aretha FRANKLIN). The other is a big, slow, aching, soul ballad, with a heart-rending, minor-key bridge or middle eight, that squeezes all emotion out of singer and listener alike, a style that was truly Redding's forte. 'These Arms of Mine' (his first single), 'Pain in My Heart', 'That's How Strong My Love Is', 'I've Been Loving You Too Long' and 'I've Got Dreams to Remember' are among the finest examples of the second pattern.

Occasionally he would combine both styles in one performance – witness his volcanic rendition of 'Try a Little Tenderness'. This old Bing Crosby number was adapted by Redding from a later version by his idol Sam Cooke. Building from slow, anguished beginnings, Redding takes the number to a searing finale with blaring horns and a four-in-the-bar snare romping out in the fade.

Although his artistic standing was inviolate for many years after his death, in more recent times Redding has been taken to task by some of the fussier critics for his stubbornly narrow approach and for his tendency to confuse vocal improvisation with grandstanding blarney.

Yet he could turn his hand to pretty well anything, provided the song had enough meat to give his hard, throaty voice something to chew on. Over the course of his career he recorded rousing versions of the Jagger/Richards anti-everything broadside '(I Can't Get No) Satisfaction', LENNON/McCARTNEY's 'Day Tripper', Sam Cooke's 'A Change is Gonna Come' and 'Shake' and Eddie Floyd's perennial dance-floor favourite 'Knock On Wood', all of them generous and animated performances, and all full to overflowing with the kind of sweet soul juice which Redding seemed able to dispense by the yard.

The Otis Redding Story is an indispensable 60-track set which incorporates all the aforementioned titles and many besides: 'Tramp', his good-natured spat with Carla Thomas; a live version of James BROWN's funky call-to-arms 'Papa's Got a Brand New Bag', and even a dubious reworking of 'White Christmas', described rather fancifully as 'the definitive soul version' by one reviewer. The compilation includes nine of the 11 tracks on Redding's best album, *Otis Blue* (1965; unavailable), but even this is a disappointment since one of the missing tracks from that magnum opus is his sublime version of Smokey Robinson's 'My Girl', the song which provided Redding with his first UK hit, peaking at No.11 in 1965.

It wasn't until just before his death that Redding came up with the design for his third song. This one was more carefully moderated and delicately tuneful than the other two, and he only had the one chance to get it right. '(Sittin' On) The Dock of the Bay', the number which signalled a new realm of possibilities for him as a major player in the mainstream pop marketplace, was recorded just three days before his death. It is a track of gentle but heartfelt reflection which, released posthumously, became his biggest hit of all. It stirs sorrowful memories even now.

Ironically, this song which suggested a new beginning in fact closed Redding's account, just as it closes this collection. The track itself ends on a delicately poignant note with Redding whistling the melody against the noise of surf breaking on the shore. There have been some portentous theories regarding the significance of this unusual yet highly affecting touch. American critic Dave Marsh declared that it was Redding's attempt 'to speak of things for which there are no words.' But guitarist Steve Cropper, a rather more prosaic customer who, as it happens, co-wrote the song and played on the record, remembers it as the result of a cock-up: 'We had worked out this little fade-out rap he was gonna do, an ad-lib thing. He forgot what it was, so he started whistling.'

Lou Reed

Born: Louis Firbank, March 2 1942, Freeport, Long Island, New York
UK No.6 album: 1992: *Magic and Loss* (Sire/Warner Bros 926 662-2)

Lou Reed is the least likely member of that select school of composer/musicians from the Sixties who now find themselves able to draw on a broad raft of adult experience in order to produce what Keith Richards calls 'mature rock'n'roll'. In the early Seventies, Reed's (and indeed Richards') ostentatious and widely publicised junkie lifestyle suggested a performer destined for an early demise.

He has confounded such expectations and, although much of his work has been a jumble of half-baked ideas couched either in starkly minimalist chord sequences or else in a clumsy neo-heavy rock format, there has never been any doubt that his experiences have given him an enduring comprehension of the way life is lived on the margins of urban American society.

What distinguishes mature rock'n'roll from its castrated cousin, the ubiquitous adult-orientated rock, is a degree of honesty and a certain pungency of expression, both of which Reed has delivered in spades on his most recent albums.

His rehabilitation from the excesses of the Seventies began in 1979 when he met Sylvia Morales, whom he married the following year. Almost overnight he dispensed with drugs, announcing that he found self-destructive people 'very, very boring'. Over the next decade his writing and singing became more focused, and by the start of the Nineties he was producing some of the best work of his career, as well as giving readings of his lyrics at theatres and sitting in on music business seminars.

At the time of writing, 1992 is shaping up to be Reed's big year. As well as his widely acclaimed album *Magic and Loss* (see below), he has a a triple-CD compilation of his past recordings, *Between Thought and Expression* (RCA PD 90621), incorporating previously unreleased material, issued in March; a book of lyrics also called *Between Thought and Expression*, published at the same time; and a UK tour timed to coincide with both.

Even so, two-fifths of his solo repertoire remains unavailable on CD, a high percentage for an artist of his stature.

- *Transformer* (RCA ND 83806) [1973]
- *Berlin* (RCA ND 84388) [1973]

Produced by David BOWIE and Mick Ronson, *Transformer* finds Reed at his most tuneful and accessible, yet demonstrating no loss of appetite for the hard sensation. Undoubtedly the best of his early albums, it incorporates 'Vicious', 'Satellite of Love' and 'Walk on the Wild Side', a sublime evocation of New York lowlife that remains his best known hit.

Coming so soon on its heels, *Berlin* enjoyed unusually strong sales, but is one of several 'difficult' Reed albums which are usually described as 'bleak' – or, in the case of *Metal Machine Music* (Great Expectations; 1975), 'unlistenable'.

The story of a doomed, drug-impaired relationship that ends in suicide, *Berlin* features a stellar cast of musicians – Steve WINWOOD, Jack Bruce, Aynsley Dunbar – but with mixed results.

- *Rock'n'Roll Animal* [1974]
- *Sally Can't Dance* [1974]

Rock'n'Roll Animal is a patchy live album in full heavy-rock mode, chiefly memorable for the long, duelling guitar blitzkrieg that leads into 'Sweet Jane'. *Sally Can't Dance* was his biggest US hit to date (No.10), yet boasts virtually nothing of lasting merit. 'It sucked,' Reed was later heard to declare.

Similar reservations would have to be voiced concerning the majority of Reed's work between then and the end of the Eighties, although several of the better albums are unavailable on CD, namely *Street Hassle* (1978), *The Blue Mask* (1982) and *Legendary Hearts* (1983).

- *New York* (WEA 925 829-2) [1989]

A funny, sad, restless, caustic elegy to the city with which his destiny has always been inextricably entwined, *New York* was a landmark in Reed's career.

In 'Hold On' he paints a Hogarthian picture of a community that is falling apart at the seams: 'There's blacks with knives and whites with guns/Fighting in Howard Beach/There's no such thing as human rights/When you walk the New York streets.'

The view from the bottom of the heap has rarely been more starkly expressed by Reed or anyone else, than it is in the song 'Dirty Blvd'. Over a neatly clipped riff, mined from the same seam of gold that produced his 'Sweet Jane' classic, Reed sings with a dead-pan air of resignation: 'No one here dreams of being a doctor or a lawyer or anything/They dream of dealing on the dirty boulevard'.

For Reed it is American society that is the failure, its original ideals reduced to a sham: 'Give me your tired, your poor, I'll piss on 'em/That's what the Statue of Bigotry says/Your poor huddled masses, let's club 'em to death/And get it over with and just dump 'em on the boulevard'.

With this album Reed not only reclaimed from the realms of comic stereotype the idea of the rock star with street credibility, but also struck a blow on behalf of those who still see in rock'n'roll the scope for more than a series of carefully rehearsed moves and empty gestures. If Bob DYLAN was plugged in to the Eighties the way he was to the Sixties, perhaps he could have come up with a commentary on the times to match this. Otherwise it's hard to think of anyone else who has come close.

- **Lou Reed/John Cale: *Songs for Drella*** (Sire/Warner Bros 7599-26140-2) [1990]

In the wake of their old mentor Andy Warhol's death, Reed and his ex-Velvet Underground (see below) colleague Cale defend Warhol's life and art, sometimes with startling vehemence.

With only guitar, piano and occasional viola accompanying Reed's disinterested drone or Cale's more dignified baritone, attention is fixed entirely on the lyrical content of a homage which is never less than fulsome and sometimes has the cloying sensibility of sixth-form poetry.

- **Magic and Loss** (Sire/Warner Bros 926 662-2) [1992]

Written as a response to the loss of two of Reed's close friends – the songwriter Doc Pomus and one of the Warhol Factory crowd called Rotten Rita, both of whom died of cancer – *Magic and Loss* casts an unblinking eye on the horrific mechanics of disease, death and the disposal of mortal remains. 'I've seen lots of people die, from car crashes or drugs,' he sings in his matter-of-fact drawl, but he finds the slow, painful progress of his friends' inexorable disintegration an infinitely worse experience to behold.

It has become a cliché to talk about rock musicians who have 'grown up' and tackled the adult dilemmas of middle age, parenthood and so forth. But this is the first rock album to venture beyond that and confront the utter finality of death and the ravaging effects of bereavement.

That it is a work of major artistic significance is not in doubt, but its success as a body of music is open to question. Although the 'loss' side of the equation is plain to see, the 'magic' is harder to find.

The Velvet Underground

Convened: 1965, New York. Split up: 1973
John Cale (f) – bass/viola/keyboards/vocals; Sterling Morrison (f) – guitar/bass; Nico (died 18.7.88) – vocals; Lou Reed (f) – vocals/guitar; Maureen Tucker – drums
UK No.47 album: 1985: *VU* (Polydor 825 092-2)

The Velvet Underground was not, on the face of it, a conspicuously successful group. They enjoyed no hit albums or singles, their sporadic attempts at touring usually ended in disaster and their unstable existence was marked by personality conflicts and a constantly changing line-up.

Adopted by the doyen of Sixties underground art, Andy Warhol, they initially worked out of Warhol's Factory HQ at 231 East 47th Street as part of his Exploding Plastic Inevitable multimedia show.

'People hated us,' Morrison recalled in 1986, and according to Cale the feeling was reciprocal: 'The only reason we wore dark glasses on stage,' he told *The South Bank Show*, 'was that we couldn't stand the sight of the audience.'

Even so, they planted an alien seed in the hippy flower-bed and many years later a deep and widespread antipathy towards the values of the Sixties took hold among a generation of pre-punks. These people rejected The BEATLES' message of love, peace and sound musicianship in favour of The Velvet Underground's dry menace, unhealthy pallor and intuitive instrumentation. The strand which the Velvets had initiated continued in the New York underground, with acts like TALKING HEADS, Patti Smith and Richard Hell providing the link to punk.

Although they denied it, The SEX PISTOLS and the UK punk movement adopted The Velvet Underground's musical and ethical framework wholesale and from there it was a relatively short jump to Eighties groups like The CURE, New Order and The Jesus and Mary Chain and on to groundbreaking acts of the Nineties like My Bloody Valentine, PIXIES, Cowboy Junkies and Primal Scream.

As the American critic Robert Christgau explained, 'Even bands which don't like The Velvet Underground, or don't use any of their treatments, still owe them a debt. Because those groups come out of the negative energy, the critical energy that The Velvet Underground instilled in the first generation of punk bands.'

- *The Velvet Underground with Nico* (Polydor 823 290-2) [1967]
- *White Light White Heat* (Polydor 825 119-2) [1968]

Their hugely influential début, bearing Andy Warhol's celebrated illustration of a banana on the cover, introduced a new dimension to rock. At a time when vague eulogies to marijuana, LSD and 'free love' were all the rage, the Velvets weighed in with chilling, amoral glimpses of the twilight world of pain and ecstasy that the serious junkie inhabits. Reed's compositions, in particular 'I'm Waiting for the Man' and 'Heroin' (reputedly written when he was just 15 years old), illuminate extremes of moral turpitude that rock'n'roll had previously barely hinted at.

The follow-up, *White Light White Heat*, continues to mine much the same vein and provides further evidence of Reed's laconic yet vivid narrative style. The stand-out cuts are the title track, 'Sister Ray' and the long, surreal story of 'The Gift'.

- *Best of The Velvet Underground* (Verve 841 164-2) [1989]

Although the Velvets' last proper album, *Loaded* (1970), is unavailable, its two essential contributions to the Velvets' legacy, 'Rock and Roll' and 'Sweet Jane', are both included on this compilation, along with 'Femme Fatale', 'All Tomorrow's Parties', 'Heroin' and others.

R.E.M.

Convened: 1980, Athens, Georgia
Bill Berry (f) – drums/vocals; Peter Buck (f) – guitar; Mike Mills (f) – bass/vocals; Michael Stipe (f) – vocals
UK/US No.1 album: 1991: *Out of Time* (Warner Bros 7599-26496-2)

It was The ROLLING STONES who initiated the questionable tradition of a rock'n'roll championship title. Their brash self-billing as 'the Greatest Rock'n'Roll Band in the World' went unchallenged for the best part of a decade, but subsequent holders of the crown have not clung on for so long: Bruce SPRINGSTEEN and U2 were able to maintain the required combination of massive global sales and across-the-board credibility for little more than a year each. Now it's R.E.M.'s turn.

Rolling Stone magazine opened the bidding as early as 1987 in a cover story billing them as 'America's Best Rock & Roll Band' just after the release of *Document* (see below). This was bold stuff considering that none of the group's preceding albums had even broached the US Top 20.

'The best band in the world?' pondered the *Q* magazine reviewer, mulling over the merits of *Green* in 1988. 'I think so.' The *NME* rather coyly ventured a description of them as 'the world's smartest, most mysterious group in motion' but it took *The Observer* to come straight out and say it, in a 1989 story simply titled 'The Best Band in the World'.

At that time such critical adulation was still out of all proportion to the group's relatively limited commercial standing. *Green* had sold two million copies in America, certainly, but in Britain it had barely scraped into the Top 30, and in Europe, as with all the group's previous albums, it had faded without trace.

But with the release of *Out of Time* in 1991 the band finally grew into the expansive cloth that had been cut for it. A transatlantic No.1 with sales well past the five million mark, at the time of writing, *Out of Time* remains firmly lodged in the American Top

10, five months after its release.

R.E.M.'s rise to this state of grace was as long and steady as it was ineluctable. They got together when Stipe, Berry and Mills were students at the University of Georgia in Athens and Buck worked in a local record store. As individuals they are not great technical musicians (with the exception of the classically trained Mills), but as a combination of musical personalities they immediately created a powerful and unusual chemistry.

Like The SMITHS in Britain, with whom they have often been compared, R.E.M. are the acceptable face of rock'n'roll weirdness, one of those rare groups in an increasingly formula-dominated market which becomes widely popular for doing things entirely its own way. Such patent integrity has been bolstered by their appetite for touring. They have done this incessantly, building an unshakable grass-roots following which, given the overheated acclaim in the media, has anchored their progress over the years in some sort of reality.

It was therefore an irony that when the really big one came, with *Out of Time* in 1991, the band was for once not on tour. Sitting back in their mansions in Athens, they could reflect on a success which, having owed nothing to the textbooks, has proved all the greater and sweeter for that.

• *Murmur* (A&M CDMID 129) [1983]

R.E.M.'s début, now available on mid-price, remains a minor, offbeat classic combining elements of folk, rock and bookish oddness in captivating proportions. Buck's chiming BYRDS-like guitar and the studied melancholia of Stipe's indecipherable vocals invest long-standing favourites like 'Radio Free Europe' and '9-9' with an air of timelessness and mystery. College radio and America's alternative rock fans picked up on the album immediately, but it also proved accessible to significant areas of the mainstream, and to everyone's surprise, reached No.36 in the American chart.

• *Document* (IRS DMIRG 1025) [1987]

Having steadily built an uncontainable following over the preceding five years and five albums, the group were finally converted from cult heroes into a major arena attraction within America by Document. It remains their most overtly political album, with Stipe employing some of his most direct lyrics yet to rail against the state of the world on tracks like 'Disturbance at the Heron House', 'Exhuming McCarthy' and 'It's the End of the World As We Know It (and I Feel Fine)'. It also yielded the group's first US hit single, 'The One I Love', a song which Stipe has strenuously denied is a love song, even if 95% of the people who bought it think otherwise.

- *Green* (Warner Bros 7599-25795-2) [1988]

The first fruit of R.E.M.'s alliance with the multinational might of Warner Bros, and Stipe's air of aggrieved whimsy is more Morrissey-like than ever. 'This is my world and I am world leader pretend,' he warbles in typically idiosyncratic fashion on 'World Leader Pretend', one of several songs with gold-plated riffs buried under a ton of lyrical angst.

The absence of drums on 'You Are Everything', 'Wrong Child' and 'Hairshirt' leaves these numbers dependent on Buck's jangling mandolin and the limited drama of Stipe's ruminative vocalising. Yet when the gloves come off, as on the single 'Orange Crush' and the tinglingly evocative 'California' with its sub-Blue Oyster Cult riff, the group demonstrate the kind of savvy that eventually lifted them to the top of the international first division.

- *Out of Time* (Warner Bros 7599-26496-2) [1991]

Despite its phenomenal success, this is hardly an album constructed in the traditional blockbuster mode. Unlike, say, *The Joshua Tree* or *Born in the USA*, *Out of Time* does not go in for bold statements painted on a huge canvas. There are no rousing chants or clenched-fist anthems designed for maximum stadium impact. Indeed, the fact that the band decided from the outset not to tour the album was entirely in keeping with the relatively modest tone of its intent.

The 11 songs – all credited to Berry, Buck, Mills and Stipe – are rarely arranged for a conventional rock-band format. As before, there are no drums on several tracks, such as the Neil YOUNG-influenced 'Country Feedback', while on many numbers Peter

Buck's ringing guitar is superseded by the more austere tones of a nine-piece string section.

This chamber-pop approach is all very well in its place – 'Low' for instance has a marvellously brooding presence and the hit single 'Losing My Religion' bounces along on a sparky mandolin part from Buck – but if anything the album seems oddly lacking in backbone. Only 'Texarcana' and another hit, 'Shiny Happy People', chime out in the 'classic' R.E.M. way, but here the usual nuggets of brilliance gleam.

- *The Best of R.E.M.* (IRS DMIRH 1) [1991]

An impressive compilation of the group's most popular work during their time with IRS (1983–1987), this includes 'Radio Free Europe', 'The One I Love', 'Finest Worksong' and 'So. Central Rain' along with many more. The often amateurish sound and unabashed vitality of these performances is the stuff of legend.

This album supersedes a previous compilation, *Eponymous* (IRS DMIRG 1038; 1988), which covers much the same territory but includes fewer tracks, a severe irritation for anyone who has already bought *Eponymous* and doesn't wish to shell out for at least seven of the same songs again.

Cliff Richard

Born: Harry Rodger Webb, October 14 1940, Lucknow, India
UK No.1 albums: 1961: *21 Today* (unavailable)
1961: *The Young Ones* (MFP CDB 752 057-2)
1963: *Summer Holiday* (MFP CDB 752 058-2)
1977: *40 Golden Greats* (EMI CDS 792 425-2)
1981: *Love Songs* (EMI CDP 748 049-2)
1988: *Private Collection* (EMI CDP 791 370-2)

No other act comes close to replicating Cliff Richard's phenomenal longevity. From the Fifties' skiffle boom to the era of Stock

Aitken and Waterman and beyond, he ranks as the most successful British singles chart act of all time and he's not finished yet. Since 1958 there have only been three years (1975, 1978 and 1986) when he has not enjoyed a UK Top 30 single, and he has been responsible for two of the last four Christmas No.1s. Elvis PRESLEY alone can boast a longer sequence of chart entries, and it seems likely that Richard will beat even his colossal tally in plenty of time for the millennium.

But what has it all been worth? Starting as the English answer to PRESLEY with his first hit 'Move It' in 1958, Richard and his redoubtable Shadows were the biggest pop sensation on this side of the Atlantic until the emergence of The BEATLES in 1963. However, the rise of mop-top mania nullified Richard's credentials as a teen idol virtually overnight, and from the mid-Sixties he prematurely abandoned his career to the tender mercies of the blue-rinse brigade, adapting his light, clean tenor voice to the anodyne demands of the Eurovision pop constituency.

Religion struck at about the same time and, while his popularity has held good, his credibility rating has been hovering at or below the zero mark ever since. The man may have outlasted psychedelia, glam-rock, punk, and the new romantics and be showing no signs of losing out to either house or rap, but even Phil COLLINS seems tough and radical by comparison.

It is a curious anomaly that an artist of such long-term popularity should be so little known in America. Despite making several tantalising beach-heads into the US charts (his 1976 single 'Devil Woman' went gold in the US and sold 1.4 million worldwide) Richard remains, like STATUS QUO, an English institution that the Americans simply won't take to their hearts.

He was awarded an OBE in the New Year's Honours list of 1980, but even as an establishment figure he seems to carry little weight. He was notable for his absence from Live Aid (though he did contribute to the *second* Band Aid single in 1989).

By the end of the Eighties his UK tours were on a comparable scale to those of DIRE STRAITS, Elton JOHN, GENESIS or even his fellow Christians U2, incorporating two-week residencies at the arenas in Wembley and Birmingham and even a two-night stand at the 72,000-capacity Wembley Stadium in 1989, recorded and later released as *From a Distance – The Event* (EMI CDCRTV 31; 1990).

But having immersed himself with such unabashed fervour in

the pop mainstream during the late Sixties and Seventies, he has emerged in the Nineties with none of the gravitas which other comparably successful veterans can now claim. It is a cruel irony that the man who laid one of the foundation stones of contemporary popular music should end up such an outsider, the lonely missing link between rock'n'roll and Barry Manilow.

- *40 Golden Greats* (EMI CDS 792 425-2) [1977]
- *Private Collection* (EMI CDP 791 370-2) [1988]

Not the least unlikely aspect of Richard's career, but odd just the same, is that after more than three decades at the top, he should still be regarded primarily as a singles act. Of his six UK No.1 albums, three are compilations of singles, two are film soundtracks and one has not been deemed significant enough to transfer to CD (a fate which has befallen much of his portfolio). Like PRESLEY, who also failed to make the transition to the demands of 'album rock', Richard has never been much of a writer, and his regular albums tend to be *ad hoc* collections of material, culled from various sources, with little sense of artistic development or thematic coherence to bind them together. Among the exceptions have been *Rock'n'Roll Juvenile* (EMI CDP 792 422-2; 1979) and *Wired for Sound* (Fame CDM 752 027-2; 1981), but it is the compilations which provide the most meaningful barometer of Richard's recorded legacy.

40 Golden Greats is a neat, chronological collection of the early hits which charts a course from the peaks of 'Move It', 'Living Doll', 'The Young Ones' and 'It'll Be Me' (his greatest rocker ever), through sloughs of wearying banality ('Congratulations', 'Power to All Our Friends') and through to a renaissance of sorts with the mildly sophisticated pop of 'Miss You Nights' and 'Devil Woman'.

Private Collection rounds up the subsequent decade's-worth of hits, from the affecting 'We Don't Talk Anymore' (1979) to the insipid 'Mistletoe and Wine' (1988).

The Shadows

Convened: 1959, London
Brian Bennett – drums; Hank Marvin (f) – guitar; Bruce Welch (f) – guitar

UK No.1 albums: 1961: *The Shadows* (with *Out of the Shadows*
 EMI CZ 378)
 1962: *Out of the Shadows* (with *The Shadows*
 EMI CZ 378)
 1977: *20 Golden Greats* (EMI CDP 746
 243-2)
 1979: *String of Hits* (EMI CDP 748 278-2)

If they had started out as the backing group for any of Cliff
Richard's contemporaries – Billy Fury or Marty Wilde or Adam
Faith, for instance – The Shadows would long since have eclipsed
their leader's achievements. Their UK chart legacy is formidable
and although they have never had a hit in America, only Jimi
HENDRIX has had a greater individual influence than Hank Marvin
on the course of rock guitar playing. Those mysterious twanging
instrumental hits in the early Sixties and the sheer exotic glamour
of Marvin's red electric guitar affected and inspired the first
generation of British rock musicians, steering the instrument into
the forefront of their consciousness.

 Eric CLAPTON described Marvin's playing as '. . . a marvellous
mixture of clear, sweet melody over a strong rock beat. On top of
all this, he looked like Buddy Holly and played a real Stratocaster!
Unbeatable . . .', while according to Pete Townshend the very
existence of The Shadows 'made me feel that I could aspire to
create music of my own.'

● *20 Golden Greats* (EMI CDP 746 243-2) [1977]

Now that The Shadows make records which give your living
room the ambience of a motorway services area, there's a
fashionable tendency to dismiss Marvin as a minor talent who
was lucky enough to be in the right place at the right time. But
anyone who goes back and listens seriously to such wonderfully
crisp and colourful vignettes as 'The Rise and Fall of Flingel Bunt',
'Wonderful Land', 'FBI', 'Apache' or 'Dance On' will surely be
disabused of such an idea. For, in terms of his clear, economic
enunciation, his uniquely integrated use of the tremolo arm and
his impeccable sense of timing, Marvin was, and still is, a virtuoso.
The uncluttered arrangements of the songs and the rest of the
band's clean, incisive delivery provide the perfect conditions for
his uncomplicated genius to shine.

There will never be another British instrumental group to top the achievements of The Shadows, and here are 20 good reasons why.

Robbie Robertson See The BAND

The Rolling Stones

Convened: 1963, London

Mick Jagger (f) – vocals/harmonica/guitar/keyboards; Keith Richards (f) – guitar/vocals/keyboards/bass; Charlie Watts (f) – drums; Ron Wood – guitar/vocals/bass; Bill Wyman (f) – bass

UK/US No.1 albums:	1971:	*Sticky Fingers* (Rolling Stones 450 195-2)
	1972:	*Exile on Main St* (Rolling Stones 450 196-2)
	1973:	*Goat's Head Soup* (Rolling Stones 450 207-2)
	1980:	*Emotional Rescue* (Rolling Stones 450 206-2)
UK No.1 albums:	1964:	*The Rolling Stones* (London 820 047-2)
	1965:	* *The Rolling Stones No.2* (London 820 048-2)
	1966:	*Aftermath* (London 820 050-2)
	1969:	*Let It Bleed* (London 820 052-2)
	1970:	*Get Yer Ya-Ya's Out!* (London 820 131-2)
US No.1 albums:	1965:	*Out of Our Heads* (London 820 049-2)
	1974:	*It's Only Rock'n'Roll* (Rolling Stones 450 202-2)
	1976:	*Black and Blue* (Rolling Stones 450 203-2)
	1978:	*Some Girls* (Rolling Stones 450 197-2)

* *The Rolling Stones No.2* is only available in the format of its American equivalent, which was re-titled *12 × 5* and features several different tracks.

1981: *Tattoo You* (Rolling Stones 450
198-2)

It has been the unbelievable and unrivalled achievement of The
Rolling Stones to hold together as essentially the same group and
remain at or near the very top of the greasy pole of rock for more
than a quarter of a century. They have accomplished this with no
compromise or dilution of their original musical spirit, garnering
good reviews and platinum sales all the way up to 1989's *Steel
Wheels* (see below) and 1991's *Flashpoint* (Rolling Stones 468 135-2).
It is an odyssey which has run like the backbone through the body
of rock's history, and with a new contract, transferring the
distribution of their Rolling Stones imprint from Columbia to
Virgin records with effect from March 1993, it looks as if they're
far from finished yet.

After The BEATLES had given up touring in 1966, The Rolling
Stones took to billing themselves as 'the greatest rock'n'roll band
in the world', a typically arrogant boast, but one which went
unchallenged until the punk revolution of the late-Seventies.
Even then, they went on to become during the Eighties and
Nineties the most colossal touring attraction the rock world has
ever known, despite having made relatively few modifications to
the slobbish musical etiquette of their English bar-band roots.

At the outset Jagger, Richards and founder member Brian Jones
(died 3.7.69) were all highly motivated disciples of rhythm and
blues. It was in converting this love of traditional black American
music into a modern popular formula that The Stones earned
their status as one of the principal architects of rock.

They achieved success in 1963 with their first single, a swift,
loutish reworking of an obscure Chuck BERRY song called 'Come
On'. Their sullen performing style and uncouth image was an
affront to conservative opinion and came as a welcome contrast to
the more wholesome musical revolution being pioneered by The
BEATLES.

It was not long before Jagger and Richards started writing their
own material, embarking on a partnership which remains second
only to that of LENNON and McCARTNEY. In the period 1963–1969 the
Stones scored 15 UK hit singles, eight of them reaching No.1, and
the coarse, grainy guitar motifs which were the hallmark of songs
like 'Jumpin' Jack Flash', 'Honky Tonk Women' and others have

become universally recognised insignia on the fabric of rock. In 1988 '(I Can't Get No) Satisfaction' was voted the best record of the past 25 years in a *Rolling Stone* magazine critics' poll, the accompanying commentary suggesting that the opening riff was 'the rock'n'roll equivalent to Beethoven's Fifth'.

'I'm flattered,' said Richards of the accolade, 'but I wonder what Beethoven would have to say about it.'

Far from waning in the Seventies, The Stones grew in popularity and produced some of their most critically acclaimed and enduring work. Yet even that long ago, the limits of the group's stamina strained belief, especially as by the mid-Seventies Richards had become one of the world's most celebrated heroin addicts. In 1977 he was arrested in Canada for possession of the drug in quantities sufficient to warrant a maximum sentence of life imprisonment. The jolt provided sufficient encouragement for him to kick the habit once and for all, since when the astonishing reserves of his iron constitution have been matched only by the supernatural resilience of the group itself.

As they enter their fourth decade, visibly marked but unbowed by the vicissitudes which have either finished off or greatly diminished all their contemporaries, The Stones still show no sign of passing on the baton. At this point 'the greatest rock'n'roll band in the world' begins to sound like an understatement.

In contrast to the meticulous attention to detail which went into the CD repackaging of The BEATLES' back catalogue, the early Stones albums were released on CD between 1984 and 1985 with a minimum of fuss and even less care. The rights to the group's Sixties repertoire belong to their former business manager, Allen Klein, who administers them through his ABKCO company, and neither Jagger nor Richards had anything to do with the remixing, remastering or repackaging of the albums from this first golden era (from *The Rolling Stones* [1964] up to and including *Get Yer Ya-Ya's Out!* [1970]).

Instead, on hand to supervise the digital transfer was Andrew Loog Oldham, The Stones' flamboyant ex-manager, image-maker and producer of their first nine albums. Oldham, it will be recalled, was so inexperienced to begin with that when he was supervising the recording of The Stones' first single, 'Come On', he didn't know what the engineer was talking about when towards the end of the session he asked what Oldham proposed to do about mixing the recording. 'I'll pick it up in the morning,' Oldham replied, before it was explained to him that there was still a lot of complex work to be done *after* the voices and instruments had been captured on tape.

Oldham's work sheet has not exactly been overcrowded since he parted company with The Stones in 1967, and it is doubtful whether he knows a great deal more about the latter-day intricacies of transferring analogue recordings on to digital masters for CD than he did about mixing on to two-track tape in the Sixties.

'What's the three things that make up a hit record?' Oldham asked rhetorically in an interview with *Musician* magazine in 1987. 'A great song, a great song and a great song. . . . It doesn't matter: scratch, hiss, pop – if you're gonna convert the world.'

Oldham's cavalier and defiantly untutored approach to the technical processes involved in the transfer to CD has been matched by Klein's lack of respect for the integrity of this early body of work. He has allowed some of the albums to be rendered in their original form (as released in the UK), others to be represented by their less satisfactory American equivalents.

On the earliest discs there is a hotch-potch of mono and stereo mixes, slapdash packaging, incomplete track details and a depressing lack of sensitivity to the weight of history encoded within the magnetic particles of those original recordings. As a whole the programme smacks of a 'roll the tapes and call the plant' operation.

The best compilation of singles from this period, *Rolled Gold* (1975), is unavailable, while in its place the less satisfactory *Hot Rocks 1964–1971* (London 820 140-2) – an oddly rejigged combination of the old *Hot Rocks 1* and *2* – was released in 1990 to cash in on the resounding success of that year's *Steel Wheels/Urban Jungle* tour.

Yet among these first recordings (and the later ones too) there is still to be found some of the finest rock music ever committed to disc, and Oldham has a point when he belittles the quest for audio perfection. Certainly, The Stones themselves have never been especially bothered about eliminating rattle and hum from their sessions and at the end of the day, even in a book called *Rock on CD*, it is the music, not the medium that is on trial.

- *The Rolling Stones* (London 820 047-2) [1964]

Fuelled by the group's visionary R'n'B fervour, this album is without doubt one of the most incendiary premières ever, surpassing even such celebrated débuts as *The Clash* and *Led Zeppelin*.

Pitching their tone in direct contrast to the cute harmonies and lovey-dovey lyrics of The BEATLES, The Stones whip through a catalogue of material, mostly American in origin, but customised with the taut, clanky arrangements that became the unmistakable hallmark of the group's sound. Jagger bawls the lyrics to '(Get Your Kicks on) Route 66', 'Can I Get a Witness' and 'I Just Want to Make Love to You' with all the untamed declamatory truculence at his command and affects a leer on 'King Bee' that it will take more than a pristine CD renovation to clean up.

Thankfully the original UK track listing and mono mix of the album has survived intact (even though the information printed on the disc says it is in stereo).

- *12 × 5* (Originally *The Rolling Stones No.2*; London 820 048-2) [1965]
- *Out of Our Heads* (London 820 049-2) [1965]

Troubles begin with the second and third albums, both of which are only available in their American versions. *12 × 5* combines bits of *The Rolling Stones No.2* with the whole of the EP *5 × 5*. On the plus side there is 'Confessin' the Blues', 'Around and Around' and 'If You Need Me', but among the many numbers pushed out are 'Down the Road Apiece', 'Pain in my Heart' and 'Off the Hook'. The total running time is a mere 31 minutes, so all the tracks on the original album *and* all the tracks from *5 × 5* could have been included with capacity to spare. For a full-price CD this is poor value.

The same thing happens with *Out of Our Heads* which, as well as sacrificing half its original tracks in crossing the Atlantic, also loses its modish cover photograph (by Gered Mankowitz) and notorious Andrew Oldham sleeve notes about knocking down and robbing blind men. While the missing tracks are now languishing in magnetic oblivion, some of the 'new' tracks are duplicated elsewhere, not least the hit singles 'Satisfaction' and 'The Last

Time'. At least they left in the heroic version of Don Covay's 'Mercy Mercy'. Total running time: 34 minutes.

● *Aftermath* (London 820 050-2) [1966]

The first album to be comprised entirely of Jagger/Richards compositions is marred by some utterly bizarre 'stereo' mixes. The vocals are totally isolated during some tracks, and if you switch to the right-hand channel during the marathon 'Goin' Home', you get nothing but a few stray guitar notes and an otherwise unaccompanied bout of shrieks and grunts from a furiously ad-libbing Jagger. The same happens on 'Mother's Little Helper', where voices and Jones' sitar are given a channel to themselves and everything else is scrunched up into the remaining space on the other side. A fascinating insight into the nuts and bolts of the song, perhaps, but not what you'd call a finished or harmonious mix.

● *Between The Buttons* (London 820 138-2) [1967]
● *Their Satanic Majesties Request* (London 820 129-2) [1967]

The Stones had maintained a phenomenal rate of productivity (four albums in two years, plus singles), but the cracks began to show on numbers five and six, released at either end of the same calendar year and overshadowed by the towering edifice of The BEATLES' *Sergeant Pepper's Lonely Hearts Club Band*, released midway between the two.

Tracks are once again messed around and, as the Q reviewer so memorably put it, 'There are holes in the mix big enough to deliver a fridge through.'

● *Beggars Banquet* (London 800 084-2) [1968]
● *Let it Bleed* (London 820 052-2) [1969]

Even by this stage in the game, The Stones were maintaining a work-rate which acts of today would regard as unthinkable. *Beggars Banquet* was preceded by 'Jumpin' Jack Flash' and followed by 'Honky Tonk Women', but neither of those classic singles was included on it or any other contemporaneous album.

The first Stones set to be produced by Jimmy Miller, *Beggars*

Banquet marked a return to basics after the variable flights of fancy that had characterised *Their Satanic Majesties Request*. Ironically, although a debilitated Brian Jones could muster only a marginal contribution to tracks including 'Sympathy for the Devil', 'Street Fighting Man' and 'Stray Cat Blues', this was the beginning of a run of great Stones albums.

Let It Bleed (a tart contrast to The BEATLES' title of the same era, *Let It Be*) was again produced by Miller, and marked guitarist Mick Taylor's début. Jones' dismissal and Taylor's recruitment meant that the band could tour again, the key factor in the subsequent divergence between the fortunes of The BEATLES and The Stones. The creative engine was thus kicked back to full throttle as they mined a rich seam of outrage and sleaze with increasing confidence and maturity. 'Gimme Shelter', 'Country Honk' (a hick country reprise of 'Honky Tonk Women'), 'Midnight Rambler' and 'You Can't Always Get What You Want' are among the treasures.

- *Get Yer Ya-Ya's Out!* (London 820 131-2) [1970]

Recorded at Madison Square Garden on November 27 and 28 1969, this is the classic live Rolling Stones album, beginning with the triumphal flourish of hyperbole that was to stay with them for the rest of their working lives: 'Ladies and gentlemen, please welcome the greatest rock'n'roll band in the world.' What follows is a ragged, cocksure display of arrogant splendour, a distillation of the ramshackle performing excellence that has underpinned the success of The Stones to this day.

- *Sticky Fingers* (Rolling Stones 450 195-2) [1971]

This was the first album to be released on The Rolling Stones' record label, marking the end of the material still controlled by Klein. From this point The Stones recorded for their own label, which has been distributed by various major companies over the years, including Warners and Columbia (né CBS).

It's hard to imagine a better opening shot: a set of peak performances ranging from the outrageously salacious and irresistibly danceable 'Brown Sugar' to the gorgeous, flowing extemporisation of 'Can't You Hear Me Knocking', taking in country/blues knockabouts ('Dead Flowers', 'You Gotta Move'), ballads ('Wild Horses', 'Moonlight Mile') and a searing Stax pastiche ('I Got the Blues') along the way. The zip on the famous Andy-Warhol-designed cover lacks the tactile quality of its vinyl forebear, but really, what a stunner this album still is!

- *Exile on Main St* (Rolling Stones 450 196-2) [1972]

A dense, mysterious collection that doesn't surrender its charms to superficial enquiry, *Exile on Main St* remains the most acclaimed Rolling Stones album, despite the critical pasting it got at the time.

The makeshift conditions under which it was recorded, literally in (tax) exile in the basement of Richards' villa in the south of France, lent *Exile* a brooding, barbarous quality, an impression reinforced by the coarse quality of the mix, a sound as grimy and grainy as the myriad oddball photographs that grace the cover artwork.

Jagger's voice is all but buried in a weave of spiky guitar, ambient percussion and honky-tonk piano, regularly embellished by fanfares of horns which arrive mob-handed during the second verse of most tracks.

Here is a Stones album which delves well below the surface glamour of the rock'n'roll dream to a place where shadows lengthen and murk gathers. At the time, they were the one group with both the confidence to expose the raw, sinewy nerves of its music and the depth of experience to make such a revelation mean something.

Highlights include the lazy chug of 'Tumbling Dice', the countrified drawl of 'Sweet Virginia' and the glorious belt of 'Rip This Joint'. Formerly a double album, at 66 minutes it now fits comfortably on to a single, highly desirable silver disc.

- *It's Only Rock'n'Roll* (Rolling Stones 450 202-2) [1974]
- *Black and Blue* (Rolling Stones 450 203-2) [1976]

Two lesser Stones albums in the overall scheme of things, but each boasting several highly enjoyable moments nevertheless. Apart from supplying rock with one of its most naggingly familiar catchphrases, *It's Only Rock'n'Roll* is chock-a-block with those pull and tug riffs out of which Bryan ADAMS has built an entire career.

There is a sublime interpretation of Smokey Robinson's 'Ain't Too Proud to Beg' and Taylor signs off with a Santana-esque finale to the poignant 'Time Waits For No One'.

It's Only Rock'n'Roll was Taylor's last outing with the band. He left for no discernible good reason and has languished in total obscurity ever since. *Black and Blue* was the 'audition' album to find his replacement and features contributions from guitarists Harvey Mandell, Wayne Perkins and the man who looked and sounded as if he'd always had the job, Ron Wood.

- *Some Girls* (Rolling Stones 450 197-2) [1978]
- *Emotional Rescue* (Rolling Stones 450 206-2) [1980]

On *Some Girls* The Stones tackle the spectre of middle age head-on with Richards' plaintive admission of changed circumstances, 'Before They Make Me Run', while adroitly side-stepping the challenge of punk with their inimitable disco pastiche, 'Miss You', the group's eighth US No.1.

In 'Beast of Burden' the album also boasts one of the most moving ballads in the entire Stones catalogue. It was never released as a single in the UK, but provided another substantial hit in America, helping *Some Girls* to become the biggest-selling Stones album ever, until it was overtaken by *Steel Wheels* in 1989.

Emotional Rescue is too obviously *Some Girls II*. An inferior set of songs in a similar vein, it cruised to the top of the charts in the wake of its predecessor's success, but cannot be recommended as an album of any great substance.

- *Tattoo You* (Rolling Stones 450 198-2) [1981]
- *Under Cover* (Rolling Stones 450 200-2) [1983]

Despite being a patchwork of old material, stockpiled from as far back as 1972, *Tattoo You* was yet another gilt-edged (minor) classic, which stayed at No.1 in the American chart for nine weeks. The album is best known for its single 'Start Me Up' but remarkable for its freshness and vigour throughout.

In what was becoming a familiar pattern, the follow-up, *Under Cover*, is a lack-lustre affair, enlivened by a nightmarish video to promote the single 'Undercover of the Night'. Directed by Julian Temple, it enjoyed a mild frisson of controversy for its 'execution' scene where Richards, acting the part of a South American death squad hit man, 'shot' Jagger in the head. Even more extreme was the gory black humour of the video for the album's other stand-out track, 'Too Much Blood', in which Jagger was chased by a blood-spattered Richards, wielding a chainsaw. Were they trying to tell us something?

• *Dirty Work* (Rolling Stones 465 953-2) [1986]

A vastly underrated album, recorded (as all their best work has been) under trying circumstances. Jagger and Richards were by now at loggerheads over most things, but in particular about whether or not the band should tour again. Richards was packed and ready to go, but Jagger wasn't so keen, mainly because he had a solo album to promote (*She's the Boss* Columbia CD 86310; 1985). That was a sore point in itself as far as Richards was concerned, and it sometimes seemed as if the entire publicity campaign for *Dirty Work* consisted of the two of them bickering about each other in the media.

But what a dark, hard album it turned out to be, a collection which confirms The Stones' enduring ability to marshal the basic sounds of rock – loud guitars, abrasive lyrics and a hot, lean groove – with a wiry vigour that has rarely been matched. The album produced a modest hit with 'Harlem Shuffle' and drew glowing reviews from those unforgiving bastions of hipness, *Melody Maker* and *NME*.

That Jagger can still sing 'I've been climbing this tree of promises for over 40 years' with such a howl of scorn in 'Hold Back' indicates a touching measure of faith in an increasingly tatty dream.

• *Steel Wheels* (Rolling Stones 465 752-2) [1989]

Although not as good as *Dirty Work*, *Steel Wheels* was the most enthusiastically received Stones album since *Some Girls*. Made swiftly, in the wake of the over-publicised row between Jagger and Richards, it is an album of tremendous vitality that combines a general restatement of first principles ('Mixed Emotions', 'Rock and a Hard Place', 'Almost Hear You Sigh') with moments of mild experimentation (notably 'Continental Drift', recorded with The

Master Musicians of Jajouka, a troup of traditional pipers from Morocco).

In a journey that has stretched way beyond all reasonable expectations, a bunch of middle-aged men have retained a unique cachet, their music something akin to magnetic north on the rock'n'roll compass. Jagger, Richards and Watts will be in their fifties and Wyman will be nearing his *sixties* when the new Virgin contract comes into effect.

How have they done it? Apart from their resilience as individuals and their compatability as a unit, The Stones have always benefited from a broad streak of hard-headed pragmatism. As Pete Townshend knows to his cost, nothing sours the milk of creative activity worse than the taint of betrayed ideals.

The Stones managed to become counter-culture icons of the Sixties without pinning their colours to any particular mast. They simply pleased themselves. The group has thus been able to retain its essence while mutating from a youthful gang of bolshy hedonists into an avuncular collection of business partners. The biggest surprise is that they still sound as if they enjoy what they're doing.

Diana Ross

Born: Diane Earle, March 26, 1944, Detroit, Michigan
US No.1 album: 1972: *Lady Sings the Blues* (Motown ZD
72129)

Despite her surprise UK hit 'When You Tell Me That You Love Me', which reached No.2 at the end of 1991, Diana Ross' commercial role is negligible compared to the MADONNAs and Mariahs of the new pop world. The album from which the song was taken, *The Force Behind the Power* (EMI CDEMD 1023; 1991), failed to breach the US Top 100.

But, as she demonstrated at her Wembley shows the same year, Ross still enjoys the status of show-business royalty. Sailing in through the audience, she fairly oozed *noblesse oblige* as she casually negotiated the gaggle of photographers milling in her path and took up position on the spiky, star-like stage, set in the middle of the arena.

What followed was a seamless display from a woman who has probably forgotten more than most of her peers ever knew about the mores of professional entertainment. Contracted to Motown records with The Supremes (see below) before she left school, she was personally tutored by the company's far-seeing and auto- cratic supremo Berry Gordy Jr and finally groomed by him for a solo career in films as well as music. With a gleaming, fixed smile nearly as broad as her hips, and her notoriously extravagant couture, she has become the living embodiment of the middle- aged pop star as surrogate Hollywood personality.

The availability of Motown's entire back catalogue* has been subject to confusion by the changeover of UK distribution rights in 1991 from BMG to Polydor. Although those rights now belong to Polydor, BMG's 'sell off' period (for running down existing stock) extended until March 1992, and at the time of writing Polydor has yet to decide which albums they deem to be worth releasing or to ascribe new catalogue numbers.

Thus, although pre-1981 releases by Diana Ross and The Supremes will continue to appear on the Motown label, the information listed below incorporates the *old* BMG numbers – which will probably have changed by the time this book is published – and Polydor may not necessarily have issued all the same albums in the same format.

● *Diana Ross* (re-titled *Ain't No Mountain High Enough* Motown WD 72733) [1970]

There have been anything up to half a dozen albums bearing the titles *Diana*, *Ross* and *Diana Ross*, but the one that's really worth having is her solo début after leaving The Supremes in 1969.

It boasts her first hit, 'Reach Out and Touch (Somebody's Hand)', and the No.1 classic 'Ain't No Mountain High Enough'. Both of them, and all but one of the other songs, were written by the husband and wife team of Nick Ashford and Valerie Simpson, as was much of Ross' best material.

'Ain't No Mountain High Enough' in particular has got the lot: a romping beat counterpointed by delicate backing vocal harmo- nies and a stirring string arrangement which Ross tops with a

* See also Marvin GAYE, Stevie WONDER, Michael JACKSON

bravura performance. She combines drama, emotion and romance in a voice that yearns so passionately it seems to go slightly weak at the knees. Still a firm favourite in concert, it remains one of her finest moments.

● *Lady Sings the Blues* (Motown ZD 72129) [1972]

A big song and dance was made out of Ross' performance in the leading rôle of Billie Holiday in the movie *Lady Sings the Blues* and certainly she caught enough of the essence of the great, doomed jazz singer to persuade the people who know about such things to nominate her for an Oscar.

However, Ross' career in movies never really took off. The follow-up, *Mahogany* (1975), was a reasonable success despite its critical drubbing, but the megabuck adaptation of the Broadway musical *The Wiz* (1976), co-starring her close friend Michael JACKSON, was a disaster in all respects.

The soundtrack to *Lady Sings the Blues* – only half of which features Ross – captures her giving a fair impression of Holiday's elegant, husky drawl as she recreates a package of the Lady's most celebrated songs: 'T'aint Nobody's Bizness If I Do', 'The Man I Love', 'Good Morning Heartache' *et al*. It is a fine tribute to a great artist, but remains, nevertheless, a well-observed facsimile.

● *The Boss* (Motown ZD 72470) [1979]
● *Diana* (Motown WD 72430) [1980]

After several collections of cloying, sentimental pop, *The Boss* was the fruit of a welcome revival of Ross' working relationship with Ashford and Simpson, who gave her something firmer to get to grips with on material like 'No One Gets the Prize' and 'All For One'. Apart from the title track, though, the album was disappointingly light on hits.

They came when, for the follow-up, she joined hands with the writing and production team of Chic's Nile Rogers and Bernard Edwards to record *Diana*. 'Upside Down', 'I'm Coming Out' and 'My Old Piano' helped to make this one of the landmark albums of a long and erratic career.

Currently available as individual items, these albums were issued for a while as a mouthwatering two-in-one package, then swiftly deleted when BMG realised just what a bargain they were offering. Perhaps Polydor will display more largesse and reinstate them as a double header. . . .

● *Why Do Fools Fall in Love?* (Fame CDFA 3186) [1981]

In 1981 Ross did the unthinkable and severed her connection with Berry Gordy and Motown. The first album for her new label (RCA in America, Capitol in the UK) was self-produced and became a huge international hit. Although ultimately she failed to maintain the momentum, she was sitting on top of the world at this point with material like 'Mirror Mirror', 'Sweet Surrender' and 'Work That Body' registering in the chart as regularly as clockwork.

● *Greatest Hits Live* (EMI CDEMDC 1001) [1989]

The latter-day Ross roadshow, captured in full swing at Wembley Arena, comes uncomfortably close to cabaret in places, especially the medley of Supremes songs which is briskly despatched with all the enthusiasm of someone taking an idle glance at a few old holiday snaps.

But this album is certainly an accurate reflection of what she now does on stage, and gives EMI the chance to tap into a few of the old Motown hits ('Upside Down', 'Reach Out and Touch (Somebody's Hand)' and the inevitable 'Ain't No Mountain High Enough') as well as giving a second airing to more recent successes like 'Chain Reaction' and 'Muscles'.

The Supremes

Convened: 1961, Detroit, Michigan. Changed billing 1967: Diana Ross and The Supremes. Reverted to The Supremes 1969. Split up: 1977. Reconvened 1983 (Motown 25th Anniversary TV special/'Oldies' package tour)
Florence Ballard (f) (died 22.2.76) – vocals; Diana Ross (f) – vocals; Mary Wilson (f) – vocals
UK No.1 albums: 1968: *Greatest Hits* (unavailable)
              1977: *20 Golden Greats* (unavailable)

US No.1 albums: 1966: *The Supremes à Go-Go* (with *Love Child* Motown ZD 72485)

                        1969: *Diana Ross and The Supremes with The Temptations: TCB* (unavailable)

                        1970: *Diana Ross and The Supremes Greatest Hits* (with *Greatest Hits Vol.2* Motown ZD 72493)

The Supremes enjoyed more US No.1 hits than anyone except Elvis PRESLEY and The BEATLES. Between 'Where Did Our Love Go?' in 1964 and 'Stoned Love' in 1970 they scored 20 US Top 10 entries, including two with The Temptations ('I'm Livin' in Shame' and 'Someday We'll Be Together'). Detectable throughout this astounding run was the guiding spirit of Brian Holland, Eddie Dozier and Lamont Holland, a team of writers who seemed able to turn out instant pop classics some time between waking up and breakfast: 'Baby Love', 'Stop! In the Name of Love', 'You Can't Hurry Love' and 'You Keep Me Hangin' On' were just the tip of the iceberg.

Adam White, an authority on Motown, observed that The Supremes 'defined the Motown sound of the Sixties – its innovation, its influence, its popularity. Their acceptance served to bridge the gap between pop and R'n'B and helped to make the music of black America more accessible to millions worldwide.'

Yet such a towering contribution is ill-served by the medium of CD, for the memory of the group's genius and the essence of their plaintive charm lies irretrievably locked in the grooves of the three-minute single. Swiftly sculpted for the era of Dansette technology, there is simply not enough sound in these productions to fill the space available on the compact disc. Recorded when even the finest pop music was considered a genuinely disposable commodity, the production of these songs is thin, super-fizzy and lacking the sonic clout necessary to make a comfortable transition to the digital format.

Although they sold many millions of long-playing records, The Supremes did not really exist as an 'albums act'. Their better efforts tended to comprise a couple of recent hits and whatever padding came most quickly to hand (e.g. *Where Did Our Love Go?* [1964], currently available together with *I Hear a Symphony* [1966] Motown ZD 72495). The lesser ones were ghastly showbiz packages, stuff like *A Little Bit of Liverpool* (1964; unavailable) which featured the girls cooing their way through Merseybeat hits like 'A Hard Day's Night' and 'World Without Love', or *The Supremes Sing Country and Western and Pop* (1965; unavailable).

In terms of CD, then, the trio's recorded legacy is meaningful primarily in terms of hit compilations, the permutations of which have been endless. Indeed, the exploitation of The Supremes' (and Diana Ross') back catalogue has been so relentless and insensitive that it has, ultimately, eroded the integrity of a classic body of work. It remains to be seen what further repackaging and reissuing will ensue under the new distribution deal with Polydor.

• *Diana Ross and The Supremes: Anthology* (Motown WD 72532) [1987]

This double-disc collection, which crams in a vast cross-section of Supremes material (though nothing from Ross' solo career), is one of Motown's much lauded *Anthology* series, all of which provide reliable and worthwhile compendiums of the essential work of the artists concerned (others have featured Smokey Robinson and The Miracles, The Four Tops and Marvin GAYE).

As with the others in the series, this emerges as the most rounded compilation of The Supremes that we're likely to get; a carefully assembled retrospective of the most successful female trio in the history of rock.

David Lee Roth See VAN HALEN

Roxy Music

Convened: 1970, London. Split up: 1976. Reconvened: 1978. Split up: 1983
Brian Eno (f) – keyboards; Bryan Ferry (f) – vocals/keyboards; Andy Mackay (f) – saxophone/oboe; Phil Manzanera (f) – guitar; Paul Thompson – drums
UK No.1 albums: 1973: *Stranded* (EG EGCD 10)
                  1980: *Flesh and Blood* (EG EGCD 46)
                  1982: *Avalon* (EG EGCD 50)

1986: *Street Life - 20 Great Hits* (EG
EGCTV 1)

Touting a bright, non-conformist strain of art-rock nouveau, performed with a clangy, non-technical panache, Roxy Music played an important role in revitalising rock in the rather dour aftermath of the hippy era. They arrived in a burst of outré splendour, dressed to the nines in a weirdly customised version of glam-decadent chic. Leopardskin, lamé, improbably elevated heels and a generous application of eye-liner were the key elements of a fashion code that married Fifties nostalgia to Seventies sci-fi.

Founded by vocalist and songwriter Bryan Ferry and bassist Graham Simpson, who had played together in a band called The Gas Board while students at Newcastle University, Roxy Music made an instant splash with their eponymous début album and a single, 'Virginia Plain', which seemed to open the door on a vista of boundless possibilities.

Unfortunately, they burned out almost as quickly as they had arrived. Although they were still capable of the odd splutter of brilliance which produced hits like 'Street Life' and 'Love is the Drug', once Ferry had ousted *avant garde* keyboard maestro Eno from the band in 1973, they lost a vital element of strategic weirdness and their music rapidly degenerated into a tired and rather empty pastiche of the original formula.

With their strikingly sophisticated veneer and vaguely arty pretensions, Roxy Music exercised a not altogether benign influence on a succeeding generation of smoothies, style buffs and upwardly mobile consumerists. SIMPLE MINDS virtually modelled their first album on Roxy Music traits, and the hideous new romantic movement led by mannequin pop stars like Spandau Ballet and Duran Duran took their cue from the cocktail party mannerisms which Roxy Music increasingly came to embrace in the Eighties.

- *Roxy Music* (EG EGCD 6) [1972]

Roxy Music and David BOWIE made their album chart début in the same month, BOWIE with his epoch-making *The Rise and Fall of Ziggy*

* Album credited to Bryan Ferry and Roxy Music.

Stardust and the Spiders From Mars, Roxy Music with the more succinctly titled but no less influential *Roxy Music*.

Both albums challenged the post-psychedelic 'progressive' rock orthodoxy of their day – there was no room for faded jeans or 'musical integrity' where these guys were coming from – but whereas BOWIE's songs were the work of a conventional tunesmith (no matter how bizarre his dress sense), Roxy Music's creations were sleek, futuristic tableaux that dispensed with verse/chorus structures, and imported weird tonal colorations, ranging from the incongruous honk of MacKay's oboe to the loopy tonal abstractions of Eno's primitive synthesiser set-up.

Ferry's highly stylised vocal technique – half-yawn, half-yodel – enabled him to deliver numbers like 'Re-make/Re-model' and the galloping 'Ladytron' with icy detachment. His voice still conveys emotion about as convincingly as an android, coating these songs in a hard, durable gloss that obscures depth of meaning as much as it does any underlying faults.

● *For Your Pleasure* (EG EGCD 8) [1973]

The group quickly reached its apogee with this, their second and best album. The gleeful thrill of 'Do the Strand' with its stiff staccato piano chords, gaudy saxophone embellishments, romping beat and quirky left-field lyric, survives intact, while 'In Every Dream Home a Heartache' remains a compulsive and chilling glimpse into the soulless heart of urban materialist chic.

● *Avalon* (EG EGCD 50) [1982]

A timeless, drifting concoction that presaged the coming of New Age and the rise of CD as the perfect delivery system for (among other things) aural wallpaper. With the band in a mellower mood than ever before, a lot of the tracks were constructed from studio improvisations. While conceding that it wasn't the kind of album that you might call either 'up' or 'rocky', Manzanera described the mood as 'positive'. As he explained to *Rolling Stone*, the album was recorded just before Ferry got married. 'It was a period when he was searching.'

- *Street Life – 20 Great Hits* (EG EGCTV 1) [1986]

The definitive compilation, comprising the biggest of both Roxy's and Ferry's solo hits. It includes the first two singles, 'Virginia Plain' and 'Pyjamarama', which are not otherwise available on the albums contemporaneous to their original release.

Bryan Ferry

Born: September 26 1945, County Durham
UK No.1 albums: 1985: *Boys and Girls* (EG EGCD 62)
               1986: *Street Life – 20 Great Hits* (EG EGCTV 1)

Bryan Ferry, the son of a farmer-cum-mine worker, and an arts graduate who studied under conceptual pop painter Richard Hamilton, will be remembered as the man who developed a credible strand of rock with an upmarket designer tag on its coat-tails. He first appeared in a white tuxedo on the cover of his 1974 album *Another Time Another Place* (EG EGCD 14), an image so powerful and seductive that it virtually wiped out a decade of rock industry prejudice against 'straight' fashion at a stroke.

It was a look that matched his urbane but superficial musical style and which later inspired a tiresome strand of yuppie-rock, the kind of thing that encouraged suave young fogeys like Tony Hadley of Spandau Ballet and Martin Fry of ABC to think they might sound soulful while looking as if they had just emerged from a Stock Exchange luncheon.

Throughout the history of Roxy Music, it always looked as if Ferry wanted to run the show solo but could never find the bottle finally to sever the cord. He initially declined to go solo because 'being very retiring by nature, I was terrified of being onstage alone', but once Roxy Music were up and running, he embarked on a series of solo albums initially comprised entirely of cover versions.

'I'd felt I'd made a reputation as a songwriter playing fairly weird music,' Ferry told American journalist Timothy White, 'and I thought it'd be interesting to do an old-style Sinatra-like album of standards and material I'd admired from Goffin and King,

---

* Album credited to Bryan Ferry and Roxy Music.

Lieber and Stoller, The BEATLES and The STONES.' The result was *These Foolish Things* (EG EGCD 9), a collection celebrated for his bold rendition of DYLAN's 'A Hard Rain's Gonna Fall'.

But Ferry's progress has been a resounding triumph of style over substance. His interpretative abilities serve only to render any song, no matter what its provenance, into the same idiosyncratic, ululating format as all the others. It is a facile exercise that systematically denudes numbers like 'Let's Work Together' or 'The In Crowd' of their emotional resonance and substitutes a glib vocal signature instead. Worse still is the way his treatment of standards like 'Smoke Gets in Your Eyes' and 'These Foolish Things' has imported the wine-bar aesthetic into rock.

After *Avalon*, Ferry ditched Roxy Music for the last time (so far) but with no new material forthcoming since the dismal, somnambulistic *Bête Noire* (Virgin CDV 2474) in 1987, he seems to have dried as a solo act.

- *Boys and Girls* (EG EGCD 62) [1985]

Ferry is joined by a galaxy of talent including Mark Knopfler, Nile Rodgers, David Gilmour, Marcus Miller and David Sanborn, for a collection which even he admits is basically *Avalon Part Two*. Such is the quest for production perfection that he practically refines himself out of existence. 'Slave to Love' and 'Don't Stop the Dance' loom at the tip of a smooth, cold iceberg.

Run DMC

Convened: 1982, Queens, New York
Jam Master Jay (f) – DJ; Darryl 'D' McDaniels (f) – vocals;
Joseph 'Run' Simmons (f) – vocals
US No.3 album: 1986: *Raising Hell* (Profile 828 018-2)

By the start of the Nineties, when NWA were hymning the joys of gang rape, Run DMC seemed such sweet, old-fashioned dudes, but back in 1986 they were the toughest team on the block. Even if they weren't such bad-mouthed mothers as they seemed at the time or ever sufficiently depraved to impress the hard core cognoscenti, Run DMC were still primarily responsible for introducing rap (or hip hop as it was known in those days) to the rock mainstream.

Their début album, *Run DMC* (unavailable; 1983) was the first rap album to go gold (sales of half a million); *Raising Hell* (see below) the first to reach platinum (one million). It is hard to overstate the impact of their crossover hit 'Walk This Way' (1986) – performed in tandem with the song's authors Steven Tyler and Joe Perry of AEROSMITH – in breaching the barrier between rap and rock. (Even so, it was five years before rock repaid the compliment, when Anthrax recorded a version of PUBLIC ENEMY's 'Bring the Noise', featuring PE mainman Chuck D.)

Run DMC's spell at the top didn't last long, of course. As they quickly discovered, those who live by the sword of self-aggrandisement and tougher-than-thou posturing have precious little to defend themselves with when new acts emerge who are prepared to take the verbal abuse to ever wilder extremes. In the time that it took Run DMC to record the follow-up to *Raising Hell*, first PUBLIC ENEMY and then the 'gangsta' rap squads (Ice T, Ice Cube, NWA *et al*) exploded out of the West Coast and rap changed virtually beyond recognition, irrevocably. The staunchly anti-gang, anti-drugs Run DMC were like teddy bears compared to that lot, yet still insisted that they were tougher than old boots, or some such. Suddenly, all the scowling and bad-boy ranting struck a sadly hollow note.

● *Raising Hell* (Profile 828 018-2) [1986]

This is unbelievably minimalist by today's standards, but it still sounds great. The sampling racket was in its infancy when Run DMC recorded this, their third album, and a lot of the tracks, such as the opener, 'Peter Piper', are nothing more than a beat-box rhythm, snatches of clonking percussion and the voices of Run and his partner DMC. 'My Adidas' boasts a deeply malevolent bass figure and then there is the added element of heavy rock guitar thrown in on 'It's Tricky', 'Raising Hell' and, of course, 'Walk This Way'.

What really hits home is the level of self-belief that is so cheerfully advertised in these vain slogans. 'Perfection to D is quite essential/He has to fulfil his potential,' declaims a droll Run against an utterly stark drum-kit accompaniment. It's all tackled with the sort of naive vitality that suggests rap had been invented yesterday, which, in terms of rock in 1986, it had.

- *Together Forever – Greatest Hits 1983–1991* (Profile FILECD 419) [1991]

Run DMC were trailblazers again when they brought out this greatest hits album, the first such compilation by a rap act. Although their reputation had diminished, they had kept going for eight years, which for a modern rap posse is an eternity. Naturally, the best tracks are from their middle period, including 'Walk This Way', 'It's Tricky', 'Run's House' and 'What's It All About?'.

Santana

Convened: 1968, San Francisco, California
Carlos Santana: Born: July 20 1947, Autlan de Navarro, Mexico – guitar/band leader; assorted personnel
US No.1 albums: 1970: *Abraxas* (Columbia CD 32032)
                 1971: *Santana III* (Columbia CD 69015)

It should come as no surprise that one of Santana's biggest fans is Salif Keita, the celebrated world music singing star from the West African state of Mali. Yet some of the more puritan of the world music buffs who flock to Keita's concerts in search of an authentic other-cultural experience are plainly shocked to hear Keita's guitarist occasionally burst forth with explosive Santana-like solos cranked out in the overheated manner and overloaded sound that has long been the Mexican maestro's trademark.

But Carlos Santana, the son of a *mariachi* musician whose family emigrated to San Francisco in 1962, was a 'world' musician two decades before the term had even been coined. By importing for the first time the percussive rhythms of Central America and Africa into the ambit of rock, he introduced a new range of rhythmic flavours to a genre which had hitherto subsisted for the most part on a staple diet of lone timekeepers and a 4/4 beat. The rock stage has since become a natural habitat for percussionists, yet it was an astounding and revolutionary innovation when the

Santana band initially appeared with a back line which incorporated two percussionists and a drummer.

With a guitar tone which varied, in an instant, from warm and ringing to brittle and taut, and a melodic playing style interspersed with helter-skelter flurries of notes, Carlos Santana was one of rock's premier instrumental stylists and remains a player of rare emotional clout. But although the far-reaching influence of Santana's first two albums remains undeniable, subsequent developments did not fulfil their abundant promise.

'Within a year of Woodstock, everything that was honey turned into vinegar within the group,' Carlos reflected in 1990. 'By the time we did *Caravanserai* (1972, see below) I had no band.'

In his search for new horizons, Carlos began to explore the world of jazz-rock fusion, indulging in a bombastic instrumental discourse with John McLaughlin on *Love, Devotion and Surrender* (1973, unavailable). Over the years he has maintained his role as leader of the constantly changing aggregate known as Santana, while collaborating as a solo artist with musicians from a wide variety of backgrounds. These include jazz-rockers Herbie Hancock and Wayne Shorter, country veteran Willie Nelson and, in his most celebrated partnership of recent times, John Lee HOOKER on the title track of the veteran bluesman's outstanding comeback album *The Healer* (Silvertone ORECD 10, 1989).

● *Abraxas* (Columbia CD 32032) [1970]

This was Santana's second album and featured what is still the band's most fondly remembered line-up: José Chepito Areas – percussion/trumpet; Mike Carabello – percussion; David Brown – bass; Gregg Rolie – vocals/keyboards; and Mike Shrieve – drums. It was the same unit which had appeared at the Woodstock festival in August 1969, and on the eponymous début album (see below), and by the time of *Abraxas* they were in full flower. Their exotic, hot-blooded, polyrhythmic attack, so steeped in the Latin culture of Central America, is married to the finest Bay Area electric rock, in a rollercoaster set which includes 'Samba Pa Ti', 'Hope You're Feeling Better' and their perennial version of FLEETWOOD MAC's 'Black Magic Woman'.

- *Santana* [1969]/*Abraxas* [1970]/*Santana III* [1971] (Columbia 4669132)

This triple-CD set, comprising the first three Santana albums, offers reasonable value for money at around £20 and is now the only way of purchasing the first album (*Santana*) which was deleted as an individual item in 1990. Originally launched on the back of the band's legendary appearance at Woodstock, the best track on *Santana* is 'Soul Sacrifice'. Indeed, it was the fledgling Santana's performance of this percussive *tour de force* – led from behind by the mighty Mike Shrieve – which trounced all competition in the subsequent *Woodstock* movie (with the possible exception of Jimi HENDRIX).

Santana III, the band's third album, features changed personnel and some of the heaviest rock that Santana ever committed to disc. It was the album which introduced Carlos Santana's protégé guitarist Neal Schon (later, together with Gregg Rolie, a founder member of US mega-bores Journey) and the axe duels come fast and furious.

Also available in triple-CD format are the later and generally less essential Santana albums *Caravanserai* [1972]/*Barboletta* [1974]/*Amigos* [1976] (Columbia 4683352).

- *Viva Santana (The Very Best of Santana)* (K-Tel NCD 3338) [1986]

A smattering of hits including the reworked version of The Zombies' 'She's Not There' and the liquid-gold lilt of 'Samba Pa Ti', together with vintage favourites like 'Black Magic Woman', 'Well Alright' and 'Oye Como Va', provide the backbone of this robust compilation.

The Sex Pistols

Convened: 1975, London. Split up: 1978
Paul Cook (f) – drums; Steve Jones (f) – guitar; Johnny Rotten (f) – vocals; Sid Vicious (died 2.2.79) – bass
UK No.1 album: 1977: *Never Mind the Bollocks Here's The Sex Pistols* (Virgin CDV 2086)

By the mid-Seventies rock was big business. Marketing techniques were becoming increasingly sophisticated, the level of technical proficiency among some rock musicians had reached that of their formally trained classical counterparts, and with all the 'name' and 'ex-name' musicians in circulation, making music had become an activity divorced from youth and the grubby realities of the street. Rock shows had become complex operations, vastly expensive to mount, and indeed to watch – rather like they are in the Nineties, in fact. The prospect of starting a band from scratch and getting any further than your local pub or a London record company receptionist seemed remote.

The Sex Pistols were conceived as a harsh, radical antidote to all that. They were the brainchild of boutique owner and would-be music business svengali Malcolm McLaren. The brief, as he saw it, was to create a group which would be vulgar, obstreperous, anti-social and immediate, thus providing an effective conduit for the rage of a new generation of disaffected youth for whom the remote, tax-exiled, anti-heroes of yore (Jagger, DYLAN, BOWIE, *et al*) were no longer relevant.

The Pistols met all these requirements and then some. A satisfactory ballyhoo ensued as they swore on television, ransacked their record company's offices, insulted the monarch during Jubilee year with their No.2 hit 'God Save the Queen' and got themselves banned from virtually every concert stage in Britain.

In so doing, The Sex Pistols administered a jolt that freed rock's wheel from the ditch, but which shook the group itself to pieces in less than three years. It was a squalid end, leaving one bass player and his groupie girlfriend dead, and a recorded legacy reducible to just one album, the quaintly titled *Never Mind the Bollocks Here's the Sex Pistols*.

Still, in opening the door for so many new bands (especially in regions like Glasgow and Manchester) and in kick-starting the network of independent labels and charts, The Pistols had an immeasurable and enduring impact on the music and musicians which emerged in their scrappy wake.

- *Never Mind the Bollocks Here's The Sex Pistols* (Virgin CDV 2086) [1977]

As the soundtrack to one of rock's more brutish sagas, this once inflamatory recording now sounds mildly dated. Even so, it is an album laced with improbably excellent performances. 'Bodies', 'Holidays in the Sun', 'Anarchy in the UK' and 'God Save the Queen' all boast a taut, propulsive energy which gives the lie to the foolish notion that the group could not play their instruments or that this was music so basic that 'anyone could do it'.

On a strictly musical level, the playing is actually too good to be the work of a punk band – if anything it sounds more like heavy metal R'n'B – but add Rotten's whiney sneer to the mix and you have an album that was an electrifying clarion call for a generation of the musically dispossessed.

Public Image Ltd

Convened: 1978, London
John Lydon (né Rotten): born January 31 1956, London – vocals; assorted personnel
UK No.11 album: 1981: *Flowers of Romance* (Virgin CDV 2189)

After the demise of The Sex Pistols, Rotten reverted to his real name of Lydon, and formed Public Image Ltd, which he at first described as an 'anti-rock'n'roll band'. Early recordings – *Public Image* (Virgin CDV 2114; 1978) and *Metal Box* (1979, re-issued as *Second Edition* Virgin CDVD 2512; 1980) – were indeed a challenging broadside to received notions of rock. With the rumbling reggae bass of Jah Wobble well up in the mix, guitarist Keith Levene providing a screechy, atonal patchwork of noise, and Lydon's bedouin-like snarl echoing somewhere in the distance, they made music which *Rolling Stone* described as 'disco Samuel Beckett style'.

But over the years, as the personnel changed, Rotten's intent mellowed to the point where he turned his 'anti-rock'n'roll' polemic on its head. The trend started in 1986 when he hired a bemused Ginger Baker (ex-CREAM) to play drums on *Compact Disc* (Virgin CDV 2366; 1986) and was continued on *Happy?* (Virgin CDV2455; 1987), by which time PIL boasted an established, conventional, two-guitar line-up featuring John McGeogh (ex-Banshees) and Lu Edmonds (ex-Damned). The same team produced *9* (Virgin CDV 2588; 1989), a compelling study in the controlled application of the unique Lydon whine to traditional rock guitar band dynamics.

● *The Greatest Hits, So Far* (Virgin CDV 2644) [1990]

Although the temptation must be constantly with him, the admirable thing about Lydon is that he has never pretended to be any more stupid or less reactionary than he really is, which is why his music has always rung true. It may also be the reason that *bona fide* 'hits' have been a bit thin on the ground during his post-Pistols phase. There is, however, no shortage of bruising charm in a collection which boasts, among others, 'Public Image', 'This is Not a Love Song', 'Rise', 'Death Disco' and 'Flowers of Romance'.

The Shadows See CLIFF RICHARD

Paul Simon

Born: October 13 1941, Newark, New Jersey
UK No.1 albums: 1972: *Paul Simon* (WEA 925 588-2)
1986: *Graceland* (Warner Bros 925 447-2)
1990: *The Rhythm of the Saints* (Warner Bros WX 340 CD)
US No.1 album: 1975: *Still Crazy After All These Years* (WEA 925 591-2)

Whatever else he has done and wherever he goes next, Paul Simon will always be remembered for *Graceland* (see below), an album (and tour) which placed him at the epicentre of one of the major musical, cultural and political events in the rock world of the Eighties.

Not bad going for someone who enjoyed his first chart entry at the age of 15 and has 'peaked' several times since. That first hit was in 1958 when he and his high school chum Art Garfunkel, recording under the alias of Tom and Jerry, reached No.49 in the US with a song called 'Hey Schoolgirl'. It was to be seven years before the duo enjoyed another hit, by which time they had

reverted to their real names, and the song – 'Sounds of Silence' –
went all the way to No.1.

- *Paul Simon* (WEA 925 588-2) [1972]
- *There Goes Rhymin' Simon* (WEA 925 589-2) [1973]

Both of Simon's first two solo albums, after the parting of the
ways with Garfunkel, were simple, agile productions which
stripped away the gloss and bluster that had bogged down his
work during the final phase of Simon and Garfunkel (see below).
Songs like 'Mother and Child Reunion' with its tugging reggae
beat and 'Me and Julio Down By the Schoolyard' from *Paul Simon*
combine melodic acuity with a pleasing suppleness of touch, while
the New Orleans carnival atmosphere of 'Take Me To the Mardi
Gras' and the breezy acoustic romp of 'Kodachrome' on *There Goes
Rhymin' Simon* still sound as fresh as the day they were recorded.

- *Graceland* (Warner Bros 925 447-2) [1986]

Having been seduced by the airy sounds and rhythms of an album
called *Gumboots: Accordion Jive Hits, Volume II* (unavailable) by a
South African group called The Boyoyo Boys, Simon travelled to
that beleaguered country, where he collaborated with the local
musical fraternity and began recording *Graceland*. Although
technically not in breach of the UN-sanctioned cultural boycott
(which banned foreign musicians from *performing* in South Africa),
Simon was widely and roundly condemned by anti-apartheid
activists for his 'insensitivity' to the political situation and for
breaking the *spirit* of the boycott.

Simon has always vigorously denied that he gave succour to the
apartheid régime or intentionally defied the boycott. 'The thing
about culture is that it flows like water,' he told *Billboard* magazine
in 1987. 'It is impossible for cultures to survive in isolation. The
terrible danger about the boycott is that it is imposing a double
prejudice against the very people whom it's meant to help. I
believe the point's been missed entirely.'

Simon could be forgiven for feeling slightly smug when, less
than five years later, he became the first major rock act to tour
inside South Africa after the lifting of the boycott.

His argument – that he intended *Graceland* to be a cultural exchange that would benefit both his own and black South African music – was vindicated both by the nature of the album and its resounding success. There was certainly no other way, at that time, that the rest of the world would have got to hear a track like 'Homeless', a lullaby written in Zulu and sung by the eminent 10-piece South African church group Ladysmith Black Mambazo, whom Simon recruited both for the album and its tour.

For most of the other numbers on *Graceland*, Simon co-opted the vivacious rhythms and sparkling sounds of South Africa to lend a seductive ethnic frisson to his light, haunting melodies and unmistakably American lyrics. The narrative of 'Gumboots', where he discusses relationship problems in 'a taxi heading downtown', submerges the accordion *mbaqanga* (jive) soundtrack beneath a lyrical scenario more worthy of a Woody Allen movie than a township *shabeen* (illegal drinking party).

Even so, the album had a catalytic impact on the commercial potential of 'ethnic' musics the world over. Mainstream audiences seized on the novel yet mellifluous interweaving of styles, and the nascent vogue for world music was given an enormous and decisive boost.

● *Negotiations and Love Songs 1971–1986* (Warner Bros 925 789-2) [1988]

This compilation doubtless came as a pleasant surprise for the many millions of people who bought *Graceland*, but were unaware for the most part of Simon's previous solo efforts following the demise of Simon and Garfunkel.

Simon has always tended towards the twee melody and self-absorbed lyric, and sure enough, for every left-field gem included here, such as '50 Ways To Leave Your Lover', there is an inconsequential pleasantry like 'St Judy's Comet'; for each achingly romantic paean like 'Slip Slidin' Away', a pre-digested piece of supper-club schmaltz like 'Something So Right'.

Still, this is a sensitive and almost comprehensive collection which includes popular favourites like 'Mother and Child Reunion', 'You Can Call Me Al' and 'Graceland' along with less celebrated yet equally evocative numbers like the Latin romp, 'Late in the Evening', 'Hearts and Bones' and the delicate 'Train in the Distance'.

• *The Rhythm of the Saints* (Warner Bros WX 340 CD) [1990]

Continuing in his cultural raider role – a sort of Alan Whicker of rock – Simon attempts the Graceland trick with Brazilian music, achieving, perhaps inevitably, rather less startling results.

Much of the music is based on the glorious interlocking waves of percussion provided by the Brazilian groups Olodun (a 14-piece drum troup) and UAKTI (classically trained musicians using percussion instruments made out of industrial piping and the like). 'The Obvious Child' romps along to an insistent side-drum shuffle, while 'Further to Fly' proceeds in a more languid vein with the beat switching on and off a jazzy samba groove. 'She Moves On' has a dark, tropical feel, its rich percussive mix oiled by deep sensual plunges of the bass line.

Yet unlike the smooth integration of musical cultures which distinguished *Graceland*, Simon's guitar and vocal parts seem too obviously grafted on top of these pulsating foundations. The melodies bed in after repeated listenings, but lack the charm of his previous work. But if the spoils of his most recent cross-cultural excursion seem relatively commonplace, it is only because Simon is a victim of his own outstanding achievements.

Simon and Garfunkel

Convened: 1963, New York. Split up: 1970. Reconvened: 1972 (Madison Square Gardens, New York concert); 1975 (US NBC TV's *Saturday Night Live*); 1977 (Britannia Music Awards, London); 1981 (Central Park, New York concert); 1982 (European tour); 1983 (US tour)
Art Garfunkel (f) – vocals; Paul Simon (f) – vocals/guitar
UK/US No.1 albums: 1968: *Bookends* (Columbia CD 63101)
                     1970: *Bridge Over Troubled Water*
                            (Columbia CD 63699)
US No.1 album: 1968: *The Graduate* (Columbia CD
                            32359)

Although they were never a favourite of the critics, Simon and Garfunkel were outstandingly successful with a bleached fusion of Greenwich Village folk and Tin Pan Alley pop, which became gradually more overwrought as their popularity increased. On

June 15 1968 they held three of the Top Five US album chart positions with *Bookends* (see above), the soundtrack from *The Graduate* (see above) and *Parsley, Sage, Rosemary and Thyme* (Columbia CD 32031; 1966).

● *Bridge Over Troubled Water* (Columbia CD 63699) [1970]

The phenomenal success of this album and the single of the same title was instrumental in launching the tedious strand of Seventies soft rock purveyed by acts like Bread, Linda Ronstadt, Andrew Gold and Carly Simon. An over-produced album that combines gentle acoustic textures with high emotional drama, yet somehow arrives at a certain blandness of tone, it marked both the pinnacle and the end of the duo's career, netting five Grammy awards and selling in excess of 11 million copies at the latest count.

Several of the songs are solo efforts by Simon in all but name – notably 'The Boxer' and 'Baby Driver' – and it became clear during the making of the album that the partnership was nearing the end of its useful life.

● *The Definitive Simon and Garfunkel* (Columbia MOOD CD21) [1991]

Art Garfunkel may have been the non-writing, non-playing half of the partnership, but listening again to this collection of 20 of the duo's best songs (selected personally by Garfunkel) it is evident just what a marvellous singing voice he had and how much his harmonies contributed to numbers like 'The Sound of Silence', 'Homeward Bound', 'Mrs Robinson' and 'Scarborough Fair'.

There was, too, an extraordinary bond between the singers, a perfect melding of tone and pitch which is reminiscent of The Everly Brothers at their best and which has rarely been equalled. Hearing 'Wednesday Morning 3 a.m.' or 'America', it is hard to think of two voices more perfectly suited to each other.

Simple Minds

Convened: 1977, Glasgow
Charles Burchill (f) – guitar; Mel Gaynor – drums; John
Giblin – bass; Jim Kerr (f) – vocals
UK No.1 albums: 1984: *Sparkle in the Rain* (Virgin CDV
2300)
1985: *Once Upon a Time* (Virgin CDV
2364)
1986: *Live in the City of Light* (Virgin
CDSM 1)
1989: *Street Fighting Years* (Virgin PMIND
1)

From a scuffling little group of die-hard Glaswegian punks calling
themselves Johnny and the Self Abusers to a first division
European stadium act with a tendency to sound as if the worries
of the world are their copyright, the Simple Minds story is a rock
odyssey in the epic tradition.

There was no instant burst of glory, but a slow fuse was lit
when in 1979 they signed a deal with Bruce Findlay's Edinburgh-
based Zoom records. Their early albums were an uncomfortable
amalgam of new wave glam and Gary Numanoid naff, betraying
influences ranging from Euro-synth bands like Kraftwerk to the
posturing art-rock of ROXY MUSIC.

They toured and worked unremittingly and after several
moderately successful singles were eventually rewarded in 1982
with a Top 20 placing for 'Promised You a Miracle'. In 1985 they
lucked into success in America with 'Don't You (Forget About
Me)', a throwaway song (recorded for a bratpack movie *The
Breakfast Club*) which just happened to reach No.1. They played at
Live Aid in Philadelphia the same year and became part of the new
rock aristocracy which that event created overnight.

'If there's such a thing as a big league, we want to be in it,' Jim
Kerr once said and although they have subsequently slipped from
grace in the US, in Britain and Europe the blocks have all fallen
neatly into place. Original keyboard player Michael MacNeil quit
in 1990, leaving the writing team of Kerr and Burchill as the only
two founder members, with the long-standing Gaynor bringing
up the rear.

Streamlined and secure, Simple Minds enter the Nineties

having simply out-toughed and out-classed most of the competition. With no immediate sign of creative ennui, they continue to bump along the top of a very high plateau with their most recent album *Real Life* (Virgin CDV 2660; 1991), a typically fine set, but perhaps ominously their first album release since 1984 not to reach No.1.

- *New Gold Dream* (81-82-83-84) (Virgin CDV 2230) [1982]

This was the break-through album and is still conspicuously the best thing the band has ever done. Written and rehearsed in an old farmhouse in the Fife countryside, it combines the moody atmosphere of their earlier work with a newly acquired melodic flair. It also kicks like a mule and was the first Simple Minds album to feature the awesomely powerful drumming of Mel Gaynor, perhaps the single most important factor in accounting for the radical overhaul of the group's sound at this time.

It incorporates their first three (proper) hits: 'Promised You A Miracle', 'Glittering Prize' and 'Someone, Somewhere (In Summertime)' and showcases all the key elements of the Simple Minds sound at work: Gaynor's thump, Burchill's neat, uncluttered guitar chops, MacNeil's grandiose keyboard washes and Kerr's rich vocal tone and pensive lyricism.

'A lot of people ask me why we can't make *New Gold Dream Part Two*,' Kerr told *Melody Maker* some years later. 'I wish we could, but we can't. All the inspiration, all the clues, they just arrived on that record. Then they were gone.'

- *Once Upon a Time* (Virgin CDV 2364) [1985]

Their biggest-selling album, this notched up worldwide sales in excess of four million copies, and earned them their only American precious metal award when it was certified gold (500,000) in 1986. 'All the Things She Said', 'Alive and Kicking' and 'Sanctify Yourself' all reached the UK Top 10. Despite such commercial accolades, it garnered little artistic kudos and has about it the ring of a Pyrrhic victory. While rounding up the floating voters, there is too much obvious barnstorming and pushing of the right buttons to please those on the more aesthetic wing of the band's supporters.

● *Street Fighting Years* (Virgin PMIND 1) [1989]

Another landmark album which found the band shooting for that place in the constellation of superstars reserved for the act which can burn with the brightest sense of mission. The vaguely impressionistic lyrics of the past are superseded by more pointed proclamations on some of the obvious international issues of the day. With Kerr effortlessly assuming the mantle of authority, the band swings the spotlight on South Africa ('Mandela Day', Peter GABRIEL's 'Biko'), Northern Ireland ('Street Fighting Years') and indeed the world (with the eco-conscious 'This is Your Land').

Since *Once Upon a Time*, detractors have always complained about the 'bluster' and 'bombast' in Simple Minds' music, yet much of this album is actually very quiet, with Kerr often pitching his voice in that silky low register located somewhere between a note and a yawn, and several of the songs starting with wistful, meandering intros. Even among the teeming shoals of sound that propel the up-tempo 'Wall of Love' or 'Kick It In', there are placid eddies where Kerr's singing slips from a yell to a whisper.

The group's more baroque tendencies are still evident in the many vast climaxes, but these are balanced by the thematic coherence and musical maturity of the work overall. At this point Simple Minds were operating with supreme confidence and comfort on the grand scale to which they had long aspired.

Simply Red

Convened: 1984, Manchester
Gota – drums/percussion/programming; Mick Hucknall (f) – vocals; Tim Kellett (f) – keyboards/trumpet; Ian Kirkham – saxophone; Fritz McIntyre (f) – keyboards/vocals; Heitor T. Pereira – guitar; Shaun Ward – bass
UK No.1 albums: 1989: *A New Flame* (WEA 244 689-2)
                 1991: *Stars* (eastwest 9031-75284-2)

The precise relationship between vocalist Mick Hucknall and Simple Red has always been a vexed question. 'This is a solo career,' Hucknall told a surprised *Q* journalist in 1991, 'and it always has been, but it's taken me five years to realise it. I just don't like the name Mick Hucknall very much.'

Evidence to support this assertion is not hard to find. Right from the group's beginnings as The Frantic Elevators, Hucknall has been the man in charge. He has appeared, by himself, on the front covers of all four Simply Red albums; the band's repertoire is overwhelmingly comprised of his compositions; he has presided over a constantly changing line-up; and he is widely recognised as the voice, the look and the spokesman of the band.

But it was a different story in 1987 when, interviewed on Channel 4's *The Tube*, he expressed his impatience with people who constantly labelled Simply Red's music as 'white soul'. 'Hasn't anyone noticed that half the band is black?' he wondered.

Hucknall is a man well versed in the art of having his cake and eating it. In the early days of Simply Red, he would sit uncomfortably in a rehearsal studio, looking and sounding a paragon of street credibility as he reeled off lists exclusively of black singers he admired: Sam Cooke, James BROWN, Otis REDDING, Marvin GAYE, *et al*, while plugging the band's first single, a cover of The Valentine Brothers song, 'Money's Too Tight (To Mention)'.

Now, of course, money's too plentiful to mention, and insofar as Hucknall/Simply Red's music is a fizzy appropriation of black musical styles for consumption by the mass rock market, the 'white soul' label has stuck.

● *Picture Book* (Elektra 960 452-2) [1985]

This fondly regarded début holds up surprisingly well, with highlights including 'Money's Too Tight', 'Come To My Aid' and the old Frantic Elevators song 'Holding Back the Years', which took Simply Red to the top of the US chart.

But they cast the net too wide in the range of black styles which they seek to imitate: the jazz swing of 'Sad Old Red', the heavy funk of 'No Direction', the soul/disco bounce of 'Red Box' and the sluggish reggae of 'Picture Book', for starters. Such a cavalier approach leaves the impression of a band with an enthusiastic but superficial understanding of the idioms involved.

● *Men and Women* (WEA 242 071-2) [1987]

Hucknall is a capable singer, but he overreaches himself with an attempt at Cole Porter's 'Ev'ry Time We Say Goodbye', and is unable to rescue 'Move On Out' from its misplaced, lumbering rock groove.

Other than that, this is a tidy collection with galloping bass lines providing a firm musical heartbeat during the choruses to 'The Right Thing' and at least one rousing soul-funk theme ('I Won't Feel Bad') of which Leon Russell would approve.

● *A New Flame* (WEA 244 689-2) [1989]

The album that took them to the first division, this sold six million copies worldwide and provided their second US No.1 single, a version of the Gamble/Huff standard 'If You Don't Know Me By Now' (a hit for Harold Melvin and the Bluenotes in 1973).

Yet despite its overwhelming success, and the expensive tailoring of Stewart Levine' production, it is the least convincing of Simply Red's albums. Hucknall's distinctive voice is as strong and wiry as his unkempt hair, but there is often a leering quality to his delivery. Whether it be a slow ballad like 'Love Lays Its Tune' ('Last night I made love for the first time') or something a bit rockier such as 'To Be With You' (I wanna be with you . . ./Most of all/To make love with you'), he brazens rather than emotes his way through the songs.

The influences are getting more contemporary: 'Turn It Up' is a social-conscience lyric set to an up-beat Alexander-O'Neal-style melody, while 'More', with its considered, light reggae feel, strays into Sade's territory until a cranked guitar solo drops by to shatter the mood. 'She'll Have to Go', like most anti-Thatcher diatribes, sounds rather dated now that she's taken their advice.

● *Stars* (eastwest 9031-75284-2) [1991]

Another meticulously produced catalogue of blue-eyed soul, this boasts some of the best tunes and grooves that Hucknall has produced since *Picture Book*. It sold 1,320,000 copies in Britain in 12 weeks, making it the top-selling UK album of 1991 ahead of EURYTHMICS, QUEEN, Tina TURNER, Michael JACKSON and R.E.M.

The best bits are the infectious, rolling-piano stomp of 'Something Got Me Started' and the winsome chorus of 'Your Mirror', although the (synthesised) twittering in the latter, underpinning the line 'Even the birds still sing their faithful song', is laying it on a bit thick.

Sly and The Family Stone

Convened: 1966, San Francisco, California
Sly Stone (f) (born: Sylvester Stewart, March 15 1944, Dallas, Texas) – vocals/keyboards/guitar; Greg Errico (f) – drums; Larry Graham (f) – bass/vocals; Jerry Martini (f) – saxophone/keyboards; Cynthia Robinson (f) – trumpet/vocals; Freddie Stone (f) – guitar/vocals; Rose Stone (f) – piano/vocals
US No.1 album: 1971: *There's a Riot Goin' On* (Edsel EDCD 165)

Sly and The Family Stone were the first act to straddle the divide between the heavy Southern funk of James BROWN and the West Coast acid-rock of Jefferson Airplane. They broke most, if not all, the rules of black music and redefined the relationship between rock and soul in the process.

That was not all. While Freddie Stone neatly co-opted the fuzz and wah-wah guitar effects that had hitherto been the preserve of players like Eric CLAPTON (then in CREAM) and Jimi HENDRIX, Larry Graham invented the 'slap' funk style of bass playing, using his thumb to thwack the bottom strings and his fingers to pluck the higher strings in one rapid fidgeting movement – a style which has been widely assimilated, but is now most notably associated with the over-heated virtuoso playing of Mark King of LEVEL 42.

Their melodies, which seamlessly combined elements of soul and pop, were couched in a dense weave of rousing, neo-gospel vocalese. Put it all together and you had Stoned soul, a concoction which proved both deliriously engaging and profoundly influential.

Their style of presentation was no less revolutionary. In soul a line of demarcation between singers and instrumentalists had long been the norm. Individual stars or vocal groups like The Four Tops and The Temptations hired backing bands to provide instrumental accompaniment. But Sly and The Family Stone were built along the less hierarchical lines of a rock group with everyone playing an instrument and most of them singing as well.

But no rock group at that time had ever had a line-up like The Family Stone's, with its fully integrated horn section and its mixed race, mixed sex and genuinely familial composition (the band included Sly's brother Freddie, sister Rose and later another sister Vanetta). Fusing the grandstanding elements of a soul revue with all the flamboyant costumed finery and florid rhetoric of the hippy era, their performances were a riotous mixture of super-charged jamming and spontaneously choreographed stomping and cheerleading.

An excerpt from Sly and The Family Stone's set at the Woodstock festival in 1969, singing their trademark anthem 'I Want to Take You Higher', was one of the best moments of the ensuing movie.

Unfortunately, 'higher' was just what Sly did get, so high that during the next decade his increasingly erratic behaviour resulted in literally hundreds of shows being cancelled at the last minute, and the inexorable drying up of his recording career. In 1984 he issued a statement from the Lee Mental Clinic in Fort Myers, Florida, where he was undergoing treatment to kick his debilitating free-basing habit: 'Drugs can take you up, but they can also take you out. . . .'

In December 1989 Sly was sentenced to 55 days in prison after pleading guilty to driving while under the influence of cocaine. He was last spotted in 1991, busking outside the Chinese Theatre, on Hollywood's Sunset Boulevard, a sorry epilogue to the career of one of rock's most gifted peacocks.

● *The Collection* (Castle Communications CCSCD 307) [1991]

A recent release, as part of the indispensable Castle Communications 'Collector Series', this is a grand compilation which eclipses the rather patchier selection offered on *Greatest Hits* (Epic 462 524-2; 1970). Principal absentees from *The Collection* are the US hits 'Stand!' and 'Hot Fun in the Summertime', but present and correct are 'Everyday People', 'I Want to Take You Higher', 'Don't Call Me Nigger, Whitey', and all three of their US No.1s, 'Everyday People' (1969), 'Thank You (Falettinme Be Mice Elf Agin)' (1970) and 'Family Affair' (1971).

But it is still their first hit, 'Dance to the Music', which defines the group's unique sound and reverberates most clearly down the years. A joyous surge of dance-floor rhythm, hoisted aloft by a clarion call of a chorus, the song introduces each instrument and describes its own construction with a combination of knowing slickness and innocent *joie de vivre* that has rarely been heard in rock before or since.

- **There's a Riot Goin' On** (Edsel EDCD 165) [1971]

Rolling Stone called it 'One of the most bleak, despairing, yet emotionally charged albums any pop artist has ever recorded'; according to critic Andrew Weiner it was 'an elegantly constructed portrait of personal and social disintegration'; while *Vox* magazine declared it to be simply 'the most important funk LP of all time'.

Whether it is any or all of these things, this album is certainly a powerful statement that stands in stark contrast to the bright, punchy optimism of the group's earlier hits. Its cover bedecked with a plain picture of the American flag and listing a non-existent title track (which eventually had to be credited as lasting 0.00 minutes to stem the tide of complaints from people thinking they had bought a faulty pressing), *There's a Riot Goin' On* marked a watershed in Sly's music. Instead of the super-cosmic dude in ever-ready party mode, the listener is confronted by the raddled, sleepy voice of a black American whose eyes have opened to the mess that he and his country have got themselves into.

The album's sound is defined by a dense, powerful mix of guitars, horns and sinuous funk rhythms. The outstanding track, with its loping beat, croaking vocal and crying wah-wah guitar, is 'Family Affair', a stunningly anguished epistle which, despite its radical, meandering form and alarming air of distraction, nevertheless topped the American chart in 1971.

The Smiths

Convened: 1982, Manchester. Split up: 1987
Mike Joyce (f) – drums; Johnny Marr (f) – guitar; Morrissey (f) – vocals; Andy Rourke (f) – bass

UK No.1 album: 1985: *Meat is Murder* (Rough Trade
ROUGHCD 81)

The most significant rock band of the Eighties or a severe case of
the Emperor's new clothes? No other act of its era generated such
extremes of devotion *and* antipathy, and The Smiths became a
touchstone for all that was good or bad about rock during the
decade.

Revered for his melancholy portrayal of whimsy and angst and
ridiculed for carrying a bunch of gladioli in his back pocket,
Morrissey created a unique strand of miserablist chic. The
combination of his sad, distracted voice – undulating like a limp
handshake – and Johnny Marr's BYRDS-derived jangly guitar
playing was the magic formula that unlocked the barrier between
the polish of pop and the substance of the indie sector.

Throughout their career, irony was advanced as the key to
understanding The Smiths, but too often hagiographers, critics
and fans alike responded in deadly earnest to Morrissey's absurdly
melodramatic outpourings. Much of it was a huge put-on, but
Morrissey nevertheless overturned the whole notion of rock
stardom. Elvis PRESLEY was sex incarnate; The BEATLES and The
ROLLING STONES were tough, glamorous adventurers, David BOWIE
was an exotic alien and Johnny Rotten was a simple macho
bastard. But the most significant rock icon of the Eighties
foreswore sex and wore a hearing aid as a fashion accessory
(apparently as a tribute to the Fifties singer Johnnie Ray). After
Morrissey you could never again take for granted what a rock star
actually was.

• *The Smiths* (Rough Trade ROUGHCD 61) [1984]

It is difficult to over-estimate the influence of this extraordinary
début. It injected the high-minded artistic ideals of the independent sector straight into the arteries of the commercial mainstream. With no major label backing or promotional budget to
speak of, the album reached No.2 in the UK and introduced the
world to the provocative appeal of this charming band.

• *The Queen is Dead* (Rough Trade ROUGHCD 96) [1986]

Released to widespread critical acclaim, The Smiths' fourth album was generally held to be the saving grace of contemporary rock at that time. Certainly the band had rarely sounded more enthusiastic, hitting a purposeful stride with 'Vicar in a Tutu' and the title track, but the increasingly wayward touches of juvenile dementia that were affecting every aspect of Morrissey's word-play make it a difficult album to take seriously in retrospect.

● *Strangeways Here We Come* (Rough Trade ROUGHCD 106) [1987]

The album which ended their quixotic incumbency. As ever, its leitmotif is one of morbid adolescent fixations, revealed in titles like 'Girlfriend in a Coma' and 'Last Night I Dreamt That Somebody Loved Me'.

● *The World Won't Listen* (Rough Trade ROUGHCD 101)

Not even The Smiths were immune to the lure of the ubiquitous 'best of' compilation, but this rehash of singles and remixes suffers from some fairly disastrous omissions (where are 'This Charming Man', 'Heaven Knows I'm Miserable Now' and 'Sheila Take a Bow'?). Generally, the later hits are better represented, including 'Panic', 'Ask' and 'Shoplifters of the World Unite'.

Morrissey

Born: Stephen Morrissey, May 22 1959, Manchester
UK No.1 album: 1988: *Viva Hate* (HMV CDSCD 3787)

Morrissey's solo career proceeded in fits and starts. Coming within six months of the official demise of The Smiths, the début *Viva Hate* (HMV CDSCD 3787) was a predictable success. An unconstrained voyage round the Morrissey ego, it is an album which gently bathes the spirit in a joyless splurge of self-obsessional fantasy and negative emotion, while offering no apologies for the dirty water-mark it leaves behind.

It took the maestro another three years to produce the 33 minutes of music which comprises the follow-up *Kill Uncle* (HMV CDSCD 3789), much of which conforms to the familiar pattern of neurotic whimsy with a flatulent title: '(I'm) The End of the Family Line', 'There's a Place in Hell for Me and My Friends' and so forth.

Electronic

Convened: 1989, Manchester
Johnny Marr (f) – guitar/keyboards; Bernard Sumner (f) –
vocals/keyboards
UK No.2 album: 1991: *Electronic* (Factory FACD 290)

After The Smiths broke up, the robust Johnny Marr went to
work as a rather chameleon-like gun for hire. His CV includes
sessions with TALKING HEADS, Bryan FERRY, Paul McCARTNEY and
Kirsty MacColl. He (briefly) joined The PRETENDERS and toured for
the best part of 1989 with Matt Johnson's band The The.

Towards the end of that year he joined forces with Bernard
Sumner of New Order, and, as Electronic, the duo released a hit
single 'Getting Away With It'. Eighteen months later they finally
put out their début album *Electronic* (Factory FACD 290).

The album is state-of-the-art electro-pop circa 1991, dominated
more by the smooth technological poise and club-rock grooves
with which New Order is associated, despite a distinctly Smith-
sonian tilt to one or two numbers such as 'Tighten Up'.

The impression of Electronic as being simply a hipper version of
PET SHOP BOYS is confirmed by the guest appearance of Neil
Tennant and Chris Lowe on 'The Patience of a Saint'.

Bruce Springsteen

Born: September 23 1949, Freehold, New Jersey
UK/US No.1 albums: 1984: **Born in the USA** (Columbia CD
86304)
1987: **Tunnel of Love** (Columbia 460
270-2)
US No.1 albums: 1980: **The River** (Columbia CD 88510)
1986: **Live: 1975–1985** (Columbia 450
227-2)

'You know what rock'n'roll is?' asked Bruce Springsteen in 1978.
'It's me and my band going out to the audience tonight and
growing older with that audience.'

This is a definition somewhat at odds with the traditional cars
'n' girls 'n' drugs 'n' booze formula which has long hinged on the

implausible, if romantic, notion of eternal, irresponsible youth. And while there are any number of superannuated rockers around in the Nineties who might recognise the wisdom of Springsteen's words, it was a comment that demonstrated considerable prescience at a time when groups like The CLASH and TALKING HEADS were supposedly leading rock through one of its fiercely regenerative phases, and Springsteen himself was still in his twenties.

It is also interesting that of all the performers who have travelled to the ultimate frontiers of rock'n'roll superstardom – from PRESLEY to JACKSON, The BEATLES to U2 – only Springsteen waited until he was in his mid-thirties to reach his peak.

Of course he was a media phenomenon long before then, but it still seemed ludicrously premature when they put his picture on the covers of *Time* and *Newsweek* simultaneously in October 1975, not just because of the overkill, but more because his feet weren't big enough for the boots into which they had been thrust. Whatever the critics said, to the vast majority of music fans outside the informed élite Springsteen was an interesting but still peripheral phenomenon.

By the same token, there was an implicit suggestion in journalist Jon Landau's frequently misquoted comment – 'I saw rock and roll future and its name is Springsteen' – that as an act Springsteen was still a long way from reaching fruition, although the statement was, of course, widely assumed to mean something much more immediate. The marketing campaign which it inspired was hideously out of joint with the reality of Springsteen's status at the time, and those old pictures of the scrawny, bearded kid in his *faux-naif* woolly hat now seem to bear little or no relation to the muscular, block-jawed performer who finally grew big enough to match and then dwarf the misplaced hyperbole of his youth.

Springsteen was rock's first middle-aged superstar – not one of the many post-Live Aid types who had hung on or come back into fashion, but someone who had believed in a grown-up vision of rock'n'roll from the word go. His faith in the long-term power of the rock dream, however tattered, invested his work with a resonance which his more cynical contemporaries could never hope to muster.

The genus rock seemed to hold few surprises once the punk explosion had died away. Springsteen's belief in its essential worth

enabled him to nurture a brattish and often ignoble musical idiom
through the difficult phase from adolescence to adulthood.

- *Greetings From Asbury Park NJ* (Columbia CD 65480) [1973]
- *The Wild, the Innocent and the E Street Shuffle* (Columbia CD 65780)
  [1974]

Springsteen's first two albums staked out the territory and laid
the firm foundations on which his career was to be built. The
establishment of a geographical location with the postcard on the
cover of *Asbury Park* underpinned the themes of continuity and
community which were to stretch throughout his portfolio. The
other musicians on *Greetings* were all from the same New Jersey
locale – Clarence Clemons (saxophone), Vini Lopez (drums),
David Sancious (keyboards), Garry Tallent (bass) and one small
contribution from Steve Van Zandt (guitar) – and this was the
line-up which formed the core of the first E Street Band, a backing
unit that was to demonstrate unswerving loyalty and outstanding
flexibility in the years ahead.

Stand-out tracks include 'Blinded by the Light' (a hit for
Manfred Mann) and 'It's Hard to be a Saint in the City' from
Asbury Park, and the convoluted marathon 'Rosalita' from *E Street
Shuffle*.

- *Born to Run* (Columbia CD 80959) [1975]
- *Darkness on the Edge of Town* (Columbia CD 86061) [1978]

Springsteen's third album, *Born to Run*, prompted the most intense
bout of critical adulation since the rock cognoscenti first got
behind the young Bob DYLAN. It is such an overpoweringly
evocative album that much of it teeters on the brink of bombast,
but in songs like 'Thunder Road', 'Jungleland' and the title track,
Springsteen taps into the lodestone, mining a vein of searing
romanticism with the unshakable integrity that quickly became
his hallmark. The vast sonic panorama conjured by the mock-
symphonic production and the baroque complexity of several
arrangements would have sounded kitsch and melodramatic in a
less secure pair of hands (as indeed they later did: see MEAT LOAF).

Darkness on the Edge of Town is a much more incisive album than
its over-acclaimed predecessor, with numbers like 'Promised

Land', 'Adam Raised a Cain' and 'Badlands' suggesting a degree of musical and emotional retrenchment after the extravagances of *Born to Run*.

- **The River** (Columbia CD 88510) [1980]

Springsteen's second masterwork (after *Born to Run*) produces further glimpses of the small people's dreams, combined with a growing dimension of social realism, never more poignantly expressed than on the folk-tinged title track. A guy recalling a lifetime of soured hopes remembers the days when he used to take his girl down to the river, which becomes a metaphor for the incessant, uncaring flow of life and time. Here are Springsteen's narrative powers at their best, demonstrating an uncanny ability to conjure a feeling of instant nostalgia for a world the listener may only have the slightest acquaintance with.

- **Nebraska** (Columbia 463 360-2) [1982]

Whatever else he might be, Springsteen is not a folk singer. This glorified demo which features him on his own, singing and playing guitar and harmonica, is grindingly dull.

- **Born in the USA** (Columbia CD 86304) [1984]

This superb album hoisted Springsteen to the very top of the superleague while dismaying a hard core of Springsteen buffs, who decried the ambiguous, clenched-fist hyperbole of the title track, the American flag imagery on the cover and the supposed lack of nuance in the lyrics and arrangements. No less an authority than Richard Williams, writing in *Q* magazine, said of *Born in the USA* that it was 'as calculated a product as anything by Stock, Aitken and Waterman'. In reaching out so unashamedly to the hearts, minds, feet and pockets of more than 18 million purchasers, Springsteen had clearly gone a bridge too far.

And yet the instrumentation is, by and large, leaner and more sparing than the full frontal, neo-Spectorish 'wall of sound' that was the hallmark of *Born to Run*, and the arrangements are far less ornate and 'epic' than early odysseys like 'Thunder Road'. There is certainly no lack of nuance in the lilting melody of 'I'm On Fire' or the broken-man lyric of 'Downbound Train'.

What this album does is to crystallise the blue-collar, cars and girls and hardworking men strand of Springsteen's work while simultaneously abandoning the show-band presentation of vintage years for a more conventional, streamlined rock effect that was to prove especially effective in a stadium context.

As ever, The E Street Band prove a supremely adaptable unit. With saxophonist Clarence Clemons taking fewer solos and the keyboards of Roy Bittan and Danny Federici deployed relatively sparingly, it is mostly down to the guitar playing of Steve Van Zandt and Springsteen himself, and the unrestrained drumming of Max Weinberg to create the requisite propulsive effect.

● *Live: 1975-1985* (Columbia 450 227-2) [1986]

This 40-song boxed collection of live concert recordings is as painstakingly and expansively presented as the shows themselves. Dotted among the performances there is roughly 45-minutes-worth of material never previously released, including the heavy, brooding 'Seeds' and a pummelling version of Whitfield/Strong's 'War', both débuted on the 1984/5 world tour, together with older stage favourites like Woody Guthrie's 'This Land is Your Land' and Springsteen's own versions of hits he has given to other artists such as Patti Smith's 'Because the Night' and The Pointer Sisters' 'Fire'.

There may be minor quibbles over the choice of material – 'Darlington County' but no 'Glory Days'? – and even the most casual observer will wonder about the omission of 'Dancing in the Dark' (from *Born in the USA*, his biggest-ever hit single), but there can be few complaints about the consistently high standard of the recording and performances throughout.

● *Tunnel of Love* (Columbia 460 270-2) [1987]

Springsteen must have been more aware than anyone that the extremes of *Born in the USA* and its accompanying world mega-tour could not be sustained indefinitely, and that his reputation as a performer was founded on an emotional honesty which was unlikely to withstand the dehumanising effects of simply writing more grand themes and pushing the right buttons for stadium audiences. In paring down the sound and scale of his songs on *Tunnel of Love* and electing to play arenas rather than stadiums in America, he indicated his willingness to walk before they made him run.

With its quieter, reflective, even intimate tone the album won back some of his original supporters and scored several hits, including the yearning 'Tougher Than the Rest' and 'Brilliant Disguise' a heart-felt essay in duplicity and mistrust between lovers that did not bode well for the state of his recent marriage.

It was to be his last album for at least five years and proved something of a disappointment for those fair-weather fans who preferred him in the role of a mainstream rocker; for them the next Bryan ADAMS album beckoned.

Ringo Starr See The BEATLES

Status Quo

Convened: 1967, London
Andy Bown – keyboards/vocals; John Edwards – bass; Rick Parfitt (f) – vocals/guitar; Jeff Rich – drums; Francis Rossi (f) – vocals/guitar
UK No.1 albums: 1973: *Hello* (Vertigo 848172-2)
1975: *On the Level* (Vertigo 848174-2)
1976: *Blue for You* (Vertigo 848089-2)
1982: *1982* (Vertigo 800035-2)

Never was a band more aptly named (with the possible exception of Mud). So much has Status Quo traded on its image of Stonehenge-like continuity, that it is the only rock'n'roll group that has consistently pretended to be older than it really is. 'Official' accounts of the band's history suggest that it dates from 1962 when drummer John Coghlan, bassist Alan Lancaster and Rossi played, together with several other bods, in a group called The Spectres. Hence the '20th anniversary' celebrations in 1982 which helped to promote that year's retrospective package (a triple-LP, since deleted, titled *From the Makers of . . .*).

Then, in 1990, there was the much-hyped '25th anniversary' of the day in 1965 when those same Spectres (not Status Quo) met a band that Rick Parfitt was playing in at a Butlin's holiday camp in Minehead. Significant though this encounter might have been,

Parfitt didn't actually *join* Rossi and Co until two years later, in 1967, which was when they became Status Quo.

Another popular misconception, long encouraged by the group, is that they have always been masters of the allegedly 'good-time' 12-bar boogie that became their trademark in the Seventies. In reality, their salad days were spent shamelessly clambering aboard whatever passing bandwagon looked most convenient at the time.

Thus, come the Summer of Love in 1967, these ex-Butlin's entertainers had become hugely unconvincing torchbearers of the hippy revolution. They achieved their first chart break-through in 1968 with 'Pictures of Matchstick Men', an endearingly kitsch approximation of psychedelic pop, that struggled to be heard through a production so awash with phasing effects that it sounded as if it had been recorded outdoors in a very high wind.

The follow up to this opportunistic success, a number called 'Black Veils of Melancholy', failed to chart at all, and there followed a sticky period marked by one or two erratic entries in the singles chart and a complete inability even to register as an albums act.

But gradually a new look and a new sound took shape and they emerged in the mid-Seventies with the heads down, no-nonsense, denim and denim look, that has since become as generic a rock image as Jagger's sneer or Elvis' quiff. Apparently, what they now played was to be called 'boogie'. In true Quo tradition it was claimed, almost immediately, that this was a style they had been perfecting for ten years or so.

Of course, it was nothing like real boogie at all. Eschewing the fluid, shuffling swing that gives proper boogie its joyous, nimble quality, Status Quo's variant of this noble rhythmic convention (which has its provenance in the earliest forms of jazz) is a stiff, piston-like plod that has proved an ideal accompaniment for the neanderthal practice of head-banging.

Coghlan left the band in 1982, never to be heard of again, and Lancaster departed in 1984, prompting a 'farewell' tour to be slotted in among the various 'anniversary' projects. But after the so-called End of the Road Tour in 1984, Lancaster rejoined the band for its appearance at Live Aid in 1985, and was then permanently replaced by John Edwards.

By the start of the Nineties, Quo had become the rock

institution that they had always told everyone they were. In 1991 they even got themselves into the *Guinness Book of Records* for the curious feat of 'performing at the largest number of British arenas in under 12 hours' as part of their *Rock 'Til You Drop* charity promotion.

● *Rockin' All Over the Years* (Vertigo 846797-2) [1990]

Although they have enjoyed countless successful albums, it is for their singles that the band is best remembered. At the time of writing, 42 of them have been British hits and Quo has made more than 100 appearances on *Top of the Pops* – both feats being the most achieved by any band.

This compilation reflects that longevity and features the biggest singles from every stage of the group's career. Quo's rugged boogie design is plentifully featured on hits including 'Paper Plane', 'Down Down', 'Caroline', 'Whatever You Want' *et al*, and has been applied no less successfully to cover versions such as John Fogerty's 'Rockin' All Over the World' (with which they memorably opened proceedings at Live Aid) and Dion's 'The Wanderer'. An occasional deviation such as 'In The Army' or 'Marguerita Time' lends some variation to the otherwise remorseless formula.

Rod Stewart

Born: January 10 1945, London

UK/US No.1 album:	1971:	*Every Picture Tells a Story* (Mercury 822 385-2)
UK No.1 albums:	1972:	*Never a Dull Moment* (Mercury 826 263-2)
	1974:	*Smiler* (Mercury 830 056-2)
	1975:	*Atlantic Crossing* (WEA K2 56151)
	1976:	*A Night on the Town* (WEA K2 56234)
	1979:	*Greatest Hits* (unavailable)
US No.1 album:	1978:	*Blondes Have More Fun* (unavailable)

A veteran of the Sixties British R'n'B boom, Rod Stewart's boisterous personality and sandpaper-rasp singing were already tempered by a hefty weight of dues-paying experience by the time he made such a monumental international impact with 'Maggie May' and its host album *Every Picture Tells a Story* (see below) in 1971.

So perhaps it was not surprising that within three years he had succumbed to the blandishments of a Beverly Hills lifestyle, ditched his parallel career with The Faces (see below), and turned into a more soulful version of Elton JOHN.

Along with the flamboyant jet-setting behaviour, including a succession of costly imbroglios with leggy blonde partners to keep him in the gossip columns, came a depressingly middle-of-the-road musical sensibility which has won him a legion of new fans at considerable expense to his musical drive and credibility.

It is all a far cry from the start of his career as a beatnik and putative blues shouter living on the Left Bank in Paris in 1963, and probably explains why he is rarely credited for his influence on latter-day performers like Huey Lewis and Bryan ADAMS. But when he puts his back into an old soul standard like Arthur Conley's 'Sweet Soul Music', the magic is still there. It's just a shame he doesn't do it more often.

- *Gasoline Alley* (Vertigo 824 881-2) [1970]

The pieces of Stewart's solo career began falling into place with his second album, an engaging combination of covers (DYLAN's 'Only a Hobo'; Elton JOHN's 'Country Comforts') and originals ('Joe's Lament', 'Lady Day' and the title track) which skilfully deploys mandolins and acoustic guitars in an otherwise straightforward rock'n'roll setting, a trick that was later to serve R.E.M. nicely too.

- *Every Picture Tells a Story* (Mercury 822 385-2) [1971]
- *Never a Dull Moment* (Mercury 826 263-2) [1972]

The first album ever to reach the top of the charts simultaneously in Britain and America, *Every Picture Tells a Story*'s mercurial appeal rests as much in the utterly distinctive timbre of Stewart's voice as it does in the enduring charm of songs like 'Mandolin Wind', 'Reason to Believe', Chuck BERRY's 'Sweet Little Rock'n'Roller' and the perennial 'Maggie May' (which also topped the UK and US singles charts in the same week).

He repeated the formula, wrapping elements of soul and modern folk into a yobbish British R'n'B package with *Never a Dull Moment*, a delightfully gritty collection which along with 'You Wear It Well' features the hit version of Jimi HENDRIX's 'Angel', and a barnstorming retread of his hero Sam Cooke's 'Twistin' the Night Away'.

- *Atlantic Crossing* (WEA K2 56151) [1975]
- *A Night on the Town* (WEA K2 56234) [1976]

With the supremely polished *Atlantic Crossing*, which coincided with the demise of The Faces, Stewart finally drifted clear of his rock'n'roll moorings and into the murky waters of mainstream family entertainment, leaving a lot of his original fans behind in the process. It remains a bland, dependable album, notable for the stadium-friendly dirge 'Sailing', but the follow-up, *A Night on the Town*, is a more rounded set, incorporating the soulful 'The First Cut is the Deepest' and the picaresque 'The Killing of Georgie'.

- *The Best of Rod Stewart* (Warner Bros 926 034-2) [1989]

Never an especially radical or rebellious artist, Stewart has maintained his position largely thanks to his unashamedly populist instincts. Over the years he has repeatedly minted anthems that are rock'n'roll facsimiles of 'Auld Lang Syne': numbers such as 'Every Beat of my Heart', 'You're In My Heart' and, of course, 'Sailing', which induce a genial sense of euphoria whenever he dishes them up to the waving and weaving throngs at his concerts.

This collection takes in most of the obvious high points of a conspicuously successful career, leading off with four No.1 hits – 'Maggie May', 'You Wear It Well', 'Baby Jane' and 'Da Ya Think I'm Sexy', the song which set him up as a disco-stud for the blue-rinse brigade. But the rough-and-ready charm of his earlier work is eclipsed by too much of the over-familiar, banner-waving ballads of later years.

- *Vagabond Heart* (Warner Bros 7599-26598-2) [1991]

Come the Nineties and Stewart's stage show had turned into a hugely enjoyable trawl through his early back catalogue, but like most of his Eighties work this album betrays the creative ennui that has overtaken him in recent years, and surprisingly few of the numbers ever got an airing live.

Even so it bounced Stewart out of a lean patch, providing him with a string of hits including the typically anthemic 'Rhythm of my Heart', 'It Takes Two' (a duet with Tina TURNER on behalf of the Pepsi corporation) and 'Downtown Train' (a well-spotted Tom WAITS tune).

Full marks for tenacity, then, but it nevertheless sounds more like a marketing exercise than the work of a man who is still more than capable of shooting from the hip when he wants to.

The Faces

> Convened: 1969, London. Split up: 1975
> Kenney Jones (f) – drums/vocals; Ronnie Lane (f) – bass/vocals; Ian McLagan (f) – keyboards/vocals; Rod Stewart (f) – vocals; Ron Wood (f) – guitar/vocals
> UK No.1 album: 1973: *Ooh La La* (unavailable)

Jones, Lane and McLagan of The Small Faces were left in the lurch when vocalist Steve Marriott (died 20.4.91) departed to form Humble Pie. Wood and Stewart were likewise on the look-out for gainful employment, their services no longer being required in The Jeff BECK Group. Thus The Faces were born, but the seeds of the group's downfall were sown from the outset, when Stewart signed a parallel solo contract with Mercury in the same month that the group signed to Warner Bros.

Within two years, Stewart's solo career was already overshadowing anything which The Faces had achieved, and the widely voiced assumption that they were merely Stewart's backing band caused rancour and contributed to the instability which eventually shook the group apart.

Emerging at a time when the trend was for 'progressive' rock played with serious intent by musicians of increasingly advanced technical prowess, The Faces brought a welcome shot of rough-

and-ready bar-room bonhomie to many fondly remembered songs, including 'Cindy Incidentally', 'Stay With Me', 'Pool Hall Richard' and 'You Can Make Me Dance Sing or Anything'. Their laddish (mis)behaviour, feather-cut hairstyles and loose, boozy style of rock'n'roll proved an enduring rôle model in later years for groups like The Quireboys, Dogs D'Amour and The BLACK CROWES.

Always a great night out, they never captured the essence of their live shows on disc and ultimately lacked the variety which Stewart brought to his solo work. In this country, their entire portfolio remains unreleased on CD. However, Japanese imports of *Ooh La La* (Warner Bros WPCP 4039) and *Snakes and Ladders – Best of The Faces* (Warner Bros WPCP 4040) are widely available for a stiff £21 or so (each!).

Sting

Born: Gordon Matthew Sumner, October 2 1951, Wallsend, Tyne and Wear

UK No.1 albums: 1987: *Nothing Like the Sun* (A&M CDA 6402)

1991: *The Soul Cages* (A&M 396 405-2)

There was a period from 1984–1986 when, although The POLICE were inactive, manager Miles Copeland let it be known that he would sue anyone who reported that the band had split up. While Andy Summers and Stewart Copeland dabbled in photography and arty film soundtracks, Sting used the time to build a workmanlike solo career. Like just about everything he has ever turned his hand to – athletics, teaching, singing, acting, songwriting – he quickly found himself pushing against an open door.

For the singer of a major league group to achieve a comparable level of solo success is not the foregone conclusion that it sometimes appears to be in retrospect; ask Mick Jagger, Freddie Mercury, Roger Daltrey, Roger Waters or Jon BON JOVI. But by the start of the Nineties, Sting was a fully established mainstream performer – the thinking person's Phil COLLINS – and The POLICE were just a fond memory.

Unfortunately, notwithstanding his involvement in various

humanitarian causes – Amnesty International, saving the Brazilian rainforests and so forth – Sting became unbearably self-obsessed. His interviews abounded with pseudish references to Jung and Schoenberg, while his music became correspondingly earnest, inward-looking and burdened with self-analytical baggage.

'I almost never listen to pop music,' he said in 1987. 'I don't think Radio 1 is designed with people like me in mind.'

- **The Dream of the Blue Turtles** (A&M DREMD 1) [1985]

For his widely acclaimed solo début, Sting moved sideways, gingerly dipping a toe in the fast-flowing waters of jazz-rock. However, there was to be none of the heavy extemporisation and awkward time-signatures so beloved of the real funk/fusion merchants (although his band could certainly have dished that up if he'd let them). Rather he hired the best musicians money could buy – Omar Hakim (drums, ex-Weather Report), Darrell Jones (bass, ex-Miles Davis), Kenny Kirkland (keyboards) and Branford Marsalis (saxophone) – and used their exquisite skill and tone to lend a swinging, sophisticated burnish to his ingenious pop-rock songs: 'If You Love Somebody Set Them Free', 'Love is the Seventh Wave', 'Russians', 'Fortress Around Your Heart' *et al.* Not even the absurd title impeded the album's progress and it eventually sold in excess of six million copies.

- **. . . Nothing Like the Sun** (A&M CDA 6402) [1987]

Not jazz, not rock, not Latin, but a strange, thoughtful combination of the lot, this album of hazy, introspective material sounds as if it simply can't be bothered to tout for custom in any particular market. A long, 12-song collection of complex and unpredictable intensity, it nevertheless proved a staggering success, eventually selling somewhere in the region of 11 million copies. One explanation may be that Sting was, at this point, well ahead of the field in writing and recording with the extended playing time and broader audio-dynamic range of the CD format in mind.

The tone is set by the opening track, 'The Lazarus Heart', a song about Sting's mother's death earlier in the year, written after a vivid nightmare. The album is dedicated to 'my mum and all those who loved her', and the dominant theme is grief.

The dappled moods stretch from the playful swing of 'Englishman in New York' and 'Rock Steady' (theme tune for the TV series of the same name) to the jazz-rock *noir* of 'Sister Moon', and a moving plea on behalf of relatives of the Chilean *desaparecidos*, 'They Dance Alone'. There is a pleasing version of 'Little Wing' performed by the late Gil Evans and his orchestra, with a sympathetic vocal from Sting which teases out the jazz element that was intrinsic in much of HENDRIX's work.

The stellar supporting cast includes Branford Marsalis, Andy Summers, Mark Knopfler, Ruben Blades and Eric CLAPTON.

● *The Soul Cages* (A&M 396 405-2) [1991]

While crafted to the usual exacting standards, this woeful collection, which emerged after a protracted and well-publicised case of writer's block, is beset by a lack of urgency and focus. Sting intended it partly as an elegy to his father (who died shortly after his mother in 1987) and partly as a journey of self-discovery back to his Tyneside roots. The result is a verbose and dreary agglomeration of river, sea, ships, islands and fishing metaphors which flap about the instrumental scaffolding of the songs like loose canvas in the wind.

The single 'All This Time' is a more up-beat echo of the days when The POLICE were a fixture in the pop charts and there are one or two decent choruses on the title track and 'Jeremiah Blues (Part 1)'. More typical, however, is the grey mood and formless mock-orchestral arrangement of 'When the Angels Fall' which finds Sting searching for answers among the tombstones.

The album draws on a multitude of sophisticated styles. Touches of jazz, a frisson of world music, and even a neo-classical guitar instrumental called 'Saint Agnes and the Burning Train' are effortlessly thrown into the mix. Sting handles it all with his customary aplomb, but he doesn't sound that bothered any more.

The Stooges See Iggy POP

The Stranglers

Convened: 1974, Surrey
Jet Black (f) – drums; Jean-Jacques Burnel (f) – bass/vocals;
John Ellis – guitar; Dave Greenfield (f) – keyboards; Paul
Roberts – vocals
UK No.2 albums: 1977: *No More Heroes* (Fame CDP 746
613-2)
1978: *Black and White* (EMI CDP 790 596-
2)

Despite their thuggish demeanour, The Stranglers were one of
the more sophisticated (and indeed older) groups to get caught up
in the thrust and grime of the punk revolution. Black, Burnel,
Greenfield and Hugh Cornwell (vocals/guitar) started as The
Guildford Stranglers during the latter part of the pub-rock era,
supporting acts like Brinsley Schwarz and Ducks Deluxe. 'We
were just an R'n'B band, but we couldn't play very well. So our
songs tended to be very short, and quite honestly most of the
audiences on that circuit seemed to hate us,' Burnel later recalled.

The onset of punk was thus a godsend, delivering The
Stranglers to an audience that welcomed their abrupt, aggressive
music and encouraged the group's instinctive tendency towards
anti-social behaviour. At the same time their comparative experience gave them a distinct edge over the mass of young turks
spilling out of recording studios the length and breadth of the
country. Burnel may have had the worst bass sound in recording
history, but he knew what to do with it. With Greenfield's organ
parts lending an elegiac counterpoint to the jackbooted rhythm
section, they worked up a distinctive line of sleazy voyeurism and
casual sexism on their first hit, 'Peaches' (1977), which they were
not permitted to perform on *Top of the Pops*.

Controversy followed them around like a dog at its master's
heels. 'We sought out violence,' Burnel later admitted. 'If there
was a punch-up, we would have started it. If someone spat at me,
I would go into the audience and haul the culprit on stage and give
him a good caning. We were trying to prove that we were tough,
which in retrospect doesn't prove anything.'

In 1980, only weeks after Cornwell had completed a stretch at
Pentonville prison for drug offences, the whole group were
arrested after a riot at a concert in Nice. The events of that hectic

and unhappy year signalled a sea change in The Stranglers' attitude and, although the sinister reputation has stuck, they replaced the macho bombast with a new repertoire of slightly left-field, arty pop songs which they took to performing on stage with the thoughtful demeanour of craftsmen engaged in tiring but pleasurable work.

There was a big falling out in 1990, with Cornwell departing to start a solo career. He was replaced by guitarist John Ellis (ex-Vibrators) and vocalist Paul Roberts. Whether this new line-up will be able to recapture the primal charm of the group's vintage work is open to question.

- *Stranglers IV (Rattus Norvegicus) (EMI CDP 746 362-2) [1977]*
- *No More Heroes* (Fame CDP 746 613-2) [1977]

Released within six months of each other, The Stranglers' first two albums were among the most trenchant musical statements to come out of the entire punk era. Scathing, sullen rants like '(Get a) Grip (On Yourself)', 'Ugly', 'Something Better Change' and 'I Feel Like a Wog' are rendered all the more effective by the light, trippy quality of Greenfield's organ-playing which at the time prompted many flattering comparisons with The DOORS.

- *Greatest Hits 1977–1990* (Epic 4675412) [1990]

The most striking aspect of this chronological selection of 15 of The Stranglers' 30 or so hit singles is the difference in approach on either side of the 1980 watershed. You would hardly credit early material like 'Something Better Change' and 'No More Heroes' as being the work of the same group that later produced the mellifluous 'Always the Sun' and the genteel, waltz-time strains of 'Golden Brown' (No.2 in 1982, their biggest hit).

The collection draws a neat line under the recorded achievements of the Cornwell era, and with 400,000 copies sold in the UK at the time of writing, is the biggest selling album of the group's career.

The Style Council See The JAM

The Supremes See Diana ROSS

Talking Heads

Convened: 1975, New York. Split up: 1991
David Byrne (f) – vocals/guitar; Chris Frantz (f) – drums/
vocals; Jerry Harrison (f) – keyboards/guitar/vocals; Tina
Weymouth (f) – bass/vocals
UK No.3 album: 1988: *Naked* (EMI CZ 362)

One of the most critically revered and enduringly fashionable
bands of all time, Talking Heads were ahead of the field at almost
every turn. Chief writer and visionary-in-residence David Byrne
could scent a new artistic trend a mile off. 'He hates anything
that's clichéd in modern life,' Tina Weymouth once proclaimed.
'When he sits down in a chair, he'll sit down in an unusual way,
just because he wants to be an individual.'

A pseudish rationale, to be sure, but such studied weirdness
was just the ticket during the mid-Seventies when the band were
getting themselves established as regulars at New York's famed
CBGB club, the epicentre of the American New Wave explosion.

The four Heads had all gone through the further education mill
and were a far more sophisticated proposition than contemporaries like Patti Smith, Television, The Ramones and Blondie. Their
combination of nervous energy and radical underground chic
made them the darlings of the cognoscenti, while their clean-cut
image and sharp ear for a tune made them accessible to the
brighter mainstream rock fan and upwardly mobile style buff
alike.

By the start of the Eighties, they had taken funk, disco and
African rhythms on board, effectively becoming the first 'world
music' rock band (although such a term had yet to be coined).

There was always a sharp contrast between the personalities of
Byrne (strange, remote, creative), Weymouth (practical, go-
getting) her husband Frantz (deferential) and Harrison (the last to
join up and always something of an outsider), and the lack of
communication within the band was legendary. In the event, it
took them three years after they last worked together to decide
that they had split up, with Byrne finally announcing in a 1991
interview with the *Los Angeles Times*: 'You could say "broken up" or
call it whatever you like. As far as I'm concerned . . . things ran
their course.'

In another interview an exasperated Frantz voiced his feelings on behalf of the rest of the band: 'What are we – doormats?'

A Talking Heads boxed set *Sand in the Vaseline* is scheduled for release in the summer of 1992.

- **Talking Heads: 77** (Sire K 256 647) [1977]
- **More Songs About Food and Buildings** (Sire K 256 531) [1978]

Their début is a seductive strain of straight-ahead rock, gilded with modest intellectual pretensions and a large dollop of jittery, art-school angst. From it they fielded the single that became their unofficial anthem, 'Psycho Killer'.

The album was produced under tense conditions by Tony Bongiovi, whose commercial ear was frequently at odds with Byrne's angular approach to songwriting and Weymouth's undeveloped bass-playing technique. Released at the height of punk, its many sophisticated touches – such as the odd tempo changes and Harrison's gliding slide guitar in 'No Compassion' – immediately set the Heads apart from the rabble.

For the follow-up, *More Songs About Food and Buildings*, they enlisted the kindred spirit of Brian Eno (ex-ROXY MUSIC) as producer, and the tumblers started to click into place. The result is a more rounded and confident album, notable for its surprise hit version of Al Green's soul standard 'Take Me to the River', the only cover Talking Heads ever recorded.

- **Fear of Music** (Sire 256 707) [1979]

With Brian Eno retained as producer, Talking Heads took a great leap forward with their third album, hiring in outside musicians and harnessing elements of funk and African music to arrangements that are both danceable and listenable. 'I Zimbra' features a pair of African drummers and some freaky guitar work from the redoubtable Robert Fripp of King Crimson; 'Life During Wartime' boasts a driving funk rhythm and a sharp paranoid edge to the lyric; and further glimpses of a stressed psyche surface on 'Memories Can't Wait', later to be given an intriguing full metal racket treatment by Living Colour.

- **_Remain in Light_** (Sire 256 867) [1980]
- **_Speaking in Tongues_** (Sire 923 883-2) [1983]

Remain in Light – the fourth best album of the Eighties, according to _Rolling Stone_ magazine – pursues the African angle to its logical extreme, with Byrne's distracted vocals (sounding more than ever like David Thomas of Pere Ubu) emerging from a coruscating mosaic of percussion, slap bass, click-funk rhythm guitar, blips, bleeps and anything else Eno thought would aid their cause.

From such organised chaos there emerged several of the group's best ever recordings, including the urgent funk of 'Crosseyed and Painless' and the fiendish groove of 'Once in a Lifetime', with its strangely haunting, if nonsensical lyric ('And you may ask yourself/What is that beautiful house?' etc). There were also a lot of arguments about who was due what songwriting royalties, though in the event the lion's share went to Byrne and Eno.

The follow-up, _Speaking in Tongues_, was a retreat to a more conventional pop-funk position and provided their biggest US hit, 'Burning Down the House'.

- **_Stop Making Sense_** (EMI CZ 289) [1984]

There is no Talking Heads greatest hits compilation, which makes this live album the next best thing. It is also the soundtrack to the Jonathan Demme movie which starts with Byrne on his own, playing 'Psycho Killer', and builds up to massed ensemble renditions of 'Once in a Lifetime' and 'Take Me to the River'. In the movie, Byrne wears an improbably ill-fitting suit, which one suspects remains the primary image most people have of him to this day.

- **_Little Creatures_** (EMI CZ 288) [1985]

A return to the sparse, four-piece sound of the early days produced a disposable batch of conventionally structured songs, many with a country-folk tilt. The main exception is 'Road to Nowhere', the band's only UK Top 10 hit.

- *True Stories* (Fame CDFA 3231) [1986]

A frequently overlooked item of merit, this neat collection is also the soundtrack to a tedious film of the same name, directed by Byrne himself. Inspired by the 'unbelievable yet true' stories of ordinary people as profiled in magazine and newspaper cuttings, Byrne slips into his persona of the distanced commentator whose rôle is to observe the surreal details of mundane lifestyles.

Guitars crunch with gravelly bravado on the opening rocker, 'Love For Sale', but it's not long before the usual pot pourri of unlikely influences makes itself felt: voodoo chants on 'Papa Legba', Nashville pedal steel on 'People Like Us' and a bluesy waltz-time on 'Dream Operator' for starters.

- *Naked* (EMI CZ 362) [1988]

The final Heads album was recorded in the cultural melting pot of Paris, where a cosmopolitan army of musicians turned out to lend a riot of regional colour to Byrne's typically oblique observations.

Elements of Algerian-Moroccan *rai* music jostle with big-band brass sections, African high-life guitar, and on a few tracks some marginal contributions from ex-SMITHS guitarist, Johnny Marr.

'Blind' is a James BROWN homage with lyrics that flit past like trees outside a train window. 'Mr Jones' has neo-Joe Loss latino interludes and 'The Facts of Life' bounces spookily along on a synthesised riff that suggests the stiff, mechanised rhythms of a factory production line.

The group has been here before (*Remain in Light*, *Speaking in Tongues*), only this time the songs are not well structured and the album a bit slapdash overall.

- David Byrne: *Rei Momo* (Sire 925 990-2) [1989]

As well as the North African influences long evident in the work of Talking Heads, Byrne found inspiration for his solo projects in the music of Brazil, supervising at least four compilations of music by indigenous acts, of which the best is *Brazil Classics 1: Beleza Tropical* (EMI CDP 791 948-2; 1989).

On his own album, *Rei Momo*, Byrne takes this a step further, smoothly harnessing a bunch of familiar-sounding Heads-type themes to the breezy Latin rhythms of the cha cha cha, the bolero, the charanga *et al*, thoughtfully identifying each of the exotic brands on offer beneath the song titles on the sleeve.

More than just a tourist, Byrne is an aloof and systematic cultural adventurer with an eye for fine detail. But while the musicians – including the fabled Cuban singer Celia Cruz – turn in vibrant supporting performances, there remains a peculiarly lifeless quality to Byrne's own singing, and his clipped, robotic delivery often sounds over-stylised and out of place.

Richard Thompson

Born: April 3 1949, London
UK No.32 album: 1991: *Rumor and Sigh* (Capitol CDP 95713-2)

As a founder member of FAIRPORT CONVENTION, Richard Thompson was instrumental in transplanting key elements of English folk music into an electric rock setting. After leaving the group in 1971, he embarked on a solo career, but it was not until his wife Linda came into the picture that he established his métier. Between 1974 and 1982, they released seven albums as a duo before their liaison, both private and professional, ended in a sticky divorce.

Having developed into a technically élite player, a richly characterful singer, a literate and emotional songwriter and a truly original stylist, there was never any doubt that Thompson would continue on his own. What surprised most observers was the astonishingly high standard of work that he maintained and the near total lack of popular recognition which it earned him.

The ice began to break with the relative success of *Amnesia* (100,000 copies sold worldwide since 1988) and *Rumor and Sigh* (his first chart placing in the Top 75). He has always toured, either with a band or solo with an acoustic guitar, and never fails to draw a respectable crowd. On a good night he can make you feel that he is the best in the world.

● **Richard and Linda Thompson:** *I Want to See the Bright Lights Tonight* (Island CID 9266) [1974]

The wedding of Linda's pure, fragile voice to Thompson's harsh guitar tone and bittersweet lyrics was, in the end, a lot more idyllic than the marriage of the couple themselves. This was the first fruit of their union and the title track, with its ascetic guitar chords and merry brass band accompaniment, still conjures an unbelievably poignant ache. 'When I Get to the Border' finds Thompson in his best electric-folk mode with an instrumental coda bounced this way and that between an accordion, a krummhorn and a clanging guitar with a tone that haunts the ear to the very last moment of the fade.

- **Richard and Linda Thompson:** *Shoot Out the Lights* (Hannibal HNCD 1303) [1982]

The last of the duo's albums together, *Shoot Out the Lights* received widespread critical acclaim, most notably from *Rolling Stone* magazine, which placed it at No.9 in its list of 'The 100 Best Albums of the Eighties', even though it got nowhere near the American chart. Essentially a musical documentation of the couple's disintegrating relationship, written and recorded as it was happening, the album carries the sort of heightened emotional payload that you don't find too often in any walk of artistic endeavour. The two stand-out tracks are the darkly menacing, slow-tempo thud of 'Shoot Out the Lights' and the spine-tingling 'Wall of Death', both of which feature prominently in Thompson's live show to this day.

- *Amnesia* (Capitol CDEST 2075) [1988]

Thompson's solo albums have all been good, but this one is superlative. The deep, slow riff of 'Gypsy Love Songs' has the sort of primeval quality that Muddy WATERS used to conjure, while its end sequence of shrieking hammered trills is pure voodoo. Similarly the codas of 'Jerusalem on the Jukebox' and 'You Can't Win' both sign off with glorious, supernova bursts of brittle Stratocaster noise.

Having long nursed a sizeable chip on his shoulder about women, Thompson's lyrical forte remains the vicious put-down, of which there are plenty here ('Turning of the Tide', 'Yankee, Go Home'). But the stinging attack of his playing is balanced both by the cleanness of his tone and by the gentleness of material like the ballad 'The Reckless Kind' and a country-flavoured song with fiddle accompaniment, 'Waltzing's For Dreamers'. Another masterpiece to add to his portfolio.

● *Rumor and Sigh* (Capitol CDP 95713-2) [1991]

Rather like Van MORRISON (a similarly roots-orientated performer), Thompson has maintained an unlikely consistency in his work. Here there is a slight but noticeable shift of the spotlight away from the taut, acidic guitar motifs towards the taut, acidic words and melodies of the songs as a whole. There is a tough blues-wailing solo in the comically quasi-metal 'Backlash Love Affair', but otherwise the guitar tends to be held in reserve for moments such as the understated but devastating codas of 'Why Must I Plead', 'Grey Walls' and 'Mystery Wind'.

A broad sweep of songs ranges from the itchy rock'n'roll belt of 'You Dream Too Much' to the joky trad-folk of 'Don't Sit on My Jimmy Shands' and the gorgeous, drifting soft rock of 'Keep Your Distance'. Innovative, imaginative, entertaining and pertinent; really, there is no praise too high for work as good as this.

Tin Machine See David BOWIE

Traffic See Steve WINWOOD

The Traveling Wilburys See George HARRISON

Tina Turner

Born: Annie Mae Bullock, November 26 1938, Brownsville, Tennessee
UK No.1 album: 1989: *Foreign Affair* (Capitol CDP 791 837-2)

A performer of tremendous vigour, good humour and resilience, Tina Turner is a trooper of the old school, a woman who has kept singing and smiling through long spells of wretched physical abuse at the hands of her former husband Ike Turner, and who made no fuss about playing at McDonald's Hamburgers' staff conventions if that's what it took to make ends meet when her career was at its lowest ebb.

Her assisted autobiography, *I, Tina*, which was an American best-seller, is notable both for its frank catalogue of her trials and triumphs and for its stark lack of any value judgements. Even so, her story of escape from marital subjugation and subsequent solo success has led to her canonisation in feminist circles, as surely as her stage costumes and dance routines have continued to guarantee her status as a sex symbol.

She is regal in her dismissal of both accolades. 'I have nothing to do with the labels people put on me,' she said in 1987. 'I was never promoting any cause by what I did, I was just living my life. As for those dresses, I wore them then, I wear them now because they're practical for the work I do and the way I'm built; they're just my style.'

It's a style which has made her one of the most commercially successful female acts ever. MADONNA and Whitney HOUSTON have sold more records, but Turner outranks even them as a crowd-puller; indeed in 1988 she won an entry in the *Guinness Book of Records* for attracting the largest paying audience for a solo artist (of either sex) in history, 182,000 at the Maracana Soccer Stadium in Brazil.

● *Private Dancer* (Capitol CDP 746 041-2) [1984]

A fitting testament to the durability and adaptability of Turner's talent, this ten-million-selling album was recorded on the hoof in little more than two weeks, using five different producers and a variety of material cobbled together at the very last moment. 'I had no direction,' she told radio interviewer John Pidgeon in 1989. 'We were just trying to get songs for an album, because we needed an album then. We were following a hit single ["Let's Stay Together"] and we weren't prepared, so it was like whatever we could get.'

'What's Love Got To Do With It', written and produced by Terry Britten, was a US No.1, and 'Better Be Good To Me' and 'Private Dancer' (written by Mark Knopfler) both reached the US Top 10.

Although prior to this album Turner had been known for her gutsy R'n'B vocal style, she is actually much happier applying her forceful voice to music in the mainstream adult-rock tradition. With this hastily assembled collection she found both her métier and her market.

● *Proud Mary – The Best of Ike and Tina Turner* (EMI CZ 422) [1991]

When she was a girl, growing up in the hamlet of Nutbush, Tennessee, Annie Bullock did her share of picking cotton in the fields. There were no telephones, and if she wanted to catch someone's attention in the next house she yelled across the fields. This was when she discovered that she had an exceptionally powerful voice. Not an especially pretty voice, but a loud, throaty, gospel-derived holler that commanded attention. She joined Ike Turner's band The Kings Of Rhythm as featured vocalist in 1956, and two years later she married the boss.

This is the definitive compilation of material from her days with The Ike and Tina Turner Revue, an 18-year stretch which ended when Mrs Turner walked out on her slave-driving husband in 1976 to face an uncertain future.

On earlier hits like 'A Fool in Love' (1960), 'It's Gonna Work Out Fine' (1961) and 'Poor Fool' (1962), Turner has clearly modelled her performances on the great soul singers of the day, particularly Sam Cooke and Ray CHARLES. Later on, as Ike supervised a rearguard attempt to gain a slice of the action from the rock revolution of the Sixties, they turned out capable and successful versions of SLY AND THE FAMILY STONE's 'I Want to Take You Higher', The ROLLING STONES' 'Honky Tonk Women' and Creedence Clearwater Revival's 'Proud Mary'. Tina's own composition, 'Nutbush City Limits' (1973), provided their last hit together, although the Phil-Spector-produced epic 'River Deep Mountain High' from 1966 remains their *pièce de résistance*, even though it never hit the chart in America.

● *Simply the Best* (Capitol CDP 796 630-2) [1991]

This is a reasonable 18-track collection of greatest hits from Turner's solo career, albeit omitting her cracking 1985 duet with Bryan ADAMS 'It's Only Love' (recorded on ADAMS' label A&M) and her version of the old Temptations' hit 'Ball of Confusion', which appeared on the first BEF album *Music of Quality and Distinction* (unavailable; 1982) and was instrumental in planting her feet on the road to solo stardom. Instead there are a trio of new songs – 'I Want You Near Me', 'Way of the World' and an undistinguished chunk of soft metal called 'Love Thing'.

'River Deep Mountain High' has been remastered and equalised by Phil Spector himself, but it still comes out sounding thinner and weedier than the much-vaunted 'wall of sound' that one remembers at the time, especially when it is heard in such close proximity to the beefy modern productions of all the other tracks.

Otherwise, 'What's Love Got to Do With It?', 'I Don't Want to Lose You', 'Let's Stay Together', 'We Don't Need Another Hero (Thunderdome)' and 'Private Dancer' are all present and correct, together with her steamy live recording of Robert PALMER's 'Addicted to Love', her perky duet with Rod STEWART ('It Takes Two') and a dinky electro-pop version of 'Nutbush City Limits' which succeeds against all the odds in compensating for the absence of the gut-bucket guitar-and-brass stomp of the original.

U2

Convened: 1978, Dublin

Bono – (f) vocals/guitar/harmonica; Adam Clayton (f) – bass; The Edge (f) – guitar/keyboards/vocals; Larry Mullen Jr (f) – drums

UK/US No.1 albums:	1987:	*The Joshua Tree* (Island CID U26)
	1988:	*Rattle and Hum* (Island CID U27)
UK No.1 albums:	1983:	*War* (Island CID 112)
	1984:	*The Unforgettable Fire* (Island CID 102)
US No.1 album:	1991:	*Achtung Baby* (Island U28 510347 2)

'We started writing our own songs because we couldn't play anybody else's,' Bono remarked in 1987. In their search for a style with which they felt comfortable, U2 hit on an unlikely distillation of post-punk evangelist rock, which eventually generated unimaginable fervour as they took it again and again to the stadiums of Europe and North America.

Like most of the great rock groups, they became friends first and good musicians afterwards. The four were pupils at the Mount Temple Comprehensive School and they first assembled in the autumn of 1976 together with several other young hopefuls for a jam session at Larry Mullen's house. After various name changes (Feedback, The Hype) and having whittled the band down to its four-piece line-up, U2 first attracted attention when they won a national talent competition sponsored by Harp lager in April 1978. A film producer called Paul McGuinness became their manager, and U2 is still the only act he has ever had on his books.

U2's great strengths have always been their individuality of style and the burning sense of mission in their music. Obviously, given the time that they got together, the band was inspired by the *mood* of punk – the idea that you could start from scratch, make your own luck and need not be hidebound by tradition – but they wisely avoided taking on the snarling, *faux naif style* of punk which so quickly became a cliché.

'Sometimes I have a guilt complex about our roots,' Bono once said. 'We don't have funky black roots. We don't have white rock roots. Our music almost doesn't seem to have roots. It's like, totally our own.'

Thanks partly to McGuinness' careful and undivided attention and partly to their own strong-willed temperaments, the quartet have stayed sober, taken their time and done things exactly right. There have been no horrible messes, no ugly rip-offs, no needless dissipation of their talents and energy, just a coherent and massive drive to reach their destination.

U2 believed in rock long after such faith had become unfashionable, and they, in turn, gave people something to believe in. Their 20 minutes at Live Aid in 1985 struck a particularly resonant chord, Bono going into a long, misty clinch with a girl from the audience, while 'Bad' meandered into snatches of 'Goodbye Ruby Tuesday', 'Sympathy for the Devil' and 'Walk on the Wild Side'.

They have fought the good fight, at times a little self-consciously, asserting vague Christian beliefs, supporting Amnesty International, starring at the 1986 Irish Self Aid concert, contributing to Little Steven's anti-apartheid 'Sun City' album, and generally caring about all the usual issues that exercise the thoughts of the modern conscience-stricken celebrity.

The impact of the band on the development of Irish rock has

been incalculable. In practical terms alone, they have contributed to an expansion of local facilities and employment simply by staying put in Dublin (as well as saving themselves a small fortune in income tax). In 1984 they set up Mother records, a non-profit-seeking label designed to showcase primarily Irish talent. Among the beneficiaries have been Hothouse Flowers, In Tua Nua, Cactus World News and The Subterraneans. But it was the inspiration of their example which was sufficient to turn Dublin into a place where, as *The Sunday Times* critic Robert Sandall observed, for the majority of healthy adults, doing a stint in a rock band seems to have become the new version of National Service.

- *War* (Island CID 112) [1983]

U2's third album was produced by Steve Lillywhite and their core sound is enhanced with violin, saxophone, acoustic and lap steel guitars and a squad of backing vocalists. But it is still the bold, primary tonal colours that dominate a stirring roll call of anthems, including 'Sunday Bloody Sunday', 'New Year's Day' (their first UK hit) and their perennial curtain call number, '"40"', which takes its title and lyric from the Fortieth Psalm.

The tone of the album, which was released at the height of the paperweight new romantic fad, is urgent and strident, a powerful fusion of non-specific (Irish) political commentary and hard guitar-based rock'n'roll.

- *Under a Blood Red Sky* (Island CID 113) [1983]

This phenomenally successful live album consolidated U2's reputation and stayed in the UK chart for almost four years. Following hard on the heels of *War* (see above), it repeats many of that album's highlights, giving the full, banner-waving treatment to 'Sunday Bloody Sunday' and '"40"', as well as reprising some of the better material from earlier in the group's career, notably 'Gloria' and '11 O'Clock Tick Tock'.

- *The Unforgettable Fire* (Island CID 102) [1984]

U2's symbolism was clearly not getting any less messianic, the fire in question being that produced by the atomic bombing of

Hiroshima and Nagasaki, but thanks in part to the production work of Brian Eno assisted by Daniel Lanois, this is a more rounded set of songs than on any of their previous albums. The lyrics also tend to have more literal substance than in the past; 'Pride (In the Name of Love)' and 'MLK' are both elegies for the late Martin Luther King, while the haunting 'Bad' is a powerful indictment of the heroin trade in Dublin.

• *The Joshua Tree* (Island CID U26) [1987]

This was the album with which U2 wrested the unofficial title of 'world's greatest rock act' from the previous incumbent, Bruce SPRINGSTEEN. It put them on the covers of *Time* and *Rolling Stone* magazines and eventually sold in excess of 12 million copies.

Everything about it is wrought on a grand scale, from the exquisite black and gold graphics of the cover design to the Old Testament imagery of both the title and the lyrics which abound with references to fire and flood, blood running like rivers and the healing hands of love.

The sombre emotional tenor is flagged by Anton Corbijn's outstandingly evocative cover photograph of the four musicians looming out in stark relief from the emptiness of a vast desert landscape, like characters in a Sergio Leone western.

The stand-out track is 'Bullet the Blue Sky', a song of immense drama that was inspired by a visit to wartorn El Salvador. 'See the sky ripped open/See the rain through the gaping wound/The howling of women and children who run/. . . Into the arms of America.' As Bono's voice trails off, The Edge looses off a barrage of shuddering guitar shrieks and great whooshing glissandos, torching the riff with fretboard napalm.

Taken as a whole the album is stylistically open-ended. Tracks range from the heroic, tom-tom-driven soundscape of 'Where the Streets Have No Name' to the ethereal pop-song simplicity of 'With or Without You' (Bono's answer to 'Every Breath You Take'?) and the sleepy Ry COODER-inspired acoustic slide-guitar passages of 'Running to Stand Still'. But the mood is unremittingly intense throughout.

It's a bold, courageous album with a deep emotional resonance. Its colossal success, without in any way pandering to predictable commercial dictates, remains an inspiration.

- *Rattle and Hum* (Island CID U27) [1988]

'All I've got is a red guitar, three chords and the truth,' sings Bono in his customised lyric to DYLAN's 'All Along the Watchtower'. Rock group manifestos don't come much pithier than that, and with this epic album, U2 go a long way towards making such an elemental boast stick.

Part-live, part-studio, part-new, part-greatest hits and a sound-track to the movie of the same name, this is an embarrassment of riches with a fantastic dynamic range: from the boneshaking live version of The BEATLES' 'Helter Skelter', through the single guitar and stark folk poetry of 'Van Diemen's Land' to the insurgent Bo-Diddley-style vamp of 'Desire' in the first eight minutes alone.

At the heart of the album is a trio of new songs recorded at the Sun Studio in Memphis. 'Angel of Harlem', a relaxed groove incorporating the warm brass sounds of The Memphis Horns; 'Love Rescue Me', a neo-country song with ropy chorus support and a born-again lyric from Bob DYLAN; and 'Love Comes To Town', a brilliant, tom-tom-driven fire-and-brimstone rocker which features the voice and blues guitar of B.B. KING as they've never been heard before.

Here, then, is U2 making an overdue connection with the blues roots of rock'n'roll, which they bypassed during their baptism in the anti-history, post-punk climate of the late Seventies.

- *Achtung Baby* (Island U28 510347-2) [1991]

The ridiculous title and zany collage of photographs on the cover suggest a determined effort to lighten up. But U2 are never going to be in danger of sounding frivolous, and what emerges is a peculiarly amorphous collection of hard 'industrial' guitar textures ('The Fly'), post-Mancunian dance beats ('Mysterious Ways'), melodies that drift like thistledown and lyrics which bite like a venomous snake.

Again produced by Daniel Lanois (his third U2 collaboration), it is an album built on the primary rock foundations of voice, guitar and drums, but larded with many bold and off-centre touches. 'I'm ready for the laughing gas,' sings Bono at the start of the opening track, 'Zoo Station', setting a tone of sinister mischief in a voice treated to sound like a station tannoy swathed in layers of muslin.

Nearly every song combines a direct appeal with an undercurrent of mystery, whether it be the warm, old-fashioned guitar sound and gorgeous melody of 'One', or the opaque blizzard of notes counterpointed by a *Moonlight Sonata*-inspired piano part in 'Love is Blindness'. Two bitter requiems to a dead love affair, 'Who's Gonna Ride Your Wild Horses?' and 'So Cruel', sound an uncharacteristic note of disillusionment.

But, in the absence of all those heroic gestures and banner-sized sentiments which make *The Joshua Tree* (see above) and *Rattle and Hum* (see above) such bravura works, it's difficult to locate *Achtung Baby*'s centre of gravity. Although it is an impressive collection of songs, the cumulative effect is mildly disorientating.

UB40

Convened: 1978, Birmingham
Astro – vocals; Jim Brown (f) – drums; Ali Campbell (f) – vocals/guitar; Rob Campbell (f) – guitar/vocals; Earl Falconer (f) – bass; Norman Hassan (f) – percussion; Brian Travers (f) – saxophone; Mickey Virtue (f) – keyboards
UK No.1 album: 1983: *Labour of Love* (DEP International DEPCD 5)

Although routinely snubbed by the purists, UB40 is the world's most popular reggae band by a mile. In Britain with the possible exception of ASWAD, no other act has come close to sustaining such a long and commercially viable career playing reggae. Until Maxi Priest scored his US No.1 with 'Close to You' in 1990, UB40's version of 'Red Red Wine' – written by Neil Diamond, but adapted from an earlier reggae treatment by Tony Tribes – was the only 'pure' reggae single ever to have topped the American chart (although honourable mentions are due to 'I Shot the Sheriff' [1974] by Eric CLAPTON, and 'I Can See Clearly Now' [1972] by Johnny Nash).

Globally, UB40 have unobtrusively sold many millions of records, having quietly conquered all major markets and amassed a loyal following in places that most rock groups never reach. They played Russia in 1986, well before it was fashionable to do so, and their 260-date world tour which ended at Birmingham

City FC in June 1989, took them to 40 countries, including Australia, Chile, Israel, Brazil, Japan and Zimbabwe.

It seems a quaint idea now, but the band took its name from the unemployment benefit form with which they were all uncomfortably familiar at the time. Led by the brothers Ali and Rob Campbell, sons of the Scottish folk singer Ian Campbell, they were school and art college friends who gradually coalesced into a multi-racial octet operating in tandem with the 2-Tone stable of acts (Madness, The Selecter, The Specials et al) in the Midlands. They were helped at the outset by Chrissie Hynde, who championed the group and gave them vital early exposure as the support act on The PRETENDERS' 1979/80 UK tour.

Unlike their peers, UB40 has remained a tight-knit, if unenviably anonymous, collective. The only change of personnel was forced upon them temporarily when bassist Earl Falconer was jailed in July 1988 for six months on a drink-driving charge, after an accident in which his brother was killed.

With their origins rooted firmly in the era of Rock Against Racism, they started out as angry young men touting an emphatic political message. But later, when performers of a more earnest disposition such as Billy Bragg and The Style Council took over that function, UB40 gradually retired from the front line. Although they have remained with their own independent label, DEP International, they have matured over the years into a dependable pillar of the mainstream rock establishment with a bulging portfolio of hits.

- *Signing Off* (Graduate GRADCD 2) [1980]
- *Present Arms* (DEP International DEPCD 1) [1981]

There's not much to chose between UB40's first two albums. Both are graced with the languid rhythmic intricacies and sophisticated harmonic interplay between horn and voices which became their calling card. And both are shot through with polemics railing against the Thatcher clampdown which inevitably sound rather dated now. 'One in Ten' from *Present Arms* is a notable exception. The statistic refers to the number of people out of work in Britain (which, sadly, doesn't seem at all out of date in 1992) and the song is a powerful, timelessly resonant indictment of the wastage of human resources. Here was the finest hour of their 'political' period.

- **Labour of Love** (DEP International DEPCD 5) [1983]

Despite their talent as songwriters, and their capable handling of arcane reggae techniques such as dub and toasting, it was this extraordinary collection of straightforward cover versions that hoisted UB40 into the first division. 'Red Red Wine', 'Many Rivers to Cross' and 'Cherry Oh Baby' are the stand-out tracks on a collection that harnesses the relaxing ebb and flow of the reggae rhythm to songs of a traditional and generally delightful melodic persuasion. Since then, the judicious renovation of old material by other artists has been as central to their work as the insistent, bass-driven pulse that guides it.

- **The Best of UB40 Vol 1** (Virgin CDPUBTV 1) [1987]

There was certainly nothing premature about the timing of this compilation, even though there have been several major hits since its release (no doubt bound for Vol 2). *The Best of . . .* takes in the loping, pull-and-tug format of both their No.1s – 'Red Red Wine' and the revival of Sonny and Cher's 'I Got You Babe' featuring Chrissie Hynde – together with favourites including 'One in Ten', 'Please Don't Make Me Cry', 'If It Happens Again' and 'Don't Break My Heart'.

- **Labour of Love II** (DEP International DEPCD 14) [1989]

As the unnecessarily defensive sleeve notes point out, this is the album that countless UB40 fans had been awaiting ever since they became hooked on the first *Labour of Love*.

Once again UB40's talent for selection and interpretation is matched by their ability to mould the free-flowing reggae groove to the most precise melodic standards, and make it sound easy to boot.

Not as good as the first *Labour of Love*, but the versions of Al Green's classic 'Here I Am (Come and Take Me)' and the Chi-Lites 1974 hit 'Homely Girl' (both inspired by previous, little-known reggae adaptations) alone make it worth the price of admission.

Van Halen

Convened: 1975, Los Angeles, California
Michael Anthony (f) – bass/vocals; Sammy Hagar – vocals;
Alex Van Halen (f) – drums/vocals; Edward Van Halen (f) –
guitar/keyboards/vocals
US No.1 albums: 1986: *5150* (Warner Bros 925 394-2)
1988: *OU812* (Warner Bros 925 732-2)
1991: *For Unlawful Carnal Knowledge*
(Warner Bros 7599-26594-2)

Van Halen provided the link between the heavy metal prototypes
of DEEP PURPLE and LED ZEPPELIN and the slick hit-making machines
of BON JOVI and DEF LEPPARD. As such they played a vital role in
lifting heavy rock from the jealous clutches of its card-carrying
cult audience (however vast) and delivering it into the arms of Top
40 radio and the mass market. Although they sacrificed nothing in
terms of power and credibility, they were the first heavy rock
group who made it look as if what they were doing might be fun.
Sometimes, they even smiled.

Founded by the Van Halen brothers, who came originally from
Nijmegen in Holland, the band was fronted in its first incarnation
by David Lee Roth (see below), more of a shouter than a singer,
but blessed with good looks, an athletic physique, phenomenal
energy and a larger-than-life personality.

Roth's glamour sold the band, but he was only reflecting the
brilliance of Eddie Van Halen, whose artistry burned at the core of
its music. Arguably the most visionary rock guitarist since Jimi
HENDRIX, in terms of pure technical ability there were very few
players who could match Eddie Van Halen in the late Seventies.

But beyond that, he inaugurated a new style of playing, which
involved hammering down on the fretboard with his *right* (i.e.
picking) hand to create rapid, swooping volleys of harmonics.
Although he was not the first to attempt this awkward practice
(Ritchie Blackmore of DEEP PURPLE and Billy Gibbons of ZZ TOP had
both been there before him), he developed and popularised the
method, raising the overall standard of electric guitar playing by
several notches and influencing the next generation of players
such as Yngwie Malmsteen and Steve Vai.

Ironically, Van Halen's biggest hit, 'Jump', is notable not for
Eddie's guitar playing, but for his prominent use of keyboards,

while his most widely celebrated guitar solo is actually on Michael JACKSON's No.1 hit 'Beat It'. This alliance, which helped get JACKSON on MTV and into the rock market, was forged in the soul-rock tradition of The Isley Brothers and Jeff BECK's work with Stevie WONDER.

● *Van Halen* (Warner Bros 256 470) [1978]

Before Van Halen, hard rock bands traditionally used to play to a length that was as excessive as their volume. This self-titled début, produced by Ted Templeman, changed all that by introducing the world to what Roth called 'short songs – BEATLES style – with a hard rock sound.'

Although flawed by Roth's tendency to emulate the Ian Gillan death shriek on 'Runnin' With the Devil' and his not altogether successful attempt to cope with the melody of The Kinks' song 'You Really Got Me', this was nevertheless a hugely influential album. Indeed, Roth was still incorporating 'You Really Got Me' and 'Ain't Talkin' 'Bout Love' in his 1991 shows. *Van Halen* sold many millions of copies, as has every one of the group's nine albums released to date.

● *1984* (Warner Bros 923 985-2) [1984]

This was the album, more than any other, which introduced rock and heavy metal to the mainstream pop market. It did so largely thanks to Eddie's judicious use of synthesiser on several stand-out tracks, notably the US No.1 hit 'Jump', which married the pumped-up production values of heavy stadium rock to the bright, contemporary sounds of the hi-tech revolution. 'Panama' and 'Hots For Teacher' remain among the hardest driving material the band has ever recorded. Sadly, it was the last Van Halen album to feature Roth, who left to start a solo career the following year.

● *OU812* (Warner Bros 925 732-2) [1988]

The first album with Sammy Hagar (ex-Montrose) dispelled any doubts about the band's ability to carry on without the exuberant Roth. Hagar is a less demonstrative personality but a superior singer and the band went on to even greater success than before.

Yielding the hit 'Why Can't This Be Love?', *OU812* is an album which virtually defines a strand of high-class, American power and spectacle rock.

David Lee Roth

Born: October 10 1955, Bloomington, Indiana
UK No.4 album: 1991: *A Little Ain't Enough* (Warner Bros 7599-26477-2)
US No.4 album: 1986: *Eat 'Em and Smile* (Warner Bros 925 470-2)

Although David Lee Roth has successfully converted the impetus of his time with Van Halen into a million-selling solo career, there is no doubt which of the parties came off worse after his departure from the group in 1984. The firm musical foundations of Van Halen were unshaken, while Roth's fortunes have increasingly come to depend on the skin-deep appeal of his flamboyant personality, his Adonis looks and the athleticism of his performing style, rather than on his abilities as a singer, writer or musician.

Now in his late thirties, his high kicks are not quite what they used to be and he is starting to look a little frayed around the edges. His show can be a diverting spectacle, but there is an imbalance between content and chutzpah.

Prominent among his solo hits are the cabaret-metal nonsense of 'Just A Gigolo/I Ain't Got Nobody' and his ham-fisted version of the BEACH BOYS' 'California Girls', a tune which he couldn't carry in a suitcase. What the audiences still want to hear, of course, are the old Van Halen hits, and it is hard to imagine him being allowed to leave a concert venue without a final encore of 'Jump'.

● *A Little Ain't Enough* (Warner Bros 7599-26477-2) [1991]

By the time of his fourth solo album, Roth had got his formula off pat, and this is the latest in a series of matey chronicles detailing the life and times of a man who carries his pistol loaded and cocked. 'I asked her "How do you get into those tight blue jeans?" She said "For starters you can buy me a drink"' (from 'Last Call') is a typical scenario.

To be fair, Roth's is a more varied and imaginative concoction than the bulldozing grind of the archetypal heavy-rock Casanova, and there are moments of genuine pazzazz – for instance the souped-up boogie of 'It's Showtime' or the relaxed, bluesy stride of 'Tell the Truth'. But while his personality is leavened by a broad streak of good-humoured showmanship, his material lacks both depth and a commercial edge, which is why in recent times he has been outgunned by acts like BON JOVI, GUNS N' ROSES and even David Coverdale's WHITESNAKE.

The Wailers See Bob MARLEY

Tom Waits

Born: December 7 1949, Pomona, California
UK No.20 album: 1987: *Franks Wild Years* (Island IMCD 50)

A downwardly mobile, modern-day beat-poet, Tom Waits is the ultimate cult hero. Inspired by the Jack Kerouac myth of the drifting bohemian and enthralled by the world-weary romanticism of Fifties *film noir* (he once described the Sixties as a decade that he'd slept through), Waits has shone the spotlight on a host of odd, low-life characters operating on the rim of American society, and produced a richly imaginative body of work in the process.

Waits' own vagabond look and rasping, bronchial voice belie his solid, if unsettled, middle-class upbringing. His tremendous facility with words and verse was stimulated by a passion for the work of beat writers like Kerouac, Allen Ginsberg and William Burroughs, and the detective fiction of such authors as Raymond Chandler and Dashiell Hammett.

In tandem with his work as a musician, he developed an acting career, starting with a small role in a Sylvester Stallone movie, *Paradise Alley* (1978) and including parts in Francis Ford Coppola's *Rumblefish* (1983) and *The Cotton Club* (1984), and a starring role in Jim Jarmusch's *Down by Law* (1986).

Buried amid the hard-boiled wit, the *bons mots* and the impossibly gruff delivery, there is a tender, compassionate quality to Waits' writing; there is a sharp ear for melody – his songs have been successfully recorded by The Eagles ('Ol' 55'), Bruce SPRINGSTEEN ('Jersey Girl'), Paul Young ('Soldier's Things') and Rod

STEWART ('Downtown Train') among others. ('Bruce SPRINGSTEEN?' said Waits in 1987. 'Well, I've done all I can for him. He's on his own now.')

- *Nighthawks at the Diner* (WEA 960 620-2) [1975]

Recorded live in a club, yet featuring what was then new material (apart from a version of Red Sovine's ghost-story narrative 'Big Joe and Phantom 309'), Waits' third album finds him demonstrating the easy, showy rapport of a born huckster placed in front of an audience that needs no winning over. Backed by a nimble jazz quartet, he entertainingly establishes his persona as the boozy, disillusioned derelict, with a perpetual 'party in his head', propping up the piano in some smoke-filled dive, with numbers including 'Warm Beer and Cold Women', 'Putnam County' and 'Emotional Weather Report'.

- *Small Change* (WEA 960 612-2) [1976]

A minor masterpiece of poetic *and* melodic invention, this album teems with grainy, off-beat images, vivid humour and many colourful turns of phrase. Check 'Tom Traubert's Blues (Four Sheets to the Wind in Copenhagen)', 'Pasties and a G-String (at the Two O'Clock Club)' and the perennial plea of the over-stretched lounge-bar entertainer 'The Piano Has Been Drinking (Not Me)'.

- *Swordfishtrombones* (Island IMCD 48) [1983]
- *Rain Dogs* (Island IMCD 49) [1985]
- *Franks Wild Years* (IMCD 50) [1987]

By the time of *Heartattack and Vine* (1980; unavailable), Waits had moved towards the more abrasive, electric R'n'B sounds of John Lee HOOKER and Screamin' Jay Hawkins. From there he evolved the junkyard-equipped, psycho-blues band which he has employed to devastating effect on his most distinguished work, a trilogy of albums released after his arrival at Island records in the mid-Eighties.

A dramatically taut yet perilously loose musical experience, these collections are bound together by a cast of drunks, misfits and lost souls of the night whom Waits depicts in murky, often humorous narratives, barked out in his uniquely ramshackle style. Thus, the chihuahua-hating arsonist who first pops up in the song 'Frank's Wild Years' on *Swordfishtrombones*, is the same character who, several years down the road (and shorn of his apostrophe), gets to have his own album title.

Swordfishtrombones introduced the 'new' Tom Waits sound that was to distinguish all three albums (and the live album which followed them, *Big Time* [Island ITWCD 4; 1988]). This magically chaotic ensemble noise seems to have been coaxed from a drum-kit built out of the contents of a plumber's yard, guitars with cheesewire for strings and a wind section using instruments borrowed from a rag and bone man's cart. 'In the Neighborhood' is graced by the melancholy sound of a full brass band, while elsewhere there are marimbas, pipe organs, an optigan (an obsolete cross between a synthesiser and an organ), a mellotron and any number of odd percussion items. 'Most of the instruments can be found in any pawnshop,' Waits explained. 'I haven't completely joined the twentieth century.'

The album features the eccentric talent of guitarist Marc Ribot (who later worked on Elvis COSTELLO's album *Spike*) and his angular, bluesy twang combines with Waits' guttural roar to produce a feel that is often reminiscent of Captain Beefheart, especially in the hectoring, religious mumbo-jumbo of the cracked preacher in 'Way Down in the Hole' or the violent buckshot belt of '16 Shells From a Thirty-Ought-Six'.

Rain Dogs continues in much the same vein. Boasting some adequate contributions from Keith Richards ('He's been borrowing money from me for so long that I had to put a stop to it'), it features several of Waits' more readily accessible tunes, notably 'Hang Down Your Head' and 'Downtown Train'.

Franks Wild Years, subtitled *Un Operachi Romantico in Two Acts*, originated as the soundtrack to a stage musical performed in 1986 by the Steppenwolf Theatre Company in Chicago, with Waits in the starring rôle. Typical of the musical ambience is 'Innocent When You Dream' with its piano tinkling uncomfortably and an old-fashioned pump organ huffing along just behind the beat, conjuring an image of the winos carousing on Shepherds Bush Green on a Saturday afternoon.

Waits claims, facetiously but plausibly, to have sung the entire set through a police bullhorn, and his bellowing voice is frequently out on a lengthy limb, noticeably on the vaudeville dirge of 'Blow Wind Blow'.

A grotesquely farcical parody of Frank Sinatra's Vegas-showband delivery, 'I'll Take New York', opens a window on the hollow values and bankrupt lifestyles beneath the ostentatious sheen of glamour that attends the rich and successful.

Muddy Waters

Born: McKinley Morganfield, April 4 1915, Rolling Fork, Mississippi. Died: April 30 1983
US No.70 album: 1969: *Fathers and Sons* (Vogue VGCD 600134)

If, as Brownie McGhee's song puts it, 'The Blues Had a Baby and They Named It Rock and Roll', then Muddy Waters was the man most likely to be faced with the paternity suit. Although shorter-lived and less widely celebrated than his peers John Lee HOOKER and B.B. KING, it was Waters who played the pivotal role in converting the blues from a rural, acoustic, folk music into the urban, electric phenomenon that formed the basis of rock'n'roll.

Brought up by his grandmother in Clarksdale – the birthplace of John Lee HOOKER – Waters began singing and playing harmonica when he was seven. By his late teens he had switched to guitar and was supplementing his meagre earnings from picking cotton by playing at local juke joints, parties and Sunday get-togethers.

To begin with, his style was subject to a combination of influences: veteran delta blues guitarist Charley Patton (died 28.4.34), the younger bottleneck guitarist Son House (died 19.10.88), and the greatest country blues singer of them all, Robert JOHNSON. But Waters had evolved his own way of doing things by the time he moved north to Chicago in 1943. While working in a paper mill by day, he played at parties, bars and clubs by night. He quickly discovered that his acoustic guitar wasn't loud enough for these noisier venues, and bought himself an electric instrument. Then he gradually assembled the finest blues band of its day, featuring at various times, Marion 'Little Walter' Jacobs (harmonica/vocals; died 15.2.68), Jimmy Rogers (guitar/vocals/harmonica), Otis Spann (piano; died 24.4.70) and Willie

Dixon (bass; died 29.1.92) among others. In 1945 he signed to Leonard and Phil Chess' label Aristocrat (renamed Chess in 1950), although it wasn't until 1948 that he began recording under his own name.

The Muddy Waters band toured Britain in 1958. Many who went to see the show where taken aback by the intensity of their attack and the sheer volume at which they played (although it would doubtless seem very modest by today's standards), but the impact of the Waters style of blues on a future generation of UK acts was incalculable.

Among those who saw him perform at this time were guitarist, bandleader, singer and (later) DJ Alexis Korner (died 1.1.84) and Cyril Davies (bandleader/harmonica; died 7.1.64), who were inspired to form Blues Incorporated, a band which became a forcing school for young British players with a passion for the blues (graduates included Mick Jagger and Charlie Watts). Songs like 'Hoochie Coochie Man', 'Rollin' and Tumblin'', 'Baby Please Don't Go', 'I Got My Mojo Working', 'I Just Want To Make Love To You' and 'Mannish Boy', many of them written by Willie Dixon, became established as standards among the UK R'n'B fraternity of the early Sixties, while The ROLLING STONES even took their name from the Waters song 'Rollin' Stone'.

Waters had a direct influence on musicians ranging from American originals like Junior Wells and Buddy Guy right through to Sixties guitar heroes like Jimi HENDRIX and Eric CLAPTON. Yet it was a long time before Waters saw any of the benefits himself. When The ROLLING STONES arrived for a recording session at the Chess studios in 1964, they were horrified to discover Waters up a ladder painting the studio.

Later, some of the musicians he had inspired teamed up with the old master to produce albums of variable quality, which did at least get Waters noticed beyond the circles of the cognoscenti. *Fathers and Sons* (see above) was a collaboration with Mike Bloomfield, Paul Butterfield, Donald 'Duck' Dunn, Buddy Miles and Otis Spann which marked Waters' only incursion into the US Top 100. Likewise, *The London Muddy Waters Sessions* (Chess CHD 9298; 1972) featuring Rory Gallagher, Georgie Fame, Mitch Mitchell, Rick Grech and Steve WINWOOD helped to shine the spotlight on the man who had contributed so much, yet received relatively little popular recognition in return.

• *They Call Me Muddy Waters* (Instant CDINS 5036) [1971]

There are any number of Muddy Waters compilations and live albums offering selections of his best known numbers in a bewildering variety of combinations. However, in common with most of the blues musicians of his vintage Waters had a tendency to re-record his songs at fairly frequent intervals and the versions featured are often not the original (or best) recordings.

Of the many live albums, *Muddy Waters at Newport* (import MCA 31269; 1961) is recommended. Otherwise the best collection of *original* Waters recordings is *They Call Me Muddy Waters*, a chronological compilation of his recordings from 1948 to 1955, not to be confused with the album of the same title which won him a Grammy in 1972.

The earliest tracks, 'Gypsy Woman', 'I Can't Be Satisfied' and others recorded in 1948, underline the closely entangled relationship between blues and jazz with the boogie piano of Sunnyland Slim and the stride bass of Ernest 'Big' Crawford providing the only backing. In fact it is only ten numbers into this 26-title set that they are joined by a drummer (Elgin Evans) for the first time.

Some of the cuts have obviously been mastered from records (the original tapes presumably having been lost in the mists of antiquity) and come complete with scratches and surface noise. But the tremendous power of Waters' deep, hard vocals and the slicing tone of his slide guitar cut through regardless. So too does the remarkable harmonica playing of Little Walter, one of the most imaginative and influential practitioners of that much overlooked instrument.

Despite the poor sound quality, numbers including 'Rollin' Stone', 'Howlin' Wolf', 'Baby Please Don't Go', 'I Want You To Love Me', 'I'm Ready' and the original (1955) version of 'Mannish Boy', are infused with the searing voodoo that makes the best blues so utterly spellbinding, and this is a fine introduction to one of the central repertoires of rock.

• *Hard Again* (Blue Sky CDSKY 32357) [1977]

Waters finally left Chess records in 1976 and accepted an offer to sign to Blue Sky, a label run by Steve Paul, the manager of Texan albino guitarist Johnny Winter. Winter, who had long idolised

Waters, jumped at the chance to work with his hero, and as well as playing and producing this album, he subsequently toured as part of Waters' band.

Assembling a line-up primarily comprised of Waters' old buddies, including James Cotton (harmonica), Pine Top Perkins (piano) and Willie 'Big Eyes' Smith (drums), Winter resisted the temptation to tart up or in any way tamper with the original Fifties arrangements of the songs, merely utilising the much superior recording facilities of the Seventies to get a great 'live in the studio' sound.

There is a tremendous *joie de vivre* – with lots of excited banter at the end of each track – as the band romps through classics like 'I Want To Be Loved', 'I Can't Be Satisfied' (Winter playing the slide guitar part with surpassing grace on a national steel), 'Deep Down in Florida' and 'Mannish Boy'.

It was this recording of 'Mannish Boy' which was used in the soundtrack for a Levis jeans TV commercial in 1988 (the one where the guy comes down the stairs in his underpants and takes his jeans out of the fridge). Subsequently released as a single, 'Mannish Boy' became Waters' only UK chart entry, peaking at No.51 in 1988.

● *Hoochie Coochie Man* (Epic 461 186-2) [1983]

During the six years before his death, Waters recorded four albums under the sympathetic hand of Johnny Winter: *Hard Again* (see above), *I'm Ready* (unavailable), *Muddy 'Mississippi' Waters Live* (unavailable) and *King Bee* (unavailable).

The tracks on *Hoochie Coochie Man* are drawn from all four albums and include 'Mannish Boy', 'I'm Ready' and 'I'm Your Hoochie Coochie Man', together with one or two adopted standards such as Slim Harpo's 'I'm a King Bee' and 'The Blues Had a Baby and They Named It Rock and Roll'.

Much of the spirit of the original recordings is recaptured with a predictably improved sound quality, and with contributions from old cohorts like James Cotton, Walter Horton (harmonica; died 8.12.81) and Jimmy Rogers, Waters lovingly recreates the core of his repertoire in tremendous performances (especially the live ones) which sizzle with a sense of occasion.

Even allowing for omissions like 'Rollin' Stone' and 'Got My

Mojo Working', it is hardly a 'definitive' collection. But as well as providing evidence of this music's resilience, it stands as a joyful and authentic companion to the original works.

Wham! See George MICHAEL

Whitesnake

Convened: 1978, London·
David Coverdale: born: September 22 1949, Saltburn-on-Sea, Yorkshire – vocals/leader; assorted personnel
UK No.2 album: 1981: *Come and Get It* (EMI 790 305-2)
US No.2 album: 1987: *Whitesnake 1987* (EMI CDEMC 3528)

He may be the undisputed cock of the Whitesnake roost now, but at the start of 1973 young David Coverdale was a complete unknown. He worked in a clothes shop in Redcar and sang in semi-pro bands of doubtful provenance with names like The Fabulosa Brothers. Nevertheless, on hearing that Ian Gillan had left DEEP PURPLE, he decided to apply for the post and sent an unsolicited tape to the group. 'I was conceited enough to think I might stand a chance,' he subsequently explained. His brass neck and his throaty voice got him the job and later that same year he was on stage at the California Jam, performing as the main attraction in front of an estimated audience of 750,000.

After DEEP PURPLE split up in 1976, Coverdale recorded two solo albums, *Whitesnake* [1977] and *Northwinds* [1978] (both available on one CD on the Connoisseur Collection label, VSOPCD 118), neither of which made the slightest commercial impact. Although he relished the control which solo status afforded him, Coverdale was forced to recognise the need to get out on the road with a band.

Thus the first Whitesnake line-up, which included bassist Neil Murray and guitarists Micky Moody and Bernie Marsden, was put together. To list in detail the changes in the Whitesnake roll call since then would be an exercise of tortuous and tedious complexity, but the best known and most durable of the early line-ups incorporated Murray, Moody and Marsden together with ex-

DEEP PURPLE cronies Ian Paice (drums) and Jon Lord (keyboards).

This was the period when the so-called New Wave of British Heavy Metal was in its primacy, and though Coverdale's gang was too seasoned a bunch of campaigners to fit comfortably in to this young, gung-ho class of warriors, they were nevertheless vigorously championed by the now-defunct *Sounds* and its then newly established offshoot, *Kerrang!*, and benefited in general from the upsurge of interest in hard rock that brought groups like Iron Maiden and DEF LEPPARD to prominence.

Coverdale's style of singing is based on that of the two classic heavy-mannered rock prototypes, Paul Rodgers of FREE and Robert Plant of LED ZEPPELIN. Latterly, as his curls have grown ever longer and more beautifully tangled, Coverdale seems gradually to be turning into Robert Plant. A memorable pair of pictures in one of the music papers showed Plant with the caption 'I come from the land of the ice and snow' next to an almost identical-looking picture of Coverdale accompanied by the words, 'That's funny, so do I.'

At the end of a British tour in August 1983, Whitesnake headlined Castle Donington, the premier event in the head-bangers' calendar. Since then, no line-up of Whitesnake that has recorded an album has survived intact to tour that album. The list of sackings is formidable: Moody, Marsden, Paice, Murray (twice), guitarist John Sykes, bassist Colin Hodgkinson, guitarist Mel Galley, drummer Aynsley Dunbar, together with sundry managers and producers have all received the order of the Coverdale boot. Only Lord and drummer Cozy Powell are known to have left Whitesnake on their own terms.

By the start of the Nineties, Coverdale's constant headhunting of 'name' musicians had turned Whitesnake into a virtual who's who of heavy rock. At the time of writing, the recruitment of wunderkind guitarist Steve Vai (ex-Frank ZAPPA, and a distinguished solo act in his own right) had provided the most recent jewel in the constantly renewed Whitesnake crown.

● *Saints an' Sinners* (Fame CDP 746 725-2) [1982]

Most of the early Whitesnake albums are interchangeable combinations of heavy blues rock and unapologetically macho innuendo: *Ready and Willing* (Fame CDP 752 054-2; 1980), *Come and*

Get It (EMI 790 305-2; 1981), *Slide It In* (EMI CDP 790 306-2; 1984) – the titles say it all, really.

Saints an' Sinners is the best by a short neck. Both 'Crying in the Rain' and 'Here I Go Again' were later tarted up and included on *Whitesnake 1987* and other strong items include 'Victim of Love', 'Bloody Luxury' and the title track.

● *Whitesnake* 1987 (EMI CDEMC 3528) [1987]

With this album Coverdale successfully adapted the spirit of the Seventies' rough and ready blues-rock tradition to the melodic spit and polish of the BON JOVI era. The formula proved a massive success, particularly in America, where 'Here I Go Again' was a No.1 single and the follow-up, 'Is This Love?', made No.2. 1987 stayed in the Top 10 for nearly six months, being held off the top slot in succession by U2, Whitney HOUSTON and Michael JACKSON. It eventually sold 8.5 million copies.

The band which actually recorded the album had, of course, been dismissed by the time it was released. The Whitesnake which appeared in the videos and which toured to promote the album comprised an Irishman, Vivian Campbell (guitar; ex-Dio); a Dutchman, Adrian Vandenberg (guitar; ex-solo act); a Puerto Rican, Rudy Sarzo (bass; ex-Quiet Riot); and a Texan, Tommy Aldridge (drums; ex-Ozzy Osbourne). Ironic that it should have been this multinational quartet of convenience, together with its bronzed, windswept leader, which received a BPI nomination for Best British Group of 1987 (along with the Bee Gees, LEVEL 42 and The PET SHOP BOYS, who won the award).

The Who

Convened: 1964, London. Split up: 1983. Reconvened: 1985 (Live Aid), 1988 (BPI Awards), 1989 (world tour)
Roger Daltrey (f) – vocals; John Entwistle (f) – bass/brass/vocals; Keith Moon (f) (died 8.9.78) – drums/vocals; Pete Townshend (f) – guitar/vocals/keyboards
UK No.1 album: 1971: *Who's Next* (Polydor 813 651-2)

Always a great stage act, but inclined to navel-gazing in the studio,

The Who's career swung from the violent, proto-punk energy of early singles like 'Anyway, Anyhow, Anywhere' and 'My Generation' to the overblown pretensions of *Tommy*, the album which introduced the phrase 'rock opera' to the popular music vocabulary.

They set out in West London in the heyday of the Mod movement. Known initially as The High Numbers, they played a truculent, but otherwise unexceptional brand of hand-me-down R'n'B that was popular in clubs like the Railway Hotel in Wealdstone and Watford Trade Hall. What set them apart from the pack, once they had changed their name and found their niche, was Townshend's angular but pithy songwriting style and a stage act which as often as not ended in a mesmerising display of auto-destructive mayhem. Townshend and Moon were the motivating forces, Moon booting his kit about like a gleeful child, Townshend, with a rather more psychotic air of derangement, gouging his guitar neck through the delicate membranes of his speaker cabinets, then systematically smashing the instrument to pieces on the floor.

As well as creating some of the greatest riffs, Townshend also wrote some of the most memorable lyrics in the rock canon. 'Hope I die before I get old' is a line often cited as evidence against him, but as a distillation of youthful frustration the song has never been bettered.

By the latter half of the Sixties, The Who outranked all UK competition bar The BEATLES and The STONES and many triumphs ensued as they graduated to the international super-league with outstanding performances at the great hippy gatherings of Monterey (1967), Woodstock (1969) and the Isle of Wight (1970).

The success of *Tommy* (see below) and the dawning of the Seventies heralded an era of increasing self-indulgence. Having exorcised all that physical rage, Townshend's attention turned with no less a degree of intensity to his intellectual angst. The next 'opera', *Quadrophenia* (Polydor 831 074-2; 1973), was twice as long and even more musically elaborate than *Tommy*. There was a rash of dismal solo albums from the other members of the band, and Daltrey began to fancy himself as an actor. Never an especially chummy group of individuals, their cohesion as a rock unit was ebbing fast.

With the benefit of hindsight, it is obvious that The Who should have called it a day when Moon died in 1978. Even before the drummer's demise the band had reached a creative menopause. Racked by self-doubt, Townshend could only nod his head in agreement when the angry young men of punk declared his group to be an outdated irrelevance, while simultaneously, in the case of The JAM and others, ripping off some of his best licks.

The choice of Kenney Jones as a replacement for Moon was also a grave mistake (as Daltrey never tired of pointing out). Jones' natural style, and his background in The Faces, marked him out as a drummer in the timekeeper mould, not at all the sort of player to emulate the cannoning crescendos and rollercoaster momentum that were the hallmarks of Moon's flamboyant style. Jones' appointment in 1979 ran counter to the very spirit of The Who, and it can not be entirely a coincidence that the band produced virtually nothing new of merit again.

For a while it looked as if Townshend was going to emerge as a solo artist of some note. His *Empty Glass* (Atco K 250 699; 1980) peaked at No.5 in America and was a tougher, sharper album than anything The Who ever came up with again. 'I'm not able to achieve with the band what I've achieved here,' Townshend was heard to declare. But he didn't have the stamina to maintain such a standard and a sporadic pattern of subsequent solo releases yielded consistently diminishing returns. The less said about Daltrey's and Entwistle's solo ventures, the better.

● *Tommy* (Polydor 800 077-2) [1969]

It still has its moments – the hyper-tense strumming that prefaces 'Pinball Wizard', the gothic bangs and crashes of 'The Acid Queen', the piquant desperation of '1921' – but taken as a whole and in retrospect, this is one of those 'classic' albums that has not weathered well. The story of the deaf, dumb and blind kid who becomes a pinball-playing Messiah has, of course, passed into rock folklore, prompting films, musicals, opera house performances and much pontification. Yet it now sounds irredeemably dated, an acid-spiked fable of the Aquarian age, with about as much contemporary resonance as *Hair*.

It was nevertheless an important staging post in the progress of the group, breaking them at last in America, clearing a massive accumulation of debts and supplying the sort of credibility as an albums band which had proved elusive during their initial purple patch of hit singles.

● *Live at Leeds* (Polydor 825 339-2) [1970]

This is the band at the peak of its fiery glory, punching home whirlwind deliveries of 'Substitute', 'Young Man Blues', 'Magic Bus' and 'Summertime Blues'. The performances are nearly all flawed: the sound is rough and undubbed, the vocal harmonies dreadful, Townshend's fumbled attempts at playing lead guitar simply embarrassing. But the energy, the momentum and raw spirit of this disc are like very few live albums before or since. In the wake of *Tommy*'s flatulent pretensions, *Live at Leeds* was an ideal purgative. It re-established The Who's credentials as a hard-nosed rock act with a seriously anarchistic streak, and it (briefly) turned Leeds into a minor rock'n'roll mecca for American tourists, who made it the next stop after the obligatory pilgrimage to Liverpool.

● *Who's Next* (Polydor 813 651-2) [1971]

Townshend originally intended this as another 'concept' album, to be called *Lifehouse*. Just for good measure, it was also going to provide the basis for a multi-million dollar film of the same name. Thankfully, enough people prevailed upon him to convince him that a simple nine-song selection with a nice throwaway title like *Who's Next* would actually be a better showcase for The Who than a *Tommy Mk II* with knobs on. They were right, and once Townshend's grand visions had been rigorously pruned back, songs like 'Baba O'Reilly', 'Behind Blue Eyes' and 'Won't Get Fooled Again' emerged as anthems which rank among The Who's most enduring work. The cover photograph of the group pissing against a stone monolith looks more childish and tawdry with each passing year.

● *Who's Better – Who's Best* (Polydor 835 389-2) [1988]

This greatest hits retrospective neatly encapsulates a distinguished history with a hefty sting of mediocrity in its tail. The early hits are musical acid bombs, uniquely summing up that Sixties teenage attitude which compounded swaggering confidence with spluttering frustration: 'I Can't Explain', 'Anyway Anyhow Anywhere', 'Substitute', 'I'm a Boy' and 'My Generation' are still touched by a magic that has rarely been duplicated in English rock.

Also still sounding fresh are the odd lyrical vignettes and bold, dramatic flourishes of 'Happy Jack', 'Pictures of Lily', 'I Can See For Miles' and 'Pinball Wizard'. But by that point in the chronology, the otiose horrors of rock opera were at hand, and 'I'm Free' and 'See Me, Feel Me' sound twee and overwrought, marking the moment when for Townshend the hard thinking began to overtake the hard rocking.

Worse is the lumpen style and inconsequentiality of the songs that make up the few hits which the group enjoyed after 1975 – 'Squeeze Box', 'Who Are You' and 'You Better You Bet' – the last being the only track here not to feature the drumming of Keith Moon. The case against Kenney Rogers rests.

Wings See Paul McCARTNEY

Steve Winwood

Born: May 12 1948, Birmingham
US No.1 album: 1988: *Roll With It* (Virgin CDV 2532)

With his soulful, high-ranging voice, multi-instrumental abilities, and meticulous songwriting and production skills, Steve Winwood has long been a musicians' musician, a man whose search for a higher aesthetic has tended to take precedence over the quest for a higher chart position.

Even so, he has enjoyed sustained multi-platinum success in America and cornered a lucrative niche alongside Robert PALMER and Peter GABRIEL at the tasteful end of the international adult rock market.

Through his work with The Spencer Davis Group (see below), Traffic (see below) and the ill-fated Blind Faith (see under Eric CLAPTON), Winwood had ascended to the highest ranks of the rock aristocracy by the time of his 21st birthday. But his subsequent work rate has been considerably less hurried, just six new solo albums since 1974.

- *Arc of a Diver* (Island CID 9576) [1981]
- *Talking Back to the Night* (Island CID 9777) [1982]

Something of a make-or-break affair after his undistinguished solo début *Steve Winwood* (Island CID 9494; 1977), his second album, *Arc of a Diver*, was produced, engineered and performed in its entirety by Winwood himself. The result is a formal, modern-sounding, if slightly stiff collection which nevertheless hit the mark, especially in America, where it peaked at No.3. A single from the album, 'While You See a Chance', also made the US Top 10.

Making innovative use of the emergent Moog synthesiser technology, the follow-up, *Talking Back to the Night*, was recorded in much the same way and achieved similar, if less spectacular, results. The outstanding cut, 'Valerie', was released as a single with limited success, but a remixed version from *Chronicles* (see below) later became a substantial hit.

Both albums feature songwriting collaborations with Will Jennings a former Professor of English from Texas, who remains the unsung Bernie Taupin figure to Winwood's Elton JOHN.

- *Back in the High Life* (Island CID 9844) [1986]

Throughout his career Winwood has received blanket approval for the soulful (some would even say gospel) edge to his unusually penetrating voice, even though at times he sounds uncomfortably like a man who has just sat down on a red hot poker. But this is the album which set the official seal on his achievements: a set of superlative poise which went triple-platinum (three million) in the States and from which 'Higher Love' earned him a No.1 hit and a Grammy for Best Male Pop Vocal Performance of 1986.

- *Chronicles* (Island SSWCD 1) [1987]

This rather premature 'best of' compilation, hurriedly released after Winwood jumped ship from Island records, boasts very few hits: just 'Higher Love', 'While You See a Chance' and the remixed (chart) version of 'Valerie'.

The title tracks of his three preceding albums lend an air of familiarity, but for the rest – 'Wake Me Up on Judgement Day',

'Help Me Angel', 'My Love's Leavin'' and 'Spanish Dancer' – we see Winwood's refined musical sensibility at work, though without the peaks of excitement or nostalgia you might expect to find on this sort of retrospective. All the same, it works as a fair introduction to a body of work with which his greatly expanded late-Eighties audience may not have been acquainted before.

● *Roll With It* (Virgin CDV 2532) [1988]

The warm, loose ambience of the title signposts the relaxed mood of Winwood's fifth solo album, a less studio-bound production than its predecessors, mixing Stax-influenced retro-rock with several sultry ballads.

While the earlier albums tended to be dominated by synths, the title track here boasts the old-fashioned sounds of Hammond organ and a real brass section, courtesy of The Memphis Horns, who also feature on three other songs. The soaring melody and dependable back-beat of 'Dancing Shoes' is typical of an album with more groove than all of Winwood's previous discs put together.

● *Refugees of the Heart* (Virgin CDV 2650) [1990]

A poor follow-up to the chart-topping *Roll With It*, this is a somnabulistic affair, bereft of wit or spark. The material has a threadbare, second-hand feel, especially the funky politesse of 'Come Out and Dance', which bears a suspicious resemblance to Peter GABRIEL's 'Sledgehammer'.

● *Keep On Running* (Island 848 745-2) [1991]

Featuring tracks by The Spencer Davis Group, Traffic, Blind Faith and a couple of numbers from the first solo album (see above), this is a handy retrospective of Winwood's tangled career during the early years.

Creaming off the best of The Spencer Davis Group's oeuvre is no difficult task, and 'Keep On Running', 'Gimme Some Lovin'', 'Somebody Help Me', 'I'm a Man' and 'Every Little Bit Hurts' does the trick neatly enough.

Most of the Traffic selections are pulled from *Mr Fantasy* (see below) and *John Barleycorn Must Die* (see below), together with hit singles 'Paper Sun' and 'Here We Go Round the Mulberry Bush'; but the glaring absence of 'Hole In My Shoe' suggests that neil's (see Traffic, below) version may have ruined it for ever.

The ballast is made up by Blind Faith's over-burdened arrangement of Buddy Holly's 'Well Alright' and an oddity called 'Happy Vibes' taken from the mid-Seventies album *Aiye-Keta* (unavailable) where Winwood was joined by Remi Kabaka and Abdul Lasisi Amao for an extended experimental jam session.

The Spencer Davis Group

Convened: 1963, Birmingham. Split up: 1969
Spencer Davis (f) – guitar; Muff Winwood (f) – bass; Steve Winwood (f) – vocals/keyboards/guitar; Pete York (f) – drums
UK No.3 album: 1966: *The 2nd LP* (unavailable)

Winwood was barely 16 when The Spencer Davis Group was signed up in 1964 by Chris Blackwell, owner of the then fledgeling Island records. Although led by and named after Davis, the group's success was undoubtedly based on the prodigous talent of Winwood, whose keening vocal style cut like a sharp wind through the taut arrangements of the English-style R'n'B material.

The group enjoyed a brief run of memorable UK hits, including 'Keep on Running' (No.1 in January 1966), 'Somebody Help Me' (No.1 in 1966), 'Gimme Some Loving' (No.2 in 1966) and 'I'm a Man' (1967), before Winwood left to form Traffic. Davis recruited various replacements and soldiered on, but without Winwood the group's support quickly crumbled.

The only CD collection of The Spencer Davis Group's work, *Best of Spencer Davis* (EMI CDP 746 598-2), was deleted in 1988.

Traffic

Convened: 1967, Aston Tirrold, Berkshire. Split up: 1974
Jim Capaldi (f) – drums/vocals; Dave Mason (f) – guitar/ vocals/bass; Steve Winwood (f) – vocals/keyboards/guitar/ bass; Chris Wood (f) – flute/saxophone

US No.5 album: 1970: *John Barleycorn Must Die* (Island IMCD 40)

The band for whom the cliché 'getting it together in the country' was coined, Traffic came to represent all that was most noble and risible in the British chapter of the hippy dream.

Reflecting on his life in the business, Winwood told *Musician* magazine in 1982 that Traffic was the result of 'a desire . . . to make a uniquely British form of rock and roll that incorporated or evoked traditional music like 'John Barleycorn' . . . while breaking new ground artistically.'

On one level they succeeded, creating a uniquely bucolic strand of English psychedelic rock. But history has not judged their music kindly, and by 1984 Nigel Planer – in his neil of *The Young Ones* persona – did not have to make many adjustments to turn Traffic's biggest hit, 'Hole In My Shoe' (UK No.2 in 1967), into a hideous parody of the naive, druggy charm of the original.

● *Mr Fantasy* (Island IMCD 43) [1967]

Traffic's first and best album is mildly experimental, unabashed English psychedelia ('Heaven is in Your Mind', 'Berkshire Poppies', 'Coloured Rain') with a strong streak of white soul, largely thanks to several magical vocal performances by Winwood, notably on the ballad 'No Face, No Name, No Number' and the epic title track.

But the basic design of the group was flawed from the outset, both musically and as a combination of personalities. Mason left within weeks of the album's release and the group was dogged by constant comings and goings/splits and reunions thereafter. Like The DOORS, they set off with no proper bass player and in concert their penchant for interminable, pseudo-jazz extemporisation made for a variable and often wearying listening experience, witness the group's live album *Welcome to the Canteen* (Island IMCD 39; 1971).

Stevie Wonder

Born: Steveland Morris, May 13 1950, Saginaw, Michigan
US No.1 albums: 1963: *Recorded Live – The 12-Year-Old Genius* (unavailable)

1974: *Fulfillingness' First Finale* (Motown
WD 72607)
1976: *Songs in the Key of Life* (Motown ZD
72131)

Stevie Wonder lost his way in the Eighties. The man who had sold an estimated 30 million records, most of them singles, by the time of his 21st birthday in 1971, and who spent the next decade redefining the role of black music in the white rock album marketplace, has more recently been content to knock out high class pap like 'I Just Called to Say I Love You' (1984, his only solo UK No.1), 'Ebony and Ivory' (1982, a UK No.1 with Paul McCARTNEY) and his excruciating duet with Julio Iglesias, 'My Love' (1988).

His recording schedules have become increasingly subject to delay; it took him five years to make *In Square Circle* (Motown ZD 72005; 1985) and at the time of writing, his record company has been waiting five years for the follow-up to *Characters* (Motown ZD 72001; 1987). A new album, to be called *Conversations*, has been in the pipeline for longer than anyone at Motown cares to remember, yet in the summer of 1991, like a magician pulling a rabbit out of a hat, Wonder casually turned up with a cheap and cheerful soundtrack for the Spike Lee movie *Jungle Fever* ((Motown ZD 72750). Nobody bought it, of course.

But rather like Bob DYLAN, Wonder has contributed so much to the shaping of popular music as it exists today that his place in the pantheon of the greats is secure, no matter what he does or doesn't do next.

Quite apart from his vast musical legacy (only Elvis PRESLEY has enjoyed more US hit singles), Wonder has been a hugely potent symbol of black advancement. Blind at birth, proficient at piano, drums and harmonica by the age of 11 and signed to the Detroit-based Tamla Motown label when it was still going under the cheesy name of Hitsville USA, Wonder was subjected, like all the label's other artists, to proprietor Berry Gordy's rigidly paternalistic star-making and grooming machine.

Not only did Wonder grow to the point where he could dictate his own terms to the label, but when his contract with Motown expired in 1971 he resisted the blandishments of virtually every other major record company in America, preferring to stick with the black-owned label that had nurtured him since childhood (albeit under new, unprecedentedly advantageous conditions).

His importance to Motown was eventually such that, according to the record company's biographer Nelson George, by 1984 Wonder's artistic decisions 'profoundly affected Motown's financial health' – one can only assume negatively.

Then there is Wonder's irrepressible record of political and humanitarian activism, extending from his involvement in anti-nuclear and anti-apartheid campaigns, to his practical help for a member of the White Panthers convicted of smoking marijuana. His song 'Happy Birthday' made a telling contribution to the campaign to have an official American national holiday declared in celebration of the birthday of Martin Luther King. Since 1986, the third Monday in every January has been just such a holiday, and rarely, if ever, has a single piece of music exerted a more directly observable influence on the practical course of political events.

- **Essential Stevie Wonder** (Motown ZD 72585) [1987]

Little Stevie Wonder, as he was initially known, enjoyed his first No.1 hit with 'Fingertips Pt 2' when he was just 13 years old. The song signalled more than it delivered. A rather slapdash live recording of Little Stevie's tinny harmonica and bongo improvisations interspersed with squeaky yells of 'Everybody say Yeah!', it nevertheless demonstrates the child prodigy's astounding confidence, both in his ability to entertain an audience and to dominate what is intrinsically a swing jazz band situation.

Whereas most of the Motown acts were steered rapidly to their niche and encouraged to stick with it, Wonder's talents were less easily moulded and contained. Like his hero, Ray CHARLES, he displayed a wide-ranging ability and a restless disregard for musical boundaries. Among several other, less successful follow-ups to 'Fingertips' was an essentially gospel-derived chant 'Workout Stevie, Workout' and the straight-ahead R'n'B standard 'High Heel Sneakers'.

In 1966 he enjoyed a US No.9 hit with a version of DYLAN's folk classic 'Blowin' in the Wind' (a number which he was still performing live at his Wembley shows in 1989) while his 1965 hit 'Uptight (Everything's Alright)' was inspired by the four-on-the-snare-drum beat which Charlie Watts of The ROLLING STONES employed to such devastating effect on their 1965 classic '(I Can't Get No) Satisfaction'.

But it was as the creator of a deeply soulful strand of pop that Wonder consistently made his mark in the Sixties, returning to the charts on both sides of the Atlantic with songs including 'I Was Made to Love Her', 'For Once in my Life', 'My Cherie Amour' 'Yester Me Yester You Yesterday' and 'Signed Sealed Delivered I'm Yours'.

Essential Stevie Wonder is a double-CD set which gathers together all of the above titles, along with the best of the rest of Wonder's pre-1972 material.

- *Talking Book* (Motown WD 72605) [1972]

Michael JACKSON reaped credit in 1983 for recruiting heavy rock guitarist Eddie VAN HALEN to play the solo on 'Beat it'. But as with so many aspects of black popular music, it was Stevie Wonder – the *original* Motown child-star turned crossover giant – who got there first, when he hired Jeff BECK to play guitar on *Talking Book*.

This superlative album became Wonder's passport to the rock mainstream, with numbers like 'Superstition' – the song which brought the sound of the electronic clavinet into popular musical currency – and 'You are the Sunshine of My Life' successfully running the gamut from hard, urban funk to breezy romantic pop.

Not for the first time, he promoted the album by touring as support to The ROLLING STONES on their massive American tour of 1972, further boosting his credibility among rock audiences.

Since re-negotiating his contract with Motown, Wonder had spent much of his time mastering the newly emergent synthesiser technology, knowledge which he applied to the composing and recording of *Talking Book*. His pioneering use of state-of-the-art keyboard and computer technology continued on subsequent albums throughout the Seventies and Eighties.

- *Innervisions* (Motown WD 72606) [1973]
- *Fulfillingness' First Finale* (Motown WD 72607) [1974]

Having established his credentials as an album act with significant crossover appeal, Wonder proceeded to build on those foundations with a series of outstanding albums which established him as an international superstar who transcended categorisation. On *Innervisions* he produced arguably the most resonant social commentary of his career in 'Living in the City', while the rhythmically churning 'Higher Ground' is one of several songs with a broader spiritual theme.

Fulfillingness' First Finale, which was the first album to be released after his recovery from a near-fatal car crash in August 1973, continues in the same vein, with stand-out tracks including 'Boogie On Reggae Woman', 'Creepin'', 'Too Shy To Say' and 'They Won't Go When I Go', later covered by George MICHAEL.

- *Songs in the Key of Life* (Motown Z 72131) [1976]

For many, this remains Wonder's *magnum opus*, a stirring, ambitious and sometimes rambling collection which highlights Wonder's protean playing and writing skills: the haunting pastorale of 'Pastime Paradise', the idiosyncratic jazz fusion of 'Contusion', the exuberant switchback riffing and easy swing of 'Sir Duke' (Wonder's tribute to Duke Ellington) and the mainstream soul-pop chorus of 'Isn't She Lovely?' are among the treats on this highly desirable double-CD.

- *Hotter Than July* (Motown WD 72608) [1980]

Wonder's last great album, it produced four UK Top 10 hits: the Martin Luther King eulogy 'Happy Birthday', the tribute to Bob MARLEY 'Masterblaster (Jammin')', the countrified 'I Ain't Gonna Stand For It' and the sedate ballad 'Lately'.

- *Original Musiquarium* (Motown ZD 72133) [1982]

This double-CD set, which comprises the two albums formerly known as *Original Musiquarium Vol 1* and *Original Musiquarium Vol 2*, scoops up the cream of Wonder's golden era from 1972 to 1982: 'Superstition', 'Living for the City' 'You are the Sunshine of My Life', 'Higher Ground', 'Boogie On, Reggae Woman' and 'Sir Duke', among many others. Essential stuff.

XTC

Convened: 1977, Swindon, Wiltshire
Dave Gregory – guitar; Colin Moulding (f) – bass/vocals;
Andy Partridge (f) – vocals/guitar
UK No.5 album: 1982: *English Settlement* (Virgin CDV 2223)

One of those groups that never fitted comfortably into the New
Wave mould but got swept along regardless by the hectic spirit of
those times, XTC started out as techno-punks, pogoing awk-
wardly out of step at the art school hop. The initial line-up of
Moulding, Partridge, Barry Andrews (keyboards, ex-King Crimson) and Terry Chambers (drums) was disrupted when Andrews
departed in 1979 and was replaced by Gregory. The band toured
prolifically, at home and as far afield as Australia, Venezuela, the
Middle East and South East Asia, until Partridge collapsed from
exhaustion in 1982. Chambers left later that year and although
the group has continued to function as a three-piece in the studio,
they have never played live again.

Despite their eccentrically English style of songwriting and
presentation, they have latterly enjoyed the greater measure of
their success in America, where their album *Skylarking* (Virgin
CDV 2399; 1986) quietly sold 250,000 copies and was ranked
No.48 in *Rolling Stone*'s 100 Best Albums of the Eighties.

- *White Music* (Virgin CDV 2095) [1978]

Like a hyperactively clever but gauche adolescent, XTC's first
album has a forced and comically awkward air about it, yet boasts
a rather endearing quality too. The spluttering incoherence of
Andy Partridge's vocals on 'This is Pop?' and the spiky, nervous
energy of scattergun songs like 'Science Friction' are prime early
examples of the idiosyncratic smarts that have sustained the
group as a minor force in English pop, while the mauling given to
DYLAN's 'All Along the Watchtower' is a fair indication of what has
kept them strictly on the margins.

- *The Compact XTC* (Virgin CDV 2251) [1986]

XTC have changed tack on several occasions, but their penchant
for convoluted arrangements somehow bundled into oddly

shaped pop packages has remained intact.

This distillation of their most accessible work, which includes 'Senses Working Overtime', 'Towers of London', 'Making Plans For Nigel', 'Sgt Rock (Is Going To Help Me)', 'Statue of Liberty' and 'Life Begins at the Hop', spares the listener the grief entailed in working through the more indigestible tracts of their albums.

In retrospect, there is often less to XTC's complex music than at first meets the ear. As this collection reveals, despite all their high-wire antics, they always take care to sling up the safety net of a good chorus and, paradoxically, it is this simple, traditional skill that has proved their greatest asset.

Yes

Convened: 1968, London. Split up: 1980. Reconvened: 1983
Jon Anderson (f) – vocals; Bill Bruford (f) – drums; Steve
Howe – guitar/vocals; Tony Kaye (f) – keyboards; Trevor
Rabin – guitar; Chris Squire (f) – bass/vocals; Rick Wakeman
– keyboards; Alan White – drums
UK No.1 albums: 1973: *Tales From Topographic Oceans*
(Atlantic 781325)
1977: *Going For the One* (Atlantic 250379)

The idea of applying an ostentatiously advanced musical technique to the writing and playing of rock seemed to strike a raft of English musicians simultaneously towards the end of the Sixties. Among the leading lights of this technical tendency, whose music became known as progressive rock, were King Crimson, GENESIS, Emerson, Lake And Palmer, The Moody Blues and Jethro Tull. But none produced such a bewildering fandango of complex harmonic structures, abrupt changes of tempo and florid lyrical metaphors with quite as much improbable gusto as Yes, whose album sleeves, with their distinctive Roger Dean fantasy landscape artwork, were ubiquitous in the campus coffee bars of the Seventies.

If the densely packed arrangements and highbrow aspirations of their early work made Yes' music a bit too stodgy for some people, it was but a light taster compared to the excesses that were to follow, and by the time of the neo-classical 'concept' album *Tales from Topographic Oceans* (see above), the journey of discovery had turned into a mindless meander.

They could go no further, and after a deluge of solo albums (five were released between late 1975 and the middle of 1976) the group returned to (relative) basics with *Going for the One* (see above). There were several increasingly desperate changes of personnel. Wakeman was replaced by Patrick Moraz, who was subsequently replaced by the returning Wakeman. Then Anderson and Wakeman were replaced by Trevor Horn (vocals/guitar) and Geoff Downes (keyboards), a duo later better known as Buggles (of 'Video Killed the Radio Star' fame). Eventually this strangely mutated version of Yes broke up after a three-night stand at New York's Madison Square Garden in September 1980.

After their comeback in 1983 the group muddled through the Eighties in a state of constant flux. By 1989 there were enough members and ex-members doing the rounds to form two bands, which is exactly what they did. But when Anderson, Bruford, Wakeman and Howe decided to get together and play material from the classic Yes era, Chris Squire, by then the only member to have stayed continuously in the 'official' Yes, threatened legal action to prevent them using the brand name of Yes in connection with any of their activities.

Less than two years later, in an extraordinary turn of events, the combatants united to form one mob-handed eight-piece Yes aggregate. They recorded the surprisingly coherent album *Union* (Arista 261558; 1991) and went off to line their pockets touring North America.

● *The Yes Album* (Atlantic SD 191312) [1971]

Featuring the almost classic line-up of Anderson, Bruford, Howe, Squire and Kaye (soon to be replaced by Wakeman), this remains absolutely the classic Yes album. It was the group's third long player, but the first to feature exclusively original compositions. Numbers such as 'Yours is No Disgrace', 'I've Seen All Good People', 'Starship Trooper' and guitarist Howe's acoustic rag 'The Clap' defined Yes' sound and provided the backbone of the group's live act right through to the *Union* tour of 1991. The music is a complicated mêlée of fractured melodies and abrupt changes clearly designed to show off the awesome virtuosity of the performers. Once this otiose formula had been greeted with popular acclaim – the album reached No.7 in the UK and scraped in at No.40 in America – there was no stopping them.

- *Close to the Edge* (Atlantic 250012) [1972]

For those who relished the move towards ever-longer and more ambitious quasi-symphonic pieces, this remains one of Yes' finest recordings. It also enjoyed the highest American chart placing of any Yes album when it peaked at No.3. The title track occupies half the playing time, the other half being divided between 'And You and I' and 'Siberian Khatru'. It took three months of painstaking work to record, after which a frustrated Bruford upped sticks and accepted an offer to join King Crimson. He was replaced by Alan White (ex-Plastic Ono Band).

- *90125* (Atlantic 790125-2) [1983]

This was the comeback album which marked the emergence of Yes as a musically streamlined, mainstream rock act of the Eighties, and re-established the group as a force in the international marketplace. 'Owner of a Lonely Heart' was a No.1 hit single in America and introduced the band to a new generation of fans. The line-up now comprised Anderson, Squire and White, together with South African guitarist Trevor Rabin and the group's original keyboard player Tony Kaye.

- *Yesyears* (Atco 7567-91644-2) [1991]
- *Yesstory* (Atco 7567-91747-2) [1991]

Yesyears is a 46-track, four-disc set comprising favourites from all stages of the band's career – among them 'Wondrous Stories', 'Don't Kill the Whale', 'Going For the One' and 'Owner of a Lonely Heart' – together with rare and previously unreleased material. Lavishly packaged with rare photographs, sleeve notes and the inevitable Roger Dean artwork, this is the kind of high-profile, coffee-table *objet* that the spread of CD has done so much to encourage.

    Yesstory is the condensed (two-disc) version, generally a more palatable option for all but the truly dedicated fan.

Neil Young

Born: November 12 1945, Toronto, Canada
UK/US No.1 album: 1972: *Harvest* (Reprise K 244 131)

and Crazy Horse

Convened: 1969, Los Angeles, California
Ralph Molina (f) – drums/vocals; Frank Sampedro – guitar/
vocals; Billy Talbot (f) – bass/vocals
US No.84 album: 1971: *Crazy Horse* (unavailable)

Crosby, Stills and Nash/Crosby, Stills Nash and Young

Convened: 1968, Los Angeles, California. Split up: 1970.
Reconvened 1974–75 [CSNY – US/UK tour]; 1977–78 [CSN
– album/US tour/live album]; 1979 [CSN – anti-nuclear
benefit concert, Madison Square Garden]; 1982 [CSN – *Peace
Sunday* anti-nuclear benefit concert, Rose Bowl, Pasadena/
album]; 1985 [CSN – Tour/CSNY – Live Aid]; 1988 [CSN –
Atlantic records 40th anniversary concert/CSNY – album];
1990 [CSNY – benefit concerts/CSN – album/US tour]
David Crosby (f) – vocals/guitar; Graham Nash (f) – vocals/
guitar; Stephen Stills (f) – vocals/guitar; Neil Young – guitar/
vocals
US No.1 albums [All CSNY]: 1970: *Déjà Vu* (Atlantic 250
                                       001)
                             1971: *Four Way Street* (Atlan-
                                       tic K2 60003)
                             1974: *So Far* (Atlantic K2
                                       50023)

One of rock's true mavericks, Neil Young has chopped and
changed his music and politics like a chef creating some bizarre
and exotic bouillabaisse, but he has yet to replace the one pair of
ripped-to-shreds jeans he has been wearing since Woodstock. A
man who believes that the very medium of CD is inimicable to the
creation of good rock'n'roll ('Digital music is like the dark ages of
recorded sound')*, perhaps his most extraordinary achievement is

---

* See introduction p ix.

to have amassed thirty odd years of playing and songwriting experience while still retaining access to the original garage-band thrill.

He started out in a high-school group, playing scrappy cover versions of BEATLES songs, before developing as a more serious folk singer, first in his native Canada and then in New York's Greenwich Village. His ability to combine the solitary disciplines of the unaccompanied singer/songwriter with his love of playing classic rock'n'roll in an electric band setting has been one of the distinguishing features of his outlandishly erratic career.

He founded Buffalo Springfield in 1966 together with Stephen Stills (vocals/guitar) and Richie Furay (vocals/guitar), both of whom he had met on the Greenwich Village circuit. A band whose timely combination of folk and rock had an influence out of all proportion to its brief, unstable existence, Buffalo Springfield split barely two years later. The best of their legacy is available on *Retrospective* (Atlantic 790 417-2; 1969).

Stills went off to join David Crosby (ex-BYRDS) and Graham Nash (ex-Hollies) in Crosby Stills and Nash, while Young disappeared to write the songs for his first album *Neil Young* (Reprise 7599-27444-2; 1969) and then to form his own backing group Crazy Horse, the original line-up of which featured Molina, Talbot and Danny Whitten (guitar/vocals; died 18.11.72).

Young's album was a flop, but the Crosby Stills and Nash début *Crosby Stills & Nash* (Atlantic K 240033; 1969) was a phenomenal success, selling more than two million copies within the first year. On its release in June 1969, CSN recruited Young as lead guitarist and 'occasional' vocalist, formally altering their name to Crosby Stills Nash and Young. A month later, the unit played only its second-ever gig in front of an estimated half a million people at Woodstock; Crosby Stills and Nash began with an acoustic set and were then joined by Young and the backing band for an electric set.

Parallel to his membership of CSNY, Young maintained his solo career, both with and without Crazy Horse as his backing band. Crazy Horse also attempted to carve out a separate identity without Young, recruiting guitarist Nils Lofgren (later a member of Bruce SPRINGSTEEN's E Street Band) and pianist Jack Nitzsche. They released three albums but made little headway. A Crazy Horse compilation, *Left For Dead* (World Service SERV 009CD;

1989), is currently available.

Beyond the obvious high points, little of Young's back catalogue has so far surfaced on CD in this country. Perhaps this is not so surprising given his distinction of being the only act ever to have been sued by his (former) record label (Geffen) for providing albums which were deemed to be 'not commercial in nature and musically uncharacteristic of [his] previous records'. The charge was never made to stick, but for whatever reason, Young's wilder back catalogue dabblings in everything from neo-metal to synthesiser-pop with dollops of acoustic country and Republican politics on the way remain unrepresented on CD.

- *After the Goldrush* (Reprise 7599-27243-2) [1970]
- *Harvest* (Reprise 7599-27239-2) [1972]

These are two of Young's hardier perennials, even though Crazy Horse were not involved in the recording of either. Young chose his third album, *After the Goldrush*, as the moment to emphasise both the folky side of his writing – on numbers like the lilting 'Only Love Can Break Your Heart' – while indulging the full force of his acerbic guitar playing, notably the incomparably cranky soloing on 'Southern Man'.

The album was a huge break-through for him, and to prove it was no fluke he went one better with the follow-up, *Harvest*, a collection in a similar vein which yielded the US No.1 'Heart of Gold'.

- *Freedom* (Reprise 7599-25899-2) [1989]

After making wobbly progress throughout the Eighties, the Neil Young renaissance started with this glorious return to the quavering dust-bowl laments and heavyweight country-rock blueprint which he drew up with such conspicuous success on *After the Goldrush* (see above).

His folk roots push through on the opening number, an acoustic version of 'Rockin' in the Free World', a diatribe against social injustice of the sort that has become a staple for John MELLENCAMP. Sixty minutes later, the same song is given a barnstorming electric band arrangement at the end of the disc.

Sandwiched between is an astounding catalogue of sinewy,

rough-hewn music that stands comparison with the best of his portfolio. Outrageous patches of overloaded power guitar explode like kegs of gunpowder during the moody, cowboy Mexicana of 'Eldorado'. Thunderous squalls of noise drift across the metre of 'Don't Cry', and he lays waste to Lieber and Stoller's standard 'On Broadway' with a furiously demented vocal and a gibberish solo.

No less convincing are the quiet, sparse constructions of 'Crime in the City' and 'The Ways of Love', where the appeal of the melody and the sense of conviction in Young's performance offset the variable pitching and tremulous timbre of his voice.

- **Neil Young and Crazy Horse:** *Ragged Glory* (Reprise 7599-26315-1) [1990]

Reunited with his old chums, Crazy Horse, Young conjures a spectacular display of gut-bucket country blues-rock, played with a raw spontaneity that is infectious. Sweeping aside twenty-odd years of technical innovation, producers Young and David Briggs opt for the comfortingly old-fashioned sound of guitars played through hot, overcranked valve amps on one-take sessions, overlaid by Young's plaintive love-it-or-leave-it yowl. Feel and enthusiasm triumph over technical precision every time and songs like 'Country Home' and 'Mansion on the Hill' boast simple, melodic grooves of such irresistible charm that the musicians are plainly reluctant to abandon them once they have been set in train. Instead they bash on with zestful abandon until, on many of the tracks, the final chord is left to dissolve in a welter of 'natural' drones and ambient feedback.

- **Neil Young and Crazy Horse:** *Weld/Arc-Weld* (Reprise 7599-26746-2) [1991]

If you think *Ragged Glory* is rough, wait until you hear this, a magnificent live album which rejoices in possibly the dirtiest recorded sound on an official, major-league release since CREAM's *Wheels of Fire* in 1968.

Blasting off with 'Hey Hey, My My (Into the Black)', the bass sound barks and burps, guitar solos wing in like sudden squalls at sea, and Young's feline voice wails with a wobbly, distraught fervour. Against a background of explosions and machine-gun noises, Bob DYLAN's 'Blowin' in the Wind' is put to the torch in an arrangement redolent of Jimi HENDRIX's massacre of the 'Stars and Stripes', while elsewhere new life is breathed into favourites like 'Cinnamon Girl' and 'Powderfinger' along with more recent triumphs such as 'Mansion on the Hill' and the epic 'Rockin' in the Free World'.

Weld is a long double album, 112 minutes of music which retail at about £20. For a whopping £34, however, you may still be able to purchase the limited edition *Arc-Weld*, which incorporates a third disc comprising 35 minutes of feedback shrieks and end-of-number bangs and crashes, welded together into one nightmarish collage of unadulterated rock'n'roll noise.

This surreal pulping of musical off-cuts produces an intriguing effect. Rock music has always been as much to do with the sensual celebration of noise as it has with conventional notions of melody and rhythm. People who do not like rock music always complain that it is too loud. In skimming off that element of vulgar, untramelled noisiness the *Arc* section of *Arc-Weld* identifies and celebrates one of the core components of great rock'n'roll.

● **Crosby Stills and Nash: *CSN*** (Atlantic 7567-82319-2) [1991]

This 77-track, four-disc boxed set, complete with illustrated discography, is an impressive audio documentary that begins to make some sense of the bewildering succession of comings and goings contingent upon this volatile three-man nucleus. It features recordings by Crosby Stills and Nash; Crosby Stills Nash and Young; Crosby and Nash; David Crosby; Graham Nash; Stephen Stills; and Manassas, the group founded by Stephen Stills which included Chris Hillman (guitar/vocals) and Al Perkins (guitar/pedal steel), both formerly of the Flying Burrito Brothers. None of Young's solo work is included.

The acoustic harmony-rock noodling of early CSN hits like 'Marrakesh Express' and 'Suite: Judy Blue Eyes' are pleasant enough but it was clearly the arrival of Young which put some lead in the group's pencil and resulted in some of their finest moments, notably 'Déjà Vu', the definitive version of Joni MITCHELL's 'Woodstock' and the spine-chilling 'Ohio', Young's moving commentary on the shooting of four students by the

National Guard at Kent State University in 1970.

With their airy harmonies, and earnest political idealism Crosby, Stills, Nash (and Young when he was aboard) were the musical personification of the Woodstock generation. Like the hippy ideals the group espoused, their oeuvre has become increasingly tattered over the years with each successive split and regrouping. Thus, although this boxed set is a sterling monument to their achievements, it has to be said that the quality of the output tails off alarmingly after the initial burst of creativity which fuelled the early work.

Frank Zappa

Born: December 21 1940, Baltimore, Maryland
UK No.9 album: 1969: *Hot Rats* (Music For Nations CDZAP2)

The Mothers of Invention

Convened: 1965, Los Angeles, California. Split up: 1969. Reconvened: 1970. Split up: 1975
Jim Black (f) – drums/percussion/vocals; Ray Collins (f) – vocals/harmonica/percussion; Roy Estrada (f) – bass/guitar-ron; Elliott Ingber – guitar; Frank Zappa (f) – guitar/vocals
UK No.17 album: 1970: *Burnt Weeny Sandwich* (unavailable)

A pioneering composer and an immensely gifted musician, Frank Zappa is also a bizarre humorist and waspish satirist whose work treads the fine line between genius and madness. He is as familiar with the classical music of Edgard Varèse and Igor Stravinsky as he is with the tenets of heavy rock, and as one of the first popular artists to inject elements of jazz and classical music into his work, he has profoundly enriched the vocabulary of rock.

Some years after he first played with Captain Beefheart in a high-school band called The Blackouts, Zappa emerged in the Sixties at the helm of LA's freakiest aggregate, The Mothers of Invention (formerly The Soul Giants, then The Mothers). He became an *éminence grise* of the Californian counter-culture, yet was simultaneously the movement's sternest critic. 'The whole hippy scene is wishful thinking,' he said in 1968. 'They wish they could love, but they're full of shit. It's easier to make someone mad than to make somebody love.'

This is a theory for which Zappa has never lost his enthusiasm. 'Hello, pigs,' he used to snarl by way of greeting to his audiences in the Sixties, his dark, saturnine looks emphasised by that distinctive and peculiarly threatening configuration of facial hair. Indeed, his prodigious talent has always been linked to a love of theatrical outrage, much of it gratuitous, and he employs a lampooning, often juvenile wit in his ceaseless search for new ways to 'make people mad'.

During a residency at the Garrick Theatre in New York's Greenwich Village in 1968, he incited a party of US marines in the audience to get up on stage and demonstrate their bayonetting skills on some baby dolls. Over the years his songs have poked fun at Jews, Catholics, hippies, groupies, politicians, the police; you name it and Zappa has held it in withering contempt. He famously described the practice of rock journalism as 'people who can't write interviewing people who can't talk for people who can't read'.

In 1971 he was forced to cancel a performance of *200 Motels* (1971; unavailable) with the Royal Philharmonic Orchestra at the Royal Albert Hall, after the venue's representatives declared the libretto obscene. Later that same year, at London's Rainbow Theatre, he was pushed off the edge of the stage by the jealous husband of an ardent fan. He was hospitalised for several weeks and spent most of the ensuing year in a wheelchair. For some time afterwards he was accompanied by a bodyguard in public and avoided England whenever possible.

He last performed here at London's Wembley Arena in April 1988, a breathtaking two-and-half hour show comprising a continuous segue of tortuous musical intricacy leavened by several of the old favourites and a succession of cosmic visual gags. When he wasn't playing a variety of astounding guitar solos, Zappa stood with his back to the audience, conducting his 11-piece touring band with a baton.

He has maintained a prolific output right up to the present, releasing more than 50 albums (either under his own name or under The Mothers of Invention imprint), about two-thirds of which are so far available in the CD format. He has also invested considerable time and energy in a campaign to oppose the Parents Music Resource Centre, a pressure group of Washington wives dedicated to 'cleaning up' rock lyrics by imposing censorship if necessary.

More recently, he has carved out a new (parallel) career in what he calls 'the Marco Polo business', setting up a 'trade consultancy' company called Why Not? and spending several months in 1990 jetting around the emerging market economies of Eastern Europe and the USA attempting to forge business and enterprise deals.

The American cable TV company Financial News Network hired him as a consultant, and while roaming the Eastern bloc with one of their camera crews, he arrived in Czechoslovakia just as former playwright Vaclav Havel was being installed as president. Declaring his long-standing passion for the album *Bongo Fury* (see below), Havel immediately appointed Zappa to be the country's new Trade and Culture Emissary.

In 1991, Zappa was diagnosed as suffering from cancer of the prostate and by December he was apparently too unwell to attend a concert at New York's Ritz Theatre to mark his birthday.

- **The Mothers of Invention:** *Freak Out* (Music For Nations CDZAP 1) [1966]

The Mothers' notorious début double album is now on one CD with some of the tracks remixed by Bob Stone and Zappa himself. A *tour de force* of psychedelic weirdness, the influences extend from the classical music of Edgard Varèse ('The Return of the Son of Monster Magnet') to The BEATLES ('You Didn't Try to Call Me', 'Any Way the Wind Blows'). A primitive four-track recording, larded with squeaks, bangs, shouts and other extraneous effects, it is a spotty experience, but at least on CD you can be sure that all the noises are supposed to be there.

- **The Mothers of Invention:** *We're Only In It for the Money* [1968]
- **Frank Zappa:** *Lumpy Gravy* [1968] (Music For Nations CDZAP 13)

The landmark third Mothers' album, *We're Only In It for the Money* (1968), is a deranged patchwork of styles from the hard rock of

'Flower Punk' (a parody of Jimi HENDRIX's 'Hey Joe') to the doo-wop
pastiche of 'What's the Ugliest Part of Your Body?' ('Some say
your nose/Some say your toes/But I think it's your mind . . .').

The album mocks everything held dear by the flower power
generation, most of whom lapped it up regardless. Paul McCARTNEY
did however let it be known that he was not amused by the cover
artwork, which is a rude parody of the BEATLES' hallowed *Sergeant
Pepper's Lonely Hearts Club Band*. Reduced to CD size, the effect of
the crowded design is somewhat muted, while the controversial
inner sleeve – a photograph of the band all wearing dresses – has
disappeared altogether.

At a price of around £12–£13, the album is paired on the same
disc with *Lumpy Gravy*, the first recording to be released under
Zappa's own name. Comprising two fifteen minute tracks –
'Lumpy Gravy I' and 'Lumpy Gravy II' – it is a collage of stoned
monologues, disjointed orchestral sequences and pointlessly odd
sound effects. Even with the enhanced audio fidelity it remains
heavy going.

- *Uncle Meat* (Music For Nations CDZAP 3) [1969]

A double-disc soundtrack for a movie that was imminent in 1969
and still being described as 'forthcoming' in 1988, the *Uncle Meat*
CD now boasts an extra 45 minutes of music not featured on the
original vinyl version. Philippe Carles of *Jazz Magazine* expressed
an educated opinion when he wrote of it, 'This is a group of eight
musicians who can play all kinds of music (Varèse, Stockhausen,
Ornette Coleman, The BEATLES, fanfare music, Shopp, traditional
jazz) and still succeed in establishing their own musical identity,
using all kinds of jokes, gimmicks and skills at their disposal in the
studio.'

- *Hot Rats* (Music For Nations CDZAP2) [1969]

Zappa's most impressive album, although it was a curious failure
in America where it barely registered in the chart (No.173), this
boasts the surpassing jazz-rock melody of 'Peaches en Regalia' and
features contributions from his old school chum, Captain Beefheart (a goatish vocal on 'Willie the Pimp') and violinist Jean Luc
Ponty.

For once Zappa reins in on the spontaneous happenings and stoned doodlings, and instead deploys a crack team of (mostly) jazz-tutored players – notably saxophonist/pianist Ian Underwood – on a more structured batch of material. The results are stunning.

However, he has been unable to resist a little retrospective tampering with the original tapes. 'Remixed from the original multi-track masters with added material from the original sessions,' it says on the insert. What this means is that two of the tracks have been extended from their original versions (which still leaves the total running time at a little under 48 minutes), while elsewhere there are odd little bits of extra instrumentation, which may seem intrusive to those who know and love the original. In lots of subtle ways, then, this CD version is substantially different from what you get on vinyl, though not necessarily an improvement.

- *Bongo Fury* (Disc International RY 10097) [US 1975]

Vaclav Havel's favourite Zappa recording, *Bongo Fury*, is a live album recorded at the Armadillo World Headquarters in Texas, and not previously released in Britain. Insofar as it captures for posterity Zappa's reunion tour with the reclusive Captain Beefheart, it is a remarkable item, but one that remains musically indifferent.

- *Guitar* (Music For Nations CDDZAP 6) [1988]

Although the commercial appeal of his many and varied recordings has been circumscribed by their unpredictability and often boggling complexity, Zappa could have forged a hugely profitable career as a virtuoso guitar hero had he been content to play the rôle. This double album is comprised entirely of guitar solos recorded live between 1979 and 1984, which may prove a bit of a high-fibre diet for some, but is a feast for devotees of the art of rock guitar.

Starting with the angular, bluesy licks of 'Sexual Harassment in the Workplace' it segues through many varied shades of excellence, from the mysterious, jittery phrases of 'Republicans' to the thick layers of gulping wang bar noises on 'Do Not Pass Go' and

'When No One Was No One'. Elsewhere the sounds range from cataclysmic eruptions of noise to the most delicate of crystalline sprinklings in an awesome display of technique, imagination and inspiration.

- *You Can't Do That on Stage Anymore Vol.1* (Zappa CDDZAP 8)
- *You Can't Do That on Stage Anymore Vol.2* (Zappa CDDZAP 9)
- *You Can't Do That on Stage Anymore Vol.3* (Zappa CDDZAP 17)
- *You Can't Do That on Stage Anymore Vol.4* (Zappa CDDZAP 40)

A monster project even by Zappa's outlandishly fecund standards, the plan is to issue six double-CDs – costing about £18–£20 and lasting approximately two and a half hours each – of previously unreleased live recordings, spanning the entire history of Zappa's career. So far four volumes have emerged.

The structure of the albums is non-chronological and so it is possible for the performance of any band from any year to run into the performance of any other band from any other year. Zappa intends the effect to resemble 'an impossible concert, with all the Zappa line-ups from the last two decades on stage at the same time, waiting to play their parts'.

Literally hundreds of musicians have passed through the ranks of Zappa's bands, among them Vinnie Colaiuta (drums, moving on to play with STING); Stev Vai (guitar, to David Lee Roth, WHITESNAKE, then solo); Warren Cucurrullo (guitar, to Duran Duran); Terry Bozzio (drums, to Jeff BECK); George Duke (keyboards, solo) to name a few.

In preparing these albums – essentially a colossal summary of his life's work – Zappa can claim access to a cast and a repertoire that stands unequalled in rock.

ZZ Top

Convened: 1970, Houston, Texas
Frank Beard (f) – drums; Billy Gibbons (f) – vocals/guitar;
Dusty Hill (f) – bass/vocals/keyboards
UK No.2 album: 1985: *Afterburner* (Warner Bros 925 342-2)

The longest-serving trio in the history of rock'n'roll, ZZ Top has carved an unlikely niche as the blues band of the space age. Like their native state of Texas they combine rural primitivism with urban smarts, and in so doing have created the perfect synthesis of backwoods rock'n'roll for the microchip era; a vision of hi-tech in a dusty hat.

In the world league table of entertainers' earnings compiled by *Forbes* magazine at the end of the Eighties, only one rock group, U2, was thought to have amassed more than ZZ Top's estimated income of $31 million over the 24-month period to 31 December 1987. Yet they remain curiously detached from the jet-setting rock'n'roll celebrity circus and immune to the 'rock messiah' syndrome that generally besets artists of their stature. In 21 years they have toured the planet yet never moved from their base in the deep South, and will still answer to the original wry description of them as 'that little ol' band from Texas'.

Billy Gibbons, a former graphic art student, started out playing guitar in Sixties psychedelic garage band The Moving Sidewalks, whose début single '99th Floor' topped the local Texan chart for five weeks in 1967. Dusty Hill and Frank Beard graduated from The American Blues, a Dallas-based band probably best remembered for the fact that they dyed their hair blue. The three met on a sin-infested street corner and made a pact which has withstood the ravages of time with a unique lack of deviation.

Apart from one minor rhythm guitar contribution from an outsider on one of their early albums, the three hombres have themselves provided every last note and beat that has ever featured on a ZZ Top album, even learning how to play saxophones and becoming their own three-piece horn section for some tracks on *Deguello* (see below). They have never augmented their live show with extra musicians, nor have they recorded or sat in with other bands.

They have been managed and produced since day one by Bill Ham, a Texan with a maverick management style similar to that of LED ZEPPELIN's former manager Peter Grant. Ham steadfastly kept ZZ Top off television throughout the Seventies, preferring to tour the band to success. Although this was hard going at the outset, they had built a following on unshakable foundations by the time of their Taking Texas to the People tour of 1976, a vast production which took to the road with a menagerie of livestock including a longhorn steer, a 2,000 lb black buffalo, half a dozen vultures, two six-foot rattlesnakes, a havelina pig and a lone howling wolf.

In the Eighties they became unlikely stars of the MTV age thanks to a slick trilogy of videos directed by Tim Newman for 'Gimme All Your Lovin'', 'Sharp Dressed Man' and 'Legs', all tracks from their colossally successful 1983 album *Eliminator* (see below).

By presenting themselves since the Eighties as rock'n'roll Methuselahs, ZZ Top is the only group seriously to confront the contradictions of growing old in a rock marketplace that trades forever in the currency of youth. While still in their early thirties, Gibbons and Hill opted for a look not fashionable since the days of the Old Testament. Having sold it as a *bona fide* rock'n'roll affectation, they need never worry again. Barring any dramatic weight gains, they will look no older in twenty years' time than they do now.

- **Tres Hombres** (Warner Bros K256 603) [1973]

ZZ Top's third album remains their best. The opening segue of 'Waitin' for the Bus' and 'Jesus Just Left Chicago' stands as one of the great opening salvos of all time, up there with 'Route 66' off the first ROLLING STONES album and 'Whole Lotta Love' from *Led Zeppelin II*. Indeed, the two inseparable songs have continued to be a strong feature of the live set right right through to the *Recycler* tour of 1991.

'La Grange', the lasciviously told story of a local whorehouse set against a freshened John Lee HOOKER riff, became a minor US hit, and more dubious Texan folklore was enshrined in the offbeat narratives of 'Precious and Grace' and the surreal, almost DYLANesque 'Master of Sparks'.

Although *Tres Hombres* reached No.8 in the American chart, it never registered in the UK. It remains one of the most overlooked albums of genius in the entire canon of rock, exposing the often repeated assertion that ZZ Top is some sort of American equivalent to STATUS QUO for the risible nonsense that it is.

- **Deguello** (Warner Bros 256 701) [1979]

Another collection of deceptively casual brilliance, highlighting, among other things, Gibbons' consummate control of guitar textures. These range from the perfectly clean Fender-plugged-direct-into-the-desk sound on 'A Fool for Your Stockings' to the grinding, overcranked Marshall grunge (what Gibbons calls his 'Bisarktone') on 'Cheap Sunglasses'.

Half a decade before Michael JACKSON and L.L. Cool J got on the case, ZZ demonstrated an easy familiarity with the language of the street on the perennially hip 'I'm Bad, I'm Nationwide'. The band's fascination with racing cars is also revealed through another of those surreal fantasy narratives, 'Manic Mechanic', sung by Gibbons as if through a failing megaphone. Sparkling, witty covers of Isaac Hayes' 'I Thank You' and Elmore James' 'Dust My Broom' ice a spectacularly rich cake.

● *Eliminator* (Warner Bros 23774-2) [1983]

When asked about the best way for up-and-coming guitarists to improve their technique, Gibbons advised them to go out and buy an album called *The Sound of the Drags*, a recording of drag-racing cars. 'If they can absorb that hot-rod feel,' said Gibbons, 'then, man, they will spank that plank.'

The success of *Eliminator* in capturing that 'hot-rod feel' has passed into rock'n'roll legend along with the car, the girls, the videos and the ten million copies sold.

The trick that they discovered was simple, but devastatingly effective. They souped up the guitar sound, streamlined the choruses and stripped away all rhythmic clutter. Unusually for a heavy rock album, 'Gimme All Your Lovin'', 'Got Me Under Pressure', 'Sharp Dressed Man', 'Legs', 'Dirty Dog' and 'If I Could Only Flag Her Down' are all propelled by an unwavering four-on-the-floor bass drum pulse. The rest is history.

BIBLIOGRAPHY

Those books which provided a constant source of vital information include:

The History of Rock, Volumes 1–10, edited by Ashley Brown & Michael Heatley (Orbis 1984)

Christgau's Guide – Rock Albums of the 70s by Robert Christgau (Vermilion 1982)

Pete Frame's Rock Family Trees & Pete Frame's Rock Family Trees Volume 2 by Pete Frame (Omnibus 1980 & 1983)

British Hit Albums, 4th Edition by Paul Gambaccini, Tim Rice & Jonathan Rice (Guinness Publishing 1990)

British Hit Singles, 8th Edition by Paul Gambaccini, Tim Rice & Jonathan Rice (Guinness Publishing 1991)

The Faber Companion to 20th-Century Popular Music by Phil Hardy & Dave Laing (Faber and Faber 1990)

The Illustrated New Musical Express Encyclopedia of Rock, compiled by Nick Logan & Bob Woffinden (Salamander 1977)

The Heart of Rock and Soul – The 1001 Greatest Singles Ever Made by Dave Marsh (Penguin Originals 1989)

The Official Music Master CD Catalogue, 12th Edition (Music Master 1991)

Guinness Book of Rock Stars, edited by Dafydd Rees & Luke Crampton with Barry Lazell (Guinness Publishing 1989) & 2nd Edition (Guinness Publishing 1991)

NME Who's Who in Rock & Roll, edited by John Tobler (Hamlyn 1991)

The Billboard Book of USA Top 40 Albums, 1st Edition by Joel Whitburn (Billboard Publications 1987)

The Billboard Book of USA Top 40 Hits, 4th Edition by Joel Whitburn (Billboard Publications 1989)

The Billboard Book of Gold and Platinum Records by Adam White (Billboard Books 1990)

Rock Lives – Profiles and Interviews by Timothy White (Omnibus 1991)

Much essential information has also been gleaned from articles, profiles and reviews in *Billboard*, *The Guardian*, *The Independent*, *The Independent On Sunday*, *Music Week*, *Q* magazine, *Rolling Stone*, *Select*, *The Sunday Times*, *The Times* and *Vox*.

Other valuable sources of information include:

The Rolling Stones – An Illustrated Record by Roy Carr (New English Library 1976)

Viva! Zappa by Dominique Chevalier (Omnibus 1986)

The Penguin Encyclopedia of Popular Music, edited by Donald Clarke (Viking 1989)

Backstreets – Springsteen: The Man and His Music by Charles R. Cross and the editors of *Backstreets* magazine (Sidgwick & Jackson 1989)

Talking Heads by Jerome Davis (Omnibus 1986)

The Illustrated Encyclopedia of Country Music by Fred Dellar, Alan Cackett & Roy Thompson (Salamander 1986)

When the Music's Over by Robin Denselow (Faber and Faber 1989)

Genesis – I Know What I Like by Armando Gallo (DIY 1980)

Where Did Our Love Go? The Rise and Fall of the Motown Sound by Nelson George (Omnibus 1986)

Prince – Imp of the Perverse by Barney Hoskyns (Virgin 1988)

The Boy in the Bubble – A Biography of Paul Simon by Patrick Humphries (New English Library 1988)

Small Change – A Life of Tom Waits by Patrick Humphries (Omnibus 1989)

Springsteen – Blinded by the Light by Patrick Humphries & Chris Hunt (Plexus 1985)

The International Encyclopedia of Hard Rock and Heavy Metal by Tony Jasper & Derek Oliver 2nd Revised Edition (Sidgwick & Jackson 1991)

Elvis Costello – An Illustrated Biography by Mick St. Michael (Omnibus 1986)

Crosstown Traffic: Jimi Hendrix and Post-War Pop by Charles Shaar Murray (Faber and Faber 1989)

Shots From the Hip by Charles Shaar Murray (Penguin 1991)

Elton by Philip Norman (Hutchinson 1991)

The Stones by Philip Norman (Elm Tree 1984)

Dire Straits by Michael Oldfield (Sidgwick & Jackson 1984)

Bare by George Michael & Tony Parsons (Penguin 1990)

Classic Albums – Interviews from the Radio One Series compiled by John Pidgeon (BBC Books 1991)

Van Halen – Jumpin' for the Dollar by John Shearlaw (Zomba 1984)

The Encyclopedia of Pop, Rock and Soul by Irwin Stambler (Macmillan 1989)

Rebel Rock – The Politics of Popular Music by John Street (Blackwell 1986)

The Doors by John Tobler & Andrew Doe (Bobcat 1987)

Rap Attack 2 – African Rap to Global Hip-Hop by David Toop (Serpent's Tail 1991)

The Beatles Book by Various Authors (Omnibus Press 1987)

Guns N' Roses – The Most Dangerous Band in the World by Mick Wall (Sidgwick & Jackson 1991)

John Lennon – An Illustrated Biography by Richard Wootton (Hodder and Stoughton 1984)

INDEX

Bold *type indicates a main entry*

Abba 73, 228
ABC 310
AC/DC 1
Adam Ant 73
Adams, Bryan 3
Aerosmith 7
Albert Hall, London 64, 73, 89
Albini, Steve 246
Alice in Chains 228
All About Eve 112
Allman Brothers Band 38
Alomar, Carlos 44
Amao, Abdul Lasisi 385
Amnesty International concerts 4,
    123, 344, 359
Antonioni, Michelangelo 29
Apollo, New York 52
Armadillo World Headquarters 404
Armatrading, Joan 9
Asbury Jukes 45
Ashford, Nick 303, 304
Aswad 11

Bad Company 121
Badarou, Wally 197
Baker, Ginger 317
Bambaataa, Afrika 53
The Band 13
Band Aid 4, 62, 183, 289
Bangla Desh concert 101, 143, 144
Barbican Centre, London 62
Des Barres, Michael 234
Basing Street Studio 94
Bauldie, John 106
The Beach Boys 17
The Beatles 21
Beck, Jeff 29
Beefheart, Captain 371, 400, 403, 404
Berry, Chuck 33

Big Country 36
Bilk, Acker 85
Billboard 18, 47, 52
Birmingham Arena 289
Black, Clint 47
The Black Crowes 38
Black Sabbath 86
Blackbushe Aerodrome 101
Blackwell, Chris 119, 202, 385
Blades, Ruben 346
Bloomfield, Mike 373
Blow Up 29
Blues Incorporated 372
Blur 88
Bon Jovi 39
Bond, Graham 85
Bongiovi, Tony 350
Bono 123
Booker T and the MGs 225, 277
Boston 48
Bowie, David 41
The Boyoyo Boys 319
Bozio, Terry 405
Bragg, Billy 364
Brand X 75
Branson, Richard 230
Briggs, David 398
Britten, Terry 356
Brooks, Elkie 232
Brooks, Garth 47
Brown, Bobby 50
Brown, James 49
Bruce, Jack 281
Brzezicki, Mark 10, 36, 37
Burdon, Eric 61
Buffalo Springfield 396
Buggles 393
Bush, Kate 53
Butterfield, Paul 373
The Byrds 55

411

Cale, J.J. 95
California Jam 376
Carles, Phillipe 403
Carter, June 58
Cash, Johnny 57
Castle Donington Monsters of Rock
2, 40, 377
The Charlatans 56
Chapman, Tracy 9, 10, 123, 219
Chapterhouse 88
Charles, Ray 60
Chelmsford Punk Festival 11
Chess, Leonard 33, 372
Christgau, Robert 69, 194, 284
Cinderella 40
Clapton, Eric 63
The Clash 69
Cocker, Joe 61
Colaiuta, Vinnie 405
Collins, Albert 82
Collins, Phil 72
Cooder, Ry 76
Cooke, Sam 61, 278, 326
Cool J., L.L. 408
Cooper, Alice 40
Coppola, Francis Ford 96, 369
Costello, Elvis 79
Cotton, James 375
Cowboy Junkies 284
Crawdaddy Club, Richmond 64
Crawford, Ernest 374
Crazy Horse 395
Cream 84
Creedence Clearwater Revival 357
Crosby, Stills and Nash/
Crosby, Stills, Nash & Young 395
Cropredy Festival 112
Cruz, Celia 353
Cucurrullo, Warren 405
Culture Club 263
The Cure 87

Daltrey, Roger 344
Davies, Cyril 373
Davies, Ray 261
Davis, Clive 156
Davis, Miles 62, 152
Dean, Roger 392, 394
De Curtis, Anthony 68
Deep Purple 89
Def Leppard 91
Denselow, Robin 202
Depeche Mode 44, 157
Diamond, Neil 15, 363

Dire Straits 92
Dixon, Willie 30, 85, 188, 373
The Dogs 93
The Doobie Brothers 77
The Doors 96
Dorn, Joel 226
Drakoulias, George 38
Duke, George 405
Dunbar, Aynsley 281, 377
Dunn, Donald 373
Duran Duran 234, 263, 308, 405
Dylan, Bob 99

The Eagles 369
Earls Court Arena 101
The Easybeats 2
Echo and the Bunnymen 107
Electronic 333
EMF 107
Emerson, Lake and Palmer 392
Eno, Brian 44, 73, 350, 361
Entertainment Weekly 47
The Eurythmics 108
Evans, Gil 346

The Faces 343
Fairport Convention 111
Fame, Georgie 373
Farm Aid 101, 210, 237
The Fat Boys 19
Ferry, Bryan 310
Fillmore West, San Francisco 86
Fine Young Cannibals 50
The Firm 122
Fleetwood Mac 113
Fogelberg, Dan 48
Foote, Micky 70
Foreigner 91
Fotheringay 112
Frame, Pete 32
Franklin, Aretha 117
Free 118
Frick, David 57
Fripp, Robert 350

Gabrels, Reeves 38
Gabriel, Peter 122
Gallagher, Rory 90, 373
Gardiner, Boris 12
Garfield, Simon 137
Garrick Theatre, New York 401
Gaye, Marvin 125
Geldof, Bob 160, 183, 244, 271
Genesis 127

Geordie 3
George, Nelson 125, 388
Giant's Stadium 9
Gillan, Ian 367
Gilmour, David 30, 53, 311
Gordy, Berry 125, 303, 305, 387
Grant, Peter 187, 406
Grateful Dead 132
Grech, Rick 373
Green, Al 350, 365
Guns 'n Roses 136
Guralnick, Peter 179
Guy, Buddy 64, 221, 373

Haggard, Merle 48
Haile Selassie 202, 203
Hakim, Omar 345
Hall, Terry 108
Ham, Bill 406
Hammer 138
Hammer, Jan 31, 32
Hammersmith Odeon 2, 77
Hammond, Albert 12
Hammond, John 100
Hancock, Herbie 314
Happy Mondays 140
Harris, Bob 93
Harrison, George 142
Havel, Vaclav 402, 404
Hawkins, Ronnie 14
Heart 38
The Heartbreakers 237
Hendrix, Jimi 146
Hepworth, David 42
Hill, Walter 77
Holly, Buddy 35, 291, 385
Hollywood Bowl 99
Honeyman-Scott, James 56
Hooker, John Lee 151
Horton, Walter 375
House, Son 372
The House of Love 56
Houston, Whitney 155
The Human League 157
Hynde, Chrissie 364, 365

Iglesias, Julio 387
Inspiral Carpets 107
INXS 159
Isle of Wight Festival 101, 148, 379
Iron Butterfly 86
The Isley Brothers 367
It's a Beautiful Day 113

Jackson, Alan 47
Jackson, Joe 161
Jackson, Michael 163
The Jacksons 167
Jacobs, Marion 372, 374
Jagger, Mick 7, 160, 222, 278, 344, 373
Jajouka, Master Musicians of 302
The Jam 168
James, Elmore 114, 115
Jarmusch, Jim 369
Jefferson Airplane 112, 328
Jennings, Will 383
Jesus and Mary Chain 284
Jesus Jones 171
Jethro Tull 392
Jett, Joan 137
Jimenez, Flaco 78
Joel, Billy 173
John, Dr 15
John, Elton 175
Johns, Glyn 9
Johnson, Robert 179
Jones, Darrell 345
Jones, George 48
Jones, Howard 73
Jones, Quincy 61, 62, 164, 165
Jones, Steve 34
Journey 48

Kabaka, Remi 385
Kansas 48
Katche, Manu 10
Keita, Salif 313
Kelly, Jon, 276
Kerrang! 2, 4, 137, 377
Khan, Chaka 62, 78
Kilgore, Merle 58
King, B.B. 180
King, Bobby 78
King Crimson 121, 350, 391, 392, 394
King, Jonathan 128
King, Martin Luther 361, 390
The Kinks 261, 367
Kirkland, Kenny 345
Klein, Allen 294, 298
Knebworth Festival 272
Knopfler, Mark 9, 10, 100, 275, 311, 346, 356
Kool and the Gang 183
Kool Jazz Festival 62
Korner, Alexis 85, 119, 373
Korrea, Djalma 124
Kravitz, Lenny 185

Lange, Mutt 6, 91, 92
Lanois, Daniel 106, 226, 360, 362
Led Zeppelin 187
Lee, Spike 387
Lennon, John 193
Level 42 196
Levine, Stewart 327
Levin, Tony 123
Lewis, Huey 82, 341
Lillywhite, Steve 123
Little Feat 77, 232, 275
Little Richard 51, 147
Little Steven 359
Little Village 78
Live Aid 63, 73, 95, 101, 143, 206,
    210, 234, 270, 271, 289, 323, 339,
    ·340, 359
Lord, Jon 376
Los Lobos 76
Lovett, Lyle 47
Lulu 43
Lyceum, London 204
Lyngstad, Freda 73
Lynne, Jeff 101, 144, 239

McCabe, Peter 58
McCartney, Paul 204
McGregor, Freddie 12
McGuinness, Paul 359
McLaren, Malcolm 261, 316
McLaughlin, John 314
Madison Square Garden, New York
    298, 393
Madonna 198
Mahavishnu Orchestra 31, 75
Malmsteen, Yngwie 366
Manassas 399
Mandela Concert 9, 10
Manfred Mann 85, 104
Mann, William 27
Marcana Stadium, Brazil 356
Marcus, Greil 14
Marillion 129
Marley, Bob and the Wailers 201
Marotta, Jerry 123
Marr, Johnny 56
Marriott, Steve 343
Marsalis, Branford 345, 346
Marsh, Dave 51, 118, 126, 279
Martin, George 23, 24, 26, 27, 31,
    205
Martyn, John 73
Marvin, Hank 29, 85
Matthews Southern Comfort 112

May, Brian 29
Mayall, John 61, 64, 66, 85, 114, 119,
    138
Mayfield, Curtis 32, 126, 186
Meal Ticket 93
Meat Loaf 208
Mellencamp, John 209
Mensch, Peter 91
Mercury, Freddie 20, 215, 344
Metallica 212
The Meters 225, 233
Michael, George 215
Miles, Buddy 373
Miller, Jimmy 297
Miller, Marcus 311
Mingus, Charlie 31, 32, 218
Minnelli, Liza 235
Mitchell, Joni 217
Mitchell, Mitch 373
Moby Grape 132
Monterey Festival 150, 277, 379
The Moody Blues 392
Moore, Gary 29
Moran, Pat 37
Morrison, Van 221
Morrissey 332
Most, Mickie 30, 31
The Mothers of Invention 400
Mott the Hoople 121
Murray, Charles Shaar 148
My Bloody Valentine 284

Napier-Bell, Simon 217
Nash, Johnny 363
N'Dour, Youssou 123, 124
Nepstadion, Budapest 272
Neville, Aaron 81
Neville Brothers 225
New Kids on the Block 107
New Order 235, 284
Newman, Tim 407
Newmark, Andy 44
Newport Folk Festival 102
Nicks, Stevie 237
Nirvana 227
Du Noyer, Paul 191
Numan, Gary 233

O'Connor, Sinead 50
Oldfield, Mike 229
Old Grey Whistle Test 93
Oldham, Andrew 294, 295, 296
Olodun 321
Orbison, Roy 57, 101, 145

Padgham, Hugh 10
Page, Jimmy 7, 29, 90, 122
Pahinui, Gabby 78
Paice, Ian 376
Palladino, Pino 10
Palmer, Robert 231
Parents Music Resource Centre 402
Patton, Charley 372
Paul Butterfield Band 102
Paul, Steve 374
Pearl Jam 228
Pearlman, Sandy 70
Peel, John 228
Perkins, Pine Top 375
The Pet Shop Boys 234
Peter, Paul and Mary 100
Petty, Tom and the Heartbreakers
  237
Phillips, Sam 58, 258–60
Phillips, Simon 31
Pink Floyd 239
Pixies 245
Plant, Robert 192
Plastic Ono Band 193, 394
The Pogues 247
Poison 40
The Police 250
Ponty, Jean Luc 403
Pop, Iggy 254
Powell, Cozy 376
The Power Station 234
Presley, Elvis 257
The Pretenders 260
Priest, Maxi 12, 363
Primal Scream 284
Prince 262
Prince's Trust Concert 9
Public Enemy 267
Public Image Ltd 317
Purify, James and Bobby 81

Q magazine 4, 64, 95, 174, 186, 191,
  251, 285, 325
Quicksilver Messenger Service 113,
  132
Queen 270

Racing Cars 93
Rainbow Theatre, London 401
Rea, Chris 274
Redding, Otis 277
Reed, Lou 280
R.E.M. 285
Ribot, Marc 371

Richard, Cliff 288
Richards, Keith 34, 82, 100, 101, 154,
  278, 280, 371
Richardson, Tony 77
Ride 56
Riverport Centre, St Louis 136
The Robert Cray Band 81
Robertson, Robbie 16
Rock against Racism 11
Rodgers, Nile 44, 311
Rodgers, Paul 39, 377
Rogers, Jimmy 372
Rolling Stone 38, 57, 70, 98, 163, 173,
  285, 330, 350, 354
The Rolling Stones 292
Ronson, Mick 281
Ronstadt, Linda 226
Rose, Tim 30
Ross, Diana 302
Roth, David Lee 368
Roxy Music 307
Royal Philharmonic Orchestra 89
Run DMC 311

Sade 216
Sam & Dave 81
Sanborn, David 311
Sandall, Robert 360
Santana 313
Santoro, Gene 32
Saxon 91
Scott, Ronnie 85
Scott-Heron, Gil 227
Seeger, Pete 56, 210
Seger, Bob 237
Sex Pistols 315
The Shadows 290
Shorter, Wayne 314
Simon, Paul 318
Simon and Garfunkel 321
Simple Minds 323
Simply Red 325
Simpson, Valerie 303, 304
Skid Row 40
Slaughter 93
Slowdive 88
Sly and the Family Stone 328
Smith, Willie 375
The Smiths 330
Sonic Youth 46, 228
Sonny and Cher 104
Soundgarden 228
Spandau Ballet 263, 308, 310
Spann, Otis 372

415

Spector, Phil 194, 209, 357, 358
The Spencer Davis Group 385
Springfield, Dusty 235
Springsteen, Bruce 333
Starr, Ringo 28
Status Quo 338
Steel Pulse 12
Steeleye Span 112
Stevens, Guy 119
Stewart, Rod 340
Sting 344
Stone, Bob 402
Stone, Oliver 96
Stone Pony, Asbury Park 41
The Stooges 254
Strait, George 48
The Stranglers 347
Strummer, Joe 111
The Style Council 170
Sylvian, David 42
The Supremes 305
Summers, Andy 346

Taj Mahal 77
Talking Heads 349
Taupin, Bernie 177, 178, 383
Taylor, James 48
Temple, Julian 300
Templeman, Ted 367
Terrell, Tami 127
The The 333
Them 222
Thin Lizzy 91
3rd Bass 139
Thompson, Richard 353
Tin Machine 45
Townshend, Pete 65, 146, 152, 291, 302
Traffic 385
The Travelling Wilburys 145
Tribes, Tony 363
The Tube 31, 32, 326
Turner, Tina 355

UAKTI 321
U2 358
UB40 363

Vai, Steve 366, 377, 405
Valens, Ritchie 76
Vallance, Jim 3
Vanilla Fudge 86
Vanilla Ice 137

Van Halen 366
Varese, Edgard 400, 402, 403
Vaughan, Stevie Ray 44
The Velvet Underground 283
Vicious, Sid 93, 261
Vinegar, Joe 232

Wailer, Bunny 12
The Wailers 201
Waits, Tom 369
Walden, Narada Michael 118
Wall, Mick 137
Warhol, Andy 282, 283, 299
Warren, Diane 12
Waters, Muddy 372
Waters, Roger 344
Watts, Charlie 372, 388
'We are the World' 62
Weather Report 31, 75, 345
Weeks, Willie 44
Wells, Junior 373
Wembley Arena 77, 289, 302, 305, 401
Wembley Stadium 9, 12, 131, 272, 289
Wenders, Wim 77
Wexler, Jerry 117
Wham! 216
White, Adam, 306
White, Cliff 53
White, Timothy 47, 257, 310
Whitesnake 376
The Who 378
Wings 206
Winter, Johnny 154, 374, 375
Winterland Hall 15
Winwood, Steve 382
Wonder, Stevie 386
Wood, Ron 29, 30, 101
Woodstock Festival 147, 218, 314, 315, 329, 379, 395, 396
World of Music and Dance/WOMAD 123

XTC 391

The Yardbirds 29, 30, 35, 64, 152
Yes 392
Young, Neil 395
Young, Paul 369

Zappa, Frank 400
ZZ Top 405